Relational Being

Kenneth J. Gergen

Relational Being
Beyond Self and Community

UNIVERSITY PRESS
2009

OXFORD
UNIVERSITY PRESS

Oxford University Press, Inc., publishes works that further
Oxford University's objective of excellence
in research, scholarship, and education.

Oxford   New York
Auckland   Cape Town   Dar es Salaam   Hong Kong   Karachi
Kuala Lumpur   Madrid   Melbourne   Mexico City   Nairobi
New Delhi   Shanghai   Taipei   Toronto

With offices in
Argentina   Austria   Brazil   Chile   Czech Republic   France   Greece
Guatemala   Hungary   Italy   Japan   Poland   Portugal   Singapore
South Korea   Switzerland   Thailand   Turkey   Ukraine   Vietnam

Published by Oxford University Press, Inc.
198 Madison Avenue, New York, New York 10016
www.oup.com

Library of Congress Cataloging-in-Publication Data
Gergen, Kenneth J.
Relational being: Beyond Self and Community / Kenneth J. Gergen.
p. cm.
Includes index.
ISBN 978-0-19-530538-8 (alk. paper)
1. Psychology—Philosophy. 2. Self. 3. Individualism. I. Title.
BF38.G46 2009
150.1—dc22   2008040521

3 5 7 9 8 6 4

Printed in the United States of America on acid-free paper

Note to Readers
This publication is designed to provide accurate and authoritative information in regard to the subject matter
covered. It is based upon sources believed to be accurate and reliable and is intended to be current as of the
time it was written. It is sold with the understanding that the publisher is not engaged in rendering legal,
accounting, or other professional services. If legal advice or other expert assistance is required, the services of a
competent professional person should be sought. Also, to confirm that the information has not been affected
or changed by recent developments, traditional legal research techniques should be used, including checking
primary sources where appropriate.

*(Based on the Declaration of Principles jointly adopted by a Committee of the
American Bar Association and a Committee of Publishers and Associations.)*

**You may order this or any other Oxford University Press publication by
visiting the Oxford University Press website at www.oup.com**

First to Mary
my relational inspiration without equal

To my friends and colleagues of the Taos Institute
for opening doors unimagined

To Anne Marie Rijsman and Regine Walter
for their photographic and graphic gems

To Bernard Stehle
for his caring and catalytic advice

To my friends, family, and colleagues throughout the world
for sustaining the generative flow

To all those scholars—past and present—
who invited me into the dialogue

And to Julian my dog
for being a teddy-bear

CONTENTS

PROLOGUE

TOWARD A NEW ENLIGHTENMENT

How should I describe myself to you at this moment? You would scarcely be surprised if I told you that I am now at my desk, absorbed in thought. I entertain an idea, consider its shortcomings, play with another, extend its possibilities, and slowly I am moved to write. I try fitfully to transform these fleeting states of mind into words, hoping that these pages will allow you, the reader, to understand my thoughts. Doesn't this sound quite reasonable?

Consider again: How does this commonplace passage define me as a writer? And in defining me, what does it tell us about our conceptions of being human? In important respects, we find here a picture of me as an individual thinker, dwelling in an interior world of consciousness that is all my own. And by implication, isn't this to say that we are each alone in our inner worlds? We have no direct access to each other's thoughts, and it is often difficult to translate thoughts into words. It is a world in which you can never plumb the depths of my mind; you will never fully understand me. And too, your private world will always be a mystery to me. In effect, this common account is one that defines us in terms of alienated beings.

"So what," you may respond. "It is simply a fact that we are separate individuals, each living in a private consciousness. That's just life." Or is it? If we accept this view of ourselves as bounded beings, the essential "me" dwelling behind the eyeballs, then we must continuously confront issues of separation. I must always be on guard, lest others see the faults in my thinking, the cesspools of my emotions, and the embarrassing motives behind my actions. It is also a world in which I must worry about how I compare to others, and whether I will be judged inferior. This view pervades our schools and organizations, where individual evaluation haunts our steps from the first moment we step into a classroom to our ultimate retirement. And thus we compete, tooth and claw, for ascendance over others. Self-esteem continuously hangs in the balance; the possibility of failure and depression is always at the doorstep. Under these conditions, what is the value of other people? Are they not primarily instruments for our own pleasure or self-gain? If they do not contribute to our well-being, should we not avoid or abandon them? If they actively interfere with our well-being, are we not justified in punishing, incarcerating or even eliminating them? This same attitude of me versus you insinuates itself as well into our views, nature and other cultures. It is always a matter of whose welfare is at stake.

Again, you may resist: "Yes, I can see there are problems, and sometimes we do take steps to correct them. At the same time, however, competition is also valuable. And winning is one of life's great pleasures. Besides, we are speaking of human nature here. So stop complaining and pull up your socks." Yet, is this human nature after all? As historians report, the view of the individual as singular and separate, one whose abilities to think and feel are central to life, and whose capacity for voluntary action is prized, is of recent origin. It is a conception of human nature that took root only four centuries ago, during a period that we now view as the Enlightenment. It was during this period that the soul or spirit, as the central ingredient of being human, was largely replaced by individual reason. Because each of us possesses the power of reason, it was (and is) maintained, we may challenge the right of any authority—religious or otherwise—to declare what is real, rational, or good for all. It is this Enlightenment view that has since been used to justify the institutions of democracy, public education, and judicial procedure, among others. It is by living within such institutions that we come to accept the conception as "the natural condition of being human."

Anthropologists largely concur in this conclusion. As Clifford Geertz, a doyen of the discipline, once wrote:

> The Western conception of the person as a bounded, unique, more or less integrated motivational and cognitive universe, a dynamic center of awareness, emotion, judgment, and action organized into a distinctive whole and set contrastively both against other such wholes and against a social and natural background is, however incorrigible

it may seem to us, a rather peculiar idea within the context of the world's cultures.[1]

In effect, this common view of bounded being and its realization in individualist forms of life is one that we have collectively created. And if this construction is delimiting, oppressive, and destructive, we may also create alternatives.[2]

It is the challenge of the present work to search beyond the traditions of the Enlightenment. My attempt is to generate an account of human action that can replace the presumption of bounded selves with a vision of relationship. I do not mean relationships between otherwise separate selves, but rather, a process of coordination that precedes the very concept of the self. My hope is to demonstrate that virtually all intelligible action is born, sustained, and/or extinguished within the ongoing process of relationship. From this standpoint there is no isolated self or fully private experience. Rather, we exist in a world of co-constitution. We are always already emerging from relationship; we cannot step out of relationship; even in our most private moments we are never alone. Further, as I will suggest, the future well-being of the planet depends significantly on the extent to which we can nourish and protect not individuals, or even groups, but the generative processes of relating.

Although the central challenge is that of bringing the reality of relationship into clear view, I do not intend this work as an exercise in theory. I am not interested in creating a work fit only for academic consumption. Rather, my attempt is to link this view of relationship to our daily lives. The concept of relational being should ultimately gain its meaning from our ways of going on together. By cementing the concept to forms of action, my hope is also to invite transformation in our institutions—in our classrooms, organizations, research laboratories, therapy offices, places of worship, and chambers of government. It is the future of our lives together that is at stake here, both locally and globally.

The reader must be warned. This proposal for a relation-centered alternative to the traditional view of self will be discomforting. A critical

[1]Geertz, C . (1979). From the native's point of view: On the nature of anthropological understanding. In P. Rabinow and W. M. Sullivan (Eds.) *Interpretive social science*. Berkeley, CA: University of California Press. (p. 59).

[2]Excellent overviews of the historical shifts in the Western understanding of the self since the Enlightenment are contained in Taylor, C. (1992). *Sources of the self, the making of modern identity*. Cambridge, MA: Harvard University Press; and Seigel, J. (2005). *The idea of the self*. Cambridge: Cambridge University Press.

challenge to the self has broad ramifications. We commonly suppose, for example, that people have effects on each other. As we say, parents mold their children's personality, schools have effects on students' minds, and the mass media have an impact on the attitudes and values of the population. Yet, this common presumption of cause and effect is at one with the tradition of bounded being. That is, it relies on conception of fundamentally separate entities, related to each other like the collision of billiard balls. In the present work I will propose that we move beyond cause and effect in understanding relationships. Nor, by bracketing the presumption of cause and effect, do I mean to celebrate determinism's alter, namely free will. The view of a freely choosing agent also sustains the tradition of bounded being. The vision of relational being will invite us, then, to set aside the freedom/determinism opposition, and to consider the world in terms of relational confluence.

This is not to say that I wish to destroy the traditional views of self, causality, and agency. I am not proposing that these traditional views are somehow false, that our traditions are fundamentally mistaken. Such assumptions are neither true nor false; they are simply human constructions around which we organize our lives. For example, we cannot ask whether the concept of justice is true; however, we may live or die depending on whether we believe a law is just or unjust. It is the fact that we live our lives within these understandings of independent selves, freedom, and determinism that make them worthy of serious reflection. And, if human connection can become as real to us as the traditional sense of individual separation, so do we enrich our potentials for living. Our traditions do have value; they are worth sustaining. However, such traditions should be treated as optional as opposed to defining the limits of our world. It is the development of a new alternative to which the present work is dedicated.

With this said, the reader may be willing to reflect with me as well on the utility of other assumptions and practices consistent with the tradition of bounded being. In the following pages I will also call into question the reality of mental illness, the significance of the brain in determining human behavior, the presumption of Truth, and the importance of educating individual minds. Questions will also be raised concerning the ultimate value of community, of democracy, and individual responsibility. Again, my attempt is not to judge the truth or falsity of these traditions, only their implications for our lives today. But consider: By presuming that people are "mentally ill" we obliterate more hopeful interpretations; by presuming the brain determines our actions, we fail to see that the brain is a servant in our quest for meaningful lives; by embracing Truth we eliminate the voices of all those who do not view the world in the same way; by stressing the education of individual minds we obscure the dependence of knowledge on relationships. Further, when we prize the community we invite ruptures between communities; by viewing the individual as the basis of democracy we suppress the importance of dialogue in fostering critical deliberation; and in holding individuals responsible we obscure our own contribution to untoward outcomes. We can do better.

Textual Companions

It should be clear that I do not embark on this journey into relational being as a lone thinker. Mine is not the first attempt to articulate a relationship-centered alternative to the tradition of bounded being. Indeed, it is largely to an array of textual companions that the present work owes its existence. I carry with me myriad voices, supportive, challenging, inspiring. It is appropriate to acknowledge this debt. In doing so the historical location of the work will become more apparent. Of equal importance, this précis will illuminate the major ways in which the present work deviates from the past. Scholars from the social sciences and philosophy have been especially important companions.

The Social Science Legacy

Paramount among my "textual friends" is a family of innovative social theorists whose writings span more than a century. In my graduate school days, imagined conversations with the classic work of William James,[3] Charles Horton Cooley,[4] and George Herbert Mead[5] were especially important. Each of these theorists painted a picture of the person as one whose self-understanding depended upon the views of others. The concepts of "the social self," the "looking glass self," and symbolic interaction formed a major challenge to the dominant view of the mind as a self-contained entity. For these theorists, one's sense of self was not so much a personal possession as a reflection of one's social existence. In my later graduate years, I had the good fortune of working with the social psychologist John Thibaut. For Thibaut the mental world took on a more rugged cast, with the maximization of personal gain viewed as the major goal. However, as

[3]James, W. (1890). *Principles of psychology*. New York: Henry Holt.

[4]Cooley, C. H. (1902). *Human nature and the social order*. New York: Charles Scribner.

[5]Mead, G. H. (1934). *Mind, self and society*. Chicago: University of Chicago Press. For more on the early development of thought on the social mind, see also Valsiner, J. and van der Veer, R. (2000). *The social mind: Construction of the idea*. Cambridge: Cambridge University Press; and Burkitt, I. (2008). *Social selves* (2nd ed.). London: Sage.

Thibaut and Kelley proposed,[6] individual maximization cannot be cut away from the relationship in which one is engaged. One's outcomes are intricately linked to processes of bargaining and negotiation. The mental world and social worlds were inextricably linked.

After graduate school I had the good fortune of teaching in Harvard's Department of Social Relations. It was here that I discovered the revolutionary work of the Russian developmentalist Lev Vygotsky. His writings also challenged the dominant view of isolated minds.[7] As he proposed, at least for the higher mental processes, everything that is in mind is first in the social world. In this sense, individual psychological functioning is a cultural derivative. These ideas also informed the work of numerous other theorists whose work has since been a deeply nourishing. John Shotter has been a dialogic companion for many years, and there is little in this book that has not been touched in some way by this cherished relationship.[8] Similarly, Jerome Bruner,[9] Rom Harré,[10] Richard Shweder,[11] Jaan Valsiner,[12] and Michael Cole[13] offered lively conversation in addition to their stimulating writings in cultural psychology. In all these works, the cultural context is celebrated for its impact on mental function.

The Department of Social Relations also offered me the good fortune of working with the sociologist, Chad Gordon. It was through Chad that I also became intrigued with the writings of Harold Garfinkel and other ethnomethodological scholars.[14] These works were enormously stimulating as they shifted the focus from the psychological world to the interactive processes responsible for mental attributions. Erving Goffman's presence at

[6]Thibaut, J. and Kelley, H. (1959). *The social psychology of groups*. New York: Wiley.

[7]Vygotsky, L. (1978). *Mind and society: Development of higher psychological processes*. Cambridge, MA: Harvard University Press.

[8]Shotter, J. (1993). *Cultural politics of everyday life: Social constructionism, rhetoric and knowing of the third kind*. Toronto: University of Toronto Press; (2008) *Conversational realities revisited: Life, language, body and world*. Chagrin Falls, OH: Taos Institute Publications.

[9]See, for example, Bruner, J. S. (1990). *Acts of meaning: Four lectures on mind and culture*. Cambridge, MA: Harvard University Press, Bruner, J. S. (1996). *The culture of education*. Cambridge, MA: Harvard University Press.

[10]Harré, R. (1979). *Social being*. Oxford: Basil Blackwell. (Also, issued in 1993 in a 2nd edition by the same publisher).

[11]Shweder, R. (1991). *Thinking through cultures: Expeditions in cultural psychology*. Cambridge, MA: Harvard University Press.

[12]See, for example, Valsiner J., and R. Van Der Veer, *op cit*.

[13]Cole, M. (1996). *Cultural psychology: A once and future discipline*. Cambridge, MA: Harvard University Press.

[14]Garfinkel, H. (1967). *Studies in ethnomethodology*. Englewood Cliffs, NJ: Prentice-Hall. See also Coulter, J. (1979). *The social construction of mind: Studies in ethnomethodology and linguistic philosophy*. Totowa, NJ: Rowman and Littlefield.

Harvard and the University of Pennsylvania generated an enriching colle-gial relationship extending to his death in 1982. His work also shifted the focus from the individual actor to the plane of relationship. For Goffman human action was largely social performance, and thus, the self was a byproduct of the theatrical conditions of the moment.[15] Much of this early work was ultimately collected in an edited volume, with Chad Gordon, *The self in social interaction.*[16]

Perhaps the next major watershed in deliberations on relational being issued from feminist theory. I owe my education here largely to my wife and feminist scholar, Mary Gergen.[17] Our friendship with Carol Gilligan[18] was also significant, and her challenge to Kohlberg's cognitive view of moral decision was the subject of many engaging conversations. Here, one could discern most clearly the political implications of shifting from an individualist to a relational conception of the person. The works of Jean Baker Miller,[19] Judith Jordan,[20] and their colleagues at at Wellesley College's Stone Center greatly expanded the relational vision. From their perspective there is a natural yearning for relationship. In order for this yearning to be fulfilled, one must experience growth-fostering relationships in which mutual empathy and empowerment are central.

I have also drawn continuing stimulation from writings in the thera-peutic tradition. For me, the work of socially oriented psychiatrists such as Erich Fromm[21] and Karen Horney[22] had always seemed more relevant to my life than Freud's rather hermetic conception of psychological process. Both saw culture and mind as fundamentally interdependent. Mental conditions were reflections of our social institutions, and in turn, our institutions were byproducts of our personal needs and desires. These views were resonant as well with Harry Stack Sullivan's interpersonal approach to psychiatry,

[15]See especially, Goffman, E. (1959). The *presentation of self in everyday life.* Garden City, NY: Doubleday; Goffman, E. (1961). *Asylums: Essays on the social situation of mental patients and other inmates.* Bolton, MA: Anchor.

[16]New York: Wiley, 1968.

[17]See especially her volumes, *Feminist thought and the structure of knowledge.* New York: New York University Press, 1988; *Feminist reconstructions in psychology: Narrative, gender & perfor-mance.* Thousand Oaks, CA: Sage, 2001.

[18]See Gilligan, C. (1993). *In a different voice: Psychological theory and women's development.* Cambridge, MA: Harvard University Press.

[19]Miller, J. B. (1976). *Toward a new psychology of women.* Boston, MA: Beacon Press.

[20]Jordan, J., Kaplan, A., Miller, J. B., Stiver, I., Surrey, J. L. (1991). *Women's growth in connection.* New York: Guilford; Jordan, J. V. (1997). *Women's growth in diversity: More writings from the Stone Center.* New York: Guilford.

[21]Fromm, E. (1941). *Escape from freedom.* New York: Rinehart.

[22]Horney, K. (1950). *Neurosis and human growth.* New York: Norton.

and Carl Rogers' humanist theory and practice.[23] Similar to the Stone Center feminists, both saw the development of individual well-being as fully dependent on relationships. The Stone Center group also drew heavily from the writings of object relations theorists in psychiatry.[24] Abandoning Freud's emphasis on pleasure seeking, the emphasis was placed instead on the individual's attachments with significant others. Early patterns of attachment (and rejection) laid down tracks of life-long consequence. This work has been extended by the fascinating work of Stephen Mitchell and his colleagues to provide a relational account of the therapeutic process. On this view, the meeting of the client and therapist is the inter-twining of two complex and dynamic, relational histories.[25]

This rich history of social science writing poses a significant challenge to the individualist tradition. Why is it necessary to add yet a further treatise? What does the present work offer that is not already in place? For me the major agitation derives from the inability of most of these formulations to separate themselves sufficiently from the individualist tradition. There are three significant residues that can be found in one form or another in most all these formulations. First, for many there is the continued focus on a mental world in itself, a world that ultimately functions as the source of individual action. It is variously a world of symbols, experience, cognition, emotion, motives, and/or dynamic processes. In each case attention is directed to an inner region, one that is importantly influenced by the social surrounds, but significant in its own right. The strong sense of a psychological center of action remains solid. My attempt in this work is to remove the reality of a distinctly inner or mental world. This is not to replace it with a behaviorist view of "everything on the surface." Rather, the attempt is to eliminate the very distinction between inner and outer, and to replace it with a view of relationally embodied action.

Second, there is strong tendency in many of these writings to theorize in terms of separate units, the self and other, the person and culture, the individual and society. Relationships on this account are the result of distinct entities coming into contact, they are derivative of the fundamentally

[23]Sullivan, H. S. (1953). *The interpersonal theory of psychiatry*. William Alanson White Psychiatric Foundation. Reissued by Norton, 1997; Rogers, C. (1961). *On becoming a person: A therapist's view of psychotherapy*. New York: Houghton Mifflin.

[24]For an overview, see Mitchell, S. (1988). *Relational conceptions in psychoanalysis: An integration*. Cambridge, MA: Harvard University Press. See also, Curtis, R. C. (Ed.) (1991). *The relational self: Theoretical convergences in psychoanalysis and social psychology*. New York: Guilford.

[25]See for example, Mitchell, S. A. (1993). *Hope and dread in psychoanalysis*. New York: Basic Books; Pizer, S. A. (1998). *Building bridges: The negotiation of paradox in psychoanalysis*. New York: Analytic Press.

separate units. My attempt here is to reverse the order, and to treat what we take to be the individual units as derivative of relational process. Closely related, there is a strong tendency within many of these writings to employ a causal template in explaining human action. Thus, there is a tendency to speak of the culture, society, family, or intimate others as "influencing," "having an effect on," or "determining the actions of" the individual. Again, such an analytic posture sustains the presumption of independent beings, and defines relationships as their derivative.

With this said, however, there are passages, metaphors, and insights within these traditions that will make their way into the present work. My attempt here is not to abandon this rich and significant work so much as to stretch its implications to the point that a more fundamental paradigm shift can be take place. As Brent Slife would put it, many of the existing attempts represent a weak relationality, or social inter-action; the attempt here is to generate a "strong relationality," one in which there is no condition of independence.[26] In this respect, there are other social science scholars and practitioners whose writings are more immediately congenial with the proposals of the present work. Their writings, and often our conversations, play an integral role in the emerging thesis, and will later be acknowledged.

Philosophic Inheritance

From the early writings of Descartes, Locke, and Kant to contemporary discussions of mind and brain, philosophers have lent strong support to the reality of bounded being. In many respects, the hallmark of Western philosophy was its presumption of dualism: mind and world, subject and object, self and other. Yet, the field of philosophy also thrives on disputation. Thus, while the individualist view of human functioning has been dominant, there are significant defectors. In developing the proposals for relational being, a number of these have made lively textual companions. An early enchantment with existentialism lead me, for one, to the work of Maurice Merleau-Ponty. Although placing individual consciousness at the center of his writings, Merleau-Ponty also argued for a consciousness that was deeply inhabited by the other.[27] One's perception of the other, he proposed, contains within it a consciousness of being perceived by the

[26]Slife, B. (2004). Taking practices seriously: Toward a relational ontology. *Journal of Theoretical and Philosophical Psychology. 24*, 179–195.
[27]cf. Merleau-Ponty, M. (1968). *The visible and the invisible.* Evanston, IL: Northwestern University Press.

other. As one observes the other during a conversation, for example, one is simultaneously conscious of being observed. The two forms of consciousness are inextricable. Or again, the consciousness of touching another also embodies consciousness of being touched by another. As we caress another, we are also conscious of what it is to be caressed by another.

Closely related was the work of Martin Heidegger. Like Merleau-Ponty, much of Heidegger's analysis treats the phenomenological world of consciousness. At the same time, Heidegger attempted to subvert the traditional subject/object dichotomy, in which there are conscious subjects contrasted with a separate world of objects "out there."[28] For Heidegger, consciousness is always consciousness of something. Remove all objects of consciousness, and there is no consciousness; remove all consciousness and objects cease to exist. Thus subject and object are fundamentally co-existent. The insertion of dashes between the words of his pivotal concept, Being-in-the-world, functions as a visual illustration of the conceptual breaking of the traditional binary. Although emerging from the soil of American pragmatism, the work of John Dewey and Arthur Bentley resonates with Heidegger's binary-breaking innovation. As they saw it, there is a mutually constituting relationship between the person and the object (mind and world).[29] Thus they argued for replacing the traditional view of inter-action (independent objects in causal relationship with experience), with the concept of transaction.

Although fascinated by these attempts, they do not take me far enough. Again, they begin with the presumption of a private space of consciousness, and through various analytic strategies, attempt to escape. My hope, on the contrary, is to begin with an account of relational process and derive from it a conception of individual consciousness. Further, to appreciate the works of these philosophers one must crawl inside a highly complex and exotic world of words. The major concepts acquire their meaning largely from the way they are used within the philosophic texts. There is little exit to social practice, a concern that is central to my efforts.

I have also drawn significant inspiration from a number of moral philosophers whose work blurs the boundaries between self and other. John MacMurray's *Persons in Relationship*[30] was of early interest. Here the chief concern was the preeminent value of relationship or community as opposed to individual well-being. For MacMurray special stress was placed on individual sacrifice to the communal good. Echoing this latter view is the more

---

[28]Heidegger, M. (1962). *Being and time*. New York: Harper & Row.
[29]Dewey, J., and Bentley, A. F. (1949). *Knowing and the known*. Boston: Beacon.
[30]MacMurray, J. (1961). *Persons in relation*. Atlantic Highlands, NJ: Humanities Press.

widely known phenomenological work of Emmanuel Levinas.[31] For Levinas, individual subjectivity is not independent of others. Rather, personal consciousness is constituted by the existence of the other (metaphorically, "the face of the other"). In this sense one is fundamentally responsible for the other; ethics and consciousness are co-terminal. Perhaps the most significant contribution to the present work is Martin Buber's volume, *I and Thou.*[32] Buber distinguishes between two modes of consciousness (phenomenological states), in terms of one's relation to the other. In the most common mode (I–It), the other is an object, fundamentally separate from self. Sacred for Buber, however, is the I–Thou relationship in which the other is encountered without boundaries. In this sense there is a mutually absorbing unity; the conceptual distinction between persons disappears.

Yet, while these works have been inspiring, they still retain what for me are problematic vestiges of the individualist tradition. Although the community is ultimately prized by MacMurray, it is achieved through the voluntary acts of individual agents. For all their concern with relationship, the works of both Levinas and Buber still remain allied with the phenomenological or subjectivity-centered tradition. Moral action is ultimately dependent on the voluntary decision of the actor. Further, it is not clear in these cases what kind of action is entailed. In Levinas' case, a strong emphasis is placed on self-sacrifice. However, the landscape of relevant action is never made apparent. For Buber, the I–Thou encounter is the exception to the common condition of I–It separation. However, if moved by Buber's analysis to embrace the sacred posture of I–Thou, it is not clear what follows in terms of action. What is it, exactly, to encounter another as Thou? In contrast, my hope is to link the vision of relational being to particular forms of social practice.

There is also an enormously important line of scholarship stemming from sociological and political theory. This work is especially important in its critique of liberal individualism, both in terms of its influence on cultural life and its adequacy as an orientation to civil society and politics. In terms of the injuries to daily life, the volume, *Habits of the Heart: Individualism and Commitment in American Life*, by Robert Bellah and his colleagues, was pivotal in its significance.[33] This work revealed in touching detail the insidious implications of individualist ideology for human relationships. This volume also resonated with the initiatives of the communitarian

[31]Levinas. E. (1985). *Ethics and infinity.* (R. A. Cohen, Trans.). Pittsburgh: Duquesne University Press.

[32]New York: Free Press, 1971. (Original English edition, 1937).

[33]Bellah, R. N., Madsen, R., Sullivan, W. M., Swidler, A., and Tipton, S. M. (1985). *Habits of the heart: Individuals and commitment in American life.* Berkeley: University of California Press.

movement, spearheaded by Amitai Etzioni and his colleagues.[34] Here the strong emphasis is on one's obligations to the community as opposed to claims to individual rights. The work of political theorist, Michael Sandel,[35] and philosopher, Alasdair MacIntyre[36] add important conceptual dimension to this movement. They draw attention to the deep lodgment of the individual in relationships, and find the idea of the unencumbered, free agent seriously flawed. These various works have been invaluable sources of illumination for me. However, I have been less content with the valorization of community favored as the alternative to individualism. There is not only the problem of determining the boundaries of what constitutes one's community. There are additional complications resulting from the very drawing of these boundaries. Communities are also bounded entities and create the same kinds of conflicts that attend our viewing persons as fundamentally separated. In the case of communal commitments—including the religious and political—the consequences can be disastrous.

In the pages that follow, there will be echoes of these important works. However, there are other philosophical writings that are more congenial to the present undertaking. Foremost are the latter writings of Ludwig Wittgenstein. His textual companionship has been of enormous significance, and without his *Philosophical Investigations*,[37] I suspect the present undertaking would never have gotten under way. The literary theorist, Mikhail Bakhtin, is also a prominent voice throughout this work. Although never fully severing mind from action, his multi-hued concept of dialogism has been richly stimulating.

At the same time, there is one important difference that separates the present work from all the preceding theorists (save Wittgenstein). These various philosophers have labored in a tradition concerned with establishing foundations, that is, grounding accounts of reason, truth, human nature, ethical value, and so on. Sometimes such accounts are called "first philosophies." In contrast, the present work holds no such aspirations. Although the form of writing may sometimes suggest the contrary, my aim is not to articulate what simply is, or must be, the nature of human nature. My aim is neither to be true nor accurate in traditional terms. Rather, my hope is to offer a compelling construction of the world, an inviting vision,

---

[34]See, for example, Etzioni, A. (1993). *The spirit of community: Rights, responsibilities and the communitarian agenda.* New York: Crown.

[35]See, for example, Sandel, M. (1996). *Democracy's discontent: America in search of a public philosophy.* Cambridge, MA: Harvard University Press.

[36]See especially, MacIntyre, A. (1981). *After virtue.* Notre Dame: University of Notre Dame Press.

[37]Wittgenstein, L. (1978). *Philosophical investigations.* Oxford: Blackwell.

or a lens of understanding—all realized or embodied in relevant action. The account is not a set of marching orders, but an invitation to a dance.

Engaging the Writing

Challenging traditions always carries risks. Even when our traditions are flawed, at least they are comfortable flaws. Change invites fear of what follows. These are also my experiences in writing this work. With the slow unfolding of this vision of relational being, I have also come to reflect critically on my own ways of being in the world. One comfortable convention targeted by my critical gaze was my practice of professional writing. As I came to see, traditional scholarly writing also carries with it strong traces of the individualist tradition. It is a genre that separates the knowing author from the ignorant reader; it positions the author as the owner of his or her own ideas; it often portrays the author as one whose mind is fully coherent, confident, and conflict free. I will have more to say about this tradition in Chapter 7. Yet, one's form of writing is also a medium that carries a message, and in the present work it is a message that undermines the relational thesis I wish to advance.

My aim in the pages that follow is to explore a form of writing that more fully embodies the relational thesis. How is this so? As you will find, the writing proceeds as a series of "punctuated layers." The layers will also embody different traditions of communication. At times, my scholarly voice will dominate; at other times I will write in a way that is more congenial to practitioners: I also include personal experiences relevant to the subject at hand. In addition to these layers, I have added aesthetic voices— art, poetry, photography—and even touches of humor. At times I will weave into the mix the expressions of friends, both textual and personal.

There are several ways in which I hope this form of writing serves to convey content. First, the use of multiple voices makes it more difficult to identify who I am, as the author. Without a single, coherent voice it is more difficult to define the boundaries of my being. Further, as the thesis unfolds I will characterize persons as embedded within multiple relationships. Who and what we are is constituted quite differently in many of these relationships. Thus, we all carry many different voices, each born of a specific history of relationship. By using multiple "voices" in the text, my hope is that the reader will come to appreciate the many relations from which "I as author" have sprung. Moreover, in using these various voices, my hope is to open a relationship with a broader range of readers. In writing for a single audience—for example, scholars, practitioners, or students—I strengthen the walls between groups in society. By using multiple genres perhaps a step can be taken to cross the existing boundaries, and to invite more inclusive dialogue. Finally, in contrast to traditional writing, the attempt is to relinquish some control over how the words are to be understood. By juxtaposing mixed genres, my hope is to avoid distinct closure of meaning. A space is opened for the reader to generate new associations and images.

Challenges of Language

In addition to the form of writing, a preliminary note on issues of language use will be helpful. First, I had a strong urge in writing this book to use the phrase, *relational self*, as opposed to *relational being*. This would have placed the volume more clearly in the long and estimable tradition of writings on the self. However, the term "self" carries with it strong traces of the individualist tradition. It suggests again a bounded unit, one that *interacts* with other distinct units. Further, the "self" is a noun, and thus suggests a static and enduring entity. However, the term "being," ambiguously poised as participle, noun, and gerund, subverts the image of a bounded unit. In being, we are in motion, carrying with us a past as we move through the present into a becoming.

The second issue of language use is more complex. Central to this work is a view of relationship that is not defined in terms of two or more persons coming together. Rather, as I will propose, the very idea of individual persons is a byproduct of relational process. But how can I describe this process without using a language that inherently divides the world into bounded entities? To be more specific, by relying on common conventions of writing, I will invariably rely on nouns and pronouns, both of which designate bounded or identifiable units. The very phrase," I rely on you...." already defines *me* as separate from *you*. Similarly, transitive verbs typically imply causal relations, with the action of one unit impinging on another. To say, "He invited her," or "she treated him nicely" again creates a world of separation. Try as I may to create a sense of process that precedes the construction of entities, the conventions of language resist. They virtually insist that separate entities exist prior to relationship.

It is tempting here to experiment with new linguistic forms that might erase the troublesome boundaries. Both Heidegger and Derrida have done so, the first by placing hyphens between words, and the second by striking through them. However, there is a danger in abandoning the common conventions of communication; the major thesis may be thrust into obscurity. My choice, then, is to retain the common usages, and to rely on the good will of the reader to appreciate the dilemma. I will thus write of relationships in the traditional way—of this person's relation to that, of her relationship to him, of this organization related to another. However, the reader may also benefit from a heuristic I found useful in writing, namely a *logic of placeholders*. When I write about the individual, the person, myself, I, me, you, and so on I will use the words in the conventional way. However, I will hold out a place in which they can be understood as emergents of relationship. For example, I may write of "Ronald's relationship to Maria," as if they existed independently. The convention helps me to communicate with you as reader. However, as I write I also hold a place for realizing that both these names are constructions created in a relational process that preceded the names. Further, even the common separation we make between one physical body and the other, are constructions born of relationship. The belief that the skin marks the separation of the body from the world is a useful fiction that we have developed together. Yet, the moment I try to describe what a word like "together" means, the language will grasp me by the throat. I will speak as if two physically separate entities were meeting. I can only hope that you can join me in being aware that we are holding out a place in which we can understand the very idea of "physical entities" as a byproduct of relational process.

The Unfolding Narrative

In the choice of layered writing, the reader may sometimes lose the over-arching logic of this work. Thus, a guide to the unfolding tale may be useful. In the initial chapter I hope to make clear why the search for relational being is so important, why this is not an exercise in theoretical gymnastics, but an invitation to explore new and more promising forms of life. Here I am joined by many scholars who share in their discontent with the individualist tradition. The initial chapter will assemble many of these voices into a "chorus of critique." With the chorus in place, we can then embark on the exploration of relational being.

I will use the next three chapters to introduce the concept of relational being. Chapter 2 will focus on the pivotal concept of co-action, or the process of collaborative action from which all meaning is generated. Or in general terms, it is from co-action that we develop meaningful realities, rationalities, and moralities. It is in this process that a world of bounded entities is created, and through which alternative worlds may be established. This argument also prepares the way for Chapters 3 and 4, in which I will revisit the vast vocabulary of mental life so central to the individualist tradition. If all meaning issues from relationship, then we may include the very idea of mental life. Unlike Descartes, individual reason is not the source of human action; rather, the concept of individual reason is an outcome of relationship. In these two chapters I will thus attempt to recast the vocabulary of the psychological world in relational terms. I will develop the thesis that terms such as "thinking," "remembering," "experiencing," and "feeling," do not refer to events inside the head of the individual, but to coordinated actions within relationship.

In the two chapters (Part II) that follow, I begin to shift the focus from theory to practice, and particularly to matters of everyday life and death. New conceptual territory will be opened, but with a sharper eye to its implications for action. In Chapter 5, the pivotal concept of multi-being will be developed. As an outcome of immersion in multiple relationships, I will propose, we emerge as rich in potential for relationship. However, the realization of this potential can also be radically diminished in any given relationship. This discussion will give way to a concern with the art of coordinating action. In Chapter 6 the issue of social bonding will become focal. While social bonding can be deeply nurturing, my particular concern in this case is with the destructive repercussions. This treatment will invite a discussion of dialogic practices for restoring relationship between antagonistic parties.

The next four chapters (comprising Part III) are more specifically devoted to societal practices. If our sense of bounded being is fortified by existing practices, what kinds of changes are necessary to appreciate the power of relationship? In my view, there is a sea change taking place across many professions, in which the focus on the single individual is being replaced with fostering effective relationships. These chapters will bring many of these offerings into concert. In Chapter 7 the focus is on knowledge as a relational achievement. Replacing the heroic accounts of the individual discoverer, I will propose that what we call knowledge emerges from the process of co-action. I will then consider three relevant sites of practice—the creation of disciplines, the act of writing, and the practice of social science research. In each of these instances, there is a need for replacing fragmentation and conflict with productive coordination. This discussion will prepare the way for an extended treatment of education in Chapter 8. If knowledge is achieved through relationship, then educators should shift their attention from the individual student to the nexus of relationships in which education occurs. In this discussion I will focus most particularly on pedagogical practices as they are fostered in relations between teachers and students, among students themselves, between classroom and community, and between classroom and global communities.

Therapeutic practices take center stage in Chapter 9. Here I suspend the traditional focus of therapy on the individual and replace it with a view of therapy as relational recovery. If human anguish is born within the process of collaborative action, then collaborative process should serve as the central focus of therapy. This does not demand so much an abandonment of traditional therapy, as a rethinking of the way these practices contribute (or not) to relational well-being. This discussion of relational recovery prepares the way for the subsequent treatment of organizational life (Chapter 10). Traditional organizations are viewed as collections of single individuals, each hired, advanced, or terminated on the basis of individual knowledge, skills, and motivation. In this chapter I replace this view with relational process as the critical element to effective organizing. Within this context I will take up specific practices of decision making, leadership, personnel evaluation, and the relationship of the organization to its surrounds.

In the concluding chapters (Part IV) I step back to reflect on broader implications of relational being. In Chapter 11, I consider the moral consequences of these deliberations. There is a strong relativist message that follows from the view that all moral values emerge from relational histories. Must relativism be our conclusion? Here I make a case for relational responsibility, that is, the shared responsibility for sustaining those processes out of which moral values are generated. In the final chapter, I take up issues of spirituality. Can a bridge be formed, I ask, between the secular account of relational being developed and traditions of spirituality? A bridge to dialogue between these traditions is found in the ultimate impossibility of grasping the nature of relational process. This same inability is also found in numerous theological attempts to locate the nature of the sacred. There is a space, then, for appreciating the sacred potential of collaborative practices. Daily life takes on spiritual significance.

One

From Bounded to Relational Being

I

Bounded Being

If I ask you to tell me about your childhood years, how will you respond? Chances are you will talk about your mother, your father, a brother or a sister or two; you may tell me about your house, your dog, and so on. Nothing remarkable here. But consider again: the world of your description is filled with separate or bounded beings—yourself to begin, and then there is mother, and then father, sister.... What lies between these commas, each insuring that we understand these as individual beings? What is it, for example, that separates you and your mother? Skin and space you might venture....

•

When you were very young and tried with crayons to depict the world, chances are you began with bounded beings. This stick figure is "my mommy," "that blob is "my house," and so on. Each may be clearly delineated...perhaps with the unmistakable force of black crayon. For young children the individual figures simply float in empty space. For older children a background may be recognized—vast splotches of green or blue or yellow. There are first the bounded beings; the remainder is irrelevant.

•

Is daily life not understood in just this way: me here, you there, a space between?
For us it is a world of fundamental separation.

•

If I ask you to tell me about yourself—what drives your actions in life, what motivates you—how will you proceed? Chances are that you will tell me about the way you think about life...and possibly death. You will describe your desires, what you want from life, what you hope to achieve. And if comfortable with me, you may tell me about your feelings, your love, your passions, and your repulsions. Your inner world is bursting with content. Some slips out in your words and gestures, the remainder lies hidden from view...perhaps, you think, even from yourself. Such accounts suggest a profound separation. What is most important to us, we believe, lies buried within—in thoughts, feelings, desires, hopes, and so on. You are there within your shell, and I am here within mine. We proclaim good fortune when we sense the sharing of these inner worlds.

•

In this chapter I wish to grapple with the impact of these boundaries. At this point in Western history we take them for granted. The sense of self as fundamentally independent is tissued to our daily lives; it pervades our private moments; it is insinuated into our daily relationships; it is inscribed in the objects about us; it is secreted within our institutions. We have no difficulty in speaking of "my thoughts," "my decision," "my love," "my experience," "my needs".... and we seek to know the "intentions," the "true feelings," and the "personal values" of others. Indeed, we are comfortable living within our crayoned lines. But should we be?

In what follows I wish to confront some of the liabilities. When we take these boundaries for granted—simply as the way things are—what are the results for our lives together? What is invited and what is denied in our lives? In my view, there are enormous costs entailed, costs that we have also come to take for granted. We can no longer afford such complacency. As I shall propose, there are important ways in which the presumption of persons as bounded units now emerges as a threat to the well-being of the world more generally. Such concerns are voiced within a significant corpus of writing that attacks what is characterized as the individualist tradition.[1] Much of this writing will be echoed in the present account.

---

[1]See, for example, Gelpi, D. L. (1989). *Beyond individualism, toward a retrieval of moral discourse in America*. Notre Dame, IN: University of Notre Dame Press; Hewitt, J. P. (1989). *Dilemmas of the American self*. Philadelphia: Temple University Press; Bellah, R. N. et al. (1985). *Habits of the heart: Individualism and commitment in American life*. Berkeley: University of California Press; Heller, T.C., Sosna, M., and Wellbery, D. E. (Eds.) (1986). *Reconstructing individualism, autonomy, individuality, and the self in Western thought*. Stanford: Stanford University Press; Capps, D., and Fenn, R. K. (1998). *Individualism reconsidered, Readings bearing on the endangered self in modern society*. New York: Continuum; Lasch, C. (1978). *The culture of narcissism*.

Yet, my present critique is not an end, but a beginning. It establishes the groundwork for the major challenge of this book, sketching an alternative to the tradition of bounded being. This vision, relational being, seeks to recognize a world that is not within persons but within their relationships, and that ultimately erases the traditional boundaries of separation. There is nothing that requires us to understand our world in terms of independent units; we are free to mint new and more promising understandings. As the conception of relational being is grasped, so are new forms of action invited, new forms of life made intelligible, and a more promising view of our global future made apparent. No, this does not mean abandoning the past; the traditional view of the bounded individual need not be eliminated. But once we can see it as a construction of our own making—one option among many—we may also understand that the boundary around the self is also a prison.

•

I divide this critical inquiry into three sections. In the first I take up issues related to the daily characterization of ourselves, and the deadening weight we acquire through the discourse of a bounded self. I then turn from the sense of self to the corrosive impact of bounded being on our daily relations. Finally, I take up the broader character of cultural life. What happens to the general patterns of living when we accept the tradition of independent individuals? To be sure, my account will be selective. I focus exclusively on the unfortunate fall-out of a longstanding tradition. But my attempt is not inclusive; there are still further critiques that are absent from this assay. There is also good reason for critique without apology. So deeply hallowed are the ideals of autonomy, individual reason, personal conscience, liberty, free competition, and self-knowledge—all companions to bounded being—that isolated doubts are seldom heard. If there is to be transformation, these dissenting voices must have their day.

Self as Abuse

Conceptions of the person are children of cultural history. Prior to the 16th century, there was little doubt in the West that the holy soul was the central ingredient of the self. This conception made it intelligible to seek absolution of sin from God's representatives on earth. Self-conception and the institution of religion walked hand in hand. As the conception of soul has gradually been replaced by its secular counterpart, conscious reason,

New York: Basic Books; Leary, M. R. (2004). *The curse of the self, self-awareness, egotism, and the quality of human life.* New York: Oxford University Press.

so has the influence of the church been undermined. Yet, what are the results of our enlightened sense that we are the self-determining agents of our actions? Consider first the dimensions of personal life. I focus in particular on concerns with isolation, evaluation, and self-esteem.

Fundamental Isolation

We gaze into each other's eyes with hopes of glimpsing the wellspring of action. I know that somewhere within you dwells the thoughts, hopes, dreams, feelings, and desires that center your life. Your words and deeds may give expression to these internal undulations, but imperfectly so. Yet, if what is most important about you lies somewhere inside you, then you shall remain forever unknown to me. The essential "you" is not before me, available to my gaze, but somewhere else—lurking behind the eyes. I can never penetrate the shield of the face to know what is truly there, what you truly think, feel, or want. Even in our most intimate moments I cannot know what is behind your words of endearment; I can never grasp their meaning. We remain fundamentally estranged. And you are identically placed. My private world is unavailable to you. What is essential to me is "in here," a private space that neither you nor anyone else can enter. I exist in a garden of good and evil to which there are no visitors. And so here we are, you in your world and I in mine. I was born alone, and shall die alone. It is the fundamental condition of human nature.

•

Ships that pass in the night, and speak each other in passing,
Only a signal shown, a distant voice in the darkness;
So the ocean of life, we pass and we speak one another,
Only a look and a voice, then darkness again and silence.
—Henry Wadsworth Longfellow

•

If we understand ourselves as fundamentally isolated, then living alone is a natural act. Almost half the adults living in the United States now live alone. Closely related is the fact that in 2004 the average American had only two close friends in whom they could confide on important matters. This was down from 1985 when the average was three such confidants. The number who said they had no one they could confide in jumped from 10% in 1985 to 25% in 2004.[2] Thus the prevalence of loneliness should come as

[2]McPherson, M., Smith-Lovin, L., and Brashears, M. (2006). Social isolation in America: Changes in core discussion networks over two decades. *American Sociological Review, 71*(3), 353–375.

little surprise. There are now over two million websites devoted to the challenge of loneliness in contemporary life. Loneliness is viewed not only as a deficit in itself, but is associated with dangerously elevated levels of blood pressure,[3] and to depression and suicide.[4]

•

> We suffer a lot in our society from loneliness. So much of our
> life is an attempt to not be lonely: "Let's talk to each other; let's
> do things together so we won't be lonely." And yet inevitably,
> we are really alone in these human forms. We can pretend;
> we can entertain each other; but that's about the best we can do.
> When it comes to the actual experience of life, we are very much
> alone; and to expect anyone else to take away our loneliness is asking
> too much.
>
> —Ajahn Sumedho

•

Nor should it be surprising that many therapists, scholars, and theologians describe what they feel is a distinct loss of meaning in people's lives.[5] There is a failure to locate something truly significant—worthy of a life commitment, a compass for concerted action, a reason to remain alive. Yet, we also celebrate autonomy, the "self-made man," the individual who resists social convention and marches to his own drummer. Is it this very celebration that lends itself to the loss of meaning? When asked about what is truly meaningful to them, many people speak of love, family, and God. Yet, what is the origin of such investments? Could they ever be discovered in solitary? What if we could understand all that we call thought, fantasy, or desire as originating in relationships? Even when physically isolated we might discover the remnants of relationship. We would invite a renewed appreciation of self *with* others.

•

[3]Hawkley, L. C., Masi, C. M., Berry, J. D., and Cacioppo, J. T. (2006). Loneliness is a unique predictor of age-related differences in systolic blood pressure. *Psychology and Aging, 21,* 152–164.

[4]See, for example, Stravynski, A., and Boyer, R. (2001). Loneliness in relation to suicide ideation and parasuicide: A population-wide study. *Suicide and Life-Threatening Behavior, 31,* 32–40; Hafen, B. Q., and Frandsen, K. J. (1986). *Youth suicide: Depression and loneliness.* Evergreen, CO: Cordillera Press.

[5]See, for example, Frankl, V. (1985). The unheard cry for meaning: Psychotherapy and humanism. New York: Washington Square Press; Krasko, G. (2004). *The unbearable boredom of being: A crisis of meaning in America.* New York: Universe.

I once embraced the heroics of lonely isolation. These were the days when I thrilled to the writings of Sartre and Camus, liberally laced with doses of Jack Kerouac and Alan Ginsberg. In this world I was the master of my fate; each moment was a choice-point at which the authentic act could be fundamentally redeeming. I was Sisyphus in a meaningless world. In my daily decision to painfully push the boulder to the mountaintop, I became a hero. I needed no one; I laughed at their conventional ways....until one day I became conscious of the fact that such heroism was not itself born in isolation. The image of the isolated hero was a cultural tradition. My heroism was but a performance in search of vicarious praise from my heroes.

•

The meaning of one's life for most Americans is to become one's own person, almost to give birth to oneself. Much of this process ...is negative. It involves breaking free from family, community, and inherited ideas.

—Robert Bellah

Unrelenting Evaluation

If I am fundamentally alone, the origin of my actions, then what is to be said of failure? To be sure, there are events outside my control, but by and large, my failures are of my own doing. In this sense, any inadequate performance, impropriety, or public failure throws the essential "me" into question. All insufficiencies in behavior are potentially expressions of an internal lack. To explain, "it wasn't my fault," "my parents neglected me," or "I had no knowledge of the consequences," is to defend against the dreaded accusation: you are inferior![6]

The possibility of personal inferiority begins as early as a child's first experience with competitive games. "My failure" is not taken lightly. Upon entering school, the "self in question" becomes institutionalized. From that day forward the individual exists in state of continuous evaluation: "am I good enough," "will I fail," "how will I be judged by my teachers, parents, and classmates?" "have I sinned?" The stakes become higher as one's career is on the line. There are the SATs, IQ scores, GREs, MCATs, LSATs...And then the college graduate enters adult professional life to find semi-annual

---

[6]As Karen Horney proposed, within the United States, the threat of self-insufficiency is virtually a national neurosis. See Horney, K. (1937). *The neurotic personality of our time.* New York: Norton.

performance evaluations, promotion evaluations...a life replete with threats to one's worth.[7]

•

Arriving at Yale was a harrowing experience. At the time, the dominant culture was New England prep, and entering as a scholarship boy from the South I was already déclassé. Everywhere I turned there were threats to my shaky sense of worth. There were the rich to remind me of my impecunious origins, the super-cool to illuminate my lack of sophistication, the world travelers to reveal my parochialism, the super-jocks to diminish my athletic skills, the superbly handsome to remind me of my average looks, and the dedicated scholars to suggest my shallowness. There were days that I wondered whether I had anything to offer. By what fluke was I ever accepted? Yet, there were also late night bull sessions with dorm-mates: a Jew from Florida, a Catholic from New York State, and a playboy from Connecticut. Slowly revealed through our quips and light hearted debates was the fact we all shared an over-arching sense of apprehension. And, in spite of our differences, there were important moments in which we assured each other that we just might be OK.

•

The number of ways in which we can fail is skyrocketing. As contemporary technologies bring us into an ever-expanding orbit of relationships, so do the criteria of self-evaluation multiply. Every acquaintance can remind us of some way in which we may be inadequate. A friend from California may remind you that you are not relaxing and enjoying life enough, while a successful associate from Ohio suggests that if you aren't working at least 11 hours a day you are wasting your talents. A friend from Boston reminds you that you are not keeping up with all the wonderful literature now being published, while your colleague from DC implies that your knowledge of world politics is inadequate. A visitor from Paris gives you the sense that your clothing is without style, while a ruddy companion from Colorado implies that you are growing soft. In the meantime the media confront us with a barrage of additional criteria of personal failure. Are you sufficiently adventurous, clean, well traveled, low in cholesterol,

[7]As research indicates, the apprehension of evaluation may indeed reduce one's performance. Fearing failure, one begins to fail. See, for example, Steele, C., and Aronson, J. (1995). Stereotype threat and the intellectual test performance of African Americans. *Journal of Personality and Social Psychology, 69,* 797–811.

well invested, slim, skilled in cooking, odor-free, burglarproof, family oriented? Every social gathering raises questions of one's popularity; every remark can carry hints of one's failings; and every utterance, article of clothing, or bodily blemish risks sundry and subtle forms of derision. What damage is inflicted on society's youth when it is only "Number 1" that counts?

Unrelenting evaluation is not an inherent dimension of social life; it is specifically an outcome of presuming a world of bounded beings. If we did not understand the world in terms of separated individuals, each acting according to ability and state of mind, neither failure nor blame would belong to any ONE. For a Buddhist the challenge of life is not that of struggling to avoid failure and achieve success; it is to transcend the very structures that deem the struggle significant. Such an insight invites the exploration of relational being.

The Search for Self-Esteem

If I am fundamentally alone, and confronting continuous threat of evaluation, what is my fundamental goal in life? Is it not my own survival? I can trust no one to care for me; they cannot know me; and I am always under threat of evaluation. Thus, caring for the self is paramount. In spite of my shortcomings, I must learn to love, accept, and prize myself.

So common is this form of logic that many social scientists believe it is essential to human makeup. For the eminent psychotherapist, Carl Rogers, most problems of human suffering are caused by a lack of self-regard.[8] Self-regard is natural, argued Rogers; it is there from birth. However, our problems stem from living in a world where others' regard is always conditional. "I love you *only if* you do..." In a world where conditions are placed on our value, we come to evaluate ourselves conditionally, proposes Rogers. The result is constant self-doubt, an inability to be open and loving with others, and the erection of numerous defenses. The therapist's task is primarily that of giving the client unconditional regard. By prizing the client in spite of failings, he or she will be restored to fullness.

Much the same message is evidenced in the longstanding interest of psychologists in self-esteem. The number of research studies on self-esteem now numbers in the thousands.[9] The primary concern of this research has

---

[8]Rogers, C. R. (1961). *On becoming a person, a therapist's view of psychotherapy.* Boston: Houghton Mifflin (1967 – London: Constable).

[9]See, for example, Wylie, R. (1976). *The self-concept: Theory and research on selected topics.* Lincoln, NB: University of Nebraska Press; Hewitt, J. P. (1998). *The myth of self-esteem.* New York: St. Martins; Branden, N. (2001). *The psychology of self-esteem.* San Francisco: Jossey-Bass; Mruk, C. (2006). *Self-esteem research, theory, and practice: Toward a positive psychology of self-esteem.* New York: Springer.

been to demonstrate the numerous problems in life associated with low self-esteem, and to locate ways of boosting self-regard. The impact of such research has now reached societal proportions. School programs for enhancing self-esteem, support programs for adults, and self-help exercises have become a major cultural staple. The National Association for Self-Esteem—dedicated to "integrating self-esteem into the fabric of American Society"—offers posters, games, books, toys, clothing, and tapes to help children raise their sense of self-worth. At present there are over a million websites offering materials relevant to increasing self-esteem.

•

Eva Moskowitz writes:

> We live in an age consumed by worship of the psyche. In a society plagued by divisions of race, class, and gender we are nonetheless bound together by a gospel of psychological happiness. Rich or poor, black or white, male or female, straight or gay, we share a belief that feelings are sacred and salvation lies in self-esteem, that happiness is the ultimate goal and psychological healing the means...All the institutions of American life - schools, hospitals, prisons, courts—have been shaped by the national investment in feelings. ..The intense concern with the psyche is unique historically as well as culturally. No other nation in the world puts so much faith in emotional well-being and self-help techniques.[10]

•

There is also a darker side to this clamor for esteeming the self. For we are also aware that self-love is a close companion to the less admirable characteristics of narcissism, conceit, vanity, egotism, selfishness, and arrogance. Where is the line to be drawn? We are well aware of this darker demeanor in our relations with others. Very special conditions must prevail before an acquaintance can speak of his or her accomplishments, wondrous personality, or outstanding choices without our turning cold. We may glow when our children take pride in a job well done, praise them for their self-confidence, and encourage them to be a "take charge kind of person"... until that point when they turn and say, "Don't tell me what to do..."[11]

•

[10]Moskowitz, E. S. (2001). *In therapy we trust, America's obsession with self fulfillment* (pp. 1; 279). Baltimore: Johns Hopkins University Press.

[11]As research indicates, people with high self-esteem do not thereby gain the esteem of others. See Baumeister, R. et al. (2003). Does high self-esteem cause better performance, interpersonal success, happiness, or healthier lifestyles? *Psychological Science in the Public Interest, 4,* 1–44.

Many scholars view this emphasis self-esteem as an invitation to social callousness. Even in the early 1800s, Alexis de Tocqueville commented on what he saw as a major flaw in American individualism:

> Individualism is a mature and calm feeling, which disposes each member of the community to sever himself from the mass of his fellows and to draw apart with his family and his friends, so that after he has thus formed a little circle of his own, he willingly leaves society at large to itself...individualism, at first, only saps the virtues of public life; but in the long run it attacks and destroys all others and is at length absorbed in downright selfishness."[12]

Almost 200 years later this same theme is echoed in Christopher Lasch's critique, *The culture of narcissism*.[13] As he argued, the "me first" attitude dominating contemporary life reduces emotional relationships and sexual intimacy to trivia. They become vehicles to "make us feel good." In essence, "I love you because you give me pleasure." By the same token, scholarly research is transformed from an inherent good to "good for my career." The demand to "publish or perish" does not favor the birth of new knowledge so much as the tenuring of new professors. Political activity is not so much concerned with achieving the public good as ensuring that "my party wins." When "me first" is an unquestioned reflex, political gridlock should be no surprise. More unsettling are the effects of believing one is superior to others. Research suggests, for example, that this sense of superiority is linked to violence. Violent criminals often characterize themselves as superior; their victims "deserved what they got." Street gang members and school bullies also tend to regard themselves as superior to others. Most radically there is the Holocaust, a tragic outcome of identifying oneself as a master race.[14]

I am not proposing that we abandon the multitudes suffering from an impoverished sense of self-worth, anguished at the challenges of normal life, or drawn to escape through suicide. My concern is with the possibility of an alternative future. Why must we unthinkingly sustain a tradition in which the primary site of evaluation is the individual self? Why must the prizing of one's individual mind serve as the essential ingredient of the good life? When we cease to think in terms of bounded beings, we take a step toward freedom from the ratcheting demands of self-worth.

[12]de Tocqueville, A. (1945). *Democracy in America* (p. 104). New York: Vintage.

[13]Lasch, C. (1979). *The culture of narcissism*. New York: Norton.

[14]Baumeister, R. F. (2001). Violent pride. *Scientific American, 284*, 96–101; Baumeister, R. F., Smart, L., and Boden, J. (1996). Relation of threatened egotism to violence and aggression: The dark side of self-esteem. *Psychological Review, 105*, 5–33. See also Crocker, J., and Park, L. W. (2004). The costly pursuit of self-esteem. *Psychological Bulletin, 130*, 392–414, and Leary, *op cit.*

"You have to be sensitive to the fact that other children are inferior to you."

Courtesy: The New Yorker Collection 2007, William Haefeli from the cartoonbank.com

Self and Other

In his classic work, *Celebrating the other*, Edward Sampson proposes that
we sustain our self-esteem through "self-celebratory monologues"—stories
about how good we are, how successful, how righteous.[15] To sustain these
monologues, however, we require others who are less than good. We thus
construct worlds in which others are irrational, unthinking, sinful, and so
on. There is the close relationship, then, between our presumption that we
are "self-contained" and the quality of our relations with others. We now
amplify this concern with a focus on issues of distrust, derogation, and
imposing artifice.

[15]Sampson, E. E. (2008). *Celebrating the other, a dialogic account of human nature.* Chagrin
Falls, OH: Taos Institute Publications.

Distrust and Derogation

We seek others' acceptance to ensure our worth as individuals. That is our cultural logic. Yet, how much trust can we place in others' expressions of support or love? Are they just being polite, trying to make us feel good, wanting something in return? Are we being manipulated? In trying to answer such questions we confront a profound challenge: Comprehending the other's *inner world*. As our tradition tells us, people's actions issue from these internal worlds. To understand another's actions one must grasp the other's underlying reasons, motives, or desires. Yet, how are we to penetrate the veil? Interestingly, in spite of several hundred years of inquiry on this topic, no scholar has yet been able to provide an adequate account of how such understanding can be accomplished. All we have are "outward" expressions of an inner world, never access to this world itself. I will return to this issue in later chapters. However, for now it is enough to underscore the impenetrable ambiguity of others' actions. The cranium will never open to reveal the secrets of the soul. What, then, do we ever truly know about the other? When we presume boundaries of being, we are thrust into a condition of fundamental distrust. We want to believe the sincerity of others' appreciation; we try to convince ourselves that the love is authentic. Yet, at base we also know that we do not know. The bounded mind is forever elusive and opaque.

•

Distrust is deepened by the prevailing assumption that self-gratification is the fundamental human goal. This is also an assumption to which the scientific community has added a chorus of confirmation. Freud spoke directly to the point: The primary drive of individual behavior is animal pleasure and it is present from birth. Indeed, so powerful is this energy, argued Freud, that the person must establish neurotic defenses to prevent its full expression. In more recent years socio-biologists have given Freud's pleasure principle a genetic twist. As they propose, the fundamental motive driving human action is to sustain one's own genes. Freud's emphasis on erotic desire now becomes the desire to reproduce oneself. Thus, proposes the socio-biologist, in fulfilling their genetic destiny, men are *naturally* polygamous.[16] Should we accept these scientific speculations as truth? Only if we are willing to grant that scientists such as Freud and the socio-biologists can somehow pierce the interior of human minds, that they can

[16]For more on the social science rationalization of self-gratification, see Wallach, M., and Wallach, L. (1993). *Psychology's sanction for selfishness.* San Francisco: W. H. Freeman; and Schwartz, B. (1986). *The battle for human nature.* New York: Norton.

look inward and discern the "real source" of our actions. Is the sexual act, for example, the result of a pleasure drive, a drive to reproduce, the need for security, a need for achievement, a drive for power, the urge for ultimate communion, or....

•

That humans are fundamentally motivated to gratify themselves is a cultural construction. And as such, we are scarcely obliged to incorporate this belief into our ways of life. And why should we wish to? To the extent that I believe you are fundamentally out for self-gratification, your actions become suspect. All your expressions of affection, nurturance, commitment, and personal concern cease to be genuine—from the heart. Rather, they raise questions about what you *are trying to get* from me. Aren't I simply being enlisted in the service of your pleasure, your needs, your desires? And if you try to assure me that your expressions are genuine, is this simply another layer of ruse? Should we hunger for another's love, such suspicion is poison.

•

The presumption of bounded being not only engenders distrust of others, but sets in motion an active search for others' failures. When we are chronically concerned with self-worth, we search for measures of "How good am I?" The question demands comparison with others. Am I more or less intelligent, talented, humorous, motivated, and so on. Social psychologists have long studied the process of social comparison.[17] Although research is compendious, there are two unvarying themes. The first is that people commonly choose downward comparison. That is, they scan the environment to locate people who are less worthy than they are. Self-esteem is boosted by locating what one sees as others' inferiority. If the other's inferiority is not clearly apparent, people can always locate shortcomings. "He is generous, but he's also a coward." "She looks good, but she has a blah personality."

A second major conclusion from social comparison research is that upward comparison is often painful. If I look over the field and find that everyone else is better than I am, I suffer. As the research suggests, I may go in one of two directions: First I can look selectively. I can simply avoid

[17]See, for example, Festinger, L. (1954). A theory of social comparison process. *Human Relations, 7,* 117–140; Kruglanski, A. W., and Mayseless, O. (1990). Classic and current social comparison research. *Psychological Bulletin, 108,* 195–208; Suls, J., Martin, R., and Wheeler, L. (2002). Social comparison: Why, with whom and with what effect? *Current Directions in Psychological Science, 11,* 159–163.

information about others' good qualities; after all, such information would make me feel inferior. Or, I can find ways of discounting their superiority. Again the search is for shortcomings: "He may seem intelligent, but he has to work harder than anyone else for his grades." "She may appear friendly, but behind your back she's a snake."

•

We should not be surprised that for almost any term of praise, one can find a replacement that reduces praise to derision. We have the verbal resources to destroy the character of anyone "better than me."

strong character	rigid
brave	foolish
sweet	saccharine
thrifty	tight
knowledgeable	know-it-all
articulate	bull-shitter
convincing	con artist
highly motivated	frantic
faithful	conventional
spiritual	flaky
thoughtful	indecisive
accepting	gullible
optimistic	unrealistic...

As a whole, research on social comparison paints a gloomy picture. It suggests that we enter the world each day looking through gray-lensed glasses. We avoid seeing the good in others, and take comfort in locating their failings. We scan the social world to ensure we are better than all.

•

As an author I am acutely aware of social comparison pressures. To enter a bookstore or library, for example, is a daunting experience. I want to count myself as a skilled writer, but before me stand thousands of competitors. In the face of these unending rows of books, what possible value does my work have; is it just another cover in the crowd? In a bookstore I look at the stacks of best sellers, and see an author whose work is widely discussed, my spirit sinks. "How can I ever compete with them; why go on?" But then I look for flaws. "Sure his work is popular; that's because he just says what everyone wants to hear." "That work has had a big impact, but unfortunately the arguments are totally wrong headed." "This book is really hyped, but the content is trivial." I am now ready to return to my unfinished manuscript. I resent the presence of social comparison in my life. If I hadn't absorbed the lessons of bounded being, I wouldn't enter the crippling cul de sac of comparison. Social comparison is not a fact of human nature, but an unfortunate tradition of Western culture. The challenge for all of us is to undo the boundaries of being.

Relationships as Artifice

If the fundamental atom of society is the bounded self, how are we to understand relationships? If self is the "natural" unit of being, then relationships are "artificial." They are not given in nature, but are created when two individual selves come together. As we say:

> "We must work on this relationship."
> "They developed a relationship."
> "This relationship is coming apart."
> "He needs to build a good relationship."

•

If the self is primary, then relationships are secondary in their importance to us. We must be forever cautious about connection. Relationships will inevitably place demands on the individual; expectations and obligations will develop; norms of right and wrong will be imposed. If we are not very careful, our freedom will be destroyed. As Michael and Lisa Wallach see it, in contemporary culture, "Super-ordinate loyalties tend to be viewed as an unacceptable limitation on one's personal freedom."[18]

If we see relationships as secondary and artificial, we will seek them out primarily when they are required for our personal use or satisfaction. In this sense, a committed relationship is a subtle mark of insufficiency. It suggests that we lack something. We are so vulnerable that we sacrifice our autonomy. One may view bachelor parties as rituals of derision as much as celebration. By the same token, the committed relationship remains under continuous threat—to be sustained only so long as it remains personally fulfilling. "If you are no longer fulfilling my needs, I am out of here." Commitment is dangerous. Wrapped round all relationships is the threat of expendability.[19]

•

[18]Wallach, M., and Wallach, L. (1993). *op cit.*
[19]See also Bellah et al. *op cit.*

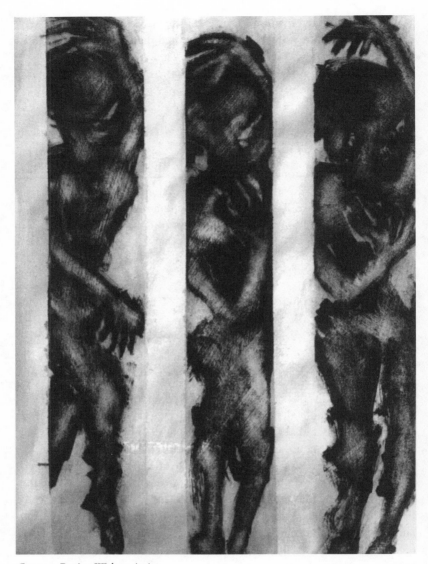

Courtesy: Regine Walter, Artist

(The English) don't spend much time in relationships
until they know what the odds are.

—Malcolm Bradbury

•

The social sciences have also contributed to this broad suspicion of
"the other." Since their beginnings in the 19th century, scientists have

frequently proposed that the individual is in some way spoiled by others. Haunted by the history of the French revolution, Gustav LeBon argued that in the crowd one's capacity for reason is destroyed.[20] Following WWII, social scientists were aghast at the submission of German citizens to Hitler's fascism. It was in this context that Asch's famous work on conformity was celebrated. As Asch demonstrated, in the face of a group that unanimously agreed in a decision that was obviously wrong, the individual could scarcely resist conforming.[21] Influenced by the horror of the Holocaust, Stanley Milgram set out to condemn those who are obedient to authority.[22] As he attempted to show, perfectly reasonable individuals could be pressured into delivering powerful electric shocks to another human being, possibly killing him. And, as Irving Janis argued with his research, when people make decisions together they are in danger of "groupthink."[23] They suppress information, fail to be self-critical, and they give in to others' opinions. In all this work, groups are dangerous; independence is honored.

It is not that such research is incorrect, as it is selective—both in terms of what it chooses to observe and how it is interpreted. Researchers choose specific conditions that cast the group in a negative light. Many other situations could be selected that would paint an opposing picture—showing how a group corrects the biases of individual judgment, creates more options, or generates high morale. Further there is also the selection of terminology for interpreting the observations. If one agrees with group opinion, is it *conformity* or an *expression of solidarity*; if one obeys an experimenter's orders to shock another subject is it *obedience* or *doing one's best for science*? In effect, such research is political in its message: Beware the group.

•

Hell is other people.
—Jean Paul Sartre

•

I was to deliver a speech on the 100th anniversary of the founding of social psychology. To conduct the necessary background research

[20]Le Bon, G. (2002). *The crowd*. Mineola, NY: Dover Publications.

[21]Asch, S. (1956). Studies of independence and conformity: A minority of one against a unanimous majority. *Psychological Monographs*, 70 (Whole no. 416).

[22]Milgram, S. (2004). *Obedience to authority*. New York, NY: HarperCollins.

[23]Janis, I. (1983). *Groupthink: Psychological studies of policy decisions and fiascoes*. Boston, MA: Houghton Mifflin.

I chose to spend two weeks in Oxford's Boudlian Library. To be sure, this would mean being away from family, friends and colleagues. But then again, I relished the vision of being completely free and on my own. No obligations, no expectations, no strings... autonomy at last. For several days the library was a robust companion. Soon, however, I began to feel restless. I needed someone to talk with, laughter, and companionship. I sought out old acquaintances at the University, journeyed to London to visit a friend, and even began talking to strangers. Within a week I was booked. Obligations cluttered every evening; expectations were strung throughout the days. Freedom had vanished. A lesson was in the making: Freedom contains an emptiness that only relationship can fill.

The Culture of Bounded Being

The tradition of bounded being carries far beyond the daily experience of self and others. It is also realized in our ways of life and the structures of our institutions—schools, businesses, and democracy itself. Indeed, we generally think of such groups as constituted by single individuals. As the French theorist, Michel Foucault, proposed, this conception of social life facilitates domination.[24] It is when individuals can be singled out by authorities, and incarcerated or eliminated, that communal resistance is discouraged. As Foucault proposes, the very idea of assigning authorship to books originated at a time when authorities wished to monitor and suppress political critique. Later in this work, I will have much to say about relational practices in such institutions as education, therapy, and organizations. However, to complete this chapter I wish to take up two orientations pervading contemporary cultural life. My concern here is with the ways in which the ideology of bounded being lends itself to a marketing of selves and a breakdown in moral deliberation.

The Costs of Calculation

As proposed, because of the primacy of the self, the significance of relationship is diminished. The question thus presents itself: Why should we care to have companions? For the bounded self the answer is clear: because they can give me pleasure. Relationships have no inherent value.

---

[24]Foucault, M. (1979). What is an author? In J. V. Harari (Ed.) *Textual strategies*. Ithaca: Cornell University Press.

It is individual well-being that counts, and the value of others is determined by whether they contribute to or detract from one's pleasure. "What are you to me?" That depends on "how much benefit you can provide, and at what cost." And thus we hear,

- You should get to know him; he can help your career.
- He just doesn't fulfill my needs.
- What have you done for me lately?
- I don't need you anymore.
- You can go places with him.
- You are holding me back.

•

Some critics speak of this calculating orientation to social life as *instrumentalist*. In effect, others are defined as instruments for achieving my goals. They are not ends in themselves; their welfare does not matter in itself; they are simply means to the goal of my well-being. To be sure, one may wish to help others to achieve their own happiness; but one sacrifices for others only so they will ultimately reciprocate. Thus we speak of, "enlightened self-interest!"

Again we find the social sciences dispensing truths that contribute to the naturalization of this orientation. Economic theory is the most obvious case. As the father of contemporary economic theory, Adam Smith, characterized human action, it is essentially based on self-interest. It is human nature for an individual to maximize gains and minimize losses.[25] As a cadre of social economists now proposes, a calculus of self-gratification is central to all human action, from buying beer to choosing a mate.[26] Many psychologists have since echoed this "economic truth." B.F. Skinner's theory of behavior is among the most prominent. For Skinner, the organism—whether a pigeon or a politician—is governed by reinforcements—or roughly, the doses of pain and pleasure provided by the environment. We are hardwired, in Skinner's view, to maximize the amount of reward and minimize punishment.[27] As psychologists also reason, social relations are all about seeking the greatest pleasure from others at a minimal cost. Human love, on this view, is a matter of making a profit. We love someone

[25]Smith, A. (1991). *The wealth of nations*. Amherst, NY: Prometheus Books.

[26]See, for example, Becker, G. S., and Murphy, K. M. (2000). *Social economics: Market behavior in a social environment*. Cambridge: Harvard University Press.

[27]Skinner, B. F. (1991). *The behavior of organisms*. Acton, MA: Copley Publishing Group Incorporated.

when they give us maximal pleasure at minimal cost.[28] When we embrace such views, every relationship is a candidate for commodification.

•

In a social world where an economic calculus prevails, the prediction and control of others becomes a virtue. In this vein, psychologists have set out to demonstrate the advantages of believing that we are in control of what happens to us. A personality scale is used to measure the degree to which a person believes they have such control, as opposed to believing they are pawns to circumstance.[29] Almost invariably, research demonstrates that those believing in internal control are better off—more optimistic, more effective in their performance, more likely to be leaders, more oriented to action, and so on.[30] This research is coupled with numerous studies that place both dogs and people in conditions where their control is removed. As they become helpless to control their outcomes, they become progressively inactive and often depressed. As Martin Seligman, doyen of helplessness research, has argued, the major cause of depression in human beings is indeed the sense of helplessness to control one's world.[31]

Let us presume for the moment that people today are benefited emotionally when they feel they are in control. The important question, then, is whether such findings tell us about human nature as opposed to the state of culture. Such research paints a picture of a culture in which each of us is out to ensure that we are in control of our surrounds. Or, in effect, we all wish to control each other; we wish others to be predictable and thus manageable. Yet, these lines of research contribute to the very beliefs that sustain the orientation. What if we ceased to view our bounded being as the center of our social universe? Would the clamor for control not subside? Is it possible that social order grows not from "my managing you" and vice versa, but from a collaborative conjoining? Perhaps there are greater benefits to be derived from rocking in the cradle of relationship—with others and with our environment.

•

[28]See, for example, Homans, G. C. (1961). *Social behavior, its elementary forms*. New York: Harcourt Brace; Blau, P. (1986). *Exchange and power in social life*. New York: Transaction; Thibaut, J. W., and Kelly, H. H. (1986). *The social psychology of groups*. New York: Wiley.

[29]Phares, J. E. (1976). *Locus of control in personality*. Morristown, NJ: General Learning Press.

[30]Lefcourt, H. M. (1982). *Locus of control: Current trends in theory and research*. Hillsdale, NJ: Erlbaum.

[31]Seligman, M. (1975). *Helplessness: On depression, development and death*. San Francisco: Freeman.

When others are defined in terms of their instrumental value, the economic metaphor creeps in the door of daily life. As social economists demonstrate, all that we value can be reduced to the precision of market value. Everything can be evaluated in terms of monetary gains and losses. What is the cost of an arm or a leg? It depends on what you would pay to have it replaced. What is the cost of a sunset? It depends on how much people would pay to see it. Thus, human beings and their actions become commodities, no different in principle from a suit of clothes or an automobile. It is not simply that human beings lose intrinsic value, but rather, that all values are abandoned save market value.

•

As we come to understand individuals as rational calculators, the nature of our relationships is altered. All "declarations of the heart"—of friendship, care, love, devotion, or commitment, become subject to suspicion. They are reduced to so much rhetoric, or at worst, to subterfuge. "I love you," loses is capacity to bond when it is translated as "you are my meal ticket." To be loved for one's money is not to be loved at all.

•

> When I was a teenager, declarations of passionate and undying love were not infrequent. The romantic spirit prevailed; there was ecstasy to be found in a lingering smile or the paralytic movements of the "last dance;" and should tender embraces give way to a deep kiss, leaping over the moon became a distinct possibility. However, should it be revealed that by chance one had secreted a "rubber" into his billfold—my God, *just in case*—the door of romance would slam shut. Obviously the swain had *planned* to have sex; not only had he thought about it, but most likely all his devout declarations and tender touches were dedicated to precisely this end. In the mere existence of the condom the relationship was transformed from communion to concupiscence.

•

Times have changed...or have they? You are enraptured by her—the sparkling conversation, the revelations of her soul, the movement of her body—and ah, the eyes, lips, hair, fragrance, soft skin—all compel you into the depths of bliss. *The moment* is approaching... when... well, you will have to address the following questions:

- Do I have the right to say "no" at any time I wish?
- Did you bring protection?

- Do you have herpes?
- Have you had an AIDS check-up?

If you answer all these questions correctly, you may then proceed...but passion will have flown from the window.

•

As Barry Schwartz proposes, the economic disciplines have "helped to justify the conditions that foster the pursuit of economic self-interest to the exclusion of almost all else."[32] To the extent that an economic calculus of relationship prevails, we may anticipate a world in which human relationships become superfluous to the good life. Under these conditions a man might ask, for example, "for my sexual pleasure, will a wife cost more than a series of girl friends, or will an occasional prostitute be cheaper? Further, "Why should I go out and spend $100 to take this woman out to dinner, when I can spend $20 for a porn video?" Might such an attitude not contribute to the fact that pornography is far and away the most lucrative e-business in the world? It is in the cyber-world that one can have access to visual pleasure that is wholly under one's control—and at a fraction of the price of having a real-life partner.[33]

Public Morality as Nuisance

In his 19th century essay, *On Liberty*, John Stuart Mill, gave voice to beliefs now engrained in the woodwork of everyday life: "Men should be free to act upon their opinions—to carry these out in their lives." (p. 84)[34] And so it is that we simply presume the right to our own opinion, ideals, values, and ways of life. In common terms we question anyone's right to tell us what we should or shouldn't do. As we might say, "Who do you think you are that you can impose your moral values on me? If you don't like what I do, well that's your problem. This is a free country."

•

These are foundational sentiments of the bounded being. Yet, these sentiments also provoke a second order concern. If everyone has the right to self-direction, how are we to achieve a viable form of collective life? Clearly,

[32]Schwartz, B., *op cit*. pp. 247–248.
[33]For a walk on the wild side, the reader can visit www. realdoll. com. Here will be found for sale a range of life size, rubber dolls. The dolls approximate the cultural ideals of beauty, and all are specifically equipped for the pursuit of erotic pleasure. Their flesh can approximate the warmth of the human body if they are allowed to soak in a tub of warm water, and with skill they may be packed in a suitcase as a traveling companion!
[34]Mill, J. S. (2003). *On liberty*. New Haven: Yale University Press. Originally published in 1859.

if we all acted upon our own private impulses, we would confront what Thomas Hobbes viewed as a world of "all against all." Under these conditions life would indeed be "nasty, brutish, and short."[35] With much the same concerns at hand, Jean Jacques Rousseau proposed a "social contract" in which each individual would freely choose to live under a code common to society.[36] The idea of the social contract is attractive, until someone proclaims that the common good is not his good. No one can be properly forced to sign up.

The problem of the common good continues into the present. For scholars it is represented in "the tragedy of the commons," Garrett Hardin's famous metaphor for the demise of the collective good when individuals maximize their private welfare.[37] If we have a common space with limited resources, and everyone thinks only of his own desires, the resources will soon be eradicated. When no one cares for the whole, it means the ultimate deterioration of individual welfare. It is a spark that ignited John Rawls' highly acclaimed, *The Theory of Justice*, a more elaborated model of the social contract.[38] It is also there in the trash-littered streets and the polluted air of our cities. It is present in the urban ghettos, sanctuary of the jobless, the street gangs, and the addicted. "These are not *my* problems," we say. "People have a choice; they don't have to live that way. My grandfather was poor, and he chose a life of hard work to pull himself up." If individual goods are primary, the common good is of secondary interest.

•

Man is not a solitary animal, and so long as social life survives, self-realization cannot be the supreme principle of ethics.

—Bertrand Russell

•

There is more to the problem than pitting individual rights against the collective good. With the primacy of the self we also fashion the common attitudes toward codes of ethics and law. As Robert Bellah and his colleagues characterize the logic,

In asserting...the uniqueness of each individual, (one) concludes that there is no moral common ground and therefore no public relevance

[35]Hobbes, T. (1950). *Leviathan, or the matter, form, and power of a commonweal, ecclesiastical and civil*. New York: Dutton. (Originally published in 1651 in London (A Crooke)).

[36]Rousseau, J. J. (1968). *The social contract*. New York: Penguin. (Originally published in 1762).

[37]Hardin, G. (1968). The tragedy of the commons. *Science, 162*, 1243–1248.

[38]Rawls, J. (1971). *A theory of justice*. Cambridge: Harvard University Press.

of morality outside the sphere of minimal procedural rules and obligations not to injure.[39]

As we find, the tradition of bounded being discourages deliberation on moral issues, and alienates us from our governing bodies. From the standpoint of bounded being, any overarching moral code is fraught with danger. Because individual liberty is threatened, it constitutes a stepping-stone to oppression. The result is a general aversion to any moral demands. Even in the academic world, moral philosophy occupies a very small corner of concern. Public laws are similarly suspect. They are not part of us as individuals; we did not personally choose or make them. We never signed the social contract. In effect, they are not "my codes," but necessary nuisances. I have no intrinsic duty to obey them; I acquiesce primarily because I may suffer if I do not obey. They are my protection, and if I disobey I may be punished. Otherwise, they are a bother.

•

In the contemporary world, the sense of community and shared social purpose are assaulted as unjust restraints on liberty, impediments to the free assertion of the self.

Robert Goodwin

•

For many of us growing up in the late 60s, this implicit logic of "law as nuisance" became a battle cry. If the government was unjust—engaging in a war that denied liberty to others—then why should we obey it? What right did they have to impose their unjust laws and unethical standards on us? We cried out in many different ways, blood was shed, a president tumbled from office, and the war ended in desolation. We could not step out of the logic: The individual is the atom of society; the State is a necessary evil (or "good," if you happened to be on the other side.) It was the Individual vs. the State—and so it is today.

•

Much the same logic also sparks the militia movements; it enlivens the spirit of the KKK; and lends subtle support to Mafia activities. All represent the right of self-determination in action. And it is so in the realm of international relations, in which separate governments represent bounded

[39]Bellah et al. *op cit.*

beings. Each claims a right to control its destiny. No other nation has a right to impose its values. The result is not simply a weakened United Nations, but a general atmosphere of relations among nations replete with alienation, competition, and distrust.[40] Yet, if the concept of bounded being is optional, then so is the concept of the bounded State. And if both are optional, can we not seek out an alternative means of understanding ethics and law? Can we move into a space of understanding in which neither individual nor state hold the right to dictate the good? We shall return to this possibility in an exploration of relational ethics (Chapter 11).

Transforming Tradition

The longstanding and much cherished tradition of the individual self carries with it enormous costs. I have emphasized here the ways in which this tradition invites a sense of fundamental separation and loneliness; encourages narcissism at the expense of relationships; generates unending threats to one's person, and transforms the self into a marketable commodity. Relationships turn both artificial and threatening, and moral demands are infringements on our autonomy. In the end, we also come to see nations as bounded units, and the result is global alienation and distrust.

Although this account has been selective, it does represent a growing consciousness within communities of scholars and practitioners. At the same time, I do not see these critiques as lethal in their intent. The point of the present work is not to eradicate tradition.[41] Rather, by placing our traditions under critical scrutiny they become denaturalized. That is, life as we know it ceases to be a reflection of human nature at work, but a tradition that has become so commonplace that we forget that it is a human creation. And if it is a human creation, we have the power to create alternatives. In the pages that follow my attempt will be to generate a vision of a world in which relationship takes precedence over bounded units. Indeed, if we can come to appreciate the reality of relationship, we will be in a position to transform tradition. We will not treat our institutions of democracy, public education, courts of law, and individual rights as celebrations of bounded being. When understood as outcomes of relational life new

[40]For an excellent illustration of this logic, see Steyne, M. (2006). *America alone: The end of the world as we know it.* New York: Regnery. Here the author presumes a fundamental antagonism between the two bounded units, Islam and the United States. A posture of aggression is invited.

[41]For an extended account of the ways in which the tradition of bounded being offers moral resources see Taylor, C. (1989). *Sources of the self, the making of the modern identity.* Cambridge: Harvard University Press.

forms of action will be invited. Similarly, there are ways of retaining the joys of individual accomplishment, romantic love, heroism, leadership, and creative action, without embracing essential separation and alienation. Again, to understand these traditions as rooted in relationship can transform our ways of life. We may not wish to abandon the fruits of the Enlightenment, but this does not mean that we must remain frozen... culture in aspic. The challenge of the ensuing chapters, then, is to open the way to relational being.

2

In the Beginning Is the Relationship

As you read these lines, isn't it clear: *You* are the reader, *this* book is before you, and *I* am the writer. We have, then, three entities—you, me, and the book—each separate and distinct. But reconsider: As I write I am using words that are not my own; I am borrowing from countless sources and shaping them for you. Are these words, then, truly my own—a unique expression of me as an independent being, or are they someone else's, and in important degree even yours? The moment at which *I* the author specifically begins and ends is clouded. Consider as well that the words on this page are not the specific property of the book itself. The book does have some distinct characteristics—a unique title, chapter names, cover design— that suggest an independent identity. But all that *it* says—the important stuff—is borrowed from elsewhere—one might have said "from me" if only we knew where I began and ended. But hold on; precisely who are *you* in this situation? As these words crowd your consciousness are they not defining who you are at this moment; aren't they at this moment *your* words. Or were they yours already? At the moment of reading, then, the words belong to neither you, the book, nor to me. At the moment of reading there is no clear separation between me, the book, and you. Not only are we joined together, but we are wedded as well to a preceding world of language without evident end. And as you put this book aside and speak to others, so will we be carried into the future.

•

My fifth grade geography teacher asked me to write an essay on Mesopotamia. I knew nothing about Mesopotamia, but dutifully began a library search. Ah, the encyclopedia was so full of wonderful information, orderly, coherent, and perfectly spelled. There were also colorful photos and a map. I took pencil in hand and slowly began to ponder. Everything I might wish to know or say about Mesopotamia was there before me. But I was supposed to write an essay in *my own words*. Virtually everything I could write would be taken from this book before me. How could my writing be *my own*? And when I converted these orderly perfections into my limited vocabulary, simplified grammar, and inventive spelling, would I not be disfiguring them? Soon my teacher would give me a grade for my degrading.

•

Consider the way we teach children about the world. One points to oneself and says "Mama," and to another and says, "Dada." Later we might take the finger of the child and point, "There is a cat," and "See the dog." Each pointing is to what we consider a *thing*, a separate and bounded entity. And from this process we emerge with a world of things—secured for us by a world of nouns. This *book*, that *reader*, the *author* over there. Are we not enchanted by a world of nouns to believe in a world of separation?[1]

•

What if there were no nouns? Would our world remain composed of distinct and separate things? What if our only language for describing the world were dance? The movements of the body are continuous, and it is difficult to separate the flow of action into discrete, noun-like entities; like waves of the ocean it is not clear where one movement ends and another begins. If we used dance to teach our children about the world, the world might not appear to us as separated entities. The child might discover a world of endless movement, not discrete "forms" but continuous "forming." The child might never ask if it were possible to separate the dancers from the dance.

•

If there were no pronouns, would *you* and *I* cease to exist as independent beings? Would there be an *I* if there were no means of designating a separate being? To employ the words *you* and *I* is to create a world of separations.

---

[1]Also see Gregory Bateson's argument for "stamping out nouns," in his *Steps toward an ecology of mind*. New York: Ballantine Books, 1972.

And so it is with proper names. Would we have a unique identity in a culture that assigned no proper names?[2] When armies are bent on destruction
of their foe—the villages, cities, and entire peoples—they do not make a
roll call of proper names. *You* and *I* become individual selves only when it
is socially useful. Utility precedes essence.

•

> In important respects "the individual self" is
> not a state of nature
> but of language.

•

In these few remarks I have attempted to blur the commonly accepted
boundaries between self and other, and to underscore the constructed character of bounded being. This is to prepare the way for an exploration of an
alternative to this longstanding tradition. We begin in the present chapter
by exploring a vision of insoluble connectivity. Thrust into presence is a
process of relationship from which the very conception of separated entities
emerges. After introducing this focal process of co-action, I explore its constraints and its potentials. This will lead to a concluding section in which
we find reason to suspend the traditional assumption of cause and effect
in explaining human relations. Here we consider human action within a
relational confluence.

Co-Action and Creation

A simple but substantial question: Have you truly "helped someone in
need" if the recipient detests your action? Can you "help" another without
his or her affirming that it is help and not hindrance? Within this question
lies an invitation to new adventure. In accepting the invitation, we shift
our gaze from singular entities to conjunctions. We move metaphorically
from the movements of individual dancers to the dance, from individual
brush strokes to the emerging painting, from individual athletes to playing
the game. More specifically, let us explore the potentials of a co-active process, in which "help" is located within a conjunction of actions. As I shall
propose, all that is meaningful to us as human beings derives from this
process. All that we take to be real, true, valuable, or good finds its origin
in coordinated action.

[2]See also, Mulhauser, P., and Harré, R. (1990). *Pronouns and people: The linguistic construction of social and personal identity.* Oxford: Blackwell.

Once this process of co-action is made clear, we are prepared to revisit the idea of the individual self. In subsequent chapters we shall find that all those properties once attributed to individual minds are the outcomes of relationship. I shall propose that reason and emotion, for example, are not possessions of individual minds, but of relations. Figuratively speaking, they are not features of the individual pigments but of the larger picture of which they are a part. The horizon will then explode as we realize the relational base of virtually all "mental phenomenon." Memory, motives, and intentions will be incorporated into the relational process, along with our sensations of pleasure and pain. We move, then, from individual being to relational being.

•

Let us begin simply. You pick up a novel and your gaze falls on a single word in the first line: "knife." Ah, adventure is afoot...but what is this all about; what kind of adventure; what is intended here? In fact, the word in itself provides no answers. What kind of knife, in whose hands, to what ends? To determine the meaning of "knife" you read further. Your eyes move to the beginning of the sentence. "He pressed the knife into..." Your intrigue now intensifies; you are perhaps bearing witness to a murder most foul. But clarity is still needed; pressing a knife means almost nothing in itself. So you read on. Now you find that the knife is pressing into "...a mound of soft butter." No murder mystery here...oh well, perhaps an interesting domestic drama is unfolding. But to determine whether this is indeed the case you must again read on.

As we find, the word "knife" has little meaning in itself. Blurt it to a passerby, scream it into the night, paint it on a billboard. All are meaning/less acts. The word alone lies fallow. It springs into life as it is placed within a context of other words. As one phrase is added, the word "knife" appears to be a murder weapon; with yet another phrase, we envision a mundane breakfast setting. Each additional phrase alters what we understand by the word. The meaning of a word is not contained within itself but derives from a process of coordinating words. Without this coordination, the single words within the novel would mean very little. If we attempt to understand a novel by placing all its words in an alphabetical list, we would find ourselves in limbo. The fun begins in the fusion.[3]

•

[3]The concept of co-action owes a debt to Herbert Blumer's *Symbolic interactionism: Perspective and method* (1969, New York: Prentice Hall), and to John Shotter's writings (especially, Action, joint action and intentionality. In Brenner, M. (Ed.) (1980). *The structure of action.*

Let us turn from the book to our daily relationships. Similar to the first line of the book, I say a few words to you: "Gorgeous day, isn't it!" You walk on past, without even a shrug. What now is the meaning of my action? If you simply failed to hear me, then I have meant nothing. I might as well have remained silent or mumbled incoherently. It is when you take some action in reply to mine that my words commence their journey toward meaning. When you reply, "Absolutely, I sure wish I didn't have classes," you have touched my words with a wand of affirmation. Now my words have become a cheery greeting.

More generally, it may be said, there is no action that has meaning in itself, that is, an action that can be isolated and identified for what it is. There are no acts of love, altruism, prejudice, or aggression as such. In order to be anything at all, they require a supplement, an action by at least one other person that ratifies their existence as something. Of course, you may supply the supplement yourself. "I did greet her," you may say to yourself. But this supplement is the child of past relationships in which someone was present to confirm your actions as a greeting. In "knowing what you are doing" you are a stand-in for another.

•

At the same time, your affirmation of my greeting is not an action in itself. This supplement comes into meaning only by virtue of my preceding action. You may go about the street muttering, "Absolutely, I sure wish I didn't have classes" to all who pass by. But they will regard you as mad. Your words bring my words into meaning, but without my words your words fall into emptiness. There is, then, a precious reciprocity. Both action and supplement alone lie fallow; only in coordinated action does meaning spring to life.

•

As a writer I come to you with a deep sense of humility. I place these words in motion, but they mean little in themselves. I say nothing at

Oxford: Oxford University Press; *Conversational realities*, 1993, London: Sage), both of whom employ the concept of *joint action*. In Blumer's case the term was an attempt to extend G.H. Mead's symbolic interactionist views by pointing to the ways in which people align themselves with each other's actions through mutual interpretation. For Shotter the term has variously been used to emphasize shared intentionality, dialogically structured relations, and the unintended consequences of dialogue. Also relevant are Westerman's concept of *coordination* and Fogel's discussion of *co-regulation*. See Westerman, M.A. (2005). What is interpersonal behavior? A post-Cartesian approach to problematic interpersonal patterns and psychotherapy process. *Review of General Psychology*, 9, 16–34; and Fogel, A. (1993). *Developing through relationships: Origins of communication, self, and culture*. Chicago: University of Chicago Press.

all on these pages until you grant me meaning. With unstinting criticism you could reduce my words to idiocy. If more charitable, you bring me as an author into life. If enthusiastic you grant me wings. And yet, if I—or someone like me—had no words to give you, never addressed you, never positioned you to reply, what are you then to say? You stand inert. Indeed, how often is there anything to say or do until there is some form of invitation? It is when someone says, "what do you think of this?" that you are animated. Suddenly you are brimming with ideas, opinions, tastes, and values. We must both be humble; for neither of us is meaning/full except for the other. We come into life through relationship. We exist in a state of inter-animation.

•

Co-action is far more than words alone. Speaking and writing are bodily actions, and in this sense equivalent to all other actions taking place while we converse—smiling, laughing, gazing into each other's eyes, shuffling the feet. All that has been said about co-action includes the entire coordination of bodies. Thus:

If I thrust out my hand and…you grasp it in yours,

I have offered a greeting.

…you push it aside to embrace me,

I have underestimated our friendship.

…you kneel and kiss it,

I have demonstrated my authority.

….you turn your back,

I have been insulting.

….you give me a manicure,

I am your customer.

•

The distinction between verbal versus non-verbal communication is an artificial one. Rather, we should attend to unified acts of coordination, with words/movements/facial expressions forming a seamless whole. Remove the threads of any, and the cloth is undone…or it becomes part of a different garment.

•

What is spoken is never, and in no language, what is said.

—Martin Heidegger

•

It was January and I had agreed to give a series of lectures at the University of St. Gallen in Switzerland. Because the town is small and there were no rooms for the weeks of my stay, it was arranged for me to have a bedroom in the apartment of an 83-year-old widow. I was not happy with the accommodation; not only would my privacy be threatened, but the requirement that I be a "perfect citizen" on a continuous basis was daunting. The latter problem was intensified by the fact that Frau Ferlin spoke only German, and I suffered from a beginner's acquaintance with the language. We would have little means of verbal communication.

On the evening of my arrival, I was intent on "no entangling alliances" and walked past the dining room to depart for dinner. There at the table was Frau Ferlin. Two places had been set. She was lighting the candles. I had no choice but to take a seat. She chattered on, I understood little, but the food and personal warmth were nourishing. The next morning, I found she had prepared my breakfast. I attempted as best I could to indicate this was unnecessary, but my remonstrations were without effect. That evening I found my bed had been made, and the covers turned down. I went to thank her, and she offered me a glass of wine. We sat, again with her laughing chatter, and my attempt to catch the gist of her humor.

As the weeks bore on, I realized that St. Gallen closed its doors early; there was little life—save by the hearth with Frau Ferlin. There I found my linguistic skills slowly improving. I also found myself becoming increasingly fond of this woman. I invited her out to a local concert; she beamed. A few days later she began to meet me at the door before my morning departure for the university, to be certain that my clothes were appropriate for Herr Professor. To ensure my good appearance, she would steal my shoes away to polish them. I began to bring food and wine to the apartment. On one weekend I drove her to the countryside where she showed me her birthplace and childhood neighborhood.

On the week before my departure, I happened to look up one morning as I left the apartment building and saw her in the window

watching me. I waved a greeting and she waved in return. A daily
ritual had been born. Frau Ferlin refused to let me pay rent;
I reciprocated by bringing her several cases of her favorite
wine. On the day of my departure, we met at the door to say
"Auf Viedersehen," knowing full well that we might never
see each other again. No words were spoken. We both broke
into tears.

The Co-Creation of Everything

Let us expand the scope of the co-active process. A father takes his little boy
to the zoo; he stops before an enclosure, grasps the boy's finger, and points
to a shape. "See the zebra," he says. "Zebra ...zebra...that is a zebra."
The boy looks puzzled...stares ahead and mumbles, "horse." "No," the
father says, "not a horse. That is a zebra." Slowly the boy burbles, "Zeeba."
"Not quite, replies the father, "*zebra*." "Zebra," responds the boy, to which
the father says, "right, now you have it, zebra...see the stripes." This
little adventure in co-action is not trivial. Indeed, for the child it has created a new world, one now inhabited by zebras. Before the co-active
steps of coordination—the initiating father, the responding child, the
correcting father, the echoing child, and so on, the child's world was
replete with horses, but no zebras. Through co-action Zebras have now
been born.

•

Consider the energetic first grader, moving, jumping, infinitely curious.
The teacher is annoyed; the movements are disrupting the class. She speaks
with a counselor who offers the teacher a new phrase, "attention deficit
disorder." "Well," she says, "he doesn't pay attention, and surely this is a
deficit ...But I wouldn't quite say it is a disorder." Yes, says the counselor
authoritatively, it is a well-known disorder, and there are very good drugs
on the market that will cure him." "Uhmmm," mutters the teacher,
"I guess you may have something...I will speak to his parents about treatment." In that brief interchange, attention deficit disorder becomes the
teacher's reality. Soon it will become the first grader's way of life, and most
likely, for a very long time.

•

When my children grew up, there was nothing called attention
deficit disorder. Some kids were more active than others, and a few
required special attention. Today there are over 500 authoritative

books on the subject, over 900,000 websites featuring it, and the drug, Ritalin, is a multi-billion dollar business.[4]

•

Consider the game of baseball. We see batters and fielders; we observe fly balls, foul balls, and home runs; we note that a runner is left on first base, and we thrill when the winning score crosses home plate. All these exist for us. Yet, until there is co-action there is no world of baseball. It is only when we jointly affirm that "this is baseball," "that is a run," "the team with the most runs wins," and so on, that the world of baseball acquires a dramatic life. Consider now the communities that have brought forth the worlds of chemistry, physics, mathematics, biology, economics, psychology, and other worlds of knowledge. All such worlds are the fruits of co-action.

•

The critic wishes a word, "Are you trying to say that nothing exists until there is some kind of relationship? There is no physical world, no mountains, trees, a sun, and so on? This just seems absurd." In reply, this is not precisely what is being proposed here. We should not conclude that "nothing exists" before the moment of co-action. Whatever exists simply exists. However, in the process of co-action whatever there is takes shape as *something for us*. It comes to be "mountains," "trees, and "sun" in terms of the way we live. Whatever exists does not require distinctions, for example, between Europe and Asia, men and women, or health and illness. It is in the process of co-action that these become distinctions around which our lives are organized. We cannot specify what exists before there is co-action, because the moment we try to enumerate these fundamentals we are indulging in the fruits of co-action.

•

With the process of co-action now in place, let us turn to the tradition of bounded being. The world of *you* and *I* is not unlike the worlds of balls and strikes, protons and neutrons, or trees and mountains. To speak of you and I is to enter a communal tradition, like baseball or physics, in which these words have developed significance. Outside this tradition, they may be meaningless. In the world of atomic physics there are no individual selves. Even when we are speaking of human beings, we do not always recognize the existence of individual selves. One is seldom struck by the reality of individual selves when policy decisions are made about crowd control, illegal workers,

[4]See Wallwork, A. (2007). Attention deficit discourse: Social and individual constructions. *Journal of Critical Psychology, Counseling and Psychotherapy, 16*, 69–84.

the Right Wing, the student body, the Lutheran Church...or collateral damage.

•

Independent persons do not come together to form a relationship; from relationships the very possibility of independent persons emerges.

•

Let us be more concrete. Consider that:

- If a policeman says "Stop where you are."...you become a suspect.
- If a salesperson says, "Can I help you?"...you become a customer.
- If your wife says, "Can you give me a hand, honey?"...you become a husband.
- If your child says, "Mommy come quick."...you become a mother.

Others call us into being as a suspect, a customer, a husband, a mother, and so on. Would we be any of these without such callings?[5]

•

Consider as well one's personality, the sort of person one is. Tom passes his business colleague, Jenna, in the hall and remarks:

"Wow, Jenna, you really look great today."

What kind of person is Tom? Consider Jenna's possible replies:

"Thanks Tom...you have made my day."

"Are you trying to flirt with me?"

"Do you think you can just bury the past with a superficial remark like that?"

"You need glasses...I've been up all night with a fever."

"Gee, I thought you would never notice."

"Haven't you ever heard of sexual harassment?"

In the moment of co-action Tom takes on character. He becomes "a morale boosting colleague," a "harmless flirt," an "insensitive male," a "clumsy idiot," an "attractive male," or "a chauvinist pig." Before Jenna spoke who was he?

•

The critic is aroused: "You seem to be suggesting that I have no existence outside of relationship. But I spend hours every day alone. I take a shower,

---

[5] Social scientists have called it many things: "interpolation," "alter-casting," and "positioning" among the most common. See Harré, R., and van Langenhove, L. (Eds.) (1999). *Positioning theory: Moral contexts of intentional action.* Oxford: Blackwell Publishers. The important idea is that when others speak to us or act toward us in a given way, so do they define us. They call us into being as this or that kind of person, cast us in a particular role, or thrust us into a self-defining position.

brush my teeth, have breakfast, take a walk...all of this alone. In what sense am I engaged in relationships? I am my own person in all this...no co-action to it. Just me, doing my thing." Surely, many of our actions are carried out alone, without others present or privy. But in what sense are these actions "our own possessions," uncontaminated by relationship? To take an obvious case, I sit here alone writing, but my actions are essentially entries into a conversation. They issue from previous conversations with others and they press these conversations forward with you, the reader. That you are not physically present, and I am not speaking the words out loud, is merely a problem of logistics. In reading the newspaper or watching television by myself I am again participating in a conversation, in this case as the recipient of words and images to which I might sometime respond.

Let's take some less obvious cases. If I were to cook for myself, am I not simply taking on the role of another person...acting, for example, in the place of my mother or my spouse as the chef? If I wash my shirts, am I not preparing myself for meeting others? The same may be said for taking a shower, combing my hair, or shaving. I may be alone, but my actions are deeply embedded in my relationships. Or, let us say, I go camping for a week, ride my bicycle for an hour, or gaze into the sunset—all alone in each case. However, I only go camping because it makes sense to do so; the same may be said about biking or watching the sunset. They are all "good things to do." Yet, the fact that we have common names for these activities— "camping," "cycling", and "watching the sunset"—along with the common value we attach to them—is a demonstration of their relational origin. The same may be said for "hiking," "whistling," "flushing the toilet," and so on. To act intelligibly at all is to participate in relationship.

•

Consider the implications: Can you carry out any action that is not in any way sensible, that would not be recognized as "something people in our culture do?" Stand on your head, do a belly flop into a pool, speak gibberish...all are sensible in some context. Perhaps you can think of an action that is total nonsense. But would this not be an action chosen because of your relationship to me in which I have challenged you with the question? In effect, all meaningful action is co-action.

•

To live means to participate in dialogue: to ask questions, to heed,
to respond, to agree, and so forth. In this dialogue a person
participates wholly and throughout his whole life: with his eyes, lips,
hands, soul, spirit, with his whole body and deeds.

—Mikhail Bakhtin

•

Let us consider the co-active process in more detail. Three issues are particularly important.

Co-Action and Constraint

Co-action is first a process of mutual constraint. Inherent in the process of coordinating is an ordering. Over time the actions of the participants typically become patterned, anticipated, and dependable. Spoken language is a good example. As languages develop and become useful to a group of people, so can they be characterized in terms of rules, both formal and informal.[6] Words are sensible only by virtue of one's acting according to the rules. You can say "the cat chases the mouse," but to announce, "the chases cat mouse the" is to step out of a tradition of coordination. In this sense, early socialization is that process by which the developing child is enabled to participate in the traditional patterns of a culture or sub-culture. Without the capacity to coordinate in this way, our actions are rendered unintelligible. "To be a person" is not to exist in a fundamental state of freedom, but of constraint. One may be "born free," but the mother's first caress is an enticement to a vitalizing enchainment.

•

Let us press further: As I converse with you, my utterances are candidates for meaning. However, these candidates are not my possession, but the byproducts of a relational history. Without this history of constraint, I would have nothing to say. At the same time, provided we share in a tradition of conversation, my utterances and actions carry a *pre-figuring* potential. That is, they indicate a domain of what is possible for you to say and do. Simply put, if I ask you a *question*, it is intelligible for you to give me an *answer*. If I ask, "Do you know the directions to the turnpike," you are virtually obliged in our tradition to reply with an answer. "Yes, you take the right fork…" or, "No, I'm sorry I don't live around here," will suffice. You can reply, "Autumn is coming," or "I am so hungry," but I will be puzzled. Nor can you be "knowledgeable" without my having asked a question. For you to approach a stranger and say, "Yes, you take the right fork…" will invoke suspicion.[7] It is not an answer until there is a question… It is only in the context of what has been said to you that your actions acquire

---

[6]We do not act according to the rules, that is, by following rules "inside the head." Rather, we generate patterns of coordination, and later, extract what seem to be the rules.

[7]See Craig, R. T., and Tracy, K. (Eds.) (1983). *Conversational coherence: Form, structure and strategy.* Sage Series in Interpersonal Communication. Beverly Hills, CA: Sage Publications.

their particular meaning. In effect, my question pre-figures your possibilities for action.

•

Yet, the process of constraint moves in both directions. In responding to me, there occurs a *post-figuring*. Without acknowledgement of some kind, my utterances cease to be candidates for meaning. They are sounds signifying nothing. The supplement post-figures my words as having a particular meaning—not this, but that. This is demonstrated in the many ways Jenna responded to Tom in the illustrations above. In her various responses, his personality was created. Tom was not free to be Tom; the "fact of his personality" was constrained by Jenna. In a broad sense, all of us are constrained in our actions by having to prepare them in such a way that they may be ratified as meaningful.

•

Consider the news analyst bent on locating the strategy behind the President's policies:

The President Promotes:	*The News Analyst Interprets:*
More funding for the military.	A strategy to secure veterans' votes.
Programs for inner-city schools.	An attempt to lure black voters.
A new social security program.	A tactic to secure the elderly vote.

The President wishes to be sincere, but in the hands of the analyst there is no sincerity—only instrumental strategizing. When the analyst interprets "the real reason behind the words," authenticity is turned to sham.

•

Can we ever be authentic unless others are willing to accept us without question? The moment our motives are thrown into doubt, our sense of authenticity is jeopardized—possibly even to ourselves. We may protest that our motives are pure, but how long will purity stand if others claim we protest too much? One cannot be authentic alone.

•

Thus far we have only treated the simple act/supplement relationship. One speaks, another responds, and in the interchange meaning is born. However, life moves on and the simplicity of the moment is soon subverted. What has been termed the supplement in these examples does not remain so. It functions twice, first serving to define the other's action, but second as an action that stands itself to be supplemented. For example in the preceding illustration, the news analyst is not the final arbiter of the President's meaning. To propose that the President's words are merely strategic is a supplement that is also an action open to supplementation. Should the President point out that the news analyst is just a spokesman for the conservative press, the analyst's words now become "mere instruments of persuasion."

Further, any turn in the conversation may be used to supplement any previous action in such a way that its meaning is altered. For example, the analyst might respond to the President's defense by failing to address it (thus discrediting it as meaning/full), and return to a critique of the President's initial proclamation to demonstrate its fallacies. Or, one may return to one's own early actions, and supplement them in a way that alters their meaning. The President might, for example, return to the initial proclamation to demonstrate its impeccable logic. Thus, at any point in a conversation, preceding actions by either party may be discarded, modified, or redefined in their meaning.[8] The actions of the participants are increasingly inter-knit, with meaning always in motion.

Multiplicity and Malleability

If there is no intelligibility outside traditions of constraint, are we forever bound to existing tradition? Can we never escape the existing rules of relationship, possibly established before our birth? These are pessimistic conclusions. And clearly, we do abandon tradition; our ways of life are continuously unfolding. The world is awash in conflict between those clinging to tradition versus those careening toward the new. Yet, if there is no intelligibility outside constraint, how are we to account for change? The major answer lies in our movement from one relational context to another. As we move from the home, to the office, to a visit with friends, to the sports field, and so on we carry with us patterns of speaking and acting. These practices are now inserted into the new contexts, and supplemented in new ways. The words and actions now acquire different functions. They become increasingly meaning/full.

•

The metaphor of the game is useful here. Let us say that every tradition of coordination forms a particular kind of game. There are the various

---

[8]Relevant is Harold Garfinkel's account of conversation as a process of "ad hocing" in which one can never be certain of what is possible until after the fact of another's utterance. See Garfinkel, H. (1984). *Studies in ethnomethodology*. Malden MA: Polity Press/Blackwell Publishing (first published in 1967).

formalized games, such as chess, checkers, bridge, soccer, Monopoly, and so on. There are also informal games, such as "how my father and I argue with each other," "how we play with our children." However, the border between games is porous. Very often the actions generated in one game are borrowed and inserted into another game. The act of crossing a goal line with a ball is thus shared across the games of American football, rugby, and Australian football. In everyday life the demarcation among games is far more ambiguous. The potential for borrowing and inserting is enormous. We borrow the embrace as a signal of endearment from, let us say, our relation with our mother at bed time, and place it in the context of our relations with, for example, an intimate partner. Yes, the act retains something of its initial significance (or pre-figuring power), while simultaneously acquiring additional potential. It no longer signals "it's time to go to sleep," but begins to suggest, "it's time for us to go to bed together." As we borrow and insert, so do the "rules of the game" become increasingly ambiguous. Consider, for example, the way in which the word "love" has traveled across contexts. The word may be used in relations with parents, partner, and children, along with relations to artists, ice cream, your shoes, and God. When we use a word like love, then, it is never fully clear what game is being played, from the superficial to the profound. In this sense, most conversations are akin to playing a multi-dimensional game in which any move on the part of any participant can be treated as a move in several other games.[9]

•

Every conversation is a potentially open field: A friend greets you in the morning and says, "You look tired." Among other things, you can define this as an expression of sympathy, or as a criticism of the way you look. Let's say you respond with, "You just don't know what I have been through." Is your friend to treat this utterance as a friendly invitation to inquire further, or possibly a criticism of his lack of sensitivity? He responds, "So, tell me, what's been happenin'" You wonder, is this an expression of sincere interest or a breezy indication of disinterest? In effect, there is a continuous bleeding of traditions into each other. Actions may constrain, but because they are ambiguous the constraints are soft. The range of intelligible supplements may be vast; the permutations and combinations in any co-active sequence is without number. With each new combination

---

[9]As linguists put it, the meaning of most words is *polysemous*, carrying the semantic traces of many contexts of usage.

lie the seeds for transforming tradition. Or, one might say, in the multiplication of constraints lies the possibility for infinite transformation.

•

Let's return to the construction of the self. Through co-action we come into being as individual identities, but the process remains forever incomplete. At any moment there are multiple options, and self-identity remains in motion. Consider the interchange between a client and her therapist:

CLIENT: "All day I seem to boil in anger. I sit at my desk and take orders from a really horrible guy. For one, he is stupid, and half the time makes mistakes in what he tells me to do. He barks at me...sort of like a marine sergeant. And then I find him staring at me...no, leering is a better word..."

THERAPIST: "Yes, authority is difficult to deal with. I wonder how long you have had this kind of problem. Let's talk a little about your relationship with your father."

The client has offered what could be seen as a definition of herself as a victim, and the therapist has subsequently defined her in terms of her "problem with authority." Yet, the client now has the floor. She may allow the therapist's utterances to stand. Or, as an alternative, she might say:

CLIENT: "No, I want to tell you some more about the guy...he is such a jerk..."

The client effectively disregards the therapist's words; his position as authority is challenged. The client might also say:

CLIENT: "I resent your trying to say this is 'my' problem. That's so patriarchal...sort of protecting the power structure where men are on top. Look, this guy is a crumb, and if you can't explore this with me, we might as well call it quits."

Here the therapist is positioned as "part of the problem." If he does not find a way to recast either his words or hers, the relationship will end. He may say:

THERAPIST: "Oh, please don't misunderstand me...I'm sure this guy is just as bad as you say. It's just that I want to explore some alternatives to just being angry."

And now the therapist waits...for precisely how he has defined himself at this moment is now in the hands of his client.

•

Human beings are constituted in conversation.
—Charles Taylor

•

We do not own what we say or do. As our words are absorbed by the continuing process of co-action so are we transformed:

> The phone call thrust me into mystery. It was unusual to receive calls in my location at a small German university where I had agreed to several weeks of lecturing. More important was the voice, that of an exotically accented woman. She asked for an appointment, but would only tell me that I might find it interesting. As to her identity, she simply said, "Although you do not know me, I know much about you?" On the appointed day of her visit, I was indeed restless. Later that morning, the heels of her shoes, clicking against the marble hallway, heralded her arrival. Her appearance matched her voice, a black sweater and long black skirt suggesting mystery on the verge of revelation. And soon the revelation was unleashed: I was responsible for transforming her life! How could this be?
>
> Ulrike had been married to a professor many years her senior, and been all consumed by a cerebral life. Everyday life revolved around books, ideas, and endless discussions. As part of her continuing education, she had attended a lecture I had given at a nearby university two years before. The crowded room was stifling, and I had removed my jacket during the lecture. As she described the event, my recall was instant: My shirt tails were too short. Thus, each time I reached out to scribble something on the blackboard my shirt front began to pull away from my trousers. With one hand I would write, and the other tuck. While I was engaged in this ritual, Ulrike related, her attention was drawn to my navel. When my shirt would begin to pull away, she could often catch a brief glimpse of it. She became mesmerized; my words ceased to be interesting; the only important question was whether she would be offered another glimpse of my belly-button. And, as she began to ponder her obsession, she also began to realize the way in which her marriage was failing. It was imperative now to restore its zest, to live fully again! Her marriage was transformed, and she wished to express her deep gratitude for "all I had done" for her!

•

Relationships move on, carrying with them the identities of the participants. An infinite unfolding over which no *one* has control. Like an ocean wave, the "I" may appear for a frozen moment to be itself alone. Yet, as the moment passes the wave disappears into the endless undulations from which it is inseparable.

Relational Flow: Failing and Flourishing

We have now scanned the ways in which the process of collaborative action is constrained, and as well its potential for infinite malleability. Any viable relationship will simultaneously require both these processes, the first essential to the creation of any meaning at all, and the second ensuring a sensitivity to the shifting context. Let us envision, then, a process of *relational flow* in which there is both continuous movement toward constraint, on the one hand, and an openness to the evolution of meaning on the other.[10] In the process of relational flow, we generate durable meaning together in our local conditions, but in doing so we continuously innovate in ways that are sensitive to the multiplicity of relationships in which we are engaged. Ideally, if there were no impediments to the relational flow, there would be a full and creative sharing of meaning from the immediate face to face relationship, to the local community, to the surrounding society, and ultimately to the world at large. In each relational moment we would resonate with our surrounds, absorb its potentials, create new amalgams, and return them to the larger flow of relations in which we are constituted.

•

The reeds give
way to the
wind and give
the wind away

—A.R. Ammons

•

Let us press this vision forward. Our daily lives are replete with tensions and alienated relations; everywhere there are the scarcely tolerated, the disliked, the disreputable, the despised, and the despicable. And in the world more generally these same conditions turn deadly. If there is harmony, it is often within closed doors, behind residential gates, or protected by fortified borders.

---

[10]Relevant is Bakhtin's distinction between *centripetal* and *centrifugal* forces in language, the former toward unification and the latter toward disorganization. Bakhtin, M. M. (1982). *The dialogic imagination: Four essays.* Austin: University of Texas Press.

This concern with alienated relationships will be central to later chapters of the book. As a preliminary, however, it is useful to consider distinctions among forms of relational flow. In particular, I wish to distinguish between relational processes that are ultimately *degenerative* as opposed to *generative*. The former are corrosive; they bring co-action to an end. The latter are *catalytic*; they inject relations with vitality.

To expand, consider your response to such common utterances as:

I think you made a mistake.

You are dead wrong.

How could you possibly think of something like that?

I don't think you did right by him.

I don't think you are fair.

By common tradition, each of these comments may be seen as an attack on the intelligibility of your behavior. And, given our traditions of supplementation, chances are you will defend your actions. You may question the person's right to comment as they have; you may criticize their judgment; you may even respond with a biting attack. With each of these supplements you move toward a condition of alienation. By common standards the sequence is perfectly normal, but the effect on the relationship is corrosive. Arguments are often of this form, as are expressions of mutual indifference. At the extreme of degenerative exchange is mortal combat. Sequences of attack and counter-attack may be highly coordinated, but the trajectory is toward mutual annihilation.

In contrast, it is useful to envision forms of generative process, those in which new and enriching potentials are opened through the flow of interchange. A successful teacher, for example, may engage students in such a way that their taken for granted assumptions about the world are suspended, and delight enkindled in new worlds of possibility. In the sciences, the generative challenge may be one that introduces a theory contradicting or suspending the commonplace assumptions of a discipline in such a way that new forms of inquiry are stimulated.[11] In day-to-day relations, generative challenges can make the difference between boredom and excitement. It is when life as usual is disrupted by humor, irony, thoughtful reflection, a compelling fantasy, and the like, that we avoid the slide into deadening repetition.

Generative processes stimulate the expansion and flow of meaning. Ultimately they may be an important key to our future well-being. Many of the rock-solid meanings by which we carry out our lives are lethal in

---

[11]For further discussion, see Gergen, K. J. (1994). *Toward transformation in social knowledge* (2nd ed.). London: Sage.

Your fear is contagious
      Your anger spreads like weeds
            Your joy moves with the speed of good news.
As you speak with me you create the world.

REGINE WALTER, ARTIST

their potential. We find it "just natural" to seek revenge, and enjoy the downfall of the victim. We are deeply satisfied when those who threaten us are imprisoned. Many advocate the torture of terrorists. Tit-for-tat struggles of attack and revenge may be sustained for centuries. Here we can appreciate the enormous importance of the generative challenge. Such challenges may open reflection on our destructive habits and open discussion on alternatives. We stand each moment at a precious juncture, gathering our pasts, thrusting them forward, and in the conjunction creating the future. As we speak together now, so do we give shape to the future world. We may sustain tradition; but we are also free to innovate and transform. Future chapters will be devoted to the practical challenge of such transformations.

From Causality to Confluence

The challenge of transforming traditions raises one final issue relevant to the forthcoming chapters, the question of cause and effect. We inherit strong traditions of understanding people's actions. In particular we inherit two major forms of explaining "why" people behave as they do. On the one hand there is *causal* explanation, favored by most social scientists. People change because of external forces impinging on them. As commonly said, for example, people can be "influenced," "educated," "rewarded," "threatened," or "forced" to change their behavior. On the other hand there are explanations lodged in the assumption of *voluntary agency*, favored in our daily relations and in courts of law. For example, we say that people are free to choose between right and wrong, or to decide what they want to do in life. Yet, in developing a relational view of human action, we find that neither of these traditional explanations is satisfactory. Both sustain the tradition of bounded being, and neither recognizes the fundamental significance of co-action in human affairs. In effect, an alternative way of explaining human action is invited, one that places the co-active *confluence* in the center of concern. In what follows, I shall first elaborate on the shortcomings of causal explanation, and then turn more briefly to voluntary explanation. This analysis will give way to a discussion of confluence explanation.

•

At the outset, it is difficult to deny the obvious reality of cause and effect. We observe that the flame on the stove brings the water to a boil, we step on the gas pedal and the car accelerates, we ask a friend to "please pass the salt," and she places the shaker before us. Is it not clear that the boiling water, the accelerating car, and the passing of the salt are the direct result of their antecedents? And without such antecedents, these events would not have occurred. This view of causal relationships—if X then Y, if not X then not Y—has ancient origins. Aristotle termed it *efficient causation*.[12] Centuries later, under Isaac Newton's influence, one could indeed begin to conceive of the universe as "one great machine," with each of its components causally related. For every event there is a cause, and to imagine an "uncaused cause" is to step outside the realm of science. This *mechanistic* view of human behavior still remains pervasive.

To illustrate, in the social sciences we observe behavior we call aggressive, altruistic, or delinquent, and we are concerned. In the service of bettering society, how can we bring about more of one and less of another? Concern gives way to the question: "What causes these behaviors?" What forces, influences, factors, or life situations bring them about? The question of cause then sets in motion mammoth programs of research. And from this research we reach such conclusions as, aggressive models cause children to act aggressively, the promise of rewards will increase altruism, or peer group pressure causes delinquency. As often proposed, social science research should be directed toward increasingly accurate prediction of human behavior, and thus, enhanced control over the future. If society can gain control over the causes of prejudice, hatred, crime, and so on, we move toward a better world.

•

For centuries philosophers have debated the concept of causal explanation. In recent decades, as quantum physicists have abandoned causal explanation in favor of field theoretical accounts, such debate has waned. Remaining unsolved, however, are major questions concerning the nature of causality. Most prominent among these, how can one event "make happen" or "produce" changes in another? We see the flame on the stove, and then we observe the boiling water. But how did the flame "make" the water boil? If you ask me to pass the salt, what if anything determines that I will pass the shaker? We are left in mystery. As many some propose, we should abandon the idea of causal force. Rather, we should simply confine ourselves to prediction. We can predict rather reliably what will happen to a pot of water placed on a flame, or a request for salt at a dinner party. The concept of causal determination is an unjustified and unnecessary addition.

[12]Aristotle distinguished among four kinds of causation, of which the prevailing view of *efficient* cause is only one. A contrasting form of causality for Aristotle was termed *final*. A final cause is the purpose or end that is served by an action. Thus, we say, the person purchased the gift *because* he wanted to please his parents. Generally, however, we now view final causation as a way of talking about freely chosen actions. Freely chosen actions are, in turn, viewed as uncaused.

•

Note our temptation to think of nature as divisible into discrete happenings, each of which has one "father" (cause) and one, or several "sons" (effects). This way of looking at the world leads to bewhiskered questions.

—Norwood Russell Hanson

•

There is further reason to bracket the concept of cause and effect. In significant ways the concept contributes to the ideology and institutions of bounded being. When we search for causal explanations for a person's actions, we begin to split the world into independent entities. There are causal conditions on the one hand and their effects on the other. Thus, we treat acts of aggression, altruism, and prejudice as effects, and search for an independent set of conditions that bring these about. In effect, we define the individual as fundamentally separated from the surrounding world, alone, and subject to its vicissitudes. In the case of social interaction, the presumption of cause and effect case is even more damaging in its implications for social life. As ventured in the preceding chapter, the ideology of bounded being places primary value on the self and its development; simultaneously we become suspicious of others and the constraints they may place on our lives. It is an ideology that invites us to see ourselves as uncaused causes. On this view, we wish to see ourselves as origins of others' behavior, but not as pawns to theirs.[13] Thus, the question hovers over every relationship, "Am I in control, or is the other controlling me?" We resent those who wish to exert control over us, and we lose respect for those over whom we have control. As I heard a philosopher once remark, "Whenever I meet another philosopher, the most important question is whether I can defeat him or he can defeat me." Where control is an issue, threat is ever at hand.

•

In a world of cause and effect, everyone clamors to be a cause.

•

I am joined here by many other critics of causal explanation as applied to human behavior.[14] However, it is at just this point that we begin to surmise

---

[13]See DeCharms, R. (1976). *Enhancing motivation: Change in the classroom.* New York: Irvington.

[14]See, for example, Taylor, C. (1964). *The explanation of behavior.* New York: Humanities Press; Harré, R., and Secord, P. (1967). *The explanation of social behavior.* Oxford: Blackwell;

the problems with the major alternative to cause and effect philosophy, namely voluntarism. For humanist scholars in particular, there is strong resistance to any account of human action that denies our voluntary agency. For them it seems so obviously true that we can decide on our actions from moment to moment.[15] If you ask me to pass the salt, I can choose to do it or not. More importantly, if we allow the assumption of causal determinism to prevail, and the concept of "freely chosen action" is demolished, we undermine the basis for moral responsibility. If we understand that all our actions are the result of causes beyond our control, then we cannot be held responsible for what we do. That we rob, rape, and torture is beyond our personal control. Yet, the debate continues. For determinist scientists such voluntarist complaints are unhelpful. To say that a man robbed a bank because he chose to do so is circular. It is to say no more than he robbed because he robbed. Nothing is discovered or learned that might help us discourage such actions in the future. All one can do is punish the robber for his choice. If we want more promising futures, it is argued, we must discover the conditions that influenced him to engage in such behavior.[16] More generally, to admit voluntary agency into the social sciences is to conclude that human behavior is not lawful. One could always choose to disobey the law. If the scientific principle predicts that I will be aggressive, I can choose otherwise. Thus, prediction and control are unreachable goals for the social sciences.[17]

•

The debates between advocates of determinism and voluntarism are long-standing and interminable. However, I propose that we simply set the debate aside, put it on the shelf of history. Why? For one, if the concept of cause-and-effect is abandoned, as suggested here, then so is its antagonist, voluntarism. In large measure, the concepts of determinism and agency draw their meaning from each other. One cannot champion determinism if there is nothing against which it can be contrasted. If I propose that the entire cosmos is composed of granite, there can be little opposition without

Merleau-Ponty, M. (1967). *The structure of behavior*. Boston: Beacon Press; Rychlak, J. F. (1977). *The psychology of rigorous humanism*. New York: Wiley-Interscience.

[15]The self-evidential grounds were indeed sufficient to form the basis for the development of existential philosophy.

[16]See, for example, Skinner, B. F. (2002). *Beyond freedom and dignity*. Indianapolis, IN: Hackett Publishing Company.

[17]For further discussion on this debate and a relational alternative, see Gergen, K. J. (2007). From voluntary to relational action: Responsibility in question. In S. Maasen and B. Sutter (Eds.) v *On willing selves*. London: Palgrave.

a concept of what is not granite. Thus, to dispense with either side of the antinomy, is to foreclose on the other.

•

Without injustice the name of justice would mean what?
—Heraclitus

•

Most important from the present standpoint, the concept of voluntary agency is similar to the concept of cause-and-effect in its support for the ideology of bounded being. For the voluntarist, we are the sole origins of our actions. We function as gods in miniature, the originators of our futures. Thus invited are all the ills outlined in the preceding chapter.

•

The critic is agitated: "Yes, there may be problems in the idea of free agency, but we are still left with the problem of moral responsibility. After all, we need to hold individuals responsible for their action. If no one was responsible for anything, then it is a world of anything goes." This is an important critique, and deserving of close attention. For the moment, I will simply point out that the tradition of holding individuals responsible is not without its problems. For example, the individualist view of moral and legal responsibility reigns supreme in the United States. We punish those who step out of line. Thus, it is not surprising that while the nation possesses only 5% of the world's population, it houses 25% of the world's prisoners. Over 7 million people in the country are either imprisoned, on probation, or on parole for their freely chosen crimes. No other nation, no matter the size, holds so many in detention. Alternative views are needed. In the next chapter I will introduce a relational view of agency. And in Chapter 11, I will take up the issue of moral responsibility from a relational standpoint.

•

How could we replace the traditional explanations of causality and agency? Is there an approach to explanation that would more fully reflect a relational view of the world? To sketch the contours of possibility, let us return to the concept of co-action. As I proposed, it is through collaborative action that all meaning emerges. Thus, the very idea of causality and agency are children of relationship. They are historically and culturally specific, and the battle between them is essentially one of competing traditions of meaning. How does the concept of co-action take us further?

Consider again the causal account of behavior. On this view, people are like billiard balls, striking against each other to bring about effects. Each ball is independent until it is struck by an alien. And yet, how can we identify a cause in itself, seperated from an effect? Without something we call "an effect" there is nothing to be called "a cause," and vice versa. Cause and effect are mutually defining.[18] Let us expand through illustration: You are walking by a park and see a man throw a ball into an open space before him. An aimless activity, you surmise, scarcely notable on a summer's day. Now, consider the same action when the ball is thrown to someone wearing a catcher's mitt. Suddenly the individual's action can be identified as "pitching." In effect, there is no pitching until there is catching, and no catching until there is pitching. We look further to find that there is a man with a bat, bags that form a diamond shape, men holding mitts in the field, and so on. At this point we might justifiably conclude that this is a "baseball game." What we traditionally view as "independent" elements—the man with the bat, the bags, the men in the field—are not truly independent. They are all mutually defining. A man standing alone in the field wearing a mitt would not be playing baseball, nor would the bags constitute a game. Alone they would be virtually without meaning. It is when we bring all these elements into a mutually defining relationship that we can speak about "playing baseball." Let us then speak of the baseball game as a *confluence*, a form of life in this case that is constituted by an array of mutually defining "entities."[19]

In attempting to explain and predict human action, let us replace the metaphors of billiard balls and unmoved movers with the metaphors of baking or doing chemistry. The concern now shifts from isolated entities to the combination of ingredients. With a combination of flour, butter, eggs,

---

[18]We are accustomed to saying that the cause precedes an effect. However, from a relational standpoint there is a sense in which the order is reversed. Normally we designate a behavior that we want to understand, and we seek its cause. However, we can only discover as a cause that which makes conventional sense as a cause. If we see acting aggressively, we ask why. However, the cause must be something that enables us to sustain the definition that we have made of the behavior, namely that it was aggressive. Thus, we cannot say it was caused by "a lucky break," as it is senseless to say that good luck causes aggression. We must search for a cause that justifies aggression, such as "bad luck," or frustration. In this sense, once we have designated an effect, we have also determined the cause. The effect, then, precedes the cause.

[19]The setting off of "entities" in quotation marks is to indicate that it has no independent identity, only an identity in relationship. As outlined in the Prologue, anything we consider an "independent entity" is a placeholder. In a more extended analysis, the entity would itself be considered a confluence.

The whole is equal to the sum of the relations.
At the turn of the 20th century an artistic movement called pointillism emerged. Pointilist painters used tiny specks of paint to create the subject matter of their painting. The subject was never painted in itself. Indeed, one might say that there was no "in itself," as the subject emerged from the juxtaposition of the points of paint. Paul Signac's painting of the harbor at Marseilles is illustrative.

milk, and a griddle, we bring about a pancake. By compounding hydrogen and oxygen we have water. From this standpoint, a lighted match does not cause the combustion of gasoline; rather the combustion is the achievement of a particular combination of flame and gasoline. In the same way, what scholars might define as an intellectual attack does not cause another to argue; the argument is achieved only when another responds with a defense.

•

Each thing, including each person, is first and always
a nexus of relations.

—Brent Slife

•

Mary and I once puzzled over the fact that every Christmas time we labored to decorate the house. The decorating cost us time and money; there was no obvious gain. Nothing dire would befall us if we failed to do so. Why, we asked, do we do it? We now see this as a misleading question. We decorate neither for a reason that lies somewhere inside, or pressures from the outside. Rather, we decorate because we exist within a confluence—an array of mutually defining relationships with each other and our surrounds. When the season is upon us, such actions are obvious ways of going on; they are congenial within the confluence. If we were at a dinner party we would eat, if we were at a concert we would applaud. We do not do so for reasons of private origin, or because someone "makes us do it," but because we are participants in a confluence of relationships in which these are intelligible actions.[20]

•

The critic takes notice: "This suggests to me that you as a physical person have no will of your own. Your actions matter little; it is the confluence that counts. Doesn't this view stifle our motivation for change? Doesn't it favor the status quo, suggesting that an individual's efforts are futile?" Not at all. You will certainly import into any situation a set of preferred performances. They don't represent "will power," so much as a set of relationally established trajectories. And they can be enormously important when injected into a given confluence. Consider the power that even a single word or phrase may have in a given context: "You are fired," "I quit," or "we are finished." The same holds true of one's movements: a raised fist, a derisive laugh, an embrace. Even one's physical presence may alter the confluence. Depending on the circumstances, simply standing there as an observer, a demonstrator, or a mourner may all change the definition of the situation. And we must also consider the objects that are present. A vase of flowers, a menorah, a dog, a weapon on the wall…all are subtle means of shifting the potentials of the situation. To be sure, it may be useful to

---

[20]There is a family resemblance between the concept of confluence developed here and Pierre Bourdieu's account of *habitus*. However, for Bourdieu, habitus was a system of individual dispositions acquired from determining structures of family, education, physical location, and the like. In this sense Bourdieu's account carries significant traces of both a mind–world dualism and cause–effect explanation. See Bourdieu, P. (1977). *Outline for a theory of practice*. Cambridge: Cambridge University Press. Philosophical writings on *contextualism* are also relevant, maintaining as they do that all word meaning is dependent upon context. If extended, such a view might suggest that whatever a thing comes to be is dependent upon the way it functions within a context.

These moments of delight cannot be carried by any single element in the photograph. Delight emerges only within the confluence.

Courtesy: Anne Marie Rijsman

distinguish between constituents of a confluence that are central to its form as opposed to peripheral. But people can also be enormously flexible and creative in sustaining a given definition of the situation as various people, objects, and actions shift over time.

•

The critic remains skeptical: "Practically speaking, I don't see where this idea of confluence takes us. What about scientific prediction? Are there any advantages here over the old mechanical model?" In response, there is nothing about the confluence orientation that rules out prediction. As pointed out, the process of co-action will tend toward reliable or repeated forms of relationship. Take the game of golf. We can rather perfectly predict what most players will do after they hit their ball into a sand trap, or when they find their ball is several inches from the cup. You can know in advance rather well what Mary and I will be up to next Christmas season, or at a dinner party or concert. The advantage of the confluence orientation, however, is that we do not depend on independent factors or variables to make predictions. Rather than looking at "the effects" of income, education, and father absence on the child's school performance, for example, the concern shifts to the condition of relational life in which the child participates. Ethnography takes precedence over experimental manipulation. We shift from influence to confluence.

A confluence orientation also opens new horizons in long-term prediction. The social sciences are notoriously weak, for example, in predicting adult behavior from early childhood events. The parental treatment of the child has but scant predictive value in terms of the child's well-being as an adult. Programs like Head Start are not able to confidently predict positive futures for low-income children. From the standpoint of confluence, however, we are drawn to issues of coherence across time. We may view home life with parents or within a Head Start program as a confluence. Life within these settings may have little to do with life outside. If one is concerned with creating positive futures, concern should be direct to *relational pathways*. How can forms of confluence be linked, such that the pathway from one to another leads in a positive direction. For low-income children, can life in the home be more closely linked to life in school, a continuity be built into life at school across the years, and school life be connected more fully with higher education and to promising employment?

•

Finally, it must be asked, why should the social sciences place so much value on the traditional practice of prediction? If we are concerned with human well-being, why examine present patterns to speculate about the future? As noted above, transformation in patterns of co-action is common. Today's research is about today; the conditions of tomorrow's world may be vastly different. If we wish to generate more promising futures, the major challenge is that of collaboratively creating new conditions of confluence. How can we draw from our relational histories in such a way that new and more promising confluences result?

•

The best way to predict the future is to invent it.

—Alan Kay

•

Understanding in terms of confluence is never complete. Unlike the misleading promise of scientific certainty, we must remain humble. This is so, in part, because what we take to be a confluence owes its existence to we who define it as such. One might say that a confluence is essentially "an action" for which our supplement is required in order to bring it into being. Every attempt to identify the confluence will issue from a particular tradition of relationship. Thus, we may commonly identify a baseball game, and explore what is required to bring it into existence. But within the traditions of physics or physiology, baseball games do not exist. Thus, whatever we say about a confluence is forever dependent upon the tradition in which it is explored.

Humility is also invited by the fact that the confluence is not bounded. We may identify a baseball game as a confluence, but in doing so we have arbitrarily cut it away from everything else. Would there be a pitcher without food, water and air; would there be a "home run" without a fence? In effect, to define anything as a confluence is temporarily to blind us to the broader context of which it may be a part. One may imagine here an ultimate confluence through which all existence comes into being, including our own. This ultimate confluence is beyond description. We are rendered mute, and possibly awed. I will return to this latter sensibility in the final chapter.

3

The Relational Self

Moments from everyday conversation:

> "I *hope* that…"
> "I am so *angry*…"
> "What do you *think* about it…"
> "I don't *remember* his name…"
> "I didn't *intend* to…"
> "I really *want* to go…"
> "Her *attitude* is so negative…"

Such phrases are unremarkable, but their consequences in social life are profound. Consider that whenever we talk we contribute to a relational process from which the sense of the real and the good are derived. In this light, consider the way these phrases construct the person. At least one thing stands out: They all assert the *reality of the mind*. Declarations of hope, anger, thought, memory, intention, want, and attitudes all "make real" mental events. With the help of a dictionary, we could assemble more than 2,000 such terms…need, fear, doubt, happiness, attitudes, imagination, creativity, ambivalence, and so on. If we consulted an encyclopedia of psychology, we might even be able to add another 1,000 terms…depression, split imago, flash bulb memory, schema, repression…How stunningly rich this world is behind our eyes!

•

The issue here is not simply about words. Rather, our daily lives revolve around the discourse of the mind. People devote the greater part of their lives to what they consider their *beliefs*, their *loves*, their *ideas*, their religious *faith*, their career *aspirations*, and so on. In matters of life, death is a close companion:

- A sense of wounded pride can be an invitation to murder.
- Feelings of hopelessness can invite suicide.
- In a court of law, estimates of intention may make the difference between freedom and execution.
- A sense of superiority can invite genocide.

It may be safely said that at least in Western culture, life is grounded in the reality of the mind.

•

Man must know who he is: He must be able to sense himself as both author and object of his actions. For the only true fulfillment of his human needs is his development as a fully individuated person, which recognizes itself as the center of its own being.

—H.M. Ruitenbeek

Being Unbound

The reality of the mind is also the reality of bounded being. Mental states constitute the very ingredients of the individual *interior*. One's ability to think, and feel, and choose are the very marks of being fully human. Would a child be normal without the ability to feel pleasure and pain, happiness or anger? Doesn't normal development include expanding one's capacities for abstract reasoning, conscience, and long-term planning? Could one function properly in society without having values, attitudes, and opinions? All such suppositions support and honor the tradition of the bounded self.

•

As I proposed in the initial chapter, the assumption of an internal or mental world invites alienation, loneliness, distrust, hierarchy, competition, and self-doubt; favored is a society in which people become commodities and relationships are devalued. Yet, as proposed in the preceding chapter, this concept of bounded being finds its origins not within the interior of individual minds, but within co-action. It is from relational process that the very idea of an "inner world" is created. Speaking of our thoughts, emotions, intentions, and the like is not required by the facts of nature. If we fail to speak in these terms, it is not that we fail to grasp reality. Rather, the language of the interior issues from a particular tradition of relationship. By the same token, we can also create together new ways of speaking and acting. We must not remain forever bound by history.

•

How could we, then, transform the language by which we live; how can we recognize the primacy of relationship in all that we do? This is the major challenge of this chapter and the next. My hope is to recast the discourse of mind in such a way that human connection replaces separation as the fundamental reality. Our understanding of the mental world will be reconstructed in such a way that the wall between inside and outside is removed; the mental will cease to exist separate from relationship. Then, with this reformulation in place, Parts II and III of this work will be devoted to

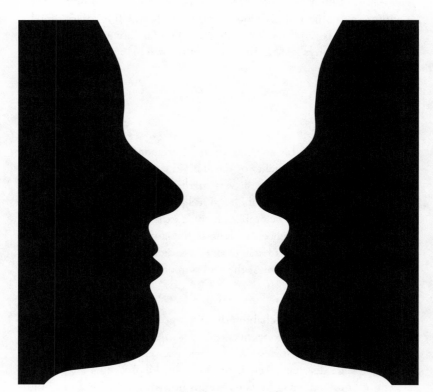

Here we confront two independent beings, spatially and mentally separated. Our present challenge is to reverse the field of understanding. Rather than focusing on the independent beings, consider instead the reality of the "between," that urn-like form emerging from the co-existence.

linking concepts to practice. If a conception of relational being is to make any difference, it must be realized in our lives together.

In this chapter I will first prepare the way by removing the idea of a distinctly mental world behind the eyes. I will propose that neither I nor anyone else could know such a world. Our words for mental life are not maps or mirrors of some interior space. At the same time, such words have enormous social consequences. Our future may depend on how and when we use them. Thus, I will propose, what we call thinking, experience, memory, and creativity are actions in relationship. Even in our private reveries, we are in relationship. In the following chapter I shall take up the question of the body and emotion.

The Very Idea of Self-Knowledge

In children's magazines we often find puzzles of the following sort: A number of words appear in one column, and in an adjoining column we find an equal number of pictured objects. The child is asked to match the word with the proper object, "tree" with a picture of a tree, "eagle" with a picture of an eagle, and so on. Each word refers to a particular kind of object. Now, as an adult, consider this possibility: Place a dozen words for mental states in a column, words like "love," "hope," "attitude," and "intention." In an adjoining column sketch a picture of these various states. When you have assembled the puzzle…"Hold on…." you say, "you want 'pictures' of mental states. What do you mean?" Yes, what could I possibly mean?

What is the color of love, the shape of hope, the size of an attitude, the contour of an intention? The questions seem nonsensical; they leave us speechless. But why are they nonsensical? For one, because whatever we mean by "an inner world," it is not like the "outer world." There is nothing in the "inner world" that allows us to make a picture of it, nothing equivalent to saying, "that is an apple and it is red." If you close your eyes, and focus all your attention within, what precisely are you looking at? And if your eyes are closed, what are you using to do the looking?

•

We often view consciousness as a mirror of the external world. But if consciousness were to function as a mirror, how could it mirror its own conditions? Two thousand years of philosophy have yielded no compelling answers to such questions. Experimental psychologists have long attempted to disclose the character of the mental world. However, in the 1930s, many abandoned the idea of "introspective knowledge," that is, knowledge of the mind resulting from inner observation. One of the major objections at the time was that the very act of trying to observe one's experience would alter the experience.

In his *Discourse on Method*, René Descartes set out to locate a foundational reality, a solid ground from which he could proceed to understand the nature of existence.[1] Descartes found good reason to doubt the opinion of authorities, the claims of his peers, and even the evidence conveyed to him by his senses. Yet, he could not doubt the existence of his own doubting... the fact that he was thinking. Yet, we must ask, how did Descartes know that he was *thinking*? What precisely is "a thought," that he could be sure he had one? What is the color, the shape, the size, the diameter, or the weight of a thought? What if Descartes was simply speaking silently to himself? Could he have mistaken his use of public speech for private thought? Could Descartes know he was doubting before he had acquired the public discourse of doubt?

•

Few ideas are both as weighty and as slippery as the notion of the self.
—Jerrold Seigel

•

Sigmund Freud proposed that the most significant content of the mind— our fundamental desires, deepest fears, and most unsettling memories—are hidden from consciousness. This was a momentous proposal, not only launching the profession of psychiatry, but laying the groundwork for much therapeutic practice since that time. Most important, Freud informed Western culture that we cannot know our own minds. What we want most to know is hidden beneath layers of repression.

Beneath a rational thought lies an unconscious desire.
Beneath professed love we may find hatred.
Beneath a wish to improve the world may lie the desire to destroy it.

Could Freud be right? On what grounds can he be refuted? And yet, how did Freud know these things? How could he peer into himself, and recognize what lies beyond consciousness? How did he go about distinguishing between a repression, a desire or a wish? What are the characteristics of these states that he could single them out? And, curiously, how did Freud manage to remove the barrier of repression to reveal the true nature of his own desires?

•

[1]Descartes, R. (2001). *Discourse on the method of rightly conducting the reason, and seeking truth in the sciences.* (Original work published in 1637). New York: Bartleby.

A great many people think they are thinking
when they are merely rearranging their prejudices.

—William James

•

Let me propose that when you...
  share your *thoughts* with me,
    tell me you *love* me,
      reveal to me your *hopes*,
        tell me what *excites* you,
          share your *fears* of the future,
            declare that this is your *opinion*,
              tell me that you *understand*,
                report on what you *remember*,

you are *not* reporting on the state of a private world. Our words do not appear to name anything about which we can be certain. As we shall see, this is not their function.

•

I have pondered these matters for many years, and not without problems. Early in my marriage, Mary asked that we exchange words of devotion before winding into sleep at night. To hear "I love you" would be the reassurance necessary for tranquility. Such a simple request...and yet I was tormented. How could I be certain of my mental state...how could I peer inward to know precisely the nature of my emotions...did emotions exist in the mind or in the body or somewhere else? I labored nightly for an answer that would allow a clear declaration. Finally, one night, exhausted by my interminable philosophizing, Mary intoned, "Just say the words...!" This I was all too happy to do, and we have slept soundly ever since...

Call in the Experts

If self-knowledge is beyond our grasp as individuals, then how are we to account for the vast vocabulary of the mind? Why do we have so many ways of talking about what's on our mind? Here the critic steps in: "OK, there are problems with individuals trying to look inside. But is this our only path to knowledge about psychological states? We have authorities to inform us about such things." To be sure, religious authorities long advised us on the nature of our spiritual lives, our desires and fears. In the

21st century such authorities have largely been replaced by mental health professionals. Our 20th century experts of the interior are typically skilled in interviewing, and may be armed as well with batteries of mental tests. Can't we then rely on such experts to inform us about our inner lives?

•

Place yourself for a moment in the chair of the psychiatrist. You listen to your client, Fred, who says:

> "Ever since the death of my father I haven't felt right. I haven't been able to do anything. I just can't seem to get started. I don't feel motivated. Work doesn't interest me. I don't know what's the matter with me."

Fred's words are clear enough. But what are these expressions telling you about his mental life? Essentially you confront the difficult challenge of using:

> words
> the exterior
> the surface
> the observable

to draw conclusions about:

> the mind
> the interior
> depth
> the unobservable.

Now the fun begins. Obviously you have no direct access to what exists beneath the client's words ("in his mind"). You can never peer behind the veil of his eyes. So, how are you to draw conclusions about his inner world, what truly drives him, what he actually feels, or is trying to say?

•

If you are hesitant in answering how it is you can discern what's on Fred's mind, you are in good company. In fact, the problem of discerning other minds has challenged some of the West's most learned scholars for several centuries.[2] It is no less profound than the challenge of trying to understand

---

[2]In philosophy the challenge here is often characterized as the "problem of other minds." See, for example, Avramides, A. (2001). *Other minds*. London: Routledge. For more on the problems of presuming minds within bodies, see Ryle, G. (1949). *The concept of mind*. London: Hutchinson; and Malcolm, N. (1971). The myth of cognitive processes and structures. In T. Mischel (Ed.) *Cognitive development and espistemology*. New York: Academic Press.

God's intentions from the words of the Bible, knowing what the authors of the Bill of Rights intended by their pronouncements, deciphering the underlying meaning of a poem, or trying to understand what a complex philosophical writing is trying to say. Much may hang on our reaching the "correct interpretation." (Indeed, individuals have hung from the gallows on the basis of others' interpretations of their words.) For some 300 years the discipline of *hermeneutic* studies has been devoted to working out a plausible rationale for justifying interpretations. Importantly, there is no commonly accepted solution.[3]

•

"Yes...but," the critic responds, "the situation is scarcely hopeless. I do have history on which I can rely. The thousands of psychiatrists before me have left a legacy of understanding to guide me; they know what I should be looking for. In the present case, for example, they might advise me to explore the client's feelings of self-esteem, the possibility of repressed anger, or perhaps a dysfunctional cognitive system." To be sure, these assumptions are congenial to the psychiatric community. But, how did this community come to know about these things? Do we have concepts of "self-esteem," "repression," or "cognitive systems" because the experts of previous generations somehow solved the hermeneutic problem? How did they accomplish such a feat?

•

A recent headline in the Science and Health section of the *Philadelphia Inquirer:*

Sometimes, Bitterness and Irritability are Really Depression.

Is this objective knowledge, divine inspiration, or something else?

•

Again the critic rebuts, "But I can check on my intuitions. I can ask my client questions bearing on my interpretations, and his answers will suggest whether I am on the right track or not. I can even share my conclusions

[3]Hermeneutic studies originated, in large measure, in the attempt to clarify the meaning of Biblical texts. Hermeneutics is derived from the Greek term for interpreter, and draws from the image of Hermes in Greek mythology. Hermes conveyed the messages of the gods to mortals, but was also known for playing tricks. Thus, special skills were essential in determining the true meaning of the messages. The most prominent work in recent hermeneutic study is that of Hans-Georg Gadamer (1975). *Truth and method* (eds. C. Barden and J. Cummming). New York: Seabury. (Original German publication in 1960.) However, Gadamer cannot account for the possibility of compelling interpretation outside one's participation in a cultural tradition.

with the patient and see if he agrees." So you suggest to the client that he may be depressed...and he nods assent. Ah, now you feel you are on the right track.

But what precisely has taken place here? Has the client considered your suggestion by turning back into himself and trying to match the term "depression" against his inner state to see if you might be correct? "Ah, yes, now I spot a depression running about in here...how could I have missed that...you are quite correct." Scarcely!

"Well..." the critic replies, "perhaps the client's self-knowledge is a bit shaky. But after all, I don't have to trust his words alone. I can observe his conduct—how much he eats or sleeps, how many days he misses work, and how he spends his leisure hours. His behavior will give me some clues as to whether he is depressed, or something else. And if I cannot observe these actions directly, I can rely on carefully developed psychological tests of depression. On these tests the client can rate how often he "feels tired," "has trouble sleeping," or "has little energy."[4]

Fair enough. Don't we all draw conclusions about people's inner life on the basis of their actions? Perhaps we do, but the question we must now ask is whether we stand on solid ground in such matters? Are people's actions truly windows to the mind? Consider: Are bodily actions any different in principle than words in drawing conclusions about what's on someone's mind? In both cases we are using external observables to draw conclusions about an unseen interior. If I smile, how can you know that it is an outward expression of happiness, as opposed to satisfaction, ecstasy, surprise, or bemusement? Could it even be an expression of anger, love, or giddiness? On what grounds could any of these interpretations be dismissed? Because I tell you so? How would I know? And if I report on a battery of tests that I often feel tired, or have trouble sleeping and eating, how could you know these were obvious symptoms of an underlying depression? After all, where did we come up with the idea that depression exists in the human mind, by observing it? In effect, our actions—whether observed or reported on a psychological test—do not speak any more fluently or transparently about mental states than our words.

•

[4]Tests such as these are now offered by professional services on myriad websites, so that individuals may learn whether or not they are mentally ill. From the present standpoint, they learn nothing more than the ungrounded interpretation of a particular group of people. If they had asked a clergyman, and imam, or a Buddhist for a major interpretation of the same behavior, "depression" would not be an option.

Try to determine how long an impression
lasts by means of a stop-watch.

       —Ludwig Wittgenstein

•

We confront the conclusion, then, that we have no means of knowing
what's on someone's mind, or indeed, whether they possess a "mind" at all.
No matter how many ways in which an individual tells you he is depressed,
and no matter how many relevant actions you take into account, you have
nothing to go on outside a tradition of co-action. You may heap one interpretation upon another to draw a conclusion, but in the end you never
move beyond the web of our own spinning.[5]

From Mind to Relationship

We now reach a turning point. We have at our disposal thousands of terms
referring to our states of mind; many of our prized institutions are based
on a belief in these mental states; life as we know it would cease to function
if such terms were expunged from our vocabulary. And yet, we find
that there is no way we could have discovered these states by looking
inward; nor do experts have any basis for their claims to know what's on
our minds. In effect, we have an enormous vocabulary for which there is no
obvious basis. More radically, one might say that mental states are wholly
fictional.

  Yet, such a conclusion is not at all a prelude to despair. To presume the
reality of mental states lends itself to all the ills of bounded being described
in Chapter 1. If we believe that human action originates in a mental interior, then the institutions of bounded being are fortified. The individualist
tradition continues unfalteringly. However, if we can suspend the assumption of minds within heads, we enter a clearing in which we can significantly expand the vision of relational being. How are we to proceed? At
the outset I do not believe we should abandon the vocabulary of mental
states. This vocabulary is all too central to the way we live our lives. What
would cultural life be like if we could no longer say things like, "I intend"…
"I think"… "I hope"…"I want"…"I need"…"I love"…and so on?
However, we can refigure our understanding of this vast vocabulary so its

---

[5]For further study in the fluidity of interpretation, see Gergen, K. J., Hepburn, A., and
Comer, D. (1986). Hermeneutics of personality description. *Journal of Personality and Social
Psychology, 6*, 1261–1270.

relational basis becomes apparent. We can begin to see that our mental vocabulary is essentially a vocabulary of relationship. If we can succeed in such an adventure, we will find that we are not selves apart, but even in our solitude, profoundly inter-knit.

•

To prepare the way, I wish to put forth four major proposals. If these logics prove clear and compelling, the way is open to understanding the entire mental vocabulary as relational in origins and functions. In the remainder of the chapter we can then take up a range of specific cases, including reason, intention, experience, memory, and creativity. Thus, the first proposal:

1. **Mental discourse originates in human relationships**. What is the origin of words like thinking, feeling, and wanting? As outlined in the preceding chapter, the answer lies within the process of co-action. All words gain their intelligibility—their capacity to communicate—within coordinated action. Without co-action the noises emitted from the mouth are little more than sounds; these sounds come into meaning as people coordinate their actions around them. In this sense, all our terms for mental life are created within relationships.

•

Children do not first recognize that they think, or feel, or intend, and then locate a label for these states. Rather, within relationships they acquire a vocabulary of the mental world that implies the existence of such states. Parents say, "Oh, I see you are *sad*," "you must be very *angry*," "can you *remember* the time....," or "You didn't *mean to* do it..." without any access to "what's in the head" of the child. It is only within their relationships that sadness, anger, and the like become realities for the child.

•

The critic seeks a word: "As we travel about the world we are scarcely struck dumb by the actions of people in other cultures. They seem reasonable enough. And when we interact it seems very clear that people everywhere are capable of rational thought, possess attitudes, motives, desires, emotions, and the like. There seems to be something equivalent to love everywhere. Isn't it reasonable to suppose that there are mental universals?" Yes, superficially this does seem reasonable. But why are we so confident that there are universals? For example, if:

a Hindu asks, "What is the state of your *Atman*?
a Japanese asks, "Do you often feel *amae*?"

a Chewaong asks "Are you really *chan?*"
an Ifalukian asks, "Did you feel *liget?*"

...how are you to reply? After all, would they not believe that people everywhere have these states? There are extraordinary variations across cultures in what people attribute to the "inner world." And in some cultures, there is virtually nothing to be said about mental life.[6]

•

The critic resists: "Well, people in different cultures may be using different words, but they may be referring to the same internal states." This is an attractive possibility. But what is "the same internal state," and how would we ever know whether it is the same? Here we return to the problem of how we can ever identify states of mind. The translator of words like *amae* and *chan* can never know to what, if anything, in the mind they refer.[7] Let us turn to the second proposal:

2. **Mental discourse functions in the service of relationship**. If mental language is not a reflection of inner states, why do we use it at all? We are guided to an answer by the preceding discussion on origins. That is, if mental language emerges from social relationships, then we can trace its utility to the same sphere. Let us not ask what it refers to in the head, but how it functions within our relationships. Consider:

When we say, "please come for a visit," "look at that sunset!" or "Is that the number 9 bus?" there are social consequences. The result of saying such things is that people board planes, cast their gaze into the distance, or give us information. In short, the words have a pragmatic function. Does mental language not function in just this way? When someone says, "You make me so angry," or "You make me so happy," something is expected of you. Bursts of anger are typically used to correct your behavior or bring you in line; expressions of happiness will invite you to repeat what you have done.

The Phrase:	**Invites:**
"I am so *sad*"	Comforting
"I am *disappointed* in you"	Questioning

---

[6]For more on cultural variations in the construction of the mind, see Lutz, C. A. (1988). *Unnatural emotions*. Chicago: University of Chicago Press; Rosaldo, M. (1980). *Knowledge and passion: Illongot notions of self and social life*. Cambridge: Cambridge University Press; Russel, J. A. et al. (1995). *Everyday conceptions of emotion: An introduction to the psychology, anthropology and linguistics of emotion*. Dordrecht: Kluwer.

[7]I will take up the question of how successful translations are achieved in the next chapter.

"These are my *beliefs*."   Respect
"I *need* your attention."   Curiosity
"I *feel bad* about what happened."   Forgiveness
"This is *depressing*."   Commiseration

•

There is something which is at the moment of uttering
being done by the person uttering.

—J.L. Austin

•

While this much seems clear, there are dangers lurking. Consider for a
moment two lovers. Each uses special expressions of love, and the consequences of using them are mutually congenial. However, let us not conclude that they use these words *in order to* bring about the consequences.
To say that mental language has social consequences is not to say that we
are always using language strategically to gain our ends. To draw this conclusion would collapse the relational view unfolding here into "social life as
manipulation." This view of persons as dramatic actors, perennially popular in the social sciences, has just such implications.[8] Words of love, from
this perspective, are necessarily inauthentic, used for purposes of stroking
one's ego or "getting laid." This is not what is being proposed here. One
could only draw such a conclusion if it were possible to identify people's
intentions—their "inner reasons" for acting. How could one act on his or
her intentions if they couldn't be recognized? Yet, it is this very problem of
knowing one's interior that we found insoluble. Thus, is a man who seems
bent on seducing every woman in sight, trying to compensate for a deep
insecurity, share the joys of sensuality, retaliate against bourgeois conventionality, or something else? And how could he know? How could he look
inward to identify which impulse was indeed in motion? As we have seen,
there is little means of doing so. If we cannot identify our motives, then we
cannot consciously treat others as means to our own ends. Let us abandon
this dismal view of social life. We turn to the third proposition:

3. **Mental discourse is action within relationships**. Consider again the
social uses of mental discourse. In doing so, we also realize that mental
discourse is itself a form of action within a relationship.[9] Return to

---

[8]Erving Goffman's dramaturgic view of social life is often held to exemplify this view. See
Goffman, E. (1956). *The presentation of self in everyday life*. New York: Doubleday.

[9]This view is foreshadowed in Roy Schafer's 1976 volume, *A new language for psychoanalysis*
(New Haven, CT: Yale University Press), in which he advocates replacing all mental terms from

our lovers. They each have their special words of endearment. But these words are not simply hovering overhead in a comic strip balloon. Their words are actions within a relationship, and in this sense, equivalent to the remainder of the body in motion—lips, eye movements, gestures, posture, and so on. The spoken language is but one component of a full social performance. Our words are notes within orchestrated patterns of action. Without the full coordination of words and action, relational life turns strange.

•

Consider the consequences if one of our erstwhile lovers, utters words of endearment while:

> pressing his thumb to his nose.
> thrusting his little fingers in his mouth.
> leaning over to peer through his legs.
> adopting the posture of a javelin thrower.
> raising the middle finger of his hand and thrusting it forward.

The words of endearment now become components of farce, insult, or nonsense.

•

We may speak of these full coordinations as *relational performances*, that is, actions with or for others. The performances in this case include the discourse of the mind.[10] In calling them performances attention is directed to their socially crafted character. For example, when you tell someone "I was thinking that…" you are not likely to be screaming or writhing on the ground. Rather, your tone of voice will probably be measured and your gestures minimal. When you say, "I am angry," you are not likely to be grinning or hopping on one foot. You are far more likely to speak with lips tightened and possibly with clenched fists. In effect, "thought" and "anger" are not inside, searching for release in expression. They are fully coordinated bodily performances in which the words, "thinking" and "anger" often (but not necessarily) figure. We perform thinking and anger in the

---

nouns to verbs. Thus we would not be inclined to view memory, for example, as a thing or a place, but as an action (as in remembering).

[10]I am indebted here to James Averill's account of emotions as cultural performances. See Averill, J. R. (1982). *Anger and aggression: An essay on emotion*. New York: Springer Verlag; Averill, J. R., and Sundarajan, L. (2004). Hope as rhetoric: Cultural narratives of wishing and coping. In J. Eliott (Ed.) *Interdisciplinary perspectives on hope*. New York: Nova Science; and Edwards, D., and Potter, J. (1992). *Discursive psychology*. London: Sage.

same sense that we might kick a ball or drive a car. "Thinking," "feeling anger," "kicking," and "driving" are all intelligible actions; it is simply that the first two carry with them words drawn from a vocabulary of mind.[11]

•

Perceptions, thoughts and feelings...are parts of practical activity.
—Michael Westerman

4. **Discursive action is embedded in traditions of co-action.** Thus far we have focused solely on the performer. However, it is essential that we draw attention once again to the process of co-action. In this context it is clear that the meaning of the performance is not the possession of the actor alone. Its meaning is born in the coordination. To illustrate, Ron has professed his love for Cindy in a beautifully coordinated way: words, gestures, tone of voice, gaze...an incandescent expression of devotion. Or is it? From the standpoint of co-action, another's supplement will ratify it as meaning one thing as opposed to another. Thus, in spite of Ron's creditable performance, its fate now lies in Cindy's hands. She may respond, "Oh Ron, I think I am in love with you too," thus identifying Ron's actions as expressions of love.

However, consider some alternative possibilities:

– Oh Ron, you are like a dependent child.
– You haven't a clue what you're talking about.
– Yea...but you said that last week to Sue.

It is also important to consider here that Cindy doesn't have complete freedom in responding to Ron. While each of these replies is sensible in Western culture, it would not be intelligible for Cindy to crow like a rooster, or respond by asking Ron if he has any popcorn. We are immersed in conventions of coordination, and to remove oneself from such conventions altogether is to cease making sense.[12] Ultimately we must consider these traditions of co-action within the broader contexts of which they are part. As Kenneth Burke reasoned, actions gain their intelligibility from the

[11]The metaphor of the performance is useful in calling attention to the fully embodied and social character of action. However, for some it may carry connotations of dissemblance or masking, or entertainment. For present purposes these are unfortunate and irrelevant traces.

[12]As Jan Smedslund proposes, in the same way that grammatical conventions govern most intelligible speech, so are there conventions that govern virtually all that we can intelligibly say about the mental events. See Smedslund, J. (1988). *Psycho-logic*. New York: Springer-Verlag; and Smedslund, J. (2004). *Dialogues about a new psychology*. Chagrin Falls, OH: Taos Institute Publications.

"I never said 'I love you.' I said 'I love ya.' Big difference!"

Courtesy: The New Yorker Collection 2002 and Leo Cullum from the cartoonbank.
com All Rights Reserved.

scene in which they occur.[13] The scene will include, for example, the physical location of the action. An expression of love shouted to one's companion at a rock concert would not generally carry the same weight as if uttered in bed after intercourse. The former could be written off as "mere exuberance;" in the latter case the moment of exuberance has passed. The relational performance occurs within a confluence that gives it legitimacy.

Here we have four proposals, first, that mental discourse originates in relationships; second, that the function of such discourse is social in nature; third, that its expression is a culturally prescribed performance; and finally, that such performances are embedded within traditions of co-action. To have a mental life is to participate in a relational life. With these proposals in place we are positioned for a full reconstruction of the psychological world.

[13]Burke, K. (1952). *A grammar of motives*. New York: Prentice Hall.

Mind as Action in Relationship

The proposals for mind as relational performance are as questionable as they are challenging. It is essential now to fill out the emerging picture, to explore the potentials and possible shortcomings as we take up more specific cases. Let us shift the focus, then, to the specific processes of reason, intention, experience, memory, and creativity. In what sense are these relational actions? I begin with these specific cases not only because talk about such processes plays such an important role in everyday life, but because they also seem so obviously "in the head." How can they be relocated in the region of the "between?" In the following chapter we can then take up mental states that are often viewed as biological, specifically the emotions, along with states of pleasure and pain.

Reason as Relationship

If I asked you about your thoughts on current politics, the national debt, or abortion rights, almost invariably you would answer with words. You would not likely flap your arms, jump up and down, or flex your muscles. When someone asks about *thoughts*, they typically anticipate *words* in reply. One reason we anticipate words, is because of the longstanding assumption in Western culture that words are the carriers of thought. As we often say today, "these words don't adequately express my ideas," or "can you express your thoughts more clearly?"[14] It is this view I have attempted to discredit in preceding sections. Let us consider reason, then, as a social performance.

•

If good reasoning is a performance within a social tradition, we may then ask about the character of a well-formed performance. In the same way we can ask about whether a given actor performed Hamlet in a convincing way, we can ask about the qualities of effectively performing reason. As a first approximation, all of the following phrases could be candidates for a good performance of reason:

It is my studied opinion that...
The superior strategy would be...
I have considered both sides of the issue...

[14]This conception of language has a long history, traced at least to Aristotle. Today it generates lively debate among scholars on the relationship between language and thought. Does language affect our thinking, it is often asked. Such debate is largely premised on the dualistic view of mind that the present account throws in question.

Yet, what if we completed the sentences in the following way:
> It is my studied opinion that we are descendents of frogs.
> The superior strategy would be to visit Hell.
> I have considered both sides of the issue, and am utterly confused.

As we find, sentences that begin to approximate good reasoning at the outset, turn strange as words are added to the sentence. Never do we have access to a "reasoning process within," but only to the shifting arrangements of words. It is the arrangement of words that we are judging, and not a mind off stage. We are not compelled or convinced by good thinking, but good words. Good reasoning and good rhetoric walk hand in hand?[15]

•

> Although we may have the feeling that we do our cognitive work in isolation, we do our most important intellectual work as connected members of cultural networks.
>
> —Merlin Donald

•

Yet, we must not make the mistake of attributing to the words alone the properties of "good" and "bad reasoning." We must again consider the tradition of relationship in which the performance is embedded. Another's words do not become "good thinking" until there is co-action, until we as listeners credit them as such. What we consider *good reasoning...*

- in economic circles is to speak in terms of maximizing economic gain and minimizing losses.
- in romanticist enclaves is to rebel against the logic of economic gain.
- in materialist camps is to honor decisions that contribute to physical well-being.
- in spiritualist groups is to invite the transcending of bodily pleasure.

•

This is to say that all utterances can be rationale within some relationship. Here I am drawn to Jerzy Kosinski's novel and award winning film, *Being There*. The major protagonist, Chauncey, is a simple-minded gardener whose scant utterances are limited to phrases he has acquired from gardening and television. Yet, within these phrases others find enormous wisdom, enough that they consider Chauncey a viable candidate for President.

---

[15]Also see, Billig, M. (1996). *Arguing and thinking*. Cambridge: Cambridge University Press; and Myerson, G. (1994). *Rhetoric, reason and society*. London: Sage.

Of course, this is the stuff of fiction. Or is it? Consider the number of social movements that have spawned totally convincing reasons for suicide, torture, and genocide.

•

I have as many sound thoughts as there are
communities in which I participate.

•

The critic remains unsatisfied, "OK, whether I am considered rational or not may depend on social convention, but even then, when I am writing or speaking it is I who produce the words. And, when it is very important to me, I silently deliberate. I take time to consider what I am writing to a grieving friend, or what I will say to my son who thinks he might be gay. This is not a public performance; it is taking place inside of me. And the word 'thinking' is a good way of referring to it. Otherwise, what sense would there be in the advice to 'think before you speak?'"

Indeed, this is a fruitful line of argument, and helps to flesh out the view of social performance. There are two important issues. First, it is important to recognize that what the critic is calling private thinking is not cut away from social life. For example, to privately formulate or solve a mathematical problem is to participate in a social tradition. In psychology this line of argument was introduced by Lev Vygotsky,[16] and is represented today in a substantial line of scholarship on the cultural basis of thought.[17] In Vygotsky's famous lines, "There is nothing in mind that is not first of all in society."[18] Thus, for example, what we call thinking is a private rendition of public conversation. How else could it be? If I asked you to *think* about the political situation, the national debt, or abortion rights, and you had never heard any of these words, what would thinking consist of?[19]

There is a second significant issue. Why must we conclude that quiet deliberation is "inside" the person? This would reinstate the dualist premise of a mind behind the words. Rather, let us consider this "something" we do

[16]Vygotsky, L.S. (1978). *Mind in society.* (M. Cole, Trans.) Cambridge, MA: Harvard University Press.

[17]See, for example, Cole, M. (1998). *Cultural psychology: A once and future discipline.* Cambridge: Belknap Press; Wertsch, J. J.V. (1991). *Voices of the mind: A sociocultural approach to mediated action.* Cambridge: Harvard University Press; Bruner, J. (1990). *Acts of meaning: Four lectures on mind and culture.* Cambridge: Harvard University Press.

[18]Vygotsky, *op cit.* p. 142.

[19]It is largely this argument—that one cannot engage in private thinking without participation in a community—that has led communitarians to reject liberal individualism. See, for example, Sandel, M. (1988). *Liberalism and the limits of justice.* Cambridge: Cambridge University Press.

alone as itself a relational performance. It is neither "in here" nor "out there." It is an embodied performance, but in this case, without an immediate audience or full expression. Michael Billig points in this direction when he asks us to consider thinking as a "silent argument."[20] In effect, it is a social performance on a minimal scale. Instead of uttering the words out loud to another, one utters them to an implied audience and without sound. In the same way an actor may rehearse his lines silently, or one may hum to herself. What we do privately is not taking place in an "inner world"—called mind—but is to participate in social life without the audience present. Implicitly there is always an audience for our private reveries. Private deliberation is, then, a *partial performance*, a topic to which we shall return.

•

In solitude we never stop communicating with our fellowmen.

—Tzvetan Todorov

Agency: Intention as Action

Precious to Western culture is the vision of the individual as a free but ultimately responsible agent. We prize our capacity to choose, to direct our actions according to our decisions. And by holding people responsible for their actions, we feel the grounds are established for a moral society. The idea of an inner wellspring of action can be traced to Aristotle. As he saw it, there is an active force within the person responsible for bodily animation. To this force he assigned the concept of what can be translated as "soul." The soul possesses the "power of producing both movement and rest."[21] As the concept evolved over later centuries, it was incorporated into the Christian tradition. To commit a sin, within this tradition, is to act voluntarily, thus bringing the soul into a state of impurity. With the Enlightenment, this view became secularized. Instead of the soul, we came to speak of conscious intent, and what had been a sin became a crime. The State replaced the Church as the arbiter of intent. One can only engage in a criminal act intentionally, that is, as an exercise of voluntary or conscious agency. In large measure we can thus trace the contemporary value placed on "free will" to the Christian tradition and the significance it placed on the soul as the center of being. Given the social origins of the concept, let us explore the discourse of agency as relational action:

•

[20] Billig, *op cit.* p. 5
[21] Aristotle (1951). *Psychology* (p. 127) (P. Wheelwright, Trans.) New York: Odyssey Press.

First it is clear that although the mind is opaque, the *discourse of agency* is both significant and pervasive. We commonly say, for example:

> I intend to be there.
> What is she trying to do?
> I choose this alternative.
> What are your intentions, sir?
> I meant no harm.
> My purpose in being here is…
> I aim to please.

It is also clear from earlier discussion that when we utter such phrases we are not giving a report on an inner state of mind. For example, what is the *intention* of a man who is simultaneously driving his car, going to Chicago, returning his mother-in-law to her home, enjoying the passing scenery, talking with his mother-in-law about family matters, and fulfilling his image of a good husband? Does this man intend only one of these actions, all of them simultaneously, each of them for a quarter of a second, or something else…? How would he go about answering such questions? What part of his mind would he examine?[22]

•

> There need not be a "doer behind the deed."
> —Judith Butler

•

Abandoning the presumption of intentions as "in the head," it is useful to consider the way the *discourse of intentions* functions in daily life. As we use this language, there are consequences:

> "I didn't intend to hurt you." reduces the likelihood of blame.
> "What I meant to say is…" is the prelude to a clarification.
> "He has the best of intentions." assigns credit to the individual.
> "He means well." serves as a form of mild derision.
> "I mean what I say." tells us to take this seriously.

The language of intentions is central to our forms of cultural life.

This is indeed the same conclusion reached by many social scientists. As reasoned here, we are often asked or required to explain our actions. Why did we act in some strange way; why did we draw such an unusual conclusion; why do we prefer this as opposed to that? We respond by giving

---

[22]Here I am indebted to G. E. M. Anscombe's 1957 book, *Intention*. Ithaca: Cornell University Press.

what social scientists call *accounts*. We are primarily called into account when there are failures or undesirable deviations of some kind. "How could you possibly have decided to….?" Such accounts are crucial to how we are treated. Depending on the account, we may be forgiven, and possibly honored; on the other hand we may be imprisoned.[23]

•

The critic grows impatient: "Surely you can't be serious. If I rammed my car into a telephone pole, I would very well know whether I intended to or not. If I were to spill my hot coffee into your lap, I would be absolutely certain that I didn't mean to. When a court of law tries to distinguish between murder and manslaughter (where the death was unintended), not just any account will do." The critic does have a point. We do make these distinctions between intentional and accidental actions, and most of the time we are pretty certain about what our intentions are in a given situation. The question, then, is how can we reconcile the fact that we can, at times, readily identify our intentions, with the proposal for intention as relational performance?

To reply, consider again what we are doing when we "recognize our intentions." As we have seen, it is nonsense to suppose that we can look inside our mind to locate the intention. But we can draw from traditions of co-action in recognizing our actions. When I am standing before a class I am engaged in a performance we traditionally call teaching. The students recognize this performance as teaching no less than I. How, then, do I know what I am trying (intending, attempting, endeavoring) to do in this situation? It is evident to me not from looking inward but from simply identifying the performance. Without hesitation I can tell you that I am trying to teach or intending to teach because I am engaged in the commonly recognizable performance of teaching. I could scarcely tell you that what I am really trying to do is cook an egg or plant tulip bulbs. I recognize my intentions in the same way an actor recognizes he is playing the part of Hamlet and not Othello. To name my intentions is to name the performance in which I am engaged.

•

[23]Shotter, J. (1984). *Social accountability and Selfhood*. Oxford: Oxford University Press. Accounts may also be used to sustain communication flows (Buttny, R. (1993). *Social accountability in communication*. London: Sage); modulate blame (Semin, G. R., and Manstead, A. S. (1984). *The accountability of conduct*. London: Academic Press), and reduce conflict (Sitkin, S. B., and Bies, R. J. (1993). Social accounts in conflict situation: Using explanations to manage conflict. *Human Relations, 46*, 349–370.)

Let us consider the question of duplicity in this light. As the critic might say, " If you cannot look inward to know your intentions, as argued, how could you lie about them? For example, how could you know if you intended to commit a crime or not?" The answer is because we recognize the performances in which we are engaged. Thus, if I recognize myself to be hunting wild boar, and the bullet strikes another hunter, I can genuinely say, "I didn't mean to." If I recognize my actions as spying for my country, and I tell my landlady that I am studying archeology, I can know that I am lying about my intentions. We are publicly labeling our actions in one way, while simultaneously suppressing an alternative definition.

•

My actions leap forward, carrying my reasons in tow.

•

The critic laments: "OK, but if you redefine agency as social performance, aren't you playing into the hands of the determinists, those who would dispense with the idea of free will? The renowned psychologist, B.F Skinner, argued that the idea of voluntary agency was not only a myth, but a harmful one at that. Social psychologists even go so far as to say that claims to voluntary choice constitute a 'fundamental attribution error.' The result of such views is a dehumanization of the person, the removal of the central ingredient of human worth, and one that separates us from machines. People become objects, just like other objects, of no particular value. Nor can we hold anyone responsible for his or her actions. To give the world to the determinists would be an enormous cultural loss."

I do appreciate the force of this argument, and share in strong reservations about the determinist project in the social sciences. However, following the logic of co-action, we must first recognize that both the concepts of free will and determinism are the outcome of people talking together. As I proposed in the preceding chapter, debates over free will and determinism are not about what is more justifiably or "truly" the case, but between two traditions of talking and their related forms of life. The primary question we must address is what happens to our lives when we embrace these forms of understanding? There are certain outcomes we might value in both cases. But as I have argued in the present work, both these concepts create a world of fundamental separation. The attempt in this case is to reconfigure agency in such a way that we move beyond the voluntarism/determinism debate, and bring relationship into the center of our concerns. By viewing agency as an action within relationship, we move in exactly this direction.

Experience and Memory: Not Mine but Ours

What is more fundamental than the fact that each of us lives in a world of our own experience? I live in my subjective world, and you in yours. And, from these daily experiences we develop a storehouse of memories. Memory, in the common tradition, is largely the accumulation of experiences. In what sense, then, can we understand experience and memory as relational phenomena, belonging not to each of us privately but to us collectively? Let us first consider experience, and then turn to its offspring, memory.

•

I begin with a story related to me by a foreign aid worker. Tim was trying to help farmers in a poor region of Africa accept new and more productive methods of crop growth. To get the message across, he and his colleagues used a film to demonstrate the optimal way of planting and harvesting. After the film was shown to a group of poor farmers, the aid workers asked them to talk about what they had seen. A farmer quickly spoke out, "The chicken, the chicken…" The audience roared their affirmation. The aid workers were dumbfounded. This was not a film about a chicken, but methods of farming. There was no chicken in the film. The audience insisted there was. So the aid workers replayed the film, and to their great surprise, in a significant segment of the film, a chicken was wandering about in what *for them* was the background.

•

For experimental psychologists such differences in our experiences of the world are understood in terms of attention. The aid workers and the farmers were attending to different aspects of the film. So central to human functioning is attention, that its study is one of the oldest traditions in psychology.[24] The most important fact about attention is the way in which it fashions what we take to be the world before us. Automobile drivers know this very well. With eyes on the road one scarcely appreciates the passing environment; and so commanding is the shift of attention to the cell phone that it is perilous. Perhaps the most vivid demonstrations in the experimental laboratory are secured by means of dichotic listening devices.

[24]For example, James Sully's 1892 volume, *Outlines of psychology* (New York: Appleton), designates attention as an "elementary" dimension of the mind, and devotes almost 20 pages to its functioning.

Participants experience different messages delivered by earphones to each ear. Such studies consistently demonstrate that the ability to understand what is presented in one ear is reduced by what is received in the other. If successful in comprehending the incoming information in one ear, people are virtually insensitive to what is heard in the opposing ear. Even if the language in the second ear is is an unknown language, participants are virtually unaware. One might say that seeing does not precede believing; believing is a prelude to seeing.

If our experience is largely dominated by the direction of our attention, we must then ask, why does attention move in one direction as opposed to another? The most obvious answer to this question lies in the realm of relationship. It is through co-action that the realities of the world become significant. Some value chickens and others methods of planting. The mother coordinates her actions with the infant's so as to secure its gaze on the teddy bear as opposed to the floor; the teacher demands that students attend to her as opposed to their cell phones; extended gazing into each other's eyes is reserved for lovers; and should we cease attending to our partners in conversation we are soon scorned. To whom, when, and where we direct our attention is no less constrained by social tradition than public speaking.

•

When peering into the microscope,
the biologist doesn't see the same world we do.
                                        —Norwood Russell Hanson

•

I have long been fascinated by a classic research study in social psychology in which investigators were interested in students' perceptions of a football game between Princeton and Dartmouth. The game was an especially rough one, with significant injuries on both sides. Yet, when queried about the game, 85% of the Princeton students said that Dartmouth had started the rough play, while only 36% of the Dartmouth students believed this was so. More dramatically, when shown a film of the game a week later, the Princeton students observed the Dartmouth team made over twice as many rule infractions as were seen by Dartmouth students. As the authors conclude, "...there is no such 'thing' as a 'game' existing 'out there' in its own right which people merely 'observe.' The game 'exists' for a person and is experienced by him only insofar as certain happenings have significance in terms of his

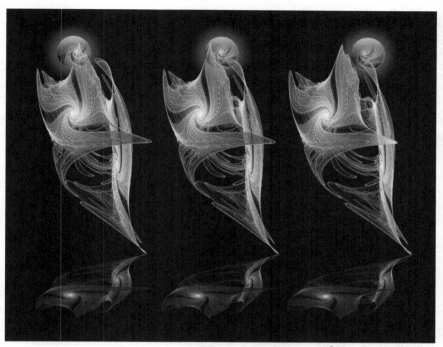

Walk In - Dance Out   ©2007 Gary W. Priester

The stereogram demonstrates the way in which our visual experience depends on the relationships of which we are a part. In following instructions on how to gaze at a stereogram—replacing the tendency to focus on the target of vision with an open and non-directed gaze—one enters into new visual worlds. The reader is invited here to view Gary Priester's stereogram, Walk In-Dance-Out, in such a way that the three figures are joined by friends.

Courtesy: Gary W. Priester

purpose."[25] Of course, "his purpose" in this case was highly dependent on school affiliation.

The critic is puzzled: "Are you trying to say that we just see what we want to see? What if a truck has lost control and headed your way, and your desire is not to be crushed? Then, are you saying, you simply wouldn't see the truck? This seems absurd." Of course it's absurd. But this is not quite what is being said here. As I pointed out in the preceding chapter,

[25]Hastorf, A. H., and Cantrill, H. (1954). They saw a game: A case study. *Journal of Abnormal Psychology, 1,* 129–134.

it is not that nothing exists before relationship. It's that nothing exists *for us*. We live in a world where trucks out of control are very important events; we place a value on not being crushed. Thus, this event is filled with meaning for us. But let's take a more subtle case. If a 4-year-old sees an open bottle of Coca Cola sitting beside the road, his eyes may brighten, and he may very well pick it up and drink the contents. The experience is a positive one. As adults most of us would not only see the bottle as "litter," but also respond negatively. And almost never would we consider drinking from the bottle. We have co-created a world in which unseen bacteria are highly significant. Even that which is not present to the human eye has meaning for us. Outside of any form of convention, there would be little to capture our attention.

•

> One must know before one can see.
> —Ludwig Fleck

•

If experience is a form of relational action, what then are we to make of memory? Traditionally we treat memory as a private event. My memories are distinctly mine, we say, they live within me alone. So, let me here recall a personally humiliating experience:

> As 6-year-olds, my friend Wilfred and I were allowed to take the bus to town. When we were crossing the street, however, Wilfred was struck by a car. A large crowd gathered; I was shoved aside. Soon an ambulance arrived, and whisked my friend away. I was stunned by the event; my head was swimming, and with the crush of the crowd, I was unable to reach the ambulance before it set off. When I arrived home an hour later, I blurted the story to my parents in a torrent of tears; and I could tell them nothing of Wilfred's welfare and whereabouts. My parents ultimately found answers to these questions, locating Wilfred at a local hospital and learning that he had only fractured his leg. I was left, however, with a lifelong feeling of ineptitude.

Now, on the face of it, this memory is very much *my own*. No one else owns this story in the way I do. However, let us explore further. My attention in this instance fastened on the accident and ambulance; a turbulent drama was unfolding. But I could have directed it elsewhere. I could have examined the shoes of the assembled crowd, the racial mixture, the facial expressions, the age variations, the weather, and so on. Yet, none of these were interesting to me or to the bystanders. Our attention was communally riveted. This is because within our culture we have come to share practices of attending. And these practices are intimately connected to our shared values, in this case the injury or possible death of a boy. In effect, my experience was mine in only a limited way. The sense organs of my body were in action; my body was in a unique position compared to others. However, the character of my experience was fully saturated with my relationship to Wilfred and to the culture more generally.

•

Let us turn from the origins of memory to its ultimate expression in words. In the story of Wilfred, there were many witnesses, each standing in a different place and coming from a different background. However, if they got together and talked, they would typically try to reach consensus on "what happened." Was it Wilfred's fault; was the driver careless; who called the ambulance; was Wilfred badly hurt? From this process of co-action will likely emerge a commonly compelling version of "what happened." For them, this account will seem "true" or "factual." This social dimension of memory has indeed stimulated the interest of many scholars over the years. The early work of Frederick Bartlett in England and Maurice Halbwalchs in France opened the way to understanding memory as a social process.[26] As Bartlett characterized it, memory is not so much a recording of sense data in the brain, as "an effort after meaning." Echoing this view, scholars from history, psychology, and sociology currently explore the process of what is variously labeled "communal," "collective," or "social memory."[27] Much of this literature demonstrates the ways in which "what happened" as a matter of social negotiation. Through the process of co-action, we construct "how we fell in love," "our vacation," or "the last family reunion." We also construct history—of "great men," nations, and peoples.

•

Common memories not only stabilize our worlds, but our social bonds. I am often struck by the urgency of couples to "get their story straight." I have seen couples ignite in irritation when they disagree on "what happened to us." To disagree is to exit the world of "with." Both my stability and my bonds were threatened by an incident with

[26]See Bartlett, F. C. (1932). *Remembering: A study in experimental social psychology.* Cambridge: Cambridge University Press; Halbwachs, M. (1925). *Les cadres sociaux de la memoire.* Paris: Albin.

[27]An excellent discussion of this work is contained in Middleton, D., and Brown, S. D. (2005). *The social psychology of experience.* London: Sage. Also see Connorton, P. (1987). *How societies remember.* Cambridge: Cambridge University Press; Misztal, B. A. (2003). *Theories of social remembering.* Buckingham: Open University Press; Wertsch, J. V. (2002). *Voices of collective remembering.* Cambridge: Cambridge University Press.

my mother. I had lived my adult years telling my children a story from my childhood, when at the age of three I wandered off from home in Cambridge. My parents were in agony, and only later did the police find me and restore me to their eager arms. I seemed far more concerned, however, with the fact that I had lost my shoe. Later, when my mother became a grandmother to my children, I listened as she began to tell them the same story. However, this time I reacted with disoriented dismay. The story being told was not about me, but my older brother, John! When a family member abandons the zone of common memory, he or she also removes the foundations from the house of being.

•

It is not simply that reports of memory are continuously created through co-action. There are also social conventions for what counts as a proper performance of memory, and when and where the performance is appropriate. To appreciate the point, consider a court of law: Several months prior to a trial you witnessed certain events and must now testify before the jury. In response to the lawyer's question about what you saw that evening, you reply black…window…light… crash… running… trees… The lawyer looks quizzically, and admonishes you, "No that won't do. I need you to tell the jury what happened." You reply, "I just did; that's what happened!" The lawyer might well be dumbfounded, and ask you to step down; you might even be held in contempt of court. Why? Because you did not tell a well-formed story or narrative. You would be acknowledged as "remembering," if you had replied: "The night was pitch black, but as I looked out my window I saw the lights of a speeding car; it careened off the side of the road and hit a parked van, at which point the driver quickly ran into the trees." This latter account is structured as a traditional narrative. There is a beginning and ending, there is a significant event (the crash); all the additional elements of the story are related to this event; the elements are arranged in chronological order. Such rules for telling a good story long pre-dated your appearance in court. Regardless of what happened, it only becomes a ratified memory if it conforms to the rules. And so it is with what we take to be the story of our lives, the history of our nation, or the evolution of the human species.[28]

---

[28]For autobiography as narrative, see MacIntyre, A. (1984). *After virtue: A study in moral theory* (2nd ed.). Danvers, MA: University of Notre Dame Press ; for history as narrative White, H. (1973). *Metahistory: The historical imagination in nineteenth-century Europe.* Baltimore: Johns Hopkins University Press; for evolution as narrative, see Landau, M. (1984). Human evolution as narrative. *American Scientist, 72,* 262–268.

•

The critic murmurs, "Yes, but these are limitations of language. What about photographs; if they are not manipulated they constitute irrefutable pictures of the past?" Yes, photographs do freeze an event in time. However, every form of representing the past—whether words, photographs, or artifacts—achieves its credibility (or not) by following social conventions. In this sense photography is a language, and like written language it must follow certain rules or it does not count as accurate. For example, the number of ways in which we can photograph a person is virtually unlimited. The photo can be taken from various distances, from different angles, with various filters, with different sharpness of focus, and so on. What we call "an accurate depiction" falls within a very narrow range of possibility.[29]

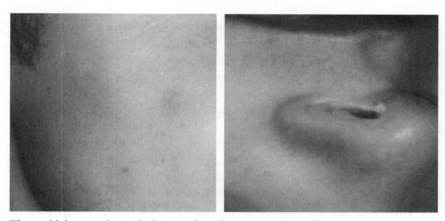

The world does not demand what we take to be our experience of it. Rather, as we emerge from relationships we come to view the world in specific ways. In effect, "direct experience" is socially fashioned. Consider the two photos here of the human face. For most viewers they will seem nonsensical or irrelevant. This is because we do not participate in a tradition that values this particular way of looking at the face.

Courtesy: Anne Marie Rijsman

[29]Related is a study of Mary Gergen in which she took photographs every 20 minutes of whatever was in front of her. When she later displayed the photos to research participants, the subject matter of most of the photos could not be identified. Cut away from a narrative of her activities, and not representing "proper" subject matters for photographs, they were largely beyond recognition. See Gergen, K. J., and Gergen, M. M. (1991). Toward reflexive methodologies. In F. Steier (Ed.) *Research and reflexivity*. London: Sage.

The critic is piqued: "Are you saying, then, that there are no accurate memories? Is it useless for jury trials to sift through evidence, to call eyewitnesses, to establish the truth about what happened? Are historians just making up stories? And what about the Holocaust? Don't your arguments play into the hands of those who try to deny it ever happened? How can you possibly take such a position?" This is a very serious criticism, and it is important to be clear in what I am proposing. As I have emphasized, through the process of co-action people create stabilized worlds of the real, the rational, and the good. Within these worlds there can be very rigorous standards for what counts as accurate. Mathematics is a good case in point. Here we have a communal achievement par excellence, and within this community there are definitive rules of accuracy. In this sense, courts of law can indeed sift the evidence in search for the truth, historians can distinguish between fact and fiction, and we can be certain about the atrocity of the Holocaust.

However, it is important to recognize that accuracy in these cases is defined within a particular tradition of relationship. This allows for very accurate records within a particular tradition. At the same time, we are invited to consider whose tradition is being honored in any given case. Whose values carry the day? What voices are absent? It is in this respect that many minority groups raise questions about standardized histories of the United States; they feel they are written out of the past. The Holocaust is an important case in point. It is not that the Holocaust is transcendentally true—that its evidence is accurate in all possible worlds of interpretation. However, the existence of this story in its present form is of enormous consequence to the future of civilization. It is a constant reminder of the horrific potentials of human beings locked within a reality of superiority and separation.[30] In effect, this story derives its importance largely from its moral imperatives, and we dare not lose it.

•

Our ways of talking about our experiences work, not primarily to represent the nature of those experiences in themselves, but to represent them in such a way as to constitute and sustain one or another kind of social order.

—John Shotter

•

[30]For an expansion of this argument, see Gergen, K. J. (2005). Narrative, moral identity, and historical consciousness: A social constructionist account. In J. Straub (Ed.) *Narrative, identity and historical consciousness*. New York: Berghahn.

Creativity as Relational Achievement

"The man of talent is like the marksman who hits a mark the others cannot hit; the man of genius is like the marksman who hits a mark they cannot even see."[31] Thus wrote the philosopher Arthur Schopenhauer in 1883. Such an accolade was not unusual for the late 19th century. This was the period of high romanticism in which the source of great works was located deep within the individual mind. One could speak of "inspired" work, or literally, generated by the spirits within. As Frank Barron sees it, this view of genius carries with it the metaphor of Genesis, or God the creator. Thus, the praise we accord to creative genius, the sense of awe that we sometimes experience, is subtly equivalent to an act of worship. In/spiration carries traces of the Divine.[32] This romantic view also finds a home within the modernist context of the 20th century. More specifically, with its emphasis on continuous progress, modernist culture grants accolades to creative innovation. This emphasis is represented in 20th century arts with the concept of the avant-garde.[33] The genius is one who breaks with tradition. Before the 20th century the demand for innovative art was largely unknown.

As we see, the very idea of a creative act, along with the esteem in which it is held, is a byproduct of a relational tradition.[34] We cannot reveal "the nature of the creative act" through careful research; indeed, most research on creativity sustains the very idea of its existence. In this light it is useful to consider Charles Hampden-Turner's view that, "We suffer from stereotyping creativity with ludicrous labels of semi-divinity, mystery, loneliness, and chaos."[35] Why do we "suffer" from this stereotype? The answer is largely owing to the tradition of bounded being. Both the romantic and modernist views praise the isolated individual; they treat separation as essential to inspired work. Thus we emerge today with hierarchies in which there are the creative geniuses at the top, the weary toilers in the

---

[31]Schopenhauer, A. (1886). *The world as will and idea.* Vol. III. (R. Haldane & J. Kemp, Trans.) London: Trubner and Ludgate. (Original work published in 1883).

[32]Barron, F. (1995). No rootless flower: An ecology of creativity. In R. E. Purser and A. Montuori (Eds.) *Social creativity.* Cresskill, NJ: Hampton Press.

[33]See, for example, Burger, P. (1984). *Theory of the avant-garde.* Minneapolis:University of Minnesota Press; Shattuck, R. (1968). *The banquet years: The origins of the avant garde in France.* New York: Vintage.

[34]A dramatic contrast is furnished by Kabuki theater. Here the demand on the actor is to replicate the tradition to the best of his ability. Deviations from tradition are scorned.

[35]Hampden-Turner, C. M. (1999). Control, chaos, control: A cybernetic view of creativity. In R. E. Purser and A. Montuori, *op cit.*

middle, and then the rabble. We are rendered insensitive to the relational roots of all that we value as creative.

•

Let us consider these relational roots in more detail. At the outset, there is the act of judging a work as creative. There is no means of discerning what goes on "within the mind" of the actor. As proposed, the very idea of a creative process inside the head is a child of co-action. However, we do make such judgments, and it is clear that they must find their origins within a history of relationships. For most of us, if a person spat on his shoe, hopped over the lines in the pavement, or wore his hat on his shoulder—all quite original acts—we would scarcely call them creative. They would simply seem weird. Yet, if Jackson Pollock flings paint at a canvas or John Cage tears the strings from the piano, the word "creative" is at the tip of our tongue. This is largely because acts we understand as creative must be wedded to a tradition of human meaning and practice. Within the tradition of modern painting, Pollock could be considered avant-garde; within the tradition of modern music, Cage was a genius. Outside these traditions they too would be simply strange. In effect, one comes into creativity through participation in a history of relationship.

•

To illustrate the force of tradition on judgments of creativity, Ilana Breger and I once carried out a study in which we exposed research participants to a series of abstract paintings.[36] Our challenge to them was to assess the works in terms of their creativity. However, the participants also learned that some of the paintings took only six minutes to complete. Others required less than six hours; and still others, more than six months. As the results demonstrated, paintings requiring six hours were judged significantly more creative than either of the others. Apparently, artistic creativity does not burst suddenly into being, nor require months of toil.

•

"Too many notes, my dear Mozart."
                    —Emperor Joseph II

•

---

[36]Gergen, K. J., and Breger, I. (1965). Two forms of inference and problems in the assessment of creativity. *Proceedings of the American Psychological Association, 20*, 215–216.

Given that judgments of creativity take place within a social tradition, we may also conclude that the activity of people we call creative is a performance that gains its reality within a tradition. As recent literary theorists propose, for example, poets are not free spirits plumbing the depths of complex thoughts and emotions. Rather, by and large they are participating in a tradition of poetry writing.[37] In this tradition there are well-developed forms, and standards of what counts as good or bad poetry. Within the tradition of the avant-garde, poets often try to "break the mold." However, whether the poetry is then recognized as creative depends on considerable negotiation. Poetic invention, then, is an intelligible act that cannot be removed from the dialogues about poetry in which it is immersed. In an important sense, poets write for other poets.[38]

•

Generative ideas emerge from joint thinking, from significant conversations, and from sustained, shared struggles to achieve new insights by partners in thought.

—Vera John-Steiner

•

The critic requires a word, "It seems right to point out that creativity is only recognized within a tradition, but within any tradition there are certain people who stand out. They tower above their peers in terms of creative capacity. Just consider the creative talents of James Joyce, T.S. Eliot, or Pablo Picasso. Don't they demonstrate the existence of a very special gift, one that permits the actor to go beyond anything that has yet been imagined by others?" I certainly share in the admiration for the works of these individuals. But, putting aside the way heroes in society are marketed (by art galleries and museums as well), the conclusion that such achievements are beyond relationship is neither necessary nor productive. To view creativity as a personal inspiration, isolated from others, suggests little about possible means of fostering the kinds of actions that we might praise as creative. One is creatively inspired or not, full stop. However, if we see

[37]See LeFevre, K. B. (1987). *Invention as a social act.* Carbondale, IL: Southern Illinois University Press; also Sawyer, R. K. (2003). *Group creativity, music, theater, collaboration.* Mahwah, NJ: Erlbaum.

[38]In her work, Suzi Gablik argues that modern art has become so self-sufficient, feeding upon itself, that it has become obscure, losing touch with issues of deeper meaning within the culture more broadly. See her 2004 work, *Has modernism failed* (2nd ed.). London: Thames and Hudson; along with her 1992 volume, *The reenchantment of art.* London: Thames and Hudson.

that creative acts are actions within relationship, then we can ask about the relational conditions favoring such innovations.

In terms of fostering creativity, it is first useful to consider the conditions favoring innovation, or "new ideas." As proposed in Chapter 2, participation in relationships typically brings about consensus on what is real, rational, and good. Once consensus is reached (and defended), it is difficult for participants to evacuate. Once swimming in the waters of "the real," one can scarcely step outside to view the bowl. Creative innovation is brought to a standstill. It is in the collision of traditions that innovation is born. Here unusual juxtapositions, new metaphors, and unsettling integrations are invited. Within common tradition, a telephone is simply a telephone. However, if one also participates in the high tech industry, a telephone begins morphing into a cell phone, a camera, a fashion item, a computer, an entertainment system, and.... As one participates in multiple traditions, creative acts take wing. It is for this reason that innovation so often occurs outside the mainstream—at the margins of acceptability.

•

In addition to asking about the conditions favoring creative activity, a relational view also draws attention to the web of relations in which the actor is enmeshed. As Howard Becker concludes from his study of artists' lives, "The artist...works in the center of a network of cooperating people whose work is essential to the final outcome."[39] Illuminating here are volumes exploring the fine-tuned interdependence of creative couples. We find genius is not a product of the individual mind but the relationship.[40] The creative individual often benefits from parents and teachers who, "recognize, encourage, and affirm a talented young person's interests and ability. Also, mentors serve as teachers, sponsors, friends, counselors, and role models."[41] Further, in the arts, the individual often faces loneliness, poverty, and doubts about his or her ability. This is especially so when iconoclasm is the signal of creativity. If one is unrecognized, and is breaking the mold, the risks of rejection are high. The availability of supporting others may be essential. As Mockros and Csikszentmihalyi see it, "social support systems

[39]Becker, H. S. (1982). *Art worlds*. Berkeley: University of California Press. Similar cases have been made in histories of the great discoveries in the sciences.

[40]See, for example, John-Steiner, V. (2000). *Creative collaboration*. New York: Oxford University Press; Pycior, H. M., Slack, N. G., and Abir-Am, P. G. (Eds.) (1996). *Creative couples in the sciences*. New Brunswick: Rutgers University Press; Chadwick, W., and de Courtivron, I. (Eds.) (1996). *Significant others: Creativity and intimate partnerships*. London: Thames and Hudson; and Sarnoff, I., and Sarnoff, S. (2002). *Intimate creativity: Partners in love and art*. Madison: University of Wisconsin Press.

[41]John-Steiner, *op cit.* p. 213.

and interactions are critical throughout the life span for the emergence of creativity."[42]

•

As we find, rational thought, intentions, experience, memory, and creativity are not prior to relational life, but are born within relationships. They are not "in the mind,"—separated from the world and from others—but embodied actions that are fashioned and sustained within relationship.

[42]Mockros, C. A., and Csikszentmihalyi, M. (1999). The social construction of creative lives. In A. Montuori and R. E. Purser (Eds.) *Social creativity* (p. 212). Vol. I. Cresskil, NJ: Hampton Press.

4

The Body as Relationship:
Emotion, Pleasure, and Pain

If asked about what is most important in your life, chances are the word love would soon surface. This could be love for a spouse, a partner, children, parents, or for humankind. It could also be love of one's work, one's avocation, or of God. Chances are the words *pleasure* or happiness would also emerge. Don't we choose those activities that give us pleasure, and avoid those we find are painful? Our lives centered, then, around emotional feelings, along with pleasure and pain. Unlike processes such as thinking, intending, remembering, and creating—the topics of the preceding chapter—the emotions, along with pleasure and pain, are closely associated with the body. They seem inherent in our bodily functioning. Metaphorically, we speak of some emotions as "matters of the heart," and we locate the source of pleasure and pain within the nervous system. We tend to believe that basic emotional capacities are present at birth.[1] And we are quite certain that we inherit genetic tendencies to seek pleasure and avoid pain. These bodily tendencies are part of the natural order; a normal and healthy life requires their expression. Or does it?

As proposed in preceding chapters, all meaning is generated within a process of co-action. It is to this same relational matrix that we must also trace the concept of emotions, pleasure, pain, and indeed, the body itself.

---

[1]See Gergen, K. J., Gloger-Tippelt, G., and Glickman, P. (1990). Everyday conceptions of the developing child. In G. Semin and K. Gergen (Eds.) *Everyday understanding: Social & scientific implications*. London: Sage.

This is to say that we don't have words like "love" "anger," "joy," "pain," because there are events in the world that must be named if we are to have a proper inventory of what exists. Rather, we have relationships from which we have come to create these as realities, and from which they derive their importance in our lives.

•

If this sounds puzzling, possibly absurd, consider the word, *body*. Commonly we view the skin as the container or defining line between what is or is not "my body." For many purposes this demarcation may be useful. However, without an enormous amount of movement across this divide, we would scarcely have a human being. Oxygen, water, foodstuffs, and waste products are among the most important elements to pass through the barrier. But in this sense, the idea of the skin as a container seems inappropriate. The metaphor of the sieve might be more relevant, with materials moving in both directions. On the one hand we could say that nothing that passes through me is distinctly mine (my body); all that I call "my body" belongs to the larger world out of which it is but a transient conglomerate.

Historical study shows that Plato believed the body was a tomb, Paul the Disciple that it is a temple of the Holy Spirit, Descartes that it is a machine, and Sartre that it is the self. [2] Physics is the most advanced of the sciences in defining the composition of the universe, and in the language of physics human bodies do not exist. In effect, what I call *my body*, I do so by virtue of my location in a tradition of relationship.

•

> While I am working I leave my body outside the door.
> —Pablo Picasso

•

The important point is that when we presume that we live in separate houses called the body, and that the natural denizens of these houses include the emotions, pleasure, and pain, then we add weight to the ideology of bounded being. We come to believe that what fundamentally drives our actions as human beings is locked somewhere within the nervous system, and made secure by both evolution and genetic composition. And in this case, there is not much we can do about our instincts or the effects of our brains on our actions.

---

[2] See Synott, A. (1992). Tomb, temple, machine and self: The social construction of the body. *British Journal of Sociology, 43*, 79–110; also, Blood, S. K. (2005). *Body work: The social construction of women's bodies.* London: Routledge.

Herein lies the challenge for the present chapter. Can we enter a new realm of understanding in which the emotions, pleasure, and pain are not manifestations of private bodies but of relationship? In what follows I will first take up the emotions. Amplifying the unfolding logic of the preceding chapter, I will propose that much like such processes as reasoning, intention, and memory, they are essentially performances in relationship. This proposal will generate a strong counter-reply. Am I not leaving out the vast literature on the biological bases of human conduct in general and the emotions in particular? Thus, the second part of the chapter will confront the challenge of biological determinism. In doing so, we shall have reason to ask how much, if anything, is left of the idea of innate dispositions. To what degree is our destiny among us, as opposed to within us? This treatment will set the stage for a final exploration of the relational basis of pleasure and pain.

The Emotions in History and Culture

Do we carry emotions within us? Like Descartes, who had no doubt that he was thinking, we scarcely doubt that we feel anger, happiness, boredom, and the like. In the case of the emotions, we just know! But do we? History cautions against the "self evidence" of our emotional states. For example, scholars have tried very carefully to identify and count the emotions for centuries. In the second book of the *Rhetoric*, Aristotle distinguished among fifteen emotional states; centuries later Aquinas' *Summa Theologiae* enumerated six "affective" and five "spirited" emotions; in his *Passions of the Soul*, Descartes distinguished among six primary passions of the soul; the 18th-century moralist, David Hartley, located ten "general passions of human nature"; and the 20th-century work of psychologists, Sylvan Tomkins and Walter Izard, describe some ten distinctive emotional states.[3] If emotional states are so obvious, why is there so little agreement on how many there are?

Nor do these scholars agree on the nature of their discoveries. For example, Aristotle identified *placability, confidence, benevolence, churlishness*, and *enthusiasm* as emotional states. None of these feature in contemporary books on the emotions. Aquinas believed *love, desire, hope*, and *courage* were all central emotions; Aristotle agreed with him about *love*, but none of the remainder. In the scientifically oriented volumes of Tomkins

---

[3]Tomkins, S. (1962). *Affect, imagery, and consciousness*, Vol. 1. New York: Springer; Izard, C. E. (1977). *Human emotions*. New York: Plenum.

and Izard, none of the above are recognized as basic emotions. Hobbes identified *covetousness, luxury, curiosity, ambition, good naturedness, superstititon,* and *will* as emotional states. None of these qualify as emotions in contemporary psychology. Tomkins and Izard agree that *surprise* is an emotion, a belief that would puzzle most of their predecessors, and perhaps most of the general public. However, where Izard believes *sadness* and *guilt* are major emotions, they fail to qualify as such in Tomkins' analysis.

If the emotions are simply there in mind, obvious to us who feel them, why should there be such disagreement? If emotions have identifiable features—like the chairs in the room— shouldn't we easily agree on the number and kinds? In fact, what precisely is an emotion that we could identify whether any state qualifies or not? This confusion in identifying the emotions again suggests that the emotions are not simply there in the head or body to be discovered. Rather, what we call emotion is created in co-action.

•

This is indeed the message of cultural anthropology. As revealed in numerous ethnographies, cultures vary enormously in what we in the West would identify as emotional terms and behavior.[4] For example, in her study of the Ifaluk people on a small atoll in the South Pacific, Catherine Lutz describes emotions like *Fago* and *Song*, neither of which have an equivalent in the Western vocabulary.[5] More extreme differences include the "wild-pig" syndrome, found in New Guinea, in which a man faced with frustrating circumstances begins to race about, looting, and shooting arrows at his neighbors. He may then run into a nearby forest, and be captured by the villagers who subject him to a "redomestication" ceremony. In Malaysia there is a more deadly form of expression called "running amok." In this case a man first engages in a period of withdrawal or meditation, during which he may mutter religious phrases while swaying back and forth.[6]

[4]See, for example, Rosaldo, M. Z. (1980). *Knowledge and passion: Ilongot notions of self and social life.* Cambridge: Cambridge University Press; Heider, K. G. (1991). *Landscapes of emotion: Mapping three cultures of emotion in Indonesia.* Cambridge: Cambridge University Press; Wulff, H. (2007). *The emotions: A cultural reader.* New York: Oxford University Press; Lynch, O. M. (1992). *Divine passions: The social construction of emotion in India.* Berkeley: University of California Press; Heelas, C. and Locke, A. (Eds.) (1981). *Indigenous psychologies: The anthropology of the self.* New York: Academic Press; Jain, U. (1994). Socio-cultural construction of emotions. *Psychology and Developing Societies, 6,* 151–168. For continuing debate on culture versus biology in understanding emotion, see the special issue of *Ethnos,* 69, 2004; Loseke, D. R., and Kusenbach, M. (2008). The social construction of emotion. In J. A. Holstein and J. F. Gubrium (Eds.) *Handbook of constructionist research.* Thousand Oaks, CA: Sage.

[5]Lutz, C. A. (1988). *Unnatural emotions.* Chicago: University of Chicago Press.

[6]Averill, J. R. (1982). *Anger and aggression: An essay on emotion.* New York: Springer Verlag.

At some point he will leap to his feet, seize a knife or sword, and commence to slay any living creature in sight. When he is finished he may turn his weapon on himself. Both "wild-pig" behavior and "running amok" are recognizable expressions in these cultures; in the West they would be most unusual.

•

Historical study also supports the idea of emotions as human constructions.[7] For example, we commonly speak of "our feelings," and we ask with concern about the feelings of others. But what exactly are we talking about in these cases? Is saying "I feel good," to report on the same state of mind as saying, "I have a good feeling about this deal," "I feel your pain," "I feel cold air coming in," "I have a gut feeling," or "I feel we shouldn't go…?" The inability to answer the question is a good indication that the word "feeling" is not a reading of an inner world. The historian Owen Barfield points out that from early Roman times until the Middle Ages, people tended to place more importance on external conditions than internal states. For example, one might say "the meeting was boring" or "his remark was embarrassing," rather than "I felt bored," or "I felt embarrassed." In fact the word "feeling" was not invented until roughly the 17th century. As Barfield proposes, it was only in the 17th century that people began speaking at length about their inner life.[8]

•

Feelings are not substances to be discovered in our blood but social practices organized by stories that we both enact and tell.
—Michelle Rosaldo

•

Consider as well the history of "melancholy." We seldom use the term today. We could scarcely call in to work and excuse our absence because we were suffering a horrid bout of melancholy. Yet, in the 17th century melancholy might have supplied just such an excuse. Robert Burton's early account, *The anatomy of melancholy*, reaches almost 600 pages, and reports in close detail the many types of melancholy, their manifestations, and cures.

[7]See for example, Stearns, P. N., and Lewis, J. (Eds.) (1998). *An emotional history of the United States*. New York: New York University Press; Harré, R. (Ed.) (1986). *The social construction of emotion*. Oxford: Blackwell; Graumann, K., and Gergen, K. J. (Eds.) (1996). *Psychological discourse in historical perspective*. New York: Cambridge University Press; Stearns, P. N. (1994). *American cool: Constructing a twentieth-century emotion*. New York: New York University Press.
[8]Barfield, O. (1962). *History in English words*. London: Faber and Faber.

Following Freud, many psychiatrists wish to view melancholy as an early term for describing what today we call "depression." However, Burton's descriptions not only undermine such a proposal, but help us to appreciate just how very different our emotional world is from this early period. Consider the following from Burton:

> (Melancholics) are prone to love, and easy to be taken…quickly enamored, and dote upon all, love one dearly till they see another, and then dote on her…they are humorous beyond all measure, sometimes profusely laughing, extraordinarily merry, and then again weeping without cause…groaning, sighing, pensive, sad…they feign many absurdities, vain, void of reason. One supposeth himself to be a dog, cock, bear, horse, glass, butter, etc.[9]

•

The critic begs for a moment: "Sure, there are variations in culture and history, but there also seem to be strong exceptions. Take the fact of romantic love. We find expressions of love throughout the ages. For example, we would have not problem resonating with the poetry of Catullus, writing in the 1st century BC:

> If I were allowed to kiss those honey eyes of yours
> As much as I'd like to,
> I'd kiss them three hundred thousand times,
> And still not have my fill.

It is true that histories of love show marked differences in its expression over the centuries; for me these are variations on a theme.[10] The fact of love as a basic emotion has never changed."

The critic has a point. Most of us feel at one time or another that there are universal emotions—like love—that could possibly unite us. But we must be very careful in drawing such conclusions. We take a significant step toward imperialism when we assume that everyone in the world has Western emotions. Why should the Ifaluk not believe in the universality of fago, or the Hindu of Atman? But consider more closely: First, in spite of the fact that we can locate instances of an emotion like romantic love in all ages, there are simply too many exceptions to suppose that it is given in nature. There are far too many people across culture and history for whom

[9]Burton, R. (1624/1982). *The anatomy of melancholy*, p. 393. New York: Vintage Press.

[10] See for example, Hunt, M. (1994). *The natural history of love*. New York: Anchor; Kern, S. (1992). *The culture of love, Victorians to moderns*. Cambridge: Harvard University Press; Luhmann, N. (1986). *Love as passion*. Cambridge: Harvard University Press.

romantic love is either irrelevant, or not recognized at all, to suppose its universality. How important is romantic love for people in prison, at war, in the mines, in the rice fields, on the playing fields, or in monasteries? Patterns of hetero and homosexual relations vary so widely across history and culture, that most contemporary scholars do not include love as an entry into the slate of basic emotions.

There is also a special problem in reading lines such as those of Catullus. Indeed, writings such as this are contributions to the Western vocabulary of emotion. We recognize ourselves in these lines primarily because they helped to mold the tradition in which we now participate. We confront additional problems when we take writings from other cultures as evidence of universality. As anthropologists are well aware, one can scarcely make an interpretation of another culture outside the confines of one's own cultural repertoire. Is the fact that people in a far away land indulge in kissing an indicator that they "know what love is?" Or is it only for those who already have the concept of romantic love at hand? Without the concept, how can we say that kissing is indeed an emotional expression at all? Interpreting the meaning of actions in other cultures is to absorb them into one's own world of intelligibility.[11]

The Dance of the Emotions

If emotional words and actions are created within cultural traditions, then the emotions can properly be viewed as relational performances.[12] They are forms of action that acquire their intelligibility within relationships, and they gain their value from their social use. It is not that we "feel emotions" so much as we *do* them.[13] And this doing is only intelligible within a particular tradition of relationship. To appreciate the force of this proposal

[11]There are also ideological issues to consider in the conception of romantic love, and particularly the way the emotions are attributed primarily to women. See, for example, Lutz, C., and Abu-Lughod, L. (Eds.) (1990). *Language and the politics of emotion.* New York: Cambridge University Press; Robin, C. (2006). *Fear: The history of a political idea.* New York: Oxford University Press; Ahmed, S. (2004). *The cultural politics of emotion.* London: Routledge.

[12]For more on emotions as cultural performances see Averill, J. (1982). *Anger and aggression: An essay on emotion.* New York: Springer-Verlag; Bodor, P. (2004). *On emotions: A developmental social constructionist account.* Budapest: L'Harmattan; Sarbin, T. R. (1989). Emotions as situated actions. In L. Cirillo, B. Kaplan, and S. Wapner (Eds.) *Emotions in human development.* Hillsdale, NJ: Erlbaum.

[13]*See also,* Schafer, R. (1976). *A new language for psychoanalysis.* New Haven, CT: Yale University Press.

consider several propositions that echo the logics of the preceding chapter:

Emotional performance is a crafted achievement. How does an action come to be identified as an emotion? At least one major means is through the use of words. We identify ourselves as having an emotion: "I feel happy today…," "That frightens me…," or, "I adore you…" No one has access to a private world in which the emotions may be identified. Yet, the claim can be very important to how we go on. Most typically the words are accompanied by fully orchestrated bodily actions. It is not only what is said, but the tone of voice, the gestures, the gaze, and the posture that accompany it. There are tears, laughter, grimacing, scowling, and so on. To properly perform anger requires an enormous amount of cultural education. To express what we take to be genuine emotion may require the furrowing of the brow, tension in the muscles of the chin, a steady gaze, an upright posture, and so on. One small movement, such as a limp wrist, may disqualify the action as anger. To identify an emotion is similar to recognizing that an actor is performing King Lear as opposed to Hamlet. The actor can do it well or poorly, and when the former we are comfortable with the part. When an emotion is performed poorly, we may doubt its existence. We are mystified by the actions of children who have not mastered the craft of doing anger, and we simply say they are having a "temper tantrum."[14]

•

There was a period in my life in which my performance of anger was a problem. I grew up in the southern United States where standards of tact and graciousness were honored. As generally agreed, "If you blow a fuse, you lose." I had also observed my father's reaction to others who irritated or failed him. He simply became silent and unsmiling, and he could remain so for long periods. This was an easy performance to master, and over time it came to feel quite natural. Then came married life. Mary's way of doing anger was through rapid explosion, and then a return to normal. Alas, our preferred forms of anger didn't match. If we crossed each other, Mary was quick to erupt and get over it, while I could remain sullen for hours. So, we talked it over, and Mary persuaded me to just "get things off my chest" when I was irritated. "Let yourself go," was the message, and then we can return to normal. And so I did. The results were

[14]For a discussion of educating the emotions, see Shields, S. E. (2002). *Speaking from the heart: Gender and the social meaning of emotion.* Cambridge: Cambridge University Press.

disastrous: broken dishes, broken furniture, a dented door.
We couldn't afford such outbursts. So we returned to the drawing
board. This time we focused on ways to avoid trouble spots that lead
to irritation. This strategy, combined with a consciousness of the
problems of performance, led us into the greener pastures where we
have remained.

•

The critic resists: "This description of emotions makes them seem so
planned or contrived. When I am emotional it is spontaneous. I am just
moved by my feelings without giving them a thought. Sometimes I have
regrets, for example, when I fly off the handle. But if I had to plan how
to have an emotion, it wouldn't feel authentic at all." Fair enough, but
consider the way we walk, read, or ride a bicycle. They all feel spontaneous
and uncontrived; yet, they are all learned performances. Repeat them often
enough and they are very thoroughly "just me." Feeling natural is a cultural
achievement.[15]

•

Why does it sound so strange to say, "He felt deep grief for one
second?" Because it so seldom happens? What if we were to imagine
people...who for hours alternate between second-long feelings of
deep grief and inner joy?

—Ludwig Wittgenstein

•

The validity of the performance depends on time and place. If a
performance is to count as an emotion, it must take place under socially
specified circumstances. If one fails to obey the rules of location, the
performance runs the risk of being discounted or censured.[16] One cannot
stop in the middle of a crowded street and shout, "I am in ecstasy," or "You
frighten me." It may be physically possible to do so, but others will quickly
move to a safe distance. To underscore the point, without common agreements about time and place of expression, there would be no emotions.

[15]See also Marsh, P., Ross, E., and Harré, R. (1978). *The rules of disorder*. London: Routledge,
for an account of the ordered character of what otherwise seem to be spontaneous eruptions of
hooliganism among soccer fans.
[16]See Shields, S. (2002). *Speaking from the heart*. New York: Cambridge University Press, for
a discussion of "emotional entitlement," or, the social conditions under which one can appropri-
ately claim to possess a certain kind of feeling.

If there were no conditions people defined as worthy of joy, there would be no joy. As we multiply the conditions that justify anger, then anger becomes epidemic. So numerous are the conditions under which expressions of love are possible, that the expression "I love..." is trivialized. After all, one just loves New York, pizza, her kitten, his Harley, dulce de leche, autumn leaves, hot pink... in addition to you.

•

The critic stirs: "Aren't you simply talking about the rules for expressing various emotions? Sure, there are conventions of expression, and these may vary from one culture to another. But they are expressions *of something*, namely the emotions themselves. The emotion is there inside, and it precedes expression. The cultural rules simply ensure that social life runs smoothly." Yes, this seems reasonable; it is indeed the position taken by many psychologists who study the emotions.[17] But, as we have seen from the preceding discussion, you rapidly run into problems when you try to identify what the "underlying" emotions are, how many, and of what kind. Indeed, why should we thus suppose there is an underlying something? If we began to remove layers of the body to locate an "inner world," where would we terminate the search? Just beneath the skin, beneath layers of skull tissue...? Isn't it more reasonable to treat bodily actions, in this case, as whole cloth, just as we would the movements of a dancer or a diver? There is not a "feeling" causing a doing; there is only embodied action.

•

The critic remains unconvinced: "Not so fast. I still know that I feel my emotions without ever expressing them. I do my best to hide my anger, for example, or not to let my disappointment show. These are private feelings, emotions without public expression. For me, a smooth running social life depends on our controlling our emotional expressions. Some people call it emotional intelligence." Again to reply: We encountered this same problem in the last chapter. We saw that in principle you could not look inward to identify an emotion. But clearly, there is something important going on that is not publicly performed. Sometimes it is an urge that you

---

[17]For the classic statement of this position, see Ekman, P., Friesen, W. V., and Ellsworth, P. (1972). *Emotion in the human face.* New York: Oxford University Press. Although evidence suggested that people from around the world used similar facial expressions when they felt various emotions, the test materials were translated into the vocabularies of the various populations in ways that would almost necessarily produce such findings.

resist, for example, to explode in irritation when you stub your toe. You sit alone in grief for an absent loved one, or anger at someone who has hurt you. Yet, we need not conclude that this something *is* the emotion, and that its expression is something else. Rather, drawing from the preceding chapter, what is taking place in these instances is *a partial performance.* You are engaged in "doing the emotion," but simply without using the full array of words and gestures that are common to public performance. You "know what you are feeling" in the same way you would have no doubt you were privately singing the *Star Spangled Banner* as opposed to *You Ain't Nothin' but a Hound Dog.* You are engaged in relational action simply carried out in privacy. The relational basis of these actions becomes clear in this final proposition.

The validity of the performance is achieved in co-action. As outlined in Chapter 2, there are no stand-alone performances; actions gain their meaning through co-action. To be sure, we typically accept well-performed expressions as authentic. In accepting them, we grant them validity and to the performer a sense of authenticity. The dance of relationship proceeds effortlessly. However, between the expression and the response there is a moment in which meaning lies suspended. And there are occasions in which the dance is disrupted:

> "You say you are happy for me, but I know you are jealous."
> "You say you love me, but you really want me in bed."
> "Those are just crocodile tears."
> "You are just crying wolf."

These are challenging moments for negotiation. Is the performance genuine or not? Again, the important point is that the emotional performance depends for its existence—its full sense of authenticity—on relationship. You may shout your sincerity, but unless affirmed by another, the shout is no more important than an echo.

Relational Scenarios

The focus on emotions allows us to add further dimension to the emerging picture of co-action. So far our major focus has been on the simple coordination of action and supplement, how for example, asking a question is given meaning in terms of someone's answering, and vice versa. In the same way, if you act sad, and a therapist treats it as depression, it remains unclear whether you were sad. Now let us extend the sequence of interchange. A friend greets you by saying, "Hi, how are you," you respond without pause, "Great, how are you," and the friend says, "not so bad, but I think we may get caught in a storm." You add, "I heard the storm wasn't coming 'til tonight." Here we have an extended but unsurprising set of moves. Each action affirms and adds to the other as the conversation moves on. Let us call these more extended sequences *relational scenarios*. Like dancing a waltz or playing tennis, relational scenarios are coordinated actions extending over time.

An emotional scenario is one in which an emotional performance plays an integral role. Emotional scenarios may also be brief, as in your responding to someone who says, "I'm so happy we finally have some sun," with, "Absolutely!"[18] But scenarios are often more extended and more complex. Consider the performance of anger: At the outset, you cannot perform anger at just any time. You cannot walk down the street and suddenly shout out, "I am angry at you," and remain intelligible within the culture. As we understand anger, it must have a justifiable cause. A justifiable cause is not furnished by biology, but through cultural negotiation. You may be angry if someone steals your car tires, but not if they run off with the dirt from the tires. It requires a culturally recognized justification to legitimate the expression of anger, and thus the beginning of the scenario.

Now, let us say that a friend's anger is directed at you. He or she enters and says, "I am angry with you!" It is now your turn in the scenario. You can scarcely respond by saying, "What are you doing this weekend?" or "I am so happy." Such responses make little sense in terms of the conventional scenario. In fact, it is almost unimaginable that you would respond in any other way than by asking, "why?" The question is asked because it is imperative to identify the justifiable cause of the expression. Or in dance terms, you need to know if the dance to which you are invited is a rumba or a foxtrot. The "name of the dance" also signals the range of possible replies to the expression of anger. If your friend said "I am angry because you always do things better than me, and I'm left feeling inadequate,"

---

[18]Also relevant is the concept of *sexual script*, though this term is more often used in referring to mental schemas. Research on sexual scripts is most interesting, however, in its demonstration that what might be seen as biologically determined behavior is significantly fashioned through cultural convention. See, for example, Gagnon, J. H., and Simon, W. (1973). *Sexual conduct: The social sources of human sexuality*. Chicago, IL: Aldine; Thorne, B., and Luria, Z. (1986). Sexuality and gender in children's daily worlds. *Social Problems, 33*, 1276–1290; Frith, H., and Kitzinger, C. (2001). Reformulating sexual script theory: Developing a discursive psychology of sexual negotiation. *Theory and psychology, 11*, 209–232.

your options would be much different from those invited by, "I am angry because you revealed a secret that I told you was private." The former scenario is both a complement and a call for nurturance; the latter is an accusation. Let's consider the options when you are accused:

Cultural conventions largely limit you to three options: First you may *apologize*. You can tell your friend how sorry you are you told the secret, a mistake in your judgment, it will never happen again. Second, you may *reconstruct* or reframe your friend's account of the cause so that the justification is removed. Many people reframe by simply denying the action for which they are blamed. "I didn't do it." Yet, you might also admit the deed, saying that you only did it to help your friend. Thus, your act was one of friendship, not disrespect, and anger is not justified. Finally, you might respond with *irritation*. After all, why did he burden you with this secret? Schematically, we have, then:

Justifiable Cause

Anger

Apology   Reconstruction   Irritation

It is important to underscore that the expression of anger acquires its legitimacy in the course of the relational scenario. In effect, the response of the apology legitimates the expression of anger as such. The move to reconstruct also authenticates the anger, but removes the grounds for its existence. Irritation also recognizes the expression as anger, but sets out to punish it. In contrast, if one responded to the expression with a laugh, "oh, come on now…" there is no acknowledgement of anger as such. It is in the response that anger is given birth. It is a *pre-hoc fallacy* to hold that the anger causes the response.

Let us press further to consider the ways in which the angered person responds to these three options. Given the common scenario, the apology can be accepted or rejected. If the former, the scenario comes to a close, and the participants are free to talk about other things. One can now ask, "What are you doing this weekend? The tango has ended; one can invite the other to polka. If the apology is rejected, the conversation continues. In the case of reconstruction, the angry person also has two major options, acceptance and rejection. If the reconstruction is accepted—"OK, I see that I flew off the handle too fast"—the scenario is again completed. You are free to do other things. Yet, the angry person can also attack the reconstruction—"That's no excuse!"—and the scenario remains unfinished. Finally, in the case of irritation, the most common response is intensified anger. If you righteously blame someone for their actions, and they turn on you in rebuke, their wrong-doing is doubled. They deserve even more punishment. Schematically:

Justifiable Cause

Anger

Apology   Reconstruction   Irritation

Accept   Reject   Accept   Reject   Intensified anger

In early research on emotional scenarios we found that angry exchanges are particularly dangerous.[19] When anger yields irritation, and the irritation intensifies the anger, heated escalation is almost certain to follow. Worse still, there are very few acceptable means of completing the scenario. One may stalk out the door, vow that the relationship is finished, or strike the other. Most other scenario forms can be brought to an end more success-fully, but escalating anger is a free-fall that few can escape. I will return to this challenge shortly.

To draw this exposition to a close, we find that emotional expressions are intelligible only within a relational sequence. They can only occur at certain specifiable points in the exchange, and without the ratifying actions of others, they do not exist as emotions. Emotions, then, are not possessions of individuals, or required by our biological make-up, but they are granted existence by scenarios of relationship as a whole. And these scenarios are in turn, inherited by us from traditions with possibly ancient origins.

•

The critic stirs: "I can see how much of our emotional life is scripted in this way, but this account doesn't leave any room for spontaneity. As I men-tioned before, some of my most moving emotional experiences—love is the best example—involve creative bursts of novelty. We act in madcap ways, and these are the most touching and memorable." This query is easily addressed, but its implications are substantial. As in the preceding chapter, we become creative at the juncture of multiple traditions. If we know only one scenario of "doing romantic love," for example, that is all we have at our disposal. Spontaneity is squashed. However, when we have witnessed thou-sands of love stories—courtesy of mass entertainment—we are free to move across genres or idioms, combining in novel ways as the moment invites. It is not that we can do anything we wish; even in our spontaneous moments

---

[19]Gergen, K. J., Harris, L., and Lannamann, J. (1986). Aggression rituals. *Communications Monographs, 53,* 252–265.

You are my delight,
And your laughter celebrates my being.
My pleasure inhabits your heart,
And my smiles are those of adoration.
Joy resides in the resonance.

Regine Walter, Artist

of passion we cannot sink to our knees and lick a stone, or stick our fingers into our beloved's ears. Such acts would fall outside the intelligibility of any genre. But we can do cartwheels, offer a small shell, express devotion through graffiti, or hold a rose between the teeth. There is room for novelty and spontaneity, but it results from living at the intersection of multiple traditions.

It is interesting that in Western culture there is continuous pressure to create new breeds of emotional performance. The first time a lover purchases a rose for a sweetheart on a summer's stroll may be charming. The third time it is a cliché. This is largely because we believe the emotions are beyond rational calculation and control. They burst from deep and unfathomable resources within. If an emotion is to be a "true" expression of self, it cannot too closely copy a common convention. When emotions appear to be staged, borrowed, or mimicked they are untrustworthy as expressions of the seething forces within.[20] Thus, fashions of expression are continuously in motion, and to sustain emotionally rich relations requires a continuous adventure of expression.

Disrupting Dangerous Dances

There is great joy in many emotional scenarios. The dance of love is the most obvious, but there are also the scenarios leading us from sadness to consolation, from conflict to reconciliation, and from failure to success. At the same time, there are many scenarios with dismal consequences. There is the escalation of anger, the intensification of jealousy, and mounting of hatred, with battering and bloodshed often the result. Worst still, we are scarcely able to prevent ourselves from participating. Once the Siren has begun to sing, we are compelled to follow. Communication scholars Barnett Pearce and Vernon Cronen call these dangerous dances, *undesired repetitive patterns*.[21] No one wants to "fight it out," and yet, once the fight has begun it is difficult to excuse oneself, to "cut and run." From a relational standpoint these corrosive patterns are not inevitable. They are not built into our genes. Together we stand as creators of the future. The question is whether we can locate new and compelling steps, moves that will enable us to leave the dance floor before disaster strikes. How then are we

[20]This is the plight of greeting card manufacturers, to generate messages that seem unique, and yet can appeal to the masses. Humorous cards are often appealing precisely because they break the common conventions of expression.

[21]Cronen, V. E., Pearce, W. B., and Snavely, L. M. (1980). A theory of role-structure and types of episodes and study of perceived enmeshment in undesired repetitive patterns ("URPSs"). *Communication Yearbook, 3,* 225–240.

to disrupt the call of the dangerous dance? I focus here on the common case of escalating anger.

•

When we were children my older brother John and I would have the most terrible fights. Whether playing with our toys in the bedroom, or building cities in the sandbox, we would often end in a heap of flailing fists, elbows, and feet. The typical pattern was a small affront from one side, followed by the other's retaliation, which in turn would provoke a more aggressive attack by the first party, and so on, until we were at each others' throats. Fortunately we could rely on our parents' intervention. As I see it now, our fisticuffs were not failures in socialization; in fact, they demonstrated that we were beginning to master common scenarios of anger. We were learning to be "real men." Parents would wonder at the genetic make-up of a son who cringed or ran away when insulted by a sibling.[22] Don't we want our children to stand up to bullies, and our nation to respond with "shock and awe" to any country or group that hints of aggression toward us? "Fight like a man" is a call to honor.

•

In my view there are few satisfactory resolutions to scenarios of escalating hostility. How many cases of wife-battering may be traced to the point at which increasingly heated words reach their ultimate expression in fists? And at the global level, how many options does a nation have when its honor is impugned by another nation? Escalated hostility seems virtually inevitable. So common are these scenarios that they have become naturalized. That is, we believe that countering hostility is "only normal," a biological tendency provided by the evolutionary necessities for fight and flight. Yet, if we can escape the thrall of the biological story, and realize the relational character of these scenarios, we can be liberated. If we have created these scenarios together, we are free to abandon them and to develop alternatives. As proposed by Jim Averill and Elma Nunley, we should open ourselves to living an "emotionally creative life."[23]

•

[22]Hollywood films provide a rich repository of scenarios in which an otherwise pleasant adolescent is threatened by an imposing bully, and either (1) pummels the bully into submission with a surprising show of strength, or (2) locates a clever means of ultimately subduing the villain.

[23]Averill, J. R., and Nunley, E. P. (1992). *Voyages of the heart*. New York: Free Press.

The fact is that many people do live such lives, and they do find ways to avoid escalating hostility. How can these be shared with others? In this context, Mary and I began to develop and perform small scenarios of escalating exchanges for audiences of therapists and communication specialists. For example, we play out an argument between spouses in which a wife criticizes her husband for spending money at a gentleman's club, he responds with irritation at all the money she spends on clothing and makeup, and so on until their voices reach a crescendo, at which point the husband turns to strike his wife. Stopping just short of the violent act, we interrupt our performance to ask the audience's help in re-writing the lines. Can they suggest words or actions that either husband or wife might use to disrupt the dangerous dance. We then try out the new lines to explore their potential. One of the most important things about this exercise is that it acts as a cure to "heart and mouth disease." That is, one rapidly sees that "acting naturally" is not a matter of some deep, biological urge bursting forth in the service of honesty and emotional health. Rather, one realizes that there are options for action, each with different implications for what follows. And, should one of these options prove satisfactory to the relationship, it too may become natural. Here I share four of the most effective innovations emerging from these exercises:

1. Reconstruct the Reality: "This is not what it seems."

From the logic of co-action we learn that nothing stands as real unless there is collaborative confirmation. You cannot truly be angry unless others agree that this is truly a performance of anger. This means that a common expression of anger does not require that we acknowledge it as such. We are free to invent other forms of reply that do not invite escalation. For example, the scenario can be transformed with such comments as, "You know, I think we are both very tense. Otherwise we wouldn't treat each other this way." Now the anger is redefined as tension. Or, "I think this anger is really saying that you are afraid." Or, "What your anger is saying is that I really matter to you." Or, "I think it's just the booze. Let's talk about this when we are sober." All these supplements invite a different trajectory of relationship.

2. The Meta-Move: "What are we doing?"

One of the most innovative and effective ways of stepping out of a mutually destructive scenarios comes from therapeutic professionals. We call it the *meta-move*, meaning a conversational move that reflects on the conversation itself. In this case, during the heat of battle, a participant might step out to ask about the nature of the battle itself. For example, "Look at what we are doing to each other; do we really want to go on like this?" Or, "Why are we fighting; we do love each other and this isn't good for us." Or, "Wait a minute, let's go back to ask what we are quarreling about. Is it really all that important?" Or, "You know, we could look at this problem in a different way, like a challenge for us to be more open with each other." Such comments are an invitation to abandon the hostility scenario, and to move in a new and more promising direction.

3. Shifting Emotional Registers: "I am hurt."

Although responding to attack with anger seems natural, there are other possibilities of emotional performance. Gandhian pacifism, for example, has had worldwide repercussions. In the present case, however, one important alternative is the expression of pain or hurt. For example, "It really hurts me when you say things like that to me;" or "I am so sad we are hurting each other like this." There is even the possibility of a positive reply, as in, "You know, I really think it's a good thing we can just get things off our chest like this;" or, "God, you look great when you are worked up." Such deviations from the traditional pattern invite the other into a new scenario.

4. The Theatrical Move: "Let's play this again."

We typically authenticate others' emotional performances by treating them as valid for the moment. Yet, we are also aware that such performances are conventional in character. Television and movies have provided myriad models. By focusing on the conventionality, a damaging scenario can be subverted. One can call into consciousness the similarity of what is taking place to a theater piece or a game. For example, "Hey, we are really making a mess of this. Why don't we start over, and see if we can do this conversation better;" or, "We are really great at fighting; we really do it well. Maybe we can give it a rest." Realizing that "life is like theater," one can more easily abandon the script.

•

These moves in an otherwise dangerous scenario are all intelligible and actionable. Yet, I suspect, they are only a fraction of what could be made available. With the continuous mix of traditions, old and new, there is continuous creativity in managing conflict. Means should ultimately be found for a broad sharing of practices. As a final illustration, I recently learned of a widower who praised his departed wife for her being the "great peace maker in the family." As he explained, when the two of them would squabble, she would say, "now come here Richard, sit down beside me." Reluctantly he would slouch into a seat at a safe distance. "No, Richard, come closer, here right beside me." When he had complied, she would say to him, as she placed a cheek near his face, "Now Richard, could you please kiss me here?" Slowly he would do so. "Oh Richard, not just a peck. Give me a real kiss right there." Richard more rapidly acceded. "Now, what about here?" as she faced him with her lips puckered. Upon this gesture, the anger flew from the window. Both would apologize, often in laughter and a mutual embrace.

Aren't the Emotions Biological?

There is an ominous cloud lurking over the discussion thus far. Its name is biology. For over a century psychologists and biologists have joined hands in searching for the biological roots of the emotions.[24] To be sure there have been perennial disagreements concerning how the brain affects our emotions,[25] whether there are specific brain centers for the various emotions,[26] and so on. However, in recent decades, with advances in neurological assessment and developments in evolutionary biology, there is a growing consensus that indeed the emotions are rooted in the brain, and the structure of the brain is prepared by evolution. In effect, the emotions are built into the neural system. There is little we can do but obey.

As you see, the biological view stands in sharp contrast to the relational view of the emotions developed here. From a relational perspective the very idea of emotions, along with the performances we associate with them, are lodged within relationship. The future of our emotional life is not fixed by biological structure, I have proposed, but is shaped and re-shaped through coordinated action. However, at this historical juncture there is such combined weight of evidence on the side of biology, that special attention is required. Just how much freedom do we have to create and abandon emotional performances?

To approach this problem, let's first return to the familiar question of how can we identify mental states or know of their existence. In this case the states in question are the emotions, and the identification markers are biological. Thus, we may ask, (1) can people identify their own emotional states by using biological indicators, and (2) can scientists, armed with brain scanning apparatus, identify the emotional states of their subjects? In the first case, if the emotions are biological, then I should be able to

---

[24]This history can be traced at least to Darwin's 1899 volume, *The expression of emotions in man and animals*. More recently, see for example, Panskepp, J. (2004). *Affective neuroscience: The foundations of human and animal emotions*, New York: Oxford University Press; and Lane, R. D., and Nadel, L. (2000). *Cognitive neuroscience of emotion*. New York: Oxford University Press.

[25]For example, at one time scientists argued that bodily changes caused emotional experience (e.g. the James–Lange theory), and at others that the bodily expressions of emotion followed psychological assessment (e.g. the Cannon–Bard theory).

[26]Schachter, S., and Singer, J. (1962). Cognitive, social, and physiological determinants of emotional state. *Psychological Review, 69*, 379–399.

recognize and distinguish among them by attending to my biological condition. And if I cannot recognize my emotions in this way, can brain technology enable scientists to do so? If neither we in our everyday life nor biological experts can successfully identify emotions in this way, then the grounds for a biological explanation are in peril. We may come to appreciate more fully the way in which emotions are not byproducts of biology but relational realities.

Now to the first question: I may speak of my love, my anxiety, my guilt, and so on, but how can I know that I feel such emotions? Could I be mistaken? In the preceding chapter we encountered the intractable problems we face in trying to "look inward" at our mind. But now we ask, armed with biological indicators, could we know that we feel anger as opposed to love or sadness? Here we do have one advantage. We can feel the heart racing, the dry mouth, or the blood surging in your groin. Aren't these signs of our mental condition? This idea has a long history, going back to the early psychology of William James. As James proposed, we know we are afraid of the bear in front of us because we experience our bodily reactions. We see the bear, we begin to run, and it is the experience of our body in flight that gives us the sense of fear.[27] If this view is extended, we might presume that every mental condition is accompanied by a discrete pattern of neural firing. Thus, by tuning in to our bodies, we can know our "true feelings."

•

Perspiration, a racing heart, a dry mouth, heaviness in the stomach: These are all evident enough. The important question is, do they tell us anything about our emotions? If my heart races, for example, what do I know about my *emotional* condition? I can know very surely that my heart is racing, can I safely draw conclusions about what this means *psychologically*? Scarcely. My heart often races as well during athletics, playing with children, watching an exciting film, climbing several flights of stairs, dancing, swimming... . Is my psychological state the same in all these cases, only in some of them, or something else? And for what particular states is a racing heart an expression? How could I possibly answer such a question? Biology tells us nothing about what psychological states, if any, are related to biological activity.

•

When I was eleven I was sent to a public school in the countryside. My closest companions were from devoutly religious families, and they were keen to invite me to attend church with them. My churchgoing was unsettling to my devoutly agnostic parents, especially when they learned that I was being swept away by religious

[27]James, W. (1884). What is an emotion? *Mind, 9,* 188–205.

fundamentalism. How could I not be? What stirring music, expressions of joy, visions of a righteous life, and fantastical promises...to say nothing of the pretty girls! Yet, one problem threatened my commitment. On communion Sundays it was announced to the congregation that *only* those who had faith in Jesus as the son of God could take part. One had to "truly believe" that the flesh and blood of the world's redeemer, was now incarnate in the bread and wine we were about to consume. I was drawn to the faith, but did I carry some residual doubts? I did *truly* believe all these things. How could I know if I *truly* accepted these fundamentals? But I scarcely had time to reach an answer before the tray of tiny glasses filled with "the blood of Christ" was traveling rapidly toward me down the aisle. What was I to do; what if I didn't truly believe; what if I were a fake? What would become of me?

My panic was the mother of invention: I grasped the glass, and began to observe the perspiration secreted onto its lip by my fingers. If there was no filmy deposit to be seen, then clearly I was not moved: I was not a believer. If the perspiration was in full evidence, then I was permitted to partake. Science and religion walked hand in hand.

•

Consider this possibility: We make two lists, lining up all the recognizable states of physiology on the one side, and all the names for the emotions on the other. Now, we may ask, how would we go about matching them? How do we know which emotions are accompanied by an elevated heartbeat, tears, or an erection? Of course, to begin this task would require that we know what states of mind actually exist and which are make-believe. Is the "feeling of spiritual presence" an actual state of mind or a myth; and what about "the taking of umbrage," or "malaise?" Are these genuine states of emotion? Indeed, on what grounds can we be certain that fear and anger are states of emotion, or whether they exist at all? So, then, how is the grand matching process to begin? If the body has an emotional voice, how could we comprehend its message?

•

I announce that I am afraid. Do I recall my thoughts of the past half hour in order to do that, or do I let a thought of the dentist quickly cross my mind in order to see how it affects me: Or can I be certain that it is really fear of the dentist, and not some other physical feeling of discomfort?

—Ludwig Wittgenstein

•

So, if biological signals fail to inform us of our "true feelings," what about the experts? Contemporary researchers are spurred by the development of various technologies for scanning brain activity (e.g. MRI, PET, EEG, MEG). Thus, as research subjects are engaged in various activities— problem solving, remembering, bargaining, watching films, meditating, and so on, measures can be taken of heightened neuro/chemical activity in various areas of the brain. The typical attempt is to locate those areas of the brain specific to a given psychological state or behavior.[28] Such research is dramatic in implication because it seems to reveal the cortical basis of the mental states. If a person is reading a funny story, for example, there will be brain activity in a different area of the brain than if reading a sad story, or an angering one. In terms of identifying emotions, no longer is it necessary to ask people about their emotions; they are revealed directly in the brain scan. We can know if they are loving, lusting, or lying. Brain scan technology is the real window to the soul. Or is it?[29]

•

Consider again the problem we confronted in the preceding chapter: How can we know what is in the mind of another? We are presented with their words and we take them to be symptoms of an underlying mind. Yet, we have no access to another's mind save through what we take to be its expressions. No matter what a person says about his or her feelings, there is no way of going behind the words to penetrate what lies beneath. Nor do their actions clarify. For example, you tell me you are depressed and I look to your actions. I see that you don't like to eat, you sleep for long periods, and you seldom engage in physical activities. But what can these tell me about your "inner state?" Perhaps you are worried, sad, fearful, or vigilant. I have no way of knowing except by taking into account other indicators, which in turn, will never reveal the particular mental condition.

In this context you can well appreciate the enthusiasm among scientists for brain scan technology. Here, for the first time in history, it seems that we can directly observe the mental condition as revealed in the neural activity. The problem of knowing what's on someone's mind seems finally solved. But consider again the problem of recognizing a mental state like depression. As an investigator you observe a location in the brain that is activated for a population of people who report they have little hunger,

[28]See, for example, Lane, R. D., and Nadel, L. (2000). *Cognitive neuroscience of emotion*. New York: Oxford University Press; Panksepp, J. (1998). *Affective neuroscience; The foundations of human and animal emotions*. New York: Oxford University Press.

[29]See also, Uttal, W. R. (2003). *The new phrenology*. Cambridge: MIT Press.

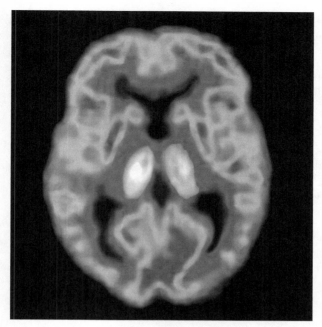

The neuro-image of the brain may reveal cortical activity when one is engaging in an emotional performance, and as well when one is playing chess or tossing the salad. But such brain activity is no more the *cause* of the performance than it is the moving of the king or adding the oil and vinegar.

don't sleep very well, and are lethargic. There we have it!: Depression! Or is it? How can we determine that the observed state of the brain is in fact indicative of "depression?" Why, is it not simply a neural correlate of sleeplessness, appetite loss, or lethargy? Or for that matter, how could we determine that the neural state is not the basis of "spiritual malaise," "anger," "withdrawal from oppressive conditions," or "cognitive integration and regrouping?"

In effect, brain scan data do not solve the problem of identifying mental states. They simply remove the problem from one site of ambiguity to another. Brain scans do not speak for themselves. To read them as evidence of depression, anger, happiness, sadness, empathy, and so on is to participate in a particular cultural tradition. A thorough assay of brain functioning could never yield a vocabulary of the emotions. Try as one may, one will not observe a brain condition of joy, hope, dread, or wonder. To draw conclusions about the emotions from brain states requires that the vocabulary is already in place. And that vocabulary is the achievement of relationship.

The culture offers us dozens of words to speak of our states of attraction, for example:

> I like you.
> I have strong feelings of friendship for you.
> I admire you.
> I am attracted to you.
> I like you very much.
> I love you.
> I love you very much.
> I am infatuated with you.
> I am passionate about you.
> I am overwhelmed by you.

We know nothing of the brain states that accompany these expressions, but a person's entire future may depend on which of them is spoken and where. The array of terms is not a reflection of cortical structure, but of the complexity of relations in a modern society.

•

> Neurology can tell us much about a blink of the eye,
> but nothing about a wink.

•

Is this to say that our brains have nothing to do with our emotions? Not at all. The brain may be essential to carrying out emotional performances, in the same way that it is essential to playing basketball or painting a portrait. The mistake is in believing that the brain *causes* or determines the performance. Consider the following experiment in brain science: We train one group of subjects to play the part of Lady Macbeth and another to master the part of Juliet. Would we wish, then, to conclude that the actions of the Macbeths and the Juliets are physiologically determined? As one plays Lady Macbeth there will surely be different states of the brain than in playing Juliet. There will also be different movements of the arms, legs, and mouth. But the playing of Macbeth and Juliet are no more determined by brain activity than they are by the movements of the arms, legs, and mouth. In performing Lady Macbeth and Juliet all these bodily functions are pressed into service. These characters and their actions are outgrowths of a communal tradition; the body is simply required for "doing relationships."[30]

---

[30]In his 2006 volume, *Descartes' error: Emotion, reason and the human brain*, Antonio Damasio relies heavily on the concept of "somatic markers" as a means of explaining how the brain informs us of what we feel, what decision is correct, and so on. Whether such a theory proves true

The body may set the limits for what is possible. We shall never "leap tall buildings in a single bound." And bodies may equip some of us to perform in better ways than others, by some standard. All intelligible action requires brain matter for its performance, but brain matter does not make the action intelligible. We must not let the body be a culture snatcher.

Bodily Pleasure: The Gift of Co-Action

> Nature has placed mankind under the governance of two sovereign masters, *pain* and *pleasure*. It is for them alone to point out what we ought to do, as well as to determine what we shall do.
>
> —Jeremy Bentham

These words from the 18th century continue to color our common consciousness. Isn't it simply natural for humans to seek pleasure and avoid pain? Aren't these inclinations built into the genetic structure of the body? As often said, pain is a signal that the body is in danger. Pain receptors give us an advantage in the Darwinian race for survival. Regarding pleasure we are more ambivalent. One long-standing tradition holds that bodily pleasure is good for us. That which gives us pleasure contributes to our well-being.[31] At the same time, many religions caution against such urges, and many pleasures are lethal. What is never denied, however, is that pleasure is a natural urge. Let us first take up the case of pleasure, and save the more difficult challenge of pain for the chapter's end.

We speak of "natural" pleasures, those we enjoy by virtue of our animal nature. No one had to tell us of the wonders of an alpine vista, the sunset, a mother's lullaby, chocolate, or the soft touch upon the skin. These, we say, are just natural. Yet, this simple presumption is not without costs. To extol the virtue of the *natural* pleasure is also to celebrate the bounded being. It is to say, "My pleasure is guaranteed by virtue of my body; no one else is needed, except as an instrument of stimulation." This is the ideology of self-sufficiency. In a similar vein we speak nostalgically of "getting back to nature," escaping the demands of social life and returning to the basic pleasures of freedom in the countryside. Yet, we must ask, are these pleasures really there prior to any relationship? At the ages of three and five, my children found sunsets in the Alps a bore, my grandson far prefers a

within the community of neuroscience, it makes little difference to the present thesis. Whatever neuroscience demonstrates will ultimately be consistent with what it is people do in cultural life.

[31] This view can be found today in the vast literature on aging that demonstrates a correlation between happiness and longevity. See www.positiveaging.net.

video game to his mother's lullaby, and whether a touch upon the genitals is pleasurable very much depends on whose touch it is. It is unlikely the touch of an examining physician.

•

Recently a friend brought a bottle of 15-year-old, first growth wine from Bordeaux. The taste was little short of ecstasy. In terms of my biological nature, my ecstasy was simply the result of a chemical composition placed in contact with my taste receptors. But consider: My first taste of wine was at six years of age when I asked my father for a sip at the dinner table. So assaulting was the experience that I almost choked. What has happened since I was six; what is it to "acquire" a taste? For me, it has been close friendships with wine enthusiasts, tête à têtes over candlelight and wine, sharing glasses at splendid dinners, and exposure to numerous images and information from the media—all immersions in relationship. When my friend served this wine, it came cloaked in relational history, and wrapped within the excitement of his sharing. We were participating in "an occasion," steeped in tradition, in which even the shape of the glass and the size of the sip were wedded to the wonder of the taste. The chemical composition of the wine and the neurological structure of my taste receptors were simply vehicles through which relationships gave shape to pleasure.

•

This simple example is fortified by wide-ranging research on the social context of pleasure. Consider:

- In his classic work on marijuana smoking, Howard Becker documents the way in which one's associates are able to reconstruct the acrid taste, the coughing, dizziness, and disorientation resulting from inhaling marijuana as an experience of pleasure. As Becker concludes, the pleasure of "getting high" is "socially acquired…not different from acquired tastes for oysters or dry martinis."[32]
- The historian Alain Corbain, charts the history of smell in 18th-century France.[33] As he proposes, as common theories about the chemistry of the air began to change, so did the experience of smell.

[32]Becker, H. (1953). Becoming a marijuana smoker. *American Journal of Sociology, 59,* 235–242.

[33]Corbin, A. (1988). *The foul and the fragrant: odor and the French social imagination: The cultural history of smell.* Cambridge: Harvard University Press. See also, Classen, C. (1994). *Aroma: The cultural history of smell.* London: Routledge.

When people began to believe that breathing the air from cesspools, swamps, and dead animals was unhealthy, these smells became "stinks."

- We typically hold that the mother's love for her children is natural. There is pleasure in nurturing, and the mother—child bond is a hereditary gift. Yet, as the historian Elizabeth Badinter demonstrates, practices of mother love are highly variable.[34] In her study of French culture, prior to the 18th century, children were considered insignificant and a mother's love to have little social or moral value. If a woman had the resources, her infants would be sent to the countryside and nurtured by a wet nurse. Children's deaths were frequent little grieved.

•

Today we are commonly struck with the vast differences among people in what gives them pleasure. For my own part, it is difficult for me to comprehend:

- the pleasure of eating marmite, kim chee, or Rocky Mountain oysters
- the fun of Polar Bear Club members swimming in the icy ocean
- the delight of industrial rock
- the ecstasy of the long distance runner
- the joy of an evening playing the slot machines
- the thrill of scaling the face of a cliff
- the pleasure derived from shooting animals.

What limits can be placed on what we can co-create as pleasurable?[35]

•

Further appreciation of the relational production of pleasure draws from a consideration of context, that is, rules for when and where the pleasure can occur. We are not likely to take pleasure in eating grilled meat while swimming in the ocean, tasting fine wine while eating a chili dog, feeling the hands of a stranger on a bus stroking the back of your neck, or listening to show tunes while attending a funeral. A touch is not a touch is not a touch, and the same is the case with all other forms of pleasure.

[34]Badinter, E. (1980). *Mother love: Myth and reality*. New York: Macmillan.

[35]For further discussion of the relationally created and controlled pleasures of sexual expression see Gagnon, J., and Simon, W. *op cit.*; Weeks, J. (1986). *Sexuality*. London: Tavistock; Seidman, S. (2003). *The social construction of sexuality*. New York: Norton.

Is this to deny the body? Not at all. Rather, it is to remove the body from its position of authority in matters of pleasure. While discrete areas of the brain may be activated when we declare our pleasure, they are not so much its determinants as its recruits.[36] To possess pleasure is a cultural act; like riding a bicycle or greeting a friend, it requires the body for its achievement. The brain does not determine the character of our joy; it provides the possibility for its relational creation.

•

"My pleasure" is scarcely mine alone. I stand in endless gratitude to:

- My mother for the pleasure of the text
- Wilfred for the beauty of the color blue
- Thomas for my joy in jazz
- Shirley for the wonder of opera
- Mary for the ecstasy of wind in the wheat field
- Karin for the charm of kletzma…
- Arthur for the joy of gardening.

The list is inexhaustible, and now I am uncertain whether "just naturally" I even liked Gerber Baby Food.

•

We now see that there are endless possibilities for creating pleasure. We accept as commonplace the pleasure of good cooking, fine music, sunrises, eros, and all the rest. But these are achievements of past generations, now set before us as a feast. What shall we create and share for future generations? What shall be our legacy? We largely assign this creative challenge to the arts. We allow the artist, the poet, and the composer, for example, to expand the domain of the pleasurable, to invite and seduce us into new worlds of wonderment—visual, verbal, auditory, tactile. But all too often we cannot follow them on their journeys; we are left cold and wondering. All too often the professionals create pleasure for the community of professionals—an unshared dialogue, a private language. Art for art's sake creates a chasm. But why should the creation of pleasure be confined to professionals? Why should we not all participate? We did so as children. "Let's pretend…" was the portal to paradise. Do we lose the knack as we settle for the petty pleasures of an orderly world? Blessed are the madcap.

•

[36]Neurological research does demonstrate that animals will endlessly continue to press a lever if it will deliver stimulation to a particular region of the cortex. Such research suggests that there are brain centers for pleasure. Yet, while there is not doubting the animals' behavior, we have no indication that they are driven by pleasure.

Let us praise the Saints of Joy among us...

• Sarah for making outlandish gifts of colored felt.
• Jane, who came to dinner dressed only in a rose.
• Maggie, for the cascade of ironic humor.
• Pru, who concocted mystery nights, in which one person was responsible for taking the other to a place they scarcely knew...an old-fashioned skating rink, a club where everyone danced to music from the 1940s, a hole in the wall restaurant where authentic Cajun food was served, a judge's chambers for a wedding ceremony.
• Wayne, whose hearty laughter moves us all to mirth.
• Norman, for generating parties from thin air.
• Little children everywhere.

The challenge is not to search for pleasure, but to create it.

•

In principle, there is no self-gratification. Even in privacy, self-pleasure feeds on a history of relationship.

Pain: The Final Challenge

We come now to a final bastion of natural being: bodily pain. In this case we are faced with overwhelming evidence of pain as both biological and universal. While the pleasures were found malleable across cultures and history, readily subject to co-active creation, pain is evident in all cultures and is clearly "there in nature" prior to relationship. Who would not recoil in agony at a door slammed on one's fingers, or a dentist's drill striking a nerve? Who can doubt the biological foundations of pain? Yet, given the preceding discussion of pleasure, there is reason to ask about limits of the biological view. In what sense, and to what degree can we understand pain as a relational achievement? The question is particularly important today. Given the enormous investment in pain management, it is essential to explore the possibilities of remedy without medical intervention.[37] As Western culture becomes increasingly dependent on pharmacological fixes to move through the day, it is imperative to locate alternatives.

•

[37]According to a 1999 products report, in the U.S., chronic back pain accounts for over 100 million workdays lost for men alone; over 40 million people suffer from chronic headaches; 8 million experience chronic facial and neck pain. Managed care programs are loathe to cover long-term pain management, not only because of the staggering costs, but because both diagnosis and treatments are deficient.

To open the door on the relational contribution to pain, consider the occasions of everyday life:

- A 3-year-old falls on the pavement, picks himself up, and runs without a sound to his mother inside the house, whereupon great wailing erupts.
- A documentary shows us children from rural China receiving inoculating injections; their faces are expressionless.
- After an evening of dancing Mary's feet show abrasions from straps that were too tight. She had a delightful time, but nursed her sore feet when she got home.
- An Olympic gymnast completes her routine despite a fractured ankle.
- An adolescent girl in the neighborhood inflicts cuts on her arms and legs.
- My friend Win walks off the Rugby field, his face bloody, his hands and legs showing serious bruises, and with a big smile, he bellows, "What a great game!"

And we know that to receive even one of the punches suffered by a boxer in a heavyweight fight would send us reeling in agony. Somehow, pain is not pain.

•

Such examples are also enriched by cultural and historical studies of pain. The historian Esther Cohen reports that before the days of Erasmus and Montaigne, very few people wrote about experiencing pain; in medieval times authors seldom wrote of their physical sensations, and autobiographies were far more likely to dwell on mental as opposed to physical anguish.[38] During the 13th –15th centuries, it was believed that pain was not primarily lodged in the body, but in the soul. In this way, the experience of pain took on a spiritual dimension. Because Christ suffered for humankind, many sought out pain as a way of both sharing Christ's pain and achieving redemption. Self-flagellation, fasting, and even martyrdom were embraced by the devout.

In his compendium, *The Culture of Pain*,[39] David Morris also describes wide historical variations in the experience of pain. During early battles, for example, wounded soldiers could become euphoric because their wounds meant they would be removed from the threat of battlefield death.

---

[38]Cohen, E. (2000). The animated pain of the body. *American Historical Review, 105*, 36–68.
[39]Berkeley: University of California Press, 1991.

For 18th- and 19th-century romantics pain took on connotations of ennobling beauty. Wordsworth could write seriously about his heart "swell'd to dear delicious pain."[40] Micronesian women in labor give so little evidence of pain that Western doctors can identify their contractions only by placing a hand on their abdomen.

•

It is here that many scholars find it useful to draw a distinction between the sensation of *pain* and the experience of *suffering*. As often proposed, the experience of suffering may have a strong cultural component. This would account for the many variations just described. However, as proposed, the sensation of pain is biological and universal, there in the body prior to relationship. While such a distinction is inviting, it is not without problems. If pain and suffering are distinct, then it should be possible to remove all suffering and still experience pain. But if we remove all suffering, do we not destroy the very concept of pain—as misery, torment, agony, and anguish? It seems wiser not to separate the inner world in this awkward fashion. Rather, let us view pain as an embodied action within a tradition of relationship.

•

Don and Donna were neighbors for several years, and because they were refreshing in their resistance to convention, I must confess a certain sense of loss when they moved away. Some years later a most peculiar postcard arrived in the mail, an invitation to a demonstration of bondage instruments. Only slowly did we realize that the hostess of this demonstration, Mistress Donna, must be our erstwhile neighbor. Coincidentally I realized that I was to speak in a symposium in the same city and on the same date as the demonstration. My curiosity was piqued.

When the day of the symposium arrived Donna was far from my mind. The demands of the day were intense, and the academic interchange continued through dinner. However, as dinner was ending, I realized that I had reached my limits of "responsible conversation," and the possibilities of a peek into the exotic drew me hither. After a long taxi ride into the bowels of the city, I finally located the decrepit apartment building in which the demonstration was taking place. I opened the apartment door with hesitation, and found myself in much the same circumstances of the entire day.

[40]From the "Sonnet on seeing Miss Helen Maria Williams weep at a tale of distress."

An audience was seated in a circle, listening attentively as the male "professor" spoke in sophisticated terms. The speech, however, was not about the genesis of self-conception, but the properties of various whips to produce pleasure without scarring the buttocks of the naked woman bent over before him. After his demonstrations the group broke up into pairs to experiment with his devices. Soon the room was filled with the thwacking sounds of leather and wood upon bare skin, accompanied by sighs of ecstasy. As I bid Mistress Donna adieu, she was beaming with pride at all the pleasure to which her work contributed.

•

Drawing from my earlier arguments, when we express our pain we are engaging in a culturally prepared performance. We are not reporting on the state of the psyche, but acting within a tradition of relationship. That is, we are engaging in an action that has achieved its intelligibility from a history of co-action. If I wrench my back I don't quietly mumble, "Heavens to Betsy," and if I fall on the ice I do not begin deliberating on the fifth decimal place of *pi*. Such actions would be laughable. However, if I shriek or curse I am a natural man (unless, of course, the shriek is too loud or the cursing too vile.)

•

The critic stirs: "Now you have gone too far. If you smack an infant on the bottom at birth, he cries. He also cries when he is hungry or a diaper needs changing. No socialization is required. Pain is there at birth." This seems convincing enough at the outset. But consider again the problem of knowing other minds. How do we know that what the infant is experiencing is pain? Perhaps these are expressions of surprise, need, fear, or something else. They may be simply primitive ways of signaling avoidance.

Let us press the case further: Bodily events do thrust their way unpredictably into the flow of activity. There are falls, blows, eruptions, cuts, stresses, contractions, and so on. Yet, like other events encountered as we move through the world, we typically attempt to absorb them into the relational worlds of which we are a part. In this sense, the physical event is much like another's action toward us. It makes no necessary demands on our behavior, but in the act of coordination it comes into being as one kind of thing as opposed to another. It is not that there is pain, and then interpretation. The fact of pain is born in the process of interpreting.

•

We gain further purchase on this relational view from Arthur Frank's classic volume, *The Wounded Storyteller*.[41] Frank illuminates three significant stories one may tell about his or her serious illness. The first is to interpret the illness as simply a deviation from the normal condition of good health; in this case the patient's task is that of *restitution*. One wishes simply to clear it up and get on with life. A more extreme story is to interpret the illness as the beginning of *chaos*. One characterizes the illness as throwing one into a state of futility or helplessness. There is no obvious means of coping or resolving. Finally, and less common, is the *quest* story. Here one understands his or her illness in terms of a journey in which significant meaning or illumination is discovered. For example, my neighbor Marge recently told me of her bout of cancer, and of all she had learned from the experience about her strengths and the significance of her family. Important for present purposes are the differences in the suffering attending these contrasting interpretations. With the restitution narrative, one simply endures the suffering while working on recovery. If illness is chaos, however, there is unrelieved anger and frustration. In contrast, when approaching illness as a quest, one may transcend the common definition of anguish. One may locate a deeper understanding of life and relationships. The result may even be serenity.

•

The critic is again at the door: "All very well and good, but biological research clearly shows the existence of pain receptors (nocioceptors), and when these receptors are fired (releasing neurotransmitters, especially glutamate), people reliably report the experience of pain. Further, because the biological makeup of the human species is more or less the same across cultures, the experience of pain must be universal." Good point. Let us for the moment, accept the reality of this research tradition. However, it is important to point out that even within this tradition the "problem of pain" remains unsolved. Not only has it been difficult to determine the relationship between central and peripheral nervous system functioning (i.e. in what degree does the central nervous system respond to the activity of the receptors, as opposed to altering input from the receptors?). There are also no fully acceptable measures of pain. If two people report they are in a state of "moderate pain," how do we know they are reporting on the same

[41]Chicago: University of Chicago Press, 2nd ed. (1997). See also, Kleinman, A. (1989). *The illness narratives: Suffering, healing, and the human condition*, New York: Basic Books; and Mattingly, C., and Garro, L. C. (Eds.) (2000). *Narrative and the cultural construction of healing and illness*. Berkeley: University of California Press.

mental state? Whether a given experience is reported as painful may vary according to the gender, age, religion, and ethnicity of the individual.[42] Earlier we concluded that to presume a private world inside is to ensure that we shall never know each other. It was partially for this reason that we abandoned the idea of minds within bodies, in favor of a view of persons as relational performers. We should move in a similar direction with pain. Let us not assume that it is isolated within, but that it is a full participant in relational life.

In conclusion, we confront a major question: If a neurological correlate of pain can be identified, in what degree can its effects be suppressed by meaningful activity? The examples cited above suggest that such activity can indeed be powerful in its effects. It makes a difference whether one is playing sports or simply at leisure as to what is experienced as pain. In this respect I am attracted, for one, to the newly developing methods of treating pain through meditation and yoga.[43] To be trained in these practices is to acquire a performance that may reduce pain without pharmacology. Given the enormous challenge of pain management, such practices deserve our concerted attention.

[42] See, for example, Unruh, A. M. (1996). Gender variations in clinical pain experience. *Pain*, 65, 123–168; Zborowski, M. (1969). *People in pain*. San Francisco: Jossey-Bass; Zatzick, D. F., and Dimsdale, J. E. (1990). Cultural variations in response to painful stimuli. *Psychosomatic Medicine*, 52, 544–557.

[43] See for example, Kabat-Zinn, J., Lipworth, L., and Burney, R. (1985). The clinical use of mindfulness meditation for the self-regulation of chronic pain. *Journal of Behavioral Medicine*, 8, 163–190; Rockers, D. M. (2002). The successful application of meditative principles to treatment of refractory pain conditions. *Pain Medicine*, 3, 188; Kabat-Zinn, J. (1990). *Full catastrophe living: Using the wisdom of your body and mind to face stress, pain, and illness*. New York: Delta; Main, D. (1991). Chronic pain and yoga therapy. *The Journal of the International Association of Yoga Therapists*, 11, 35–38; Wood, G. G. (2004). Yoga and chronic pain management—telling our story. *International Journal of Yoga Therapy*, 14, 59–67.

Two

Relational Being in Everyday Life

5

*Multi-Being and the Adventures of
Everyday Life*

In all that we say and do, we manifest conditions of relationship. In whatever we think, remember, create, and feel—in all that is meaningful to us—we participate in relationship. The word "I" does not index an origin of action, but a relational achievement.

•

These were among the central conclusions reached in the preceding chapters. Yet, these are not the end of a conversation, but a beginning. They are preparations for creative exploration, both in theory and practice. In this chapter and the next we explore the dynamics of everyday relations, their harmonies and their fatalities. In subsequent chapters we take up professional practices, in science, education, therapy, and organizations. In each case, a space opens for expanding the potentials and practices of relational being.

In the present chapter we first explore the condition of multi-being. Existence in relationship ultimately gives rise to an enormous reservoir of inchoate potentials for action. Within the ongoing stream of co-action these potentials are shaped, diminished, and expanded in unpredictable ways. Every relationship is a story in the making. This account of multi-being sets the stage for considering trajectories of relationship. How can our coordinated actions achieve vitality; what are the ingredients of stabilization; where are the trap-doors to deterioration? We consider each of these issues from a relational perspective.

Multi-Being

As his professor, I am reviewing the first draft of Leon's dissertation. On one page I find myself scribbling in the margin, "this is inconsistent with the previous chapter;" On other pages I write, "incoherent," "colloquial," or "awkward phrasing." I also have my moments of "congratulations," "elegant," "good point," or "nicely prepared." I proceed with little reflection. Am I not participating in a tradition that aims to educate individuals to become clear and coherent in their thinking?

Yet, there is a certain irony in this posture. As I sit here writing this book, I am filled with doubts and turmoil. I am acutely aware that for every sentence I write, another voice is smirking. At each moment I am confronted with dozens of ways of putting things, and dozens of criteria for judging. It is a major effort to suppress the nattering, but I am in peril if I do not. To share the turmoil of competing possibilities would quickly drive you away. In effect, I am forced by my training and your expectations to be a Leon—to create myself for you as the possessor of a unified and coherent mind.

This view of the ideal person as a coherent unity has a long tradition in the West. It is evident in the Christian tradition, with its emphasis on the purity of the soul, and the clear divide between good and evil. Philosopher Stephen Toulmin traces the emphasis on logical coherence to the rise of Modernism, and particularly the influence of the Cartesian view of reason as the center of human action.[1] Good reasoning is clear and logically consistent, ideally approximating mathematics.[2] The maturing individual should thus aspire to a coherent way of thinking about the world, one that integrates disparate facts into a single, over-arching theory. These same values are also inscribed in psychological theory and practice. At the turn of the 20th century, William James wrote of those "sick souls" whose "spirit wars with their flesh; they wish for incompatibles, wayward impulses interrupt their most deliberate plans, and their lives are one long drama of repentance and of effort to repair misdemeanors and mistakes."[3] George Kelly's widely acclaimed *Psychology of personal constructs*, asserts that all people attempt to build conceptual systems that are internally consistent.[4]

[1] Toulmin, S. (2001). *Return to reason*. Cambridge: Harvard University Press.

[2] It is not accidental that early philosophers of science sought to convert all scientific reasoning to a unified, symbolic logic, or that the arguments of contemporary analytic philosophers approximate mathematical theorems.

[3] James, W. (1958). *The varieties of religious experience*. New York: The New American Library of World Literature. (Originally published in 1902.)

[4] Kelly, G. A. (1955). *The psychology of personal constructs*. New York: Norton.

It is only natural. A legion of *cognitive dissonance* researchers assume a universal need for people to reduce inconsistency among their thoughts.[5] There are further echoes in the field of mental health. For example, as the personality theorist Prescott Lecky argues the "normally" functioning human being strives for consistency in all aspects of his life.[6] Mental suffering is equated with the inability to achieve personal coherence. It is no accident that we commonly speak of "mental *disorder*," and that the profession's labels for mental illness include schizoid thinking, bi-polarity, dissociation, and multiple personality. In my evaluation of Leon's work, I extend the reach of this tradition. All of us living in this tradition bear the burden of coherence.

•

A double-minded man is unstable in all his ways.
—*Book of James*

•

Behind the façade of unity, coherence, and wholeness lies another world. It is a world both rich in resources and incipient conflict, born in relationships and daily gaining dimension. Consider its birth: As we engage in relationships, both significant and superficial, we are continuously absorbing potentials for action. Every relationship provides three points of origin for these potentials: First, others' actions serve as *models* for what is possible. As we observe others in action, they fill our consciousness, thus providing the possibility of incorporating their actions into our own repertoire. This process, variously called imitation, modeling, mimesis, or identification, is often credited by social scientists as the fundamental engine of socialization.[7] Thus, for example, widespread research is devoted to exploring modeling as a source of gendered behavior, aggression, altruism,

---

[5]See, for example, Brehm, J., and Cohen, A. (1962). *Explorations in cognitive dissonance.* New York: Wiley.

[6]Lecky, P. (1973). *Self-consistency: A theory of personality.* New York: Island Press.

[7]Discussions of imitation may be traced to both Plato and Aristotle, and their treatments of mimesis. In the social sciences, the significance of imitation in social life can be traced to early works of Charles Horton Cooley, William McDougall, and E. A. Ross. The therapist Karl Tomm calls the resulting incorporation, "internalized others." Tomm, K., Hoyt, M., and Madigan, S. (1998). Honoring our internalized others and the ethics of caring: A conversation with Karl Tomm. In M. Hoyt (Ed.) *Handbook of constructive therapies.* San Francisco: Jossey-Bass. It is but a short step from the process of imitation to the incorporation of others to the creation of conflict. See especially Girard, R. (1977). *Violence and the sacred.* Baltimore: Johns Hopkins University Press.

and emotional behavior.[8] Through observation we incorporate the potentials of being the other.

•

"No him, no me."
    —Dizzy Gillespie speaking of Louis Armstrong

•

Yet, the accepted view of modeling does not take us far enough. Within any relationship, we also *become somebody*. That is, we come to play a certain part or adopt a certain identity. With my mother, I come into being as a child; with my children I come into being as a parent, and so on. Each relationship will bring me into being as a certain sort of person, and the actions that I acquire will enter the repository of potentials for future use. In a certain sense, we are prepared for a future in which we imitate various versions of ourselves. There is still the little boy or little girl there in waiting. But there is far more. It is not simply *the* little boy or girl but a multiplicity of them as they have come into being in our relationships with parents, friends, siblings, teachers, and so on. We are the angel, the tyrant, the meek, the show-off, and so on. As the years accumulate, so do the laminations of possibility. In this sense, one may view the "third age" as one of the richest of a lifetime. In the latter years one may—if they dare—draw from an enormous repertoire of potentials. One may re-visit and re-kindle in ways that are impossible for the young.

•

When we feel most private, most deeply "into" ourselves, we are in some other sense most deeply connected with others through whom we have learned to become a self.

    —Stephen Mitchell

•

Multi-being is also constituted by a third residue of relationship. We draw from the *form of co-action* itself, the interactive scenarios that we perform within our various relationships.[9] When we learn to dance, we acquire the ability to move our bodies in a prescribed way; we also watch our partners,

[8]There is a tendency to equate such research with a behaviorist view of development. That is, the model is viewed as a cause of the child's behavior. Yet, within the present context, we abandon the causal account in favor of a view of modeling as relational. The model only becomes a model with certain features by virtue of our participation.

[9]Richard Schwartz (1995) approaches this possibility in his work on internalized families. However, he is primarily concerned with family members as internalized others, as "inner people

and possibly could imitate them as well. Of equal importance, however, we learn the coordinated activity of the dance itself, how it goes when we move in this direction, or in that. In the same way, I learn what it is to participate in the give and take of an argument, in classroom discussion, scenarios of emotion (see Chapter 4), and so on.[10] In sum, all meaning/full relations leave us with another's way of being, a self that we become through the relationship, and a choreography of co-action. From these three sources, we emerge with enormous possibilities for being.

•

In entering any relationship I carry with me myriad ways of speaking: Depending on the occasion, I can be the formal academic, the informal and relaxed Ken, the raucous jock, the romantic, the Southerner, the aesthete, the Brit, the judgmental, the depressive, the therapist, the child, the student, the idealist, the aggressor, the humble, the spiritual, and far more. All are present, ready for use. I suspect that with a little prompting I could do a fair job as a woman, a black, a homosexual, Gary Cooper, an Asian, a therapist, Billy Graham, an Italian mobster, a Nazi officer, my editor, and my dog…for starters. Nor is it simply the words I carry. The words are wedded to action, to tone of voice, gaze, posture, movement, and so on. These too are lurking, latent but potential. Give me the right audience and enough encouragement, and who knows what I might become?

•

There are a number of important consequences of this view. At the outset is its contrast with the traditional vision of bounded being. The ideal of an internally integrated, harmonious, and coherent mind is replaced by a view of the person as fundamentally disorderly and inconsistent. In the tradition of bounded being, the person was isolated; reason functioned most perfectly in a social vacuum. In contrast, the multi-being is socially embedded, fully engaged in the flow of relationship. For the bounded being, coherence and integration are virtues; the well-ordered mind is a signal of maturity. For the multi-being, coherence and integration may be valued, but only within particular relationships. Celebrated are the myriad potentials for effective co-action across a broad and disparate field of relationships.

of different ages, temperaments, talents, and desires," (p. 57) as opposed to the patterns of family interchange. Schwartz, R. *Internalized family systems therapy*. New York: Guilford.

   [10]The founder of interpersonal psychiatry, Harry Stack Sullivan, would view these residues as "me–you patterns." See Sullivan, H. S. (1968). *The interpersonal theory of psychiatry*. New York: Norton.

There is also a more daunting implication. If we do indeed carry the residues of multiple relationships, as this vision suggests, then for anything we hold as reasonable or good, we also harbor its opposite. For every activity we embrace, we are also capable of alien activity. Every good liberal knows very well how to engage in hate talk; every religious fundamentalist knows the attractions of sin; every adult can be a baby; every responsible official has the potential for corruption; every heterosexual can entertain the possibility of homosexuality. The potential for conflict is forever with us; in our every action we carry a dissenting voice on our shoulders.

•

My conscience hath a thousand sev'ral tongues,
and every tongue brings in a sev'ral tale.
——William Shakespeare, *Richard III*

•

This is also to say that the stable worlds in which we seem to live are quite fragile. In our daily relationships we encounter only partial persons, fragments that we mistakenly presume to be whole personalities. Stability and coherence are generated in our co-active agreements. But these agreements are not binding, and disruptions can occur at any moment. I am not proposing that social life is a grand charade, in which we are all wearing masks to suit the occasion. The metaphor of the mask is misleading, as it suggests there is a "real self" just beneath the guise. For the relational being there is no inside versus outside; there is only embodied action with others. Echoing earlier chapters, authenticity is a relational achievement of the moment.

Early Precursors: Depth Psychology

To fill out this vision of multi-being and its implications, it's useful to contrast and compare with preceding accounts of personal multiplicity. Let's first consider related views in early psychoanalysis, and then turn to more recent inquiries in psychiatry and the social sciences. Curiosity about the conflicting potentials in the human personality has been present since the origins of psychiatry. Indeed, for Freud the rationally coherent self is only "a self on the surface." The most significant driving forces in our lives are repressed from consciousness. To open the floodgate to the unconscious potentials would overwhelm one with dire desires—incest, homicide, perversion and more. Both consciousness and conscience are engaged in a constant battle against the primal forces of the unconscious, and the result is a personality riven with neurotic defenses against disruption.

In this context, the aim of therapy is to bring the hidden forces into controlled expression.[11]

Carl Jung shared Freud's view of deeply dwelling, unconscious forces. However, where Freud found rudimentary destructive forces, Jung found a virtual garden of hidden impulses. Inherited from distant times in human history, he proposed, were impulses and values that clustered around the image of the wise man, the great mother, the hero, the trickster, and a state of balanced complexity, among others.[12] Within every male there was a female impulse, and vice versa. For Jung, these were not impulses to be resisted; indeed, healthy development required bringing them forth into consciousness. From this rich multiplicity life derived its meaning. The romantic vision of deeply embedded selves, and especially Freud's view of repression, continues to play a vital role in therapeutic work.[13]

There is a certain congeniality between Freud's concern with the "dark side" of personality and the potentials of multi-being. However, there are important and illuminating differences. First, there is the issue of origins. For Freud the repressed urges are biologically based, and limited to *eros* and *thanatos*, or more crudely, unbridled sexual and destructive impulses. In the case of multi-being, however, the origin of our potentials is not biological but social. In every relationship there emerge potentials for being—dominant or submissive, churlish or kind, obedient or rebellious, and so on. And this may include relations with persons both in the flesh and in film, in literature, myth, and on the web. In this sense, our potential for "doing evil" by common standards is enormous. For example, florid news accounts of rape, suicide, wife battering and the like, create the potential for just such acts. Simply put, if you know it is done, you can also entertain the possibility of doing it.[14]

•

One of my greatest delights in life is playing with children. In these relationships I draw from the residuals of my own childhood. The child I carry lives again, but now enriched through my playmate.

[11]See, for example, Freud, S. (1954). *The psychopathology of everyday life.* (A. A. Brill, Trans.) London: Penguin.

[12]See, for example, Jung, C. G. (1968). *Man and his symbols.* New York: Dell.

[13]For an excellent review of psychiatric explorations of multiplicity see Rowan, J. (1990). *Subpersonalities,* London: Routledge. Much closer to the present account are developments in relational psychoanalysis. See especially, contributors to Muran, J. C. (Ed.) (2001). *Self-relations in the psychotherapy process.* Washington, DC: APA Press.

[14]It is this view that underlies much of concern with depictions of crime and violence in the mass media. Such depictions serve as models.

What a relief to shed the responsibilities of my "adult identity!" What joy in the rollicking moments from which emerge worlds undreamt! It is against this backdrop that I have come to resent the insinuation into my life of the frequent media accounts of sexual predation. I never once thought of children as possible "objects of sexual desire" prior to my encountering such cases in the news and on the screen. Now my innocence is lost. And, as I watch children at play in the park, I find myself asking how a lurking predator might see them. For an ugly moment I am the predator…until a thundering voice intervenes to reassure me that I am normal and that they are simply children at play.

•

A second difference between the psychoanalytic and relational vision revolves around the question of why such "evil acts" are comparatively rare. In fact, most people never really consider the possibility of rape, incest, or murder. For Freud, the answer lies in *repression*, an unconscious mental process that protects the conscious mind from awareness of such desires. When evil inclinations begin seeping into consciousness, neurotic defenses (e.g. obsession, paranoia) are erected against them. Unconsciously we are perpetually struggling against our deepest desires; in our attempt to sustain an inner-order we become disordered. And indeed, without our neuroses, Freud proposed, civilization would be threatened with collapse.

In the case of relational being, however, nothing so exotic as repression is essential to our understanding. We carry with us multiple and conflicting potentials for what pass as good and evil. However, most of these potentials seldom reach consciousness, not because we defend against them, but because they are simply irrelevant to the confluence of our daily activities. One may read of murder, and thereby acquire a model of such action. One knows how to do it. However, one seldom participates in the kinds of relationships (e.g. street gangs, Mafia) in which murder is an intelligible action. In less extreme terms, most adults know how to play hop-scotch, hide and seek, and spin the bottle, but these potentials are irrelevant to the daily contexts of our lives. What holds civilization together is primarily the everyday demand for remaining intelligible within our relationships.

•

When we are absorbed in the engagement of the moment, we may be oblivious to our multiple potentials for conflict. However, we are not always so enwrapped, and conflict is always at the threshold. Freud's views on mechanisms of defense are relevant. For him, psychological defense was natural. If there were threatening impulses, there was an automatic, biologically prepared triggering of repression and the erection of mental barriers. In contrast, from the present standpoint there is no inherent resistance to incoherence. That we should live with antagonistic impulses is not in itself a problem. Incoherence becomes a problem only within relationships in which it is scorned. The child moves fluidly in a sea of incoherence; any impulse may quickly give way to its opposite. The sweet child of the moment may be the hellion of the next. It is through subsequent relations that we acquire the voice of responsible order.

•

Two plus two equals five is not without its attractions.

—Fyodor Dostoevsky

•

It is not only through relations that we come to resist conflicting impulses and to seek coherence. It is also within our relationships that we acquire the means of defending against conflict. In daily relations, for example, we all stifle impulses to criticize, to use foul language, to yawn, or to express disinterest. To do so is to have acquired social skills. It is precisely such skills that we employ in dealing with the conflicting residues of multiple relationships. Let us replace the concept of *repression*, then, with *suppression*. In this sense, what is often called "inner conflict" is the private participation in public conflict—actual or imagined. We are participating in multiple, conflicting relationships, but without full bodily engagement. As outlined in Chapter 3, these are partial performances. Or, echoing Vygotsky, every means we posses for privately suppressing impulses was acquired from participation in public life.

The metaphor of *inner dialogue* is useful here. Each impulse to "do this," and "don't do that" represents a "voice" from past relationships. These may be the voices of others, as proposed, or the voice one has acquired through relating with others. As they are juxtaposed with one another, certain voices will "win out." They will have the "best of the argument." In the words of the Russian literary theorist, Mikhail Bakhtin, some voices will prove "internally convincing."[15] To live in a heterosexual culture, for example, will encourage a naturalization of heterosexual behavior, and a view of homosexuality as deviant. Should the "deviant voice" begin to speak, ever so subtly, the "natural voice" is there to silence or reframe it: "I couldn't imagine it," "It was only adolescent fun," "well, I may be a

---

[15]See also Mikail Bakhtin on the process of internal dialogue. Bakhtin, M. (1981). *The dialogic imagination.* (M. Holquist, Ed.). Austin: University of Texas Press.

bit 'bi'." As Michael Billig suggests, the basis of what Freud called the unconscious mind is the result of our learning to change the topic of a shameful or otherwise uncomfortable topic of conversation.[16] When we carry this practice into our private lives, we simply stop the inner dialogue; over time we lose consciousness of the dialogic tension itself. We just "don't think of those things."

•

> These profiteroles look heavenly; rich cream puffs, stuffed with
> vanilla bean ice cream, and a thick Valrhona chocolate sauce drizzled
> over the three corpulent mounds. My body shivers with delight.
> Yet, suddenly my teenage companions are with me, "Going to be a
> fatty, huh?" They are soon joined by my doctor, "You should watch
> your cholesterol." But then, Harry says, "How often do you get this
> chance;" Suzie says, "Hey, you can make up for it tomorrow,"
> and there is the compelling motto "Carpe Diem. I am silent for a
> moment, and turn to my dinner companions and say, "How about
> splitting some profiteroles?"

•

It is essential here to underscore the positive social function of suppression. In the Freudian tradition defense mechanisms were neurotic. It is the task of the analyst to bring about a catharsis that will allow the individual to gain ego (cognitive) control over undesirable impulses. From a relational perspective, however, our "inner conflicts" reflect the social conflicts in which we live. And in the same way that we seek out means of reducing social conflict and finding means of going on together, we use suppressive devices to live viably in a complex sea of relationships.

At the same time, when suppressive defenses are too demanding, there is danger. In suppressing the many voices, we may "live in the moment;" in fastening on them we become inflexible. One must consider here the skill of balance: how much should we suppress, and under what conditions? The metaphor of "the voice of conscience" is apt. For Freud, the voice that warned against temptation is essentially the voice of the father. However, this super-ego constraint, as he called it, was also neurotic. It was an irrational way of dealing with destructive impulses within. In the present case, however, one's "super-ego" carries not only the father's voice,

---

[16]Billig, M. (1999). *Freudian repression: Conversation creating the unconscious mind.* Cambridge: Cambridge University Press.

"When I can't sleep, I find that it sometimes helps
to get up and jot down my anxieties."

but that of many others as well. And, rather than being neurotic, to heed
such voices is essential for living comfortably in society. To listen only to
these voices may be paralyzing. As we move across the complex contexts of
relationship, flexibility may be essential. Yet, in failing to heed such voices
we are essentially denying relational connection. It would be to say, for
example, "I don't care what my mother would say about what I am doing,"
or "My friends don't count in the choice I am making now." Those who
lack a strong sense of moral conscience are neither "bad seed," nor deficient
in their capacities for moral reasoning. Rather, they are persons without the
significant relationships in which "the good," has become an intelligible
and desirable form of life. The ability of soldiers to commit atrocities—
to rape, mutilate, or murder—is not an unleashing of primitive drives.
Rather, in a context where there is no dialogic tension—no voice of denial—
anything is possible.

I am 14 years old, it is late afternoon and the halls of my junior high school building are empty...except for three of us who have just finished football practice. We are wandering the halls, making aimless jokes about teachers, students, and the stupidity of school. On an upper floor near the staircase, I spot a set of lockers that are unhinged from the wall. Apparently they are waiting to be moved to another part of the building. I suggest in jest that to help the administration out we should take the lockers and throw them down the stairs. Wild laughter follows, and within less than a minute we heave the entire set over the balcony. As the lockers descend with a crash we are running at top speed in the opposite direction. Why, I now ask myself, would I ever do such a knuckleheaded thing? Where were the admonishing voices at this moment? Why is it that "it seemed right at the time," is so often wrong at any other time?

Contemporary Precursors: Living with Others

Lively dialogues on multiple selves have continued to the present, and many of these are congenial to the present vision of multi-being. Prominent, for example, is the shift among many psychiatrists away from Freud's early view of the person as burdened by deep and intolerable biological urges. Rather, with the writings of Karen Horney, Erich Fromm, and Harry Stack Sullivan, among others, there was a pronounced shift toward understanding persons in terms of their social relationships. The social view grew especially robust in the mid-20th century, in the guise of what came to be known as *object relations* theory. The "objects" in this case are primarily other persons, and most prominently, one's parents.[17] Such views have continued to develop, and are today represented by an active organization of relational analysts.[18]

For relational analysts, there is a continuing tendency to focus on unconscious demands and the contribution of early family relations to one's multiple and discontinuous senses of self. However, in terms of therapy, the most dramatic shift in emphasis is from the exclusive concern with the client's inner conflicts, to the relationship between the client and therapist. As it is reasoned, both bring to the analytic hour powerful

---

[17]For useful reviews, see Mitchell, S. A. (1988). *Relational concepts in psychoanalysis: An integration.* Cambridge: Harvard University Press.

[18]The major vehicle for relational writings is the journal *Psychoanalytic Dialogues, a Journal of Relational Perspectives.* See also the International Association for Relational Therapy and Psychoanalysis (http://www.iarpp.org/html/index.cfm).

residues of past relationships, and the outcome of therapy will depend importantly on the dynamics of this relationship. Both client and therapist may have ambivalent feelings toward each other, feelings that reflect their past history of relationships. There is particular concern with the alliance formed between the client and therapist, and with the significance of this alliance for the outcome of therapy. If the bond between them is successful, the therapy has a better likelihood of success.[19]

Although the relational orientation in psychiatry is primarily concerned with overcoming conflict and reducing anguish, others take a more positive view. In her casework, psychologist Mary Watkins focuses on internal conversations with "invisible guests," as she calls them. These conversations, she proposes, contribute significantly to our well-being.[20] For example, in deliberating a decision about marriage, one might hear an imagined debate between father and mother. The result could be far greater sensitivity to the pros and cons of one's own decision about marriage. For Watkins, such conversations are also linked to the development of creative artistry, and the ability to see the world through many points of view. In a similar vein, Hermans and Kempen[21] propose a view of the person as inherently dialogic. They eschew the view of the person as composed of fixed traits. Rather, through the process of internal dialogue, meaning remains under continuous development.

Echoing these views, in her work on *social ghosts*, Mary Gergen points out that the cast of potential selves is not limited to people we actually know. Some of the most significant characters in our lives can be media figures, performers, historical and fictional characters, and a deity.[22] Consider the following comments from the adolescents in her study:

- John Paul Jones was the bass and keyboard player for the rock group Led Zeppelin...when my band practices, I feel like I'm him, and it helps me play better. It gives me more energy.
- When I'm playing basketball, I like to do some monster Jams. Charles Barkley (former basketball star) and me are one.

[19]See, for example, Safran, J. D., and Muran, J. C. (2001). The therapeutic alliance as a process of intersubjective negotiation. In J. C. Muran (Ed.) *Self-relations in the psychotherapy process.* Washington: APA Press.

[20]Watkins, M. M. (2000). *Invisible guests, the development of imaginal dialogues.* New York: Continuum.

[21]Hermans, H. J. M., and Kempen, H. J. G. (1993). *The dialogical self: Meaning as movement.* San Diego: Academic Press.

[22]Gergen, M. (2001). *Feminist reconstructions in psychology: Narrative, gender & performance.* Thousand Oaks, CA: Sage.

- After watching Eddy Cheever, a famous F1 race driver, many times I became very interested in auto racing. Actually he has a major influence in my leading up to being a mechanic.

Finally, social psychologists provide engaging illustrations of multi-being in action. The capacity for people to change in chameleon-like ways generally falls under the rubric "situational effects," that is, the effects of the immediate situation on people's actions. If the situation demands, what are the limits of what people might do? This work demonstrates a remarkable plasticity in people's behavior as they move from one context to another. Most interestingly, people will often do things they otherwise deplore. In laboratory situations they will lie, exploit each other, and agree to opinions they know are incorrect. Perhaps the most famous case is that of Stanley Milgram's research on obedience to authority.[23] In this case, substantial numbers of participants were conscripted from all walks of life. Once in the laboratory, they were asked by the experimenter to deliver what they believed to be painful electric shocks to a person in an adjacent room who could not see them. They proceeded undeterred by the victim's moans and groans. Even when it appeared the shocks could be fatal to the victim, most participants obeyed the commands of the experimenter to continue delivering the shocks. Under orders, Milgram reasoned, wouldn't most of us indeed commit atrocities?[24]

•

What will people do if they find themselves alone together,
cut away from all surveillance and all ties to past or future? This was
our question in an early study of relationships in the dark.[25]
My colleagues and I advertised widely for paid volunteers to
participate in environmental research. On the appointed day, the
participants arrived separately, and were ushered into a private room.
They were told to leave their coats, purses, shoes, and the contents of
their pockets behind, as they would be taken one by one to a room
without light. After remaining there for "a period of time,"

---

[23]Milgram, S. (1974). *Obedience to authority: An experimental view*. New York: Harper & Row.

[24]Traditional social psychology attempts to measure an individual's attitudes, as if they were fixed and unitary. However, the view of multi-being suggests that an individual's views are fluid and often self-contradictory. For illustrations, see Billig, M., Condor, S., Edwards, D., Gane, M., Middleton, D., and Radley, A. (1988). *Ideological dilemmas, a social psychology of everyday thinking*. London: Sage.

[25]Gergen, K. J., Gergen, M. M., and Barton, W. (1973). Deviance in the dark. *Psychology Today*, 129–130; Gergen, K. J. (1993). *Refiguring self and psychology*. Hampshire: Dartmouth.

they would be removed one by one and sent away individually. Other than in the dark room, they would never meet each other. The room was approximately 12′ × 12′, with padded floor and walls. There was no furniture. If there were problems or anyone felt uncomfortable, a tiny red light over the door allowed one to escape. Double doors shut out any other light. About six to eight participants were included in any given session. Unsure of the outcomes, a colleague was placed in the corner of the room for security.

As we found, participants in these studies first chattered amicably about who they were and where they came from. Many lied. They also discovered the dimensions of the room and the microphones used to record the sound. After some 15 minutes the banter diminished and soon there was almost total silence. Talk was being replaced by touch. As participants described their experience, "I felt joy over the possibility of not having to look at people in clichéd ways;" "I enjoyed the wantonness of just crawling around and over other people to get from one place to another;" "As I was sitting Beth came up and we started to play touchy face and touchy body and started to neck…We decided to pass our 'love' on, to share it with other people. So we split up and Laurie took her place."

When we later approached the participants and told them it was time to leave the chamber, they frequently resisted. As we found, some 90% of the participants indicated touching each other on purpose; only 20% attempted to keep others from touching them. Some 50% hugged; 80% reported being sexually aroused. As one young woman later told us, she found herself shockingly surprised by her behavior in the dark room. She was a devout Catholic and to be married the following month. Many volunteered to return for further research, without pay. In a contrasting study, we gathered different groups of participants in the same room, but this time fully lit. None of these intimacies occurred.

Critique and Coherence

We must now allow a space for critical voices to speak. For many, the vision of multi-being is not a congenial one. These voices of resistance deserve expression and a reply that will deepen understanding:

CRITIC 1: "Doesn't this picture of multi-being run counter to a deep sense that we are durable beings. Most of us are not chameleons? We are pretty much the same day in and out, and this is precisely why we have an enormous volume of research on basic

personality traits. If we were as unstable as you suggest,
you would scarcely find such reliable traits."

REPLY: This vision of multi-being doesn't argue against the fact that
our behavior is more or less predictable from day to day.
However, let us not suppose that it is some form of "true self,"
or a "core personality" buried deep within, that drives our
actions over time. Rather, look to relationships—both past and
present; all intelligible behavior finds its origins here. I am quite
at one with myself as a professor; my behavior as a professor has
been relatively consistent over the years. But at the age of 16,
to me, there was nothing more alien than the idea of sitting at a
desk for long hours. In this sense, my professorial personality is
neither indelible, like a birthmark, nor determinant, like a
computer program. Rather, it is a form of skilled action within
relationships. Outside the university, it is often irrelevant, and
can sometimes be debilitating.

CRITIC 2: "I still feel that I am a conscious decision-maker. I think
I am aware of many facets of myself, just as you have described.
But, as a conscious agent, I can also integrate many of these
parts; I can sift and sort and decide, for example, that I can bring
my humorous side into my work. Doesn't this exercise of
consciousness constitute a central, over-seeing self? Sartre called
it a 'transcendental ego,' but for me it is simply 'I myself.'"[26]

REPLY: This common consciousness of an "I" is surely compelling,
but the meaning we attach to it is a matter of longstanding
debate. While humanists attach deep significance to the "I,"
viewing it as the very of source of action, neuro-scientists
characterize it as a mere manifestation of underlying brain
functioning. For them, the truly important activity takes place
outside the realm of consciousness. The "I" is the last to know
(Chapter 4). For Lacanian psychoanalysts, the coherent "I" is an
illusion born within an early stage of child development.
The emphasis on relational being leads us in an entirely different
direction. Recall the proposal in Chapter 3, that the content of
my consciousness is an outgrowth of a relational history.
Experience becomes meaningful through relationship. Thus, for
example, when I am giving a lecture, I am drawing on a past
history of relationship in understanding what I am doing. My
consciousness may be fully absorbed in this activity. "I" and the

---

[26]For more on psychosysnthesis see Vargiu, J. (1974). Subpersonalities. *Synthesis*. Vol. I.
Redwood City, CA: Synthesis Press; Stone, H., and Winkelman, S. (1989). *Embracing ourselves:
Voice dialogue manual*. Novato, CA: Nataraj.

act of lecturing are one. However, if by chance I slip into a state of consciousness *about* my lecturing I am likely to stumble. (For example, while once lecturing to a large audience I felt my trousers slipping down my hips. I was shocked to find that I had forgotten to wear a belt!) To become self-conscious in this way is not to enter a state untouched by relationship, but to move from one state of relational being to another.

•

We are all composites of overlapping, multiple organizations and perspectives, and our experience is smoothed over by an illusory sense of continuity.

—Stephen A. Mitchell

•

CRITIC 3: "Yet, you are the conscious being who is aware of all this. As you just described, you over-see the fragments. It seems to me, then, that the previous critic has a point. Doesn't this over-seeing consciousness constitute a core self?"

REPLY: It is true that I did integrate the fragments within a single conscious moment. But even this act of integration was given birth within relationship. Because of my relational history, one of my potentials is that of integrating. In this sense, integration is optional; there are many alternatives. For example, I could have replaced this attempt to integrate the fragments by searching for oppositions, or exploring for complementary, ying/yang impulses. Every search for "myself" is from within some tradition of meaning. And most of the time, I am not searching at all.

Picturing Multi-Being

To appreciate the vision of multi-being developed here a visual metaphor may be useful. In the figure below, various relationships in a person's life are each represented by an oval. Imagine these ovals in terms of a continuous process of coordinated activity. From every relationship there emerges a residue or a resource in the form of potential actions (e.g. language, emotional expressions, scenario movements), any of which (alone or in combination), may be activated in the moment. The person is essentially constituted, then, by a multiplicity of relationships. Some relations leave residues that are well practiced, while others leave little but whispers of possibility. The well-practiced residues are immediately at hand, such as the way one speaks to casual friends. Often we call these habits; they may also

be viewed as skills. Those less practiced may seem—for a time—to be sham or play-acting. People engaged in a rich range of relationships, such as the cosmopolite, may carry an enormous range of potentials; the sheltered or the villager may have fewer potentials. We are equipped, then, to enter any relationship with myriad potentials for being.

•

The individual represents the common intersection
of myriad relationships.

•

As the figure suggests, these relational residues resemble the wing of a butterfly. This wing enables one to soar in many directions. However, like the butterfly, two wings are required for flight. The issue we now confront is the emergence of meaning/full co-action.

Coordination: The Challenge of Flight

Many child psychologists believe the capacity for human coordination is not only innate, but is manifest at an early age. Noteworthy is the work of

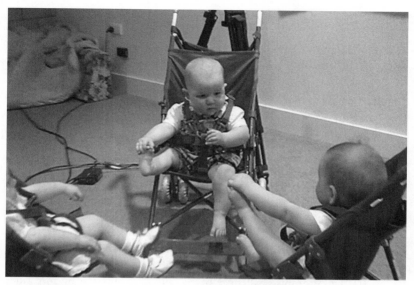

Infants under the age of one relating to each other in Benjamin Bradley's research.

Courtesy: Benjamin Bradley

Colin Trevarthan, whose classic studies of infant–mother interaction led him to conclude that, "examples of extremely close coordination of the infant's rudimentary vocalizations of pleasure or excitement with the baby talk of the mother are everywhere to be seen. Apparently, both partners are participating in a single rhythmical beat, as in music... ."[27]

Perhaps the most dramatic demonstration of this possibility is provided by Ben Bradley's research. Bradley and his colleagues observed babies interacting not with their mothers, but with other babies.[28] It is one thing for a child to coordinate with an adult who is already skilled in such matters. However, the question Bradley raises is whether infants can synchronize their actions with each other. And more challengingly, what if there

[27]Trevarthen, C. (1977). Descriptive analyses of infant communicative behaviour. In H. R. Schafer (Ed.) *Studies in mother-infant interaction*, p. 102. London: Academic Press. See also Stern, D. (1977). *The first relationship.* Cambridge: Harvard University Press; and Richards, M. P. M. (Ed.) (1974). *The integration of a child into a social world.* Cambridge: Cambridge University Press.

[28]Bradley, B. S. (2008). Early trios: Patterns of sound and movement in the genesis of meaning among infants in groups. In S. Malloch and C. B. Trevarthen (Eds.) *Communicative musicality.* Oxford: Oxford University Press. For accounts of the biological preparedness for imitation, see Meltzoff, A. N., and Prinz, W. (Eds.) (2002). *The imitative mind: Development, evolution, and brain bases.* Cambridge: Cambridge University Press.

are more than two individuals involved? To explore this possibility, conditions were arranged in which three infants of less than a year old were seated in close proximity to each other. As the researchers found, within a relatively short period of time there was a strong tendency within these trios for the infants to synchronize their actions. As Bradley concludes, "Babies are able to enter into relationships that betoken awareness of more than one other at the same time. In other words, by 9 months of age, there is evidence for a 'clan' or 'group' mentality in infants."

•

Yet, this vast potential for coordination supplies only a blank canvas, upon which an infinite range of pictures may be painted. All meaningful relationships depend on coordination, but there is no principled limit on the forms a relationship may take. Because the shape and direction of our lives depends on such coordination, it is important to explore the process in more detail. In the remainder of this chapter I will thus take up three major issues: (1) the common challenges of coordination, (2) the bumpy rides we may confront as relations unfold over time, and (3) the means of smoothing the ride and avoiding collision.

•

To appreciate the challenge of coordination, let us return to the butterfly wing. Here we add a second wing, one supplied by a second party. The question we confront is that of flight. Think here of a butterfly. How do we, as human beings who each bring with us an enormous range of potentials, take flight? And how can this flight become a thing of beauty? How can we avoid the degenerative pull to earth, and soar into the generative atmosphere of possibility? What are the resources, what are the impediments? In the discussion that follows, I begin with multi-being and the flowering of relationships. I then turn to the potentials for the suppression of potentials in relationship. Finally I take up some arts of productive coordination.

Meeting and Mutuality

The first step is simple enough, but the implications are substantial. In meeting for the first time, the central challenge is that of *generating viable scenarios*, that is, reliable sequences of relating. We must hit upon "the way we do it," our particular dance. In doing so, we establish a minimally predictable world. If we all spoke random utterances we would fail to communicate. We would not be participants in an intelligible world. The predictable scenario also breeds trust. We trust that others will "follow the

Relationships as challenges of flight.

rules" we have developed. As widely recognized, without the sense of trust there is little room for intimacy, family, organization, or community.

It is partly the demand for predictable worlds that breeds *scenarios of civility*. These are common patterns of coordination that can be used by all. Because they are not tailored to the specific identities of the participants, we view them as impersonal. Exchanging greetings, speaking of the weather, talking of the news, saying "please" and "thank you," are all scenarios of civility. We tend to view these patterns as superficial, but they are essential to a livable world. The simple exchange, "Hey, I think you left your car lights on,"…"Oh, thank you." is a vital signal that the social order is intact.

Beyond the scenarios of civility, are *context-specific scenarios*. These are the common patterns we find inside the corporation, the classroom, the courtroom, and so on. The rules of relating are clear enough and widely shared, but they are not easily transferable across contexts. Again, with continued practice in following the local rules, one may acquire a sense of authenticity. At the same time, as one moves across contexts, opposing actions may also feel "true to the core." One may feel truly oneself when engaged in work; the challenge seems to set all the vital juices flowing. Yet, on the weekend, indolent hours with a fishing rod may also seem to reveal the "natural me."

By sticking to the scenarios of civility, and those specific to our places of work, life glides by almost effortlessly. Alas, these scenarios draw so very little from our repertoires of being. So many voices are left unspoken. More challenging are situations marked by ambiguity. The common scenarios don't quite fit. Now the participants are thrust back on their resources. Together they create *hybrid scenarios*, novel forms of coordination of their very own. Here is the world of web-based dating, internet chat-rooms, new roommates at school, or the arrival of a fresh colleague at work. This is also the world of international meetings, family crises, and public calamities. Who will this person become for me; what shall I become; what shall our dance become?

•

Being young and painfully aware of my naiveté, I eagerly sought worldly experience. One particular hurdle to overcome was my virginity. My adolescent relations with girlfriends were quite idealistic, inclined toward Agape rather than Eros. But now I had met Marcy, who seemed sophisticated in ways I was not. She was a mistress of mystery and I was her servant. Late one evening we returned to her house. Her parents were asleep, and we had the living room to ourselves. Marcy lit candles, turned on a Mendelssohn concerto, and brought out wine and glasses. The lush sensuality of the occasion absorbed us both, and at a certain moment she pulled away and began to unbutton her blouse. She smiled coyly and told me that I too should "make myself comfortable." My heart began a thunderous performance. Was this finally to be my introduction into Life? I wanted to shout in anticipation. In the midst of our disrobing, however, Marcy paused and with an insouciant wink, inquired, "You are Jewish, aren't you?" I was dumbstruck.... "Well...uh... no...but...but..." My pause served as the sword upon which I was now to fall. Marcy swiftly began to dress herself, and soon the lights were on and I was expulsed into the night.

It is clear from this little slice of life, that neither Marcy nor I had ever quite played out this scenario before. It became a hybrid, all our own. Yet, if we break this novel sequence down, we realize that the hybrid was created out of recognizable sub-sequences. For example, we have here scenarios of romance, questions and answers, and ultimate rejection. In this sense, we drew from familiar residuals of past relationships to co-create the drama.

•

Depending on how we employ the resources, we may generate dramas of many kinds. Or not. Several years ago I attended a formal dinner party in Paris, during which I began to see an entire evening filled with talk about nothing in particular. I began to feel a creeping sense of boredom. We seemed doomed to repeat the endless litany of "what is appropriate to say." In a moment of small rebellion, I turned to the lovely stranger who had been seated to my right, and proposed that she play a little game with me. For 5 minutes we would exchange questions and answers. During this time we could ask each other any question we wished, and the other was required to answer it as truthfully as possible. She replied with mirthful agreement. "What fun this will be!" She had the first turn, and as she began to think through the implications, I could see her hesitation growing. After a number of uncompleted sentences, she finally admitted, "I don't think this is a good idea." I nodded, and we returned to the pleasant pastimes of our traditions.

·

Sometimes we meet someone and feel an instant sense of friendship; it's as if we have known each other forever. At other times there is immediate distaste; we yearn for an exit. We are inclined to explain such reactions in terms of personality traits. Some people are enchanting, others just plain dull and unlikable. Yet, from a relational standpoint, we draw the wrong conclusion. Our identity in a situation depends importantly on how we are positioned by others in the relationship.

Am I:

Witty	or	dull
Self-confident	or	self-doubting
Tasteful	or	slovenly
Assertive	or	obedient
Humble	or	dominant
Happy	or	sad

It depends importantly on the company I keep.[29]

·

To be sure, if we live for years within a circumscribed set of relationships, we may develop styles of action so familiar and constantly practiced that we lose flexibility. We will return to this issue in a later discussion of psychotherapy (Chapter 9). However, what we learn from this picture of multi-being is that our social surrounds do not determine us. We collaborate with others to create who we are. We are dealing here with social conventions,

[29]See Harré and Langenhove, *op cit.* Also see Althusser on the process of *interpellation.* Althusser, L. (1971). *"Lenin and philosophy" and other essays.* New York: Monthly Review Press.

not laws of nature. Thus, if someone gives me orders, I am not necessarily obedient; if someone treats me as sad, I may point to the silver lining. With significant support, a whole new array of potentials may flourish.

In many relations one's identity may shift rapidly. For example, because I am a professor I may be treated as an authority. However, I also realize that if I become authoritative, the other will be positioned as a listener. In effect, my authority will silence the other. So, I may reverse the authoritative role, and question the other about his or her ideas. Now the other is positioned as a knower, and I the learner. However, as I am listening, I am reminded of a funny story. I break in to share the story, and in doing so become a comedian. In turn, the other wants to share a funny story, and we both find ourselves now defined as friends. In effect, we flow without commanding order. We co-create our scenario, unsure of its ultimate direction, and in doing so the wings of multi-being may be spread.

•

> I sometimes fear that our abilities to generate hybrids are diminished
> during adulthood. As we grow into the accepted traditions of the
> culture, the range of hybridization becomes restricted. Life becomes
> more organized; regimentation is everywhere. When we were children
> "a cat" could variously become a lion, a monster, a baby, and much
> more. The mature adult knows that this is a cat, and nothing else.
> The rest is "merely play." When we say that children "develop,"
> are we subtly placing a value on the constricting life of adulthood?

Sustenance and Suppression

We have glimpsed the contribution of multi-being to the flowering of relationships. In principle, there is nothing within a relationship to prevent us from a full expression of our potentials for being. However, even with flexibility in convention, lasting relationships tend toward a freezing of potentials. Security, trust, and the sense of living in a meaningful world are all at stake. There is also the emerging sense of authenticity and the comfort of being known and accepted. These are sources for significant nourishment. In a sense, the movement toward reliable patterning functions as a powerful suppressive force.[30] The vast potentials we bring to the relationship are radically diminished. Most of the time we prefer to remain in character. It is simply easier to sustain the social order than to threaten it with

---

[30]As we converse we create a domain of the "not present," or that which we know but fail to make manifest. In this sense, conversation creates a form of the unconscious. See Billig, M. (1999). *op cit.*

boundary breaking expressions. It is dangerous for a business executive to reveal emotional vulnerabilities, for a professor to express ethnic prejudice, or a neighbor to reveal jealousy of your possessions. And consider the risks of coming out of the closet. Even in a close relationship, one's partner may bask in the phrase, "You are really beautiful," but not if one adds, "except for your teeth, your squeaky voice, your posture, and the way you jiggle your foot." We do not wish to hear the full chorus of all that can be said.

·

It is in this context we can better understand the emotional gravity attached to lying. We teach our children in no uncertain terms to tell the truth, and being the victim of lies can be traumatic. Lying effectively threatens the destruction of the settled world that has been established within a relationship. It is to remove the supports from under a shared reality, and thus the rationale for going on. One's identity becomes a sham. It is not the principle of honesty that is at stake in these circumstances. Most everyone will champion a lie told for good purposes (e.g. to save one's children from death). It is the shared order of reality and its accompanying way of life that is jeopardized.

A relational view of lying also opens new possibilities for action. The rage and remorse often resulting from lying are based on the mistaken presumption of a single reality and coherent selves. When we occupy an island of understanding, we tend to forget the surrounding ocean. We lose consciousness of the many relations of which we are a part. We treat the face before us as coherent and fully present. We feel we know each other; trust abounds. Lies become possible, however, when one is drawn to an alternative reality and wishes to keep it secret from someone who would be hurt or punished. In effect, the liar seeks to sustain two worlds of the real and the good. If a teenage child lies to you about where he spent his time after school, it is an attempt to sustain a positive relationship both with you and possibly his friends. "I was at Rebecca's" sustains the home reality of "I am a naïve little girl," and an opposing reality possibly shared with a boyfriend. Yes, when the bubble is burst, the result may be anguish—for all concerned. However, from a relational standpoint, this anguish is also a tribute to the relationship that has been violated. In anger, chagrin, and remorse, both the liar and the victim are proclaiming the value of their relationship. Herein lies an invitation to a new conversation.[31]

·

[31]For a more extended account of deceit within the context of relational realities, see Gergen, K. J. (1994). *Realities and relationships*. Cambridge: Harvard University Press. Chapter 12.

In spite of the comfort of remaining within circumscribed patterns of relationship, there are often strong urges for expanding the domain of potentials—of soaring with fully extended wings. In certain relationships, such as marriage or close friendships, a value is often placed on complete openness. The romantic ideal is to be completely transparent to the fullness of each other. Ideal love, we hold, requires complete knowledge of all the hidden recesses of each other. At other times the urge for expansion may be for reasons of ennui. Perfect order is perfectly boring. And too, it can be highly stressful to live in a private world that one's close associates might loathe. One may be haunted with guilt, or fearful of private desires. With self-revelation there may be relief.

Yet, these challenges to spreading the wings—of revealing the range of one's past and future potentials—also court danger. I recently read of a devout Buddhist, environmentalist, vegetarian who found, to his great surprise, that he loved guns. I know many people who strongly desire to smoke again. Thousands of men privately dress in women's clothing. How easily will those around them absorb their openness? I have also seen marriages destroyed over the revelation of an early affair, sibling relations undermined by differing choices of lifestyle, and a friendship between couples destroyed when one party revealed she had stolen the fur coat she was wearing. The challenge, then, is to locate ways in which we may sustain our nourishing ways of life without their becoming stagnant. How we can explore vistas of being without destroying the relational base from which we go forward? Such questions must be considered in the broader context of daily challenges.

Everyday Perils: Relations Among Relations

Thus far we have focused on the way relationships flourish, and begin to stabilize realities, values, and identities. Many relationships may remain locked within these predictable patterns for years, even a lifetime. Adults revisiting their elderly parents still find that they are treated as children, and friends uniting at their 50th high school anniversary often revert to adolescence. The phrase, "You haven't changed" doesn't simply refer to the body. Yet, this focus on stability is also blinding. It fails to take account of the tensions and conflicts that accompany any close relationship over time—with spouses, partners, children, sibs, and friends. Because we are participants in multiple relationships, both past and present, all actions in the moment may ripple across the range of engagement. And the repercussions may be embraced in some contexts and eschewed in others. From a relational standpoint such conflicts are not the result of defective persons, but are fully anticipated by our existence as multi-beings. Daily relations, then, may approximate small adventures in maneuvering the rapids of relational waters.

•

Picture a first-time mother and her newborn infant. Each arrives at this conjunction without a history together. Slowly and haltingly they begin to coordinate their actions with each other. They co-maneuver so that the infant soon draws nurturance from the mother's breast. From the further synchronizing of movement, gaze, facial expressions, and voice they create a meaningful world. Here we find an icon of harmonious coordination. It is also in these early months together that the mother and child are the closest to a relationship unlinked to other relationships.

•

Picture this same mother with her daughter, now a teenager. The mother serves dinner; her daughter is sullen and silent.

MOTHER: What's the matter, Trish? Aren't you hungry?
DAUGHTER: (silence)
MOTHER: Apparently you aren't talking either. What's the matter with you tonight?
DAUGHTER: (grimacing) Mom, I told you specifically last week that I really wanted to stop eating meat. Obviously you didn't listen to me, or...maybe you just don't care about what I want. Typical...
MOTHER: Now Trish, I just can't go about cooking separate meals for everyone in the family. And look, your father just loves pot roast, and your brother is gobbling it up. Why can't you just be part of the family?
DAUGHTER: You just don't understand me, do you? I'm just not going to eat this stuff, period. In fact, (getting up), I can't even stand to look at it. I'm just going to my room. (leaves the room)
FATHER: Trish, you come back here this instant!

(Trish slams the bedroom door shut.)

•

"Typical adolescent," one might say. But from a relational standpoint, problems never inhere in individual persons. The major difference between this scene and the mother with her newborn is that the mother and daughter are now each deeply immersed in relationships other than with each other. They bring to the dinner table not only the residues from long and numerous histories of relationship, but the more immediate residues of their relations with friends, family, and various media. They are fully embedded, relational beings.

The important point is this: When cut away from their networks of relationships, two individuals can create realities, rationalities, and values that remain unchallenged. Things simply are what they are; we do what we do; and it is good. It is when voices from elsewhere are imported into the immediate relationship that this shared world stands subject to reflection and rejection. One sees that things could be otherwise, this isn't as good as we thought, it could be better, it is offensive. When living in multiple relationships, disharmony lurks around every corner.

•

Many social scientists believe we can discover laws of human behavior. The hope is to generate universal principles from which people's actions can be predicted. Yet, in spite of almost a century's concerted search for reliable patterns, precious little support has been garnered. Even broad cultural patterns are subject to mercurial change. At least one major reason for the failure in prediction can be traced to the existence of multi-beings in relationship. We bring with us into relationships an enormous array of potentials, and the permutations and combinations approach infinity. Hybrids are always in the making.

This unpredictability can bring with it excitement and fascination. Herein lies the reason why many children vastly prefer playing with people than with toys. It is also a reason most adults seek to sustain an unpredict-able element in their close relationships. Novelty is no less important in relationship than in movies, art, or cooking. At the same time, it is precisely because of the fluctuating expressions and their combinatory potentials that relations are often fraught with anxiety, irritation, and conflict. Smoothly flowing coordination may be disrupted at any time with the entry of alien potentials. In the case of multi-being, for every expression there is likely a counter-expression available for action. In effect, we may view all relationships as an adventure, a journey in a vast sea of relations of which they are also a part. In the remainder of the chapter I want first to consider some of the significant shoals in this journey. Then we may take up maneuvers that make for more promising crossings.

Counter-Logics and Relational Deterioration

We may strive for harmony in relationships, but consider the chal-lenge: Because of our multiple histories of relationship, we carry with us multiple and conflicting potentials. Thus, parties in a relationship may share logics, values, or ways of being of which they are simultaneously critical. For example, both parties in a close relationship may embrace hard work, but simultaneously place value on leisure. In effect, there is a potential for conflict even for those who share traditions. I want to work; you want to play. Let us view these conflicts in terms of *counter-logics*. For any action that seems logical (rational, good), there is likely to be an oppositional action that is also logical. Each logic forms a compelling image of "ought"; the same may be said of its opposition. As we place one logic in motion, so can its opposition be called into presence. To embrace one is to invite its alter into action. And, because both logics are compelling, there is no "winning hand." Conflict is inherently insoluble. Once engaged in the battle of counter-logics, relationships often suffer and combatants may emerge with little but scars. Illustrative are the following:

> **Freedom versus Commitment**. In close relationships the most intense battles of logic often hinge on the issue of individual freedom versus commitment. The genesis of this battle can be traced to two different periods of Western history. In what is called the pre-modern period (roughly equated with medievalism), the dominant social unit was the group or collectivity. Most typical was the family, a super-ordinate unit that defined the individual participants in its terms. One's toils—regardless of age or gender—were for the family, and one could count on the family for lifetime support. All participants carried the family name, and one might sacrifice his life to protect or avenge the family. Strong and emotionally compelling logics insured commitment to this unit. In contrast, with the 17th century rise of modernism the individual began to replace the collectivity in significance. As outlined in Chapter 1, we now fall heir to several centuries of prizing the capacity of individuals to think for themselves, to find and develop themselves, and to follow their own star. These logics now reach out to us, to disturb and destroy:
>
> You owe it to the family.
>> I have to go; it's important to me.
> You aren't here when we need you.
>> I have so much to do.
> We have no time together.
>> You just don't understand my needs.
>
> •

We sometimes think of these logics as gendered, with the woman protecting the nest while the male features himself a rolling stone. There are good historical reasons for this being so, but as well, with the liberation of women and the championing of independent choice, we may be witnessing a shift in preferences. The major point, however, is that these are free-floating logics, available to anyone engaged in close relations, families, organizations, and so on.[32]

Competition versus Cooperation. Closely related to the conflict between freedom and commitment are contrasting investments in being "the best one can be," as opposed to being socially "cooperative." In the individualist tradition, with its pervasive hierarchies of individual merit, a strong value is placed on achievement, on "being number one," "being in control," "standing out." As an echo of the pre-modern value placed on the group, there are simultaneously good reasons to "work as a team," "cooperate on this," and "look out for each other." There is animosity toward the overly ambitious, the "tall poppies" among us. In organizations, such conflict is invited when "everyone should be a leader," and simultaneously "a good team-player."

Rationality versus Emotionality. With the rise of modernism and its prizing of individual reason, it became increasingly desirable to ground one's actions in "good reasons." Today, if we ask why someone acted as he or she did—for example, changed jobs, chose a vacation spot, left their school—we anticipate a compelling rationale. If the response was simply, "I don't know, I just felt like it," we would be puzzled. It is boneheaded, we say, to make choices without thinking. Countering this rhetoric of reason, we inherit from the romantic tradition a prizing of the emotions. We place enormous value on expressions of love, grief, and compassion; they seem to be emanations from deep within. To suppress our feelings is unhealthy, we say. And, we would distrust or despise such expressions if they were "calculated." Herein lies the basis for common conflict. Any action that seems wholly emotional—lavish gifts, strenuous expenditures of time and effort, self-sacrifice—may be discredited for its irrationality. "Don't you think of the cost?" "We are not made of money." "A dumb thing to do... ." Yet, the very criticism bespeaks a cold, calculating, and unfeeling personality. "All you care about is money." "Did they forget to give you a heart?" Such contests of rhetoric are particularly difficult because one can always claim that behind good reason there stirs an emotional urge, and beneath every emotion there is a subtle process of calculation.

•

---

[32] For an extended account of this counter-logic see, Bellah, R. N. et al. (1985). *op cit.*

These three counter-logics are widely pervasive in society, beckoning us all into degenerative relations. There are many others, perhaps less salient, but ready for instant deployment. To proclaim any of the following may rouse the opposition to action:

"I want..."	**"But what about..."**
Excitement	Tranquility
Having fun	Being responsible
Integrity	Getting along
Making more money	Living well enough
Solid traditions	Originality
Being in nature	Cultural life
Safety	Excitement
Progress	Sustainability

Movements in any of these directions may take place at any time. If I am in an extravagant mood, my mate may raise a voice of cautious frugality; if she suggests a quiet weekend, I may wilt at the anticipated loss of excitement; if invited for a weekend of camping I may begin to think of the fun of the city on a Saturday night; if I work late at night on a project, my mate may wonder why I can't take time off to enjoy ourselves together. Tradition serves up repertoires of conflict. And it is because the values are all so very reasonable—engrained in our sense of what is right—that they are dangerous.

Such conflicting impulses are not trouble signs in a relationship. On the contrary, any important relationship will necessarily harbor counter-logics. Vitality in a relationship may feed from the expression of multiple voices. The challenge is not that of eradicating conflict from our relationships, but of avoiding its debilitating effects. This is the topic of this final section.

The Arts of Coordination

In this chapter I have painted a picture of the person as a fountain of multiple potentials. As we join in coordination, so are these potentials brought into action, transformed, and suppressed. In effect, all relationships are potential adventures—replete with possibilities for expression, innovation, subterfuge, and conflict. In this final section we open discussion on navigating the rapids of relationship. Trajectories may lurch at any time from creative excitement to stabilized convention, and thence to alienation and outright hostility. Discussion of heated conflict will be postponed until the following chapter; more complex problems of relationship will be treated in a later discussion of therapeutic practice (Chapter 9). For now, however, it is useful to consider means of reducing the angle of lurch in most ongoing relationships. To be sure, there is no end of advice already available for improving relations. And, because the realities and values central to our relations are subject to continuous change, there are no final answers. What is unique to the present account is its concern, not with individual, but with relational well-being. Rather than treating the welfare of the bounded beings involved, we focus on the well-being of relationships. Here we touch on three contributions to sustaining productive coordination.

Understanding: Synchrony in Action

How do we move from conflict to mutual understanding? And why does understanding seem easy enough in general, but then disintegrate without warning? The answer to such questions depends importantly on what we mean by understanding each other? This is no small matter, as the long-standing vision of this process is one that links mind to mind. As long presumed, I understand you when I can apprehend the thoughts and feelings that lie behind your words and actions. Thus, an intimate relationship is one in which the participants share what's on their minds—their ideas, dreams, attitudes, memories, and emotions. We approach the understanding of written work in much the same way. We believe authors have "something on their minds," and that the written word will give us access to their thoughts. Sometimes we are frustrated that we don't understand what someone has written—in a poem, a legal brief, or a philosophic work. What is the author "trying to say" here?

As you can readily see, this view of understanding feeds from the tradition of bounded being, with minds secreted somewhere behind the eyeballs. Now recall the discussion in Chapter 3, in which we considered the problem that experts would confront in trying to determine "what's on someone's mind." As we found, there is no means of gaining access to others' psychological states. Ultimately one could do no more than guess. The accumulation of evidence in support of an interpretation would constitute no more than a multiplication of further guesses. Thus, if understanding were a process of inter-subjective connection, we would remain forever ignorant of each other.

•

Try not to think of understanding as a "mental process" at all—for *that* is the expression which confuses you. But ask yourself: In what sort of case, in what kind of circumstances, do we say, "Now I know how to go on."

—Ludwig Wittgenstein

•

Let us move then, from mental meetings, to relational action. Consider first the movements of skilled tango dancers. Each movement of the one is coordinated with the other; their actions are wholly synchronized. I propose that such synchronic coordination is the essence of understanding each other. If we meet, and you begin to tell me tearfully of the untimely death of a family member, how shall I respond? Let's say I reply with a hearty, "well, that's that...no sense crying over spilled milk. Hey, let's get a beer." Chances are you will be startled; how could I respond in this way? You thought I was your friend, and yet I seem to have no understanding at all of the importance of this loss to me. Now, contrast this with my responding with silence, and then some quiet words of consolation. In this case the chances are that you will sense my understanding. To understand each other is to coordinate our actions within the common scenarios of our culture.[33] A failure to understand is not a failure to grasp the essence of the other's feelings, but an inability to participate in the kind of scenario the other is inviting.

•

Friends recently invited us to an informal dinner. We gathered in the kitchen where the couple proceeded to prepare the meal. Their movements were transfixing. Both were highly active, but neither seemed responsible for any specific task. Sarah began dicing onions, but disappeared into the fridge to fetch mushrooms and carrots. Ben had been preparing a vinaigrette, but stopped to finish dicing the onions and placed them in a pan. Meanwhile, Sarah laid the mushrooms on the chopping board, and completed the vinaigrette. Ben began to dice the mushrooms. They continued this fluid interchange, scarcely speaking about it at all, until the meal was fully prepared. There were two cooks, but they moved as one—here was understanding in action.

•

We may speak here of *synchronic sensitivity*, that is a carefully tuned responsiveness to each other's actions. Each action flows smoothly from that which has preceded. It simultaneously provides an affirmation of what has passed, and an invitation to what follows. In effect, participants are maximally attuned to the way in which their movements are inter-twined. Individual actions are not so important in themselves as the way they contribute to the whole. Participants are focused on the relational process and its outcome.

[33]See also J. L. Austin's discussion of the "felicity conditions" for meaningful communication; Austin, J. L. (1962). *How to do things with words.* Oxford: Clarendon.

Consider the way in which synchronic sensitivity might function in a conversation.[34] In most conversations participants focus on content as opposed to process. What we are talking *about* takes precedence over the *way* we are talking. The result may sometimes lead to a rupture in relationship. When someone's comments carry content that is critical or insulting, we often fall into the familiar scenario of retaliation. Soon the relationship is in shards. With synchronic sensitivity, however, different questions are asked. "Why did it make sense for him to call me that?" "If I retaliate, how will he respond?" "What kind of relationship would be ideal for us?" "How can I respond to what he has said in a way that might move us toward this ideal?" Here a concern with process takes precedence over the specific content. Synchronic sensitivity requires a double-listening, to content on the one hand and to the relational trajectory on the other.

•

The critic stirs, "Well, I can see how this account of understanding might apply to face to face relationships. But I just don't see how this makes sense in terms of reading. When I am reading I am not synchronizing my actions with the words on the page. And when I am reading some heavy philosophy or complex poetry, I feel as if I am trying very hard to penetrate the mind or the intention of the author. How can it be otherwise?" Yes, I can resonate with this sense of trying to figure out what a complex piece of writing is trying to say. As students, perhaps all of us struggled when teachers requested that we write essays on the meaning of various novels or plays. How could we ever know if we were on the right track? And it does seem as if my mind is at work in trying to penetrate the mind of the writer. But again, let us move beyond this impossible vision of bounded beings. Rather, let us view *reading as a relational act.*

Consider first the way in which we learn to read. Someone listens—a parent or teacher—as we attempt to transform the written words before us to spoken sentences. As we convey the words to the other, he or she may accept or correct our performance. In effect, when we learn to read we are acquiring a social skill, not essentially different from learning to ride a bicycle or play the piano. Many adults continue to move their lips while reading, as if a listener were still present. Most of us no longer do so; we are engaged in a "partial performance" of a social action (see Chapter 3). As we grow older, and teachers ask us for our understanding of a complex text,

[34]The concern with synchrony in conversations is not a new one. See for example, Condon, W. S., and Ogston, W. D. (1971). Speech and body motion synchrony of the speaker-hearer. In D.L. Horton and J. J. Jenkins (Eds.) *Perception of language*. Columbus, OH: Charles E. Merrill. For the importance of synchrony in jazz ensembles, see Schogler, B. (1999–2000). Studying temporal co-ordination in Jazz duets. *Musicae Scientiae, 3* (Suppl.), 75–92.

they are not asking for a word-for-word reading. (Consider the reaction of a teacher who asks about your understanding of a poem and you simply repeated the poem.) Rather, we are being asked for a rendition of the text in a form that will be acceptable within a cultural scenario—and most particularly in the kind of scenario that are common to classrooms, and to the kinds of scenarios favored by the particular teacher. When we leave the classroom situation and find ourselves floundering in the complexity of a text, the question is not whether we can "get it right" about the author's state of mind. We should not mistake our failure for an author's brilliance. Rather, we are working to locate a means of distilling these words into a form that will enable us to participate successfully in conversation with others. Reading is altogether a social action.

•

Among my most sophisticated philosophic friends are those who find profound significance in Heidegger's complex work. I attended a dinner party some years ago for a group of largely positivist philosophers. After dinner the host took a volume of Heidegger's from the shelf and began to read, nor for profundity, but for entertainment. There ensued gales of laughter as the group demonstrated to each other the patent absurdity of the passages.

Affirmation: The Birth and Restoration of Collaboration

At the moment of my speaking, you become the midwife of my meaning. This is a critical moment in co-action; my potential to continue in the relationship vitally depends on your support. There are two major forms of supplement now possible, one that will *affirm* or invest the utterance with meaning, and the other that *denies* or empties it of significance. The former not only grants to me the status of a meaningful agent, but invests my words with value. Affirmation identifies the speaker as a worthy participant in the relationship. Negation denies the right to intelligibility. The affirming act may be as simple as a nod of the head, a smile, or an agreeable sound. But it may be pivotal in sustaining the relationship or in restoring harmony to a degenerating scenario.[35]

•

Consider: I reveal to you my fears in making a decision about a job offer. You reply, "That's really stupid; it's obvious what you have to do...." Your denial of my making sense now invites my alienation. By common convention, I might now deny the sense of your reply. "You didn't listen to me."

[35]See also, Hyde, M. J. (2005). *The life-giving gift of acknowledgement.* Lafayette, IN: Purdue University Press.

"You think things are so simple." However, I still have open to me affirming options:

"Well, I can see how you might say that…"
"Yes, from a certain standpoint that's a reasonable response…"
"It is nice someone can have such a clear vision…"

By affirming your utterance in this way I sustain our relationship, even if I go on to disagree.

•

The removal of affirmation is the end of identity.

•

The affirming voice is perhaps the easiest means of moving forward. In part this is so because we are multi-beings. We harbor multiple logics and values, even those we don't espouse. Every pro-life advocate can recite the rationale for pro-choice, and vice versa. Every pro gun enthusiast knows the arguments of the gun control activist, even if they would not be endorsed. We have, then, the means of locating an affirmative potential within many actions that might otherwise be alien.

Appreciative Exploration

At the same time, our multiple potentials do not render us omniscient. We frequently confront others' behavior that defies understanding. "How could anyone do that," we wonder. How stupid, cruel, how horrible…The daily news is replete with such jaw dropping accounts. For most Westerners, requiring women to mask their face in public is probably unthinkable; and I suspect many Arab Muslims similarly regard the depravity of the West. It is here that the logics of relational being become most useful. If we understand that all rationales and values originate within relationships, and are essential to sustaining these relationships, our options expand. We are not destined to remain ignorant, disgruntled, and possibly vengeful. In particularly, such conflict may also be used as a stimulus to curiosity. Like many people, I typically avoid talking with people who advocate "stupid" or "inhumane" positions. Likewise, I suspect they avoid talking with me. Yet, this is precisely the moment in which active inquiry into the other's realities is most needed. This is not a sneering search for the hidden foibles of their position, a gathering of ammunition for subsequent confrontation. Rather, the invitation is to explore the ways in which their positions are adequate to a tradition or form of life. In what sense do they make sense? Invited, then, are forms of appreciative exploration.

•

Critique and conflict have been common fixtures of my scholarly career. I have opposed theories and practices I have found wrong-headed, sterile, or inimical to human welfare. In turn, many have attacked me. Yet, a professional world of mutual antipathy is scarcely livable. In my experience, appreciative exploration has served as the single most powerful vehicle in securing relational well-being. Rather than singling out the problems inherent in a colleague's work (which I am altogether prepared to do), my best option is to express interest in what he or she is doing. "What ideas are turning you on these days," or "Tell me about your research," are openings to animated conversation. And, if I can focus fully on the accounts, I often find myself crawling into the logics, and indeed, appreciating the work from within this space. Bravo! Further, I often find that there are facets of such accounts that echo views in which I am invested. My sense of separation is diminished. Most fascinatingly, upon completion of such accounts, not only will my colleague make the same inquiry of me, but often listen with appreciation. Tensions remain, but affinities are also revealed.

•

The critic has waited patiently: "I find this all too cozy! In the throes of alienation, you champion synchrony, affirmation, and appreciation. But what about old-fashioned, honest disagreement, and criticism? What if I can't tolerate another's action; why shouldn't I speak up? What if I think someone is behaving irrationally; why shouldn't I drum some logic into their head? In your own words, these impulses are parts of my own multi-being. Why should I deny them expression?"

To respond, yes, to be sure, critical argument can make a valuable contribution to relationships. We scarcely want to lose the potentials of the critical voice. However, it is important to consider when and where it is productive or not, and in what ways. For example, critique can be especially useful when participants understand their "talk" as staged, that is, as a cultural performance in which they are playing roles. The roles may be formal, as in a debate; they may be professional, as in cases where I ask a colleague for critical comments; or they may be informal, as in the case of laughter-filled arguments after a meal. When there is sufficient trust, critique can be helpful. One wishes to know if his sweater is inside out, he is too fat, there is spinach in his teeth, or his fly is unzipped. However, in many contexts, critique is hazardous. This is partly owing to the individualist heritage in which critique functions as an attack on one's essence as a human being: one's ability to think. Many people tend to take critique "personally." There is brooding, antipathy, and retaliation. Time, place, and relationship are essential considerations between productive and destructive critique.

•

The conference takes place in Gerona, Spain; the hall is packed with scholars gathered to speak about the future of the social sciences. Unhappily I find that I am to be first on the stage. I have been trying for some time to avoid reading public talks. Not only are they potentially deadening in their effects on an audience, but alienating in their hiding any sign of human foibles. It is my hope to invite more humane forms of scholarly interchange. But in this case there are also a number of top philosophers in the audience, including the well-known Berkeley philosopher, John Searle. It is not an occasion on which I particularly wish to share my vulnerabilities. As I move into my talk, however, I notice Searle's foot tapping impatiently. I recall the dinner from the preceding night in which I overheard my wife talking with Searle. As I heard her exclaim, "If you think I'm crazy, just wait 'til you meet my husband." I anticipated the worst.

At the conclusion of the talk, my anticipation proved to be an underestimate. Searle's hand shot up, he was given the green light, and rather than asking a question he jumped from his seat and leapt to the stage. In a loud and surly voice, he proceeded to deliver a fusillade of criticism. At first I was stunned, but as I began to listen more carefully I began to feel there was more rhetoric here than reason. I mounted a reply, but as later informed by my colleagues, the content of our arguments was less memorable than the form: This was a bull-fight, and it was not yet finished.

Searle's presentation was scheduled on the final day. I lay in wait. When he had finished, my arm shot up, and I embarked on seven points of attack. Searle felt I should be limited to a single argument, and an acrid interchange followed. At the farewell banquet that afternoon, I avoided Searle. Life would be satisfactory for me if I never saw him again. But here he was, approaching me with a smile and his hand outstretched! "Well, Gergen," he bellowed, "we ought to take this show on the road. We could make a lot of money!" Ah, had I only shared this view of scholarship as entertainment.

•

These three arts of coordination—synchrony, affirmation, and appreciative exploration—scarcely exhaust the possibilities for passing successfully through the choppy waters of daily life. The attempt here has not been exhaustive. Rather, the hope is to generate the grounds for building an effective vocabulary for productive coordination. The door is open. The future challenge is to draw from our local vocabularies and share the resources.

6

Bonds, Barricades, and Beyond

"How could he do this to me?" I met David when I was nine years old. I was drawn by his imagination, wit, and curiosity, and we soon became fast friends. Afternoons and weekends were filled with each other and our "projects"—building a hidden village in the deep woods, dissecting crayfish, creating a museum of historical artifacts, and putting on a magic show for the neighbor children. We also had our naughty side—searching the *National Geographic* for bare breasted natives, scaring the wits out of the neighborhood children with firecrackers, and rolling tin cans under the wheels of passing cars. Our friendship was an enduring bond. Or so I thought.

One afternoon I learned from David's mother that he was at Jack's house, and I went to search him out. As I approached the shed in the rear of Jack's house, I overheard them laughing. As I drew closer and their banter became clear, I was dumbstruck. They were talking about ME, and David's wit was dissecting my every idiosyncrasy. Jack howled with each incision. I turned quietly and went home. If I weren't a *boy*, I would have cried. I never confronted David about the incident; in fact, I scarcely ever spoke with him again. Entering a new school and making new friends, I *almost* forgot him. It was only 30 years later that we were able to bridge the gulf between us.

•

As we coordinate words and actions, so do we enter a new register of relationship. We confront the possibility of creating bonds—most immediately of friendship, intimacy, marriage, family—and more extendedly with clubs, teams, communities, organizations, religions, and nations. Very often we build our lives around such relationships. Loyalty, solidarity, brotherhood, love, and commitment are cherished ideals. Many lives are sacrificed on their altars. Yet, the distressing irony is that these same significant relationships harbor powerful potentials for alienation, animosity, and mutual destruction.

In this chapter I take up the processes, potentials, and problems of bonding. I will first consider the question of origins: Why and how bonding occurs and why it does not. I will then focus on the collateral costs of cementing relationships. I will propose that every thrust toward bonding also generates dangerous barricades. In the pursuit of the ideal we lay the grounds for its destruction. It is in this context that I will take up the challenge of transformative dialogue—dialogue that moves across barriers of antipathy.

The Thrust Toward Bonding

If I were to give a quick account of my life, I suspect the milestones would carry the names of bonded relationships: My parents and brothers were there from the early years; there was David in my early adolescence; Thomas and "Greek" were my dearest friends through high school; college years were all about Mac and Gus and Merrell and Zack. And there were deep romances: Jean in my teens was to be "forever," Lenore was an exotic flower; Carol was all too perfect. And then came marriage and children, and a continued expansion of bonded relationships that remain vital today. These relationships have been the source of enormous joy, wonderment, pleasure, and fascination. Without them life would be gray pudding.[1]

•

Given the significance of such relationships, it is important to consider their source. Why is it that we become bonded to one another—or not? Of course, the answer to such a question might depend on what is meant by "bonding." Most frequently bonded relations are held to be those in which individuals are affectively fastened to one another. Such relations are said to be rewarding in themselves, and not means to some other end. It is

---

[1]For a useful survey of inquiry into the often devastating outcome of social rejection, see Leary, M. R. (Ed.) (2001). *Interpersonal rejection*. New York: Oxford University Press.

this lack of obvious reward that has also compelled scholars to search for an explanation for bonding. Much has been written about this question over the years, but I am not compelled by most of it. I do not believe that humans are "social animals," that is, genetically programmed to create herds, form friendships, fall in love, create families, or love their children.[2] There are far too many exceptions, including broken homes, broken friendships, broken love affairs, mothers who abandon their children, and individuals who prefer to live alone. Indeed in the industrialized world, the percentage of the population choosing to live alone is becoming the majority.

Nor do I wish to accept the more cynical view that bonding issues from a private form of rational calculus. As psychologists sometimes reason, love is the result of a profitable balance between the pleasure one derives from another, minus the costs.[3] It is not simply that such a view thrusts us once again into the individualist register. Rather, if we came to believe that profitability were the source of love I suspect that most would avoid such relationships; we would not wish to see another's commitment depend on the latest balance sheet of good deeds. As marriage vows attest, we wish for commitment through both sickness and health. Let us, then, consider the impetus toward bonding in relational terms.

Cementing Bonds

In the preceding chapter I treated issues of coordination in developing relationships. The question we now address is how these initial coordinations lead to bonding. Here we need to expand the account of relational process. Specifically, we must take into account at least three essential ingredients to the creation of bonds: negotiation, narration, and enchantment.

Negotiating the Real and the Good

We participate in myriad relationships; most are fleeting, periodic, or transient. Falling prey to our economic heritage, we say, "Little is

[2]See, for example, Baumeister, R. F., and Leary, M. R. (1995). The need to belong: Desire for interpersonal attachments as a fundamental human motivation. *Psychological Bulletin, 117*, 497–529; also Lawrence, P. R. and Nohria, N. (2002). *Driven, How human nature shapes our choices*. San Francisco: Jossey-Bass. The former is one of the most thorough reviews of the literature available. Interestingly, however, Baumeister and Leary conclude that, "It remains plausible (but unproved) that the need to belong is part of the human biological inheritance. ... At present, it seems fair to accept these hypotheses as tentative working assumptions while waiting for further evidence."

[3]See, for example, Hatfield, E., and Walster, G. W. (1978). *A new look at love*. Reading, MA: Addison-Wesley.

invested in them." In relational terms, what then constitutes an invested relationship? At least one central ingredient is the co-creation of a real and valued world. It is easy enough in a transient or superficial relationship to let silly or ignorant remarks slide by without comment. That's only "small talk," nothing important depends on it. What, then, is "big talk?" Consider: Mary and I are absolutely certain that this is "our house," "our dog," and "our family." We may talk with our Marxist friends about the evils of ownership, our psychiatrist friends about the dog as a surrogate child, or our humanist friends about the family of man. However, in the common rhythms of everyday life, our house, dog, and family are pillars of "the real," and failing to care for them would invite unrelenting guilt.

There is more: These valued realities are not something we simply talk about; they go hand in hand with everyday activity. We paint the rooms of our house, feed and walk the dog, and spend many nourishing hours with our children and grandchildren. The words and the activities give meaning to each other. Together they constitute what Wittgenstein would call a *form of life*. A form of life such as this may require years of negotiated language and action. As discussed in the preceding chapter, the result of establishing reliable realities, values, and action is a sense of trust. The world and its worth are in their proper place. The erosion of this reliable world invites a condition R. D. Laing described as *ontological insecurity*.[4] Its obliteration would leave us scarcely knowing how to go on. Ontological insecurity is at the doorstep when:

— Your sweetheart says, "I don't love you any more."
— Your favorite athlete is caught shaving points for money.
— Your priest is seducing altar boys.
— You find a revolver in your adolescent son's closet.
— Your affable neighbor is charged with murder.
— Someone close to you dies.[5]

•

In the contemporary world, secure realities are increasingly difficult to achieve. Technologies of communication—especially the internet and

[4]Laing, R. D. (1960). *The divided self: An existential study in sanity and madness.* Harmondsworth: Penguin. Laing's analysis is based on an individualist account of experience that emphasizes the importance of private experience. A relational analysis provides insight into the origin of such experiences.

[5]For an extensive treatment of processes by which meaningful worlds are reconstructed after the death of someone close to you, see Neimeyer, R. (2001). *Meaning reconstruction and the experience of loss.* Washington, DC: APA Books.

television—generate mercurial movements in meaning.[6] Daily we are exposed to a barrage of opinions, values, and rationalities. Traditions are everywhere questioned and defended; nothing important remains unchallenged. Consider, for example, the common reality of "the family." As developmental psychologist David Elkind notes, the traditional family in the United States prized the value of togetherness. It placed primary value on close relationships, loyalty, and love for each other; family commitments took precedence over relationships outside the family.[7] Yet, as Elkind proposes, this esteemed vision has undergone continuous erosion over recent decades. The once solid family is becoming permeable. The boundaries between the family and outside relationships are increasingly obscured; one's obligations to work, friendships, clubs, teams, and organizations often take precedence over the family. The demand for togetherness is replaced by fluidity and flexibility. There are also emerging alternatives to the nuclear family: single-parent households, gay and lesbian families, blended families, rainbow families, communal families, and so on.[8] Each alternative generates a different definition of what family life could or should be.[9] Virtually all traditional realities are now open to the shifting tides of meaning.

In sum, a first step toward bonding is the co-creation of shared realities, and the comfort, reliability, and trust that accompany them. In many respects, the contemporary erosion of secure realities may intensify the demand for bonding; indeed the threats to erosion may contribute to the growth of backlash fundamentalisms.

Narrative: From Self to Relationship

If asked about your past life, you might describe how you were brought up, attended school, experienced the dramas of success and failure, and so on. Indeed, most of us feel at times that we could write a fascinating autobiography. We could relate unique experiences—hilarious, secretive, tragic. As deeply personal as they are, however, these stories are not ours alone.

[6] See Friedman, T. (2005). *The world is flat.* New York: Farrar, Straus and Geroux. Also, see Gergen, K. J. (2001). *The saturated self* (2nd ed.), New York: Perseus, for an account of the impact of technology on the construction of meaning.

[7] Elkind, D. (1994). *Ties that stress, the new family imbalance.* Cambridge: Harvard University Press.

[8] See Chilman, C. S., Nunnally, E. W., and Cox, F. M. (Eds.) (1988). *Variant family forms, families in trouble series,* Vol. 5. Newbury Park, CA: Sage

[9] See also Skolnick, A. (1991). *Embattled paradise, the American family in an age of uncertainty.* New York: Basic Books; Reiss, D. (1981). *The family's construction of reality.* Cambridge: Harvard University Press.

Recall from Chapter 3 that in accounting for our past, we must follow the rules of story-telling, or narrative. If we wish to make sense of events across time, we have little choice but to join in this tradition.[10] So pervasive are narrative rules in self-understanding that Barbara Hardy proposes, "We dream in narrative, daydream in narrative, remember, anticipate, hope, despair, believe, doubt, plan, revise, criticize, construct, gossip, learn, hate, and love by narrative"[11] (p. 5).

Most important in the present context, the stories of our lives are intimately related to the process of bonding. Bonding requires a major transformation in the way we narrate the world. To elaborate, one of the most prominent facts about our narrative constructions of reality is the centrality of "I." In our accounts of our lives, it is the "I" who narrates, experiences, feels, decides, and so on. There is little of importance that is unrelated to this central character. "*I* was born in New York," one might say, "and then *my* parents moved to Cambridge, where *I* lived my childhood years. However, *my* most vivid memories began when *I* entered kindergarten...." This ego-centered world is scarcely a requirement of nature. As outlined in Chapter 1, it is the celebration of the *cogito* that we largely owe to the Enlightenment. The subsequent elaboration of the bounded being paved the way for the development of literary forms in which the "I" became central. It is to this heritage that we largely owe the development of the autobiography, the personal diary, and the individual protagonist of the novel.[12] Our ideology and our forms of writing often walk together.

Living our lives in the first person singular stands in the way of strong bonds. Self-narration essentially solidifies a boundary between self and other. We recognize each other as fundamentally embarked on separate journeys. In this case, bonding requires that we accept "unnatural" constraints on individual autonomy. Choosing to "go my own way" is seldom questioned. However, we may well wonder why a friend chose to marry, or join a religion. And, in replying to such questions the answer is typically in terms of some individual need, desire, or inadequacy. One desires children, wants security, needs to settle down, and so on. Or one chooses

[10]For more on narrative structure, see Gergen, K. J. (1994). *Realities and relationships*. Cambridge: Harvard University Press. Chapter 8.

[11]Hardy, B. (1968). *Towards a poetics of fiction: An approach through narrative. Novel, 2*, 5–14. See also Eakin, J. (1999). *How our lives become stories: Making selves*. Ithaca: Cornell University Press.

[12]McKeon, M. (2002). *The origins of the English novel, 1600–1740*. Baltimore: Johns Hopkins University Press; Porter, R. (Ed.) (1997). *Rewriting the self: Histories from the Renaissance to the present*. London: Routledge; Mathews, W. (1950). *British diaries: An annotated bibliography of British diaries written between 1442 and 1942*. Berkeley: University of California Press.

Here is the story of my life –
or at least of one life
The kind of life
Told by folks like us
The way we tell stories these days.
Some stories are good for laughs
Some stories are tear jerkers
Where would we be without our stories?
Where would I be without my story?

Courtesy: Regine Walter, Artist

for instrumental reasons. One marries so that she will bear *my* children; he will be a good breadwinner; she will make *me* happy; he gives *me* support.

•

Successful bonding calls for a transformation in narrative. The "I" as the center of the story must gradually be replaced by the "we." The "we" now becomes the major protagonist in the narrative of life, the central character to whom everything is related. In this context what may be called *unification myths* play a vital role. Such myths essentially depict the transformation from separate units into a whole. Exemplary are the stories couples tell about how they came together, found each other, and fell in love. There are also the stories of "how our band was formed," "our companies merged," the "nation was born," or "becoming one with Christ." Initiation rights, such as fraternity hazing and army boot camp, furnish the raw materials for unification myths, the coming into brotherhood or sisterhood. In the same way co-action gives rise to the reality of "I," so is coordination required to solidify the we.[13]

•

>   We are members one of another
>   ——Book of Ephesians

•

Narrating the *we* is seldom simple; always present and often competing is the reality of the *I*. What is good for our marriage may not be "what is good for me;" "devotion to our business" may conflict with "my personal needs," and "the success of the team" may mean "I cannot be a star." Such conflicts are endemic to life in the individualist tradition. Further, the definition of "what counts" as a marker of "we" is often ambiguous. Young singles are acutely aware of the problem of defining the *we*. Long vanished are the days when sexual relations served as clear markers of union. Such phrases as "hooking up," and "a friend with benefits" sever the equation of intercourse with bonding. Herein also lies the emptiness of the one-night stand. Such comments as "it was superficial," or "it didn't mean anything," is to say that it did not represent a movement toward bonding. The one-night stand thrives on a fantasy of communion, the death of which is often regret.

•

>   Mary and I were once asked independently to write autobiographies
>   for a volume featuring the life histories of narrative scholars. Yet,
>   we both had reservations about writing separately. This would
>   naturalize the assumption of bounded being. We thus invented a
>   *duography*, a narrative form that would replace the individual with
>   the relationship as its central protagonist. Giving birth to the form
>   was a challenge. We decided that for the first several pages we would
>   write in the first person. This allowed us to account for our lives
>   before meeting. We then generated a unification myth that described
>   our meeting and marriage. This enabled us to write the subsequent
>   story as "we." The challenge here was not easy, as we struggled
>   between relying on the discourses of "I" versus "we." At the

[13]There is an extensive literature on narratives of relationship, but it is almost exclusively concerned with the relationship among two otherwise independent beings. See, for example, Josselson, R., Lieblich, A., and McAdams, D. P. (Eds.) (2007). *The meaning of others: Narrative studies of relationships*. Washington, DC: APA Press. For more on narratives concerned with the unit of relationship, see Gergen, K. J., and Gergen, M. M. (1987). Narratives of relationship. In P. McGhee, D. Clarke, and R. Burnett (Eds.) *Accounting for relationships*. London: Methuen.

conclusion of the piece we worked toward an ultimate blurring of identities. We formed a dialogue between Me and You, neither of which had gendered identities. Thus, at one point, "Me" concludes a lengthy monologue on writing a life story with:

> ME: …the difference between the actual and the virtual is erased, and the very idea of a narrative trajectory—a life story—is subverted.
>
> YOU: (impatiently) "Whoa…hold on there. I'm still very much here."
>
> ME: "But then again, just who are you?"
>
> YOU: "You nut, I'm just *me*."
>
> ME: "But wait, that's who I am…I think we've got a problem. Maybe we should go somewhere to talk this over in private…[14]"

•

If bonding is to be sustained, the narrative achievement of "we" must be accompanied by relevant action. As commonly said, the participants must "walk the talk." The implicit rules for commitment to a relationship are varied and negotiable.[15] For many people, time is one of the most important demonstrations of bonding. Whether it is being on time or spending time together, one has a good measure of commitment. In the age of the cell phone, the measure may be the number of times one calls during periods of absence. In any case, narratives told must be accompanied by narratives lived.

The Enchanting of "We"

Building local realities and recognizing them as "ours" are important steps toward bonding. But a critical ingredient must be added: enchantment.[16] By this I mean the injection of value into the bonding unit. The unit of the partnership, the team, the club, or organization—has no value in itself. Means must be found of co-creating its worth, of injecting into its existence a sense of transcendent importance. Such enchantment goes beyond

---

[14]Gergen, K. J., and Gergen, M. M. (1994). Let's pretend: A duography. In D. J. Lee (Ed.) *Life and story, autobiographies for a narrative psychology.* Westport, CN: Praeger (p. 97).

[15]See also Erving Goffman's discussion of the implicit rules governing our ways of "being with" another person, Goffman, E. (2005). *Interaction rituals: Essays in face to face behavior* (2nd ed.). New York: Aldine.

[16]I am indebted here to Morris Berman's (1981) work, *The reenchantment of the world.* Ithaca: Cornell University Press.

the single entities making up the relationship. Traditionally we place value on specific persons: Carlos is wise, Anna is intelligent, Zack is cheerful, and so on. But when we place Carlos, Anna, and Zack on a work team together, a new domain of value can emerge, one that is not inherent in the individuals alone. It is the confluence that counts.

Enchantment can be invited in many ways. Surely language is a primary vehicle, most particularly the discourse of valuing. Relations thrive on creating their own significance. Such phrases as "we really click," "we are wonderful together," "this team is fantastic," "this school is the greatest" can be quite magical. Enchantment is also generated in rituals of celebration, such as wedding anniversaries, Bar Mitzvahs, centennial celebrations, and so on.

The Pilobolus Dance Troupe Enchants the "We".

Courtesy: John Kane

Small actions can also contribute to the aura, such as flowers set in a family room, a plate of cookies brought to the office, or a round of drinks purchased for a group of friends. The retelling of stories about "us" also touches them with significance. In all these ways, everyday banality can be gilded with the brush of the extraordinary.

•

A squeeze of the hand…a tiny gesture within the palm, a knee which doesn't move away, an arm extended, as if quite naturally, along the back of a sofa and against which the other's head gradually comes to rest—this is the paradisiacal realm of subtle and clandestine signs: a kind of festival not of the sense but of meaning.

—Roland Barthes

•

Interestingly, the enchantment process is frequently associated with emotional expression. At least in the West, emotional expressions go hand in hand with bonded relations. As we say, such relations "go deep," they involve displays of care and affection. "I love my family," we say, or "my team," or "my country." We delight when "our team" wins and suffer when they lose. We grieve at the death of someone close. It is tempting to think that such emotional expressions are natural reactions to such situations, but as advanced in Chapter 4, emotions are relational achievements. Or to put it otherwise, the link between bonding and emotions is an outcome of historically contingent construction.

In Western culture, at least one reason for the linkage between bonding and emotional expression issues from the traditional distinction between reason and emotion. We commonly associate reason with instrumental ends; we use our reason to gain rewards and avoid punishment. In contrast, the emotions are traditionally viewed as more primitive, biologically based responses. We must learn to think, it is said, but even infants have emotions. It is this traditional distinction that favors the dependency of bonding relations on emotional displays. To be emotionally involved indicates that the relationship is not the result of a reasoned act; it transcends instrumental assessment. It is a relationship that grows from more primitive, natural, and foundational origins. Thus the linkage between emotions and bonded relations is one of mutual definition. If we construct ourselves as bonded then we are emotional; if we are emotional, then we may conclude that we are bonded. To greet someone with exuberance is to signify a depth of relationship. To be indifferent at the death of a family member suggests a superficial connection.

•

In this context we can thus understand why business organizations struggle with the issue of enchantment. On the one hand, business itself is typically viewed as instrumental. The goal of business is to use powers of reasoning to turn a profit. There is little enchantment here, and indeed, businesses typically prize reasoned discussion while scorning strong displays of emotion. At the same time, businesses need members *dedicated* to the organization, who *care* about it, and *make sacrifices* for its success. To create enchantment a business may thus borrow the rhetoric of "family" or "team" to characterize itself. Yet, because individual participants are continuously being judged along instrumental lines ("what good are you to us?"), such efforts seem disingenuous. Members of a family are seldom eliminated for doing poorly.[17]

•

If the conditions are supportive, enchantment may take place rapidly. When a group is placed under threat, and their collective efforts are required for success or survival, mutual valuing may be rapid. The camaraderie of soldiers in battle is an obvious example. They rapidly become a "band of brothers." Athletic teams and community theater groups are also illustrative. As the vast number of reunions attest—sometimes occurring 50 years after disbanding—these effects may last for a lifetime. Enchantment may also take place without significant interchange. This is the plight of those "falling in love" before they are well acquainted. The aura is intense, but it is not embedded in their daily activities. Enchantment sprouts easily in Internet relations with unknown others. Participants can freely supplement each other's words in ways that amplify their emotional significance. Yet, such relations may be insufficiently embedded in the daily lives of the participants to generate a significant bond.

•

As I studied in my dormitory room at Yale, my pondering eyes often moved toward the window. There my unfocused gaze was occasionally interrupted by a figure moving about in an apartment house across the street. Normally such interruptions are momentary and unremarkable. But here was an exception, a young woman, exquisitely beautiful in face and body, wearing form-fitting clothing, and moving with grace. She was an Asian goddess! During study hours I found myself increasingly searching for her presence, and in her absence I was filled with longing. Then, one sunny Sunday

[17]See especially Smith, R. C., and Eisenberg, E. M. (1987). Conflict at Disneyland: A root-metaphor analysis. *Communication Monographs, 54*, 367–380.

afternoon, there she was lying on her couch. My imagination spun from the window, seeking entry into this sacred bower. Apparently, however, I was not alone in my reverie. A beam of light suddenly began to dance on the wall behind her couch. It was the sun's light reflected from a mirror held by another student in *my* dormitory. Soon there was a second dancing reflection on her wall. I sensed a shared intoxication. In the 15 following minutes there was a massive multiplication of dancing suitors. Her entire room pulsed with flashing lights. At last the princess acknowledged our collective attention. She sprang to her feet, opened the window, raised her arm, and shaking her fist, lustily cried out, "You Assholes!" The dancing lights were extinguished, and along with them the enchantment of a hundred young men.

Bonding and Boundaries

This is an auspicious moment to close the chapter. I have described a process through which we build the most significant relations of our lives, relations that are trusted, significant, and nourishing. And I have scanned several of the processes through which bonding is achieved. In effect, I have placed bonded relationships somewhere toward the center of what it is to live a meaningful life, and suggested routes toward its achievement. Now everyone can live happily ever after. Alas, the story has just begun and the road ahead is rocky. In many respects, the very source of worth, joy, and comfort—our bonded relationships—are also the source of enormous agony. Much of the world's bloodshed may be traced to their existence.

•

What are the grounds for such dark proposals? Here it is useful to consider again the thesis with which this volume began: As proposed, when we sustain a tradition that draws clear boundaries between self and other, there are many unfortunate consequences. Distrust, disregard, and mutual derogation are invited; injurious hierarchies of evaluation are encouraged, and the welfare of the self takes precedence over all others. In the preceding discussion we found that when deep bonds are formed, many of these problems recede. For the sake of the other and the relationship we begin to relinquish our individualist tendencies. The "we" takes precedence over the individual participants in the relationship.

However, once bonding is secured, there is an important sense in which the ravages of individualism once again return, and with a vengeance. Essentially, the process of bonding creates yet a new form of bounded entity. It is not "you" versus "me," but "us" now separated from "them." It is "my marriage," "my family," "my community," "my religion," "my country," and so on as opposed to theirs. The bonded relationship simply replaces one form of bounded being with another. This enlargement of bounded being not only opens a new range of hazards, but dangerously intensifies shortcomings inhering in the individualist tradition. In what follows I shall first take up the new threats to well-being, and then turn to the more lethal outcomes of bonded being.

Relational Severing

As outlined in the preceding chapter, we import into our relationships a vast array of potentials for action. All such potentials represent the residues of other relationships. In an important sense, we honor past relationships in all that we do. However, we also saw that as we enter new relationships, there is an accompanying tendency to eliminate certain potentials, to keep them in check. We stifle our impulses, "bite our tongue," tell "white lies," and so on to keep the relationship on an even course. Yet, each impulse that is suppressed is also a legacy from another relationship. In agreeing to "go with the group," we may also negate all those relationships from which a voice would say, "I don't think that's a good idea." In effect, commitment to the here and now of a relationship will tend to diminish the significance of all other relations of which one is a part.

•

> In every responsibility to a relationship lies irresponsibility to what lies beyond.
>
> —Bojun Hu

•

To be sure, it would be difficult to achieve good relations without a certain amount of suppression. However, suppression is highly intensified in the process of bonding. Here the stakes are high. "Are you with us or against us?" "Do we matter to you?" "Do you truly believe?" Such questions are emotionally laden, and one's answer can sometimes mean the difference between nurturing support and isolation, between life and death.

Consider the common rush to place labels on relationships. Are we friends, good friends, or best friends; is this a casual love affair or serious; are you a true friend, my best buddy, my soul mate, my partner, my ally, ...? We hasten to enclose our relationships in a box and place them on the shelf of trust. At least one good reason for this is that names secure actions. To agree on "the name of our relationship" is to ensure that we both abide by the informal rules attached to the name. Along with the

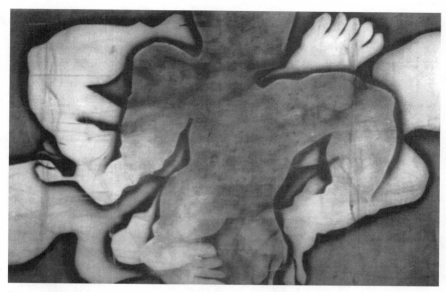

In naming you I build fences round your actions;
Your actions are the fences round my life.

In naming you our future is foreshadowed;
The names we share are the limits of our world.

If we do not name
There is infinite freedom—
But nothing to do.

Courtesy: Regine Walter, Artist

name comes an entire slate of rights and duties. In the labels for bonded relationships—"my family," "best friend," "team mate," "lover," "husband/wife" "partner"—the expectations are high. We anticipate dedication to the relationship. There is insurance that others will not destroy the private space of meaning we have created. By common standards, we do not reveal our secrets to those outside the relationship. We may enjoy analyzing those outside our relationship, but we tend to be careful about joining others in evaluating our relationship.

Thus the daily travails:

- Adolescent cliques whose participants spurn their classmates.
- Married couples who distance themselves from their in-laws.
- A mother–child relationship that is closed to the father.
- A young man whose conversion to a religious faith separates him from his family.
- A political liberal who cannot tolerate his brother's conservatism…

•

More broadly, consider the destructive consequences of political party bonding on national well-being. Out of commitment to "the party," Congressional representatives commonly sacrifice the interests of national welfare—health care, education, and social security.[18] More radically, this same lurch toward myopia within bonded groups is evident in the swindling of the public and their employees by corporate executives, and the suicide bombings of Muslims by other Muslims.

Erosion of the Interior: United We Fall

The uniformity required by bonded relationships does generate a safe, reliable, and nurturing space of being. At least for a time. The production of commitment within a relationship also has an ironic byproduct: internal division. Participants within the bonded relationship nurture seeds of their own alienation. Interior erosion has several sources:[19]

– All bonded groups create standards of good behavior, what it is to be committed to the group. Invariably, however, some participants will prove more adequate than others. Some will shine; others will struggle to meet even the minimal standards. "You were late today..." "You let us down..." "We sacrificed so much more than you...?" In effect, what amounts to a regime of righteousness emerges, where those close to perfection look with disfavor upon the blemished—and the reverse. Such resistances are common within school systems. As Willis concludes from his research on adolescence, the failure of lower class boys to live up to the imposed standards of the school, leads them to disparage those who do. The antipathy toward the "goody goods," reduces their aspirations and ultimately ensures they remain lower class.[20] Such divisiveness may also threaten marriages. Holding up standards of "the good marriage," one spouse may scold the other; in return, his or her mate may rebel at the oppression... "Why is that a crime?" "Marriage shouldn't be a prison." "I can't stand all this nagging."

[18]See also Trend, D. (1997). *Cultural democracy, politics, media, new technology*. Albany: State University of New York Press.

[19]In his theory of psychological reactance, Jack Brehm posits a universal reaction against restrictions in freedom. However, in the present account resistance is not a natural or genetically necessitated act, but one that finds its roots in relationship. See Brehm, J. (1966). *A theory of psychological reactance*. New York: Academic Press.

[20]Willis, P. (1977). *Learning to labour: How working class kids get working class jobs*. New York: Columbia University Press.

– A second source of division results from the suppression of the external relationships in which participants are engaged. For example, marital commitments will tend to threaten one's ties to friendship groups; commitments to an organization will often interfere with marriages, and so on. These are often significant relations, and when they are suppressed there may be resentment. Those who are shut out will often seek council with the now-bonded individual. Friends will chide their married buddy for his slavery to marriage; the spouse at home will inveigh against the business that steals away his/her partner's time; a friend will invite you to gossip about your other friends. As these "outside" voices are carried into the bonded relationship, they may form a source of disruptive critique. In every bonded relationship, the participants are members of a potentially dissident counter-culture.

– There is a third and more subtle stimulus to rebellion in bonded relationships. Whenever we are clear about what is valued, we create a potential world of that which is not valued.[21] A group that declares a belief in God also creates the intelligibility of non-belief; every scientific enclave defines a domain of non-science. Within the bonded relationship this negated world is typically treated as forbidden. The believer cannot simultaneously claim to be a non-believer. For example, the biologist who says that his research demonstrates the power of the holy spirit, or the business executive who reveals the flaws in the company's products, are likely to face the termination of their careers. At the same time, these forbidden worlds are intelligible to those within the bonded circle. This was the argument of multi-being. Thus, for participants in the bonded unit, the forbidden world is always potentially there at the edge of consciousness. When there are failures, irritations or disappointments in the bonded relationship, the door to the forbidden is at hand. In this way, stringent requirements in a marriage generate the intelligibility of infidelity, the orderly school establishes the possibility of vandalism, and so on. In all these ways, the thrust toward bonding carries the seeds of its undoing.

---

[21]The potential of affirmation to invite negation has a long scholarly history, to which the works of Kant, Hegel, and Saussure are significant contributions.

The Tyranny of Truth

In addition to inner frictions, strong bonds carry with them tendencies toward paralysis. I refer in particular to the satisfaction and desirability of "our way of life," behavior patterns that become so "natural" that we are virtually incapable of acting otherwise. Eating preferences are good examples. For many Westerners, breakfast without coffee would not be breakfast; steak with strawberry frosting would be intolerable. However, whether we are speaking of family life, organizations, or the classroom, we generate reliable patterns of relationship that resist disturbance. A son who takes his father's chair at dinner, a student who sits in the place of the teacher, and a janitor who occupies the chair of the CEO are all entering dangerous territories.[22] While such intolerance seems reasonable enough, it also encourages resistance to the external world. Capacities for coordination are diminished.

Normally our trusted patterns remain unchallenged; our lives are arranged so that we seldom stray from our zone of comfort. However, it is this kind of paralysis that is responsible for much of the antipathy separating ethnic, religious, and economic groups. *We* cannot stand the way *they* talk, the music they listen to, their slavish ways of worship, their silly clothes… Because of crystallized forms of relationship, our capacity to engage in productive coordination is disabled. It is far easier to remain snugly disdainful.

One of the most effective means of enchanting these comfortable patterns is to ally them with the discourse of Truth. To possess "the truth" is to be in touch with what is actually the case, beyond dispute. In the case of bonded groups, declarations of truth serve valuable functions. They first add enchantment to the group, anointing the "we who possess the truth." The U.S. Declaration of Independence unites the nation under the "self-evident truth" that "all men are created equal." Similarly, we variously treat with honor those who "speak truth to power," "proclaim the truth of God," "relentlessly seek the truth," or discover scientific truth. Claims to truth also invite trust in the realities that have been created within the relationship. For example, scientific reports on the effects of a particular treatment of cancer carry with them a promise to the scientific community. They attest that within the accepted traditions of the scientific community, the results are not fabricated, that they actually occurred. In the same way, religious groups may variously proclaim truth that Jesus was the Son of God,

---

[22]For a classic account of the incapacitating effects of the ordinary, see Garfinkel, H. (1965). *Studies in ethnomethodology*, New Jersey: Prentice Hall.

Muhammad the Prophet of God, and so on. Moreover, such declarations pay homage to the realities, rationalities, and values of a given tradition.

•

> Let us be committing ourselves to the truth, to see it like it is and to tell it like it is, to find the truth, to speak the truth and live with the truth.
>
> —Richard Nixon to the Republican Party

•

But let us examine further: Traditionally to speak "the truth" is to use words that accurately portray the world. It is to assume that somehow there is an array of words that is uniquely suited to the world as it is. Yet, as proposed in preceding chapters, the meaning of language is created through co-action; words come to mean whatever is congenial to those who are in relationship. Except for the demands of convention, we are free to employ any arrangement of words for any state of affairs. There is no privileged discourse of truth, except the privilege that is granted within a tradition. More will be said about this in later chapters on knowledge and education.

Thus, while the discourse of truth may unite a given community or tradition, its dangers begin when local certainty becomes global Truth. When "is true" leaps the boundaries of the tradition, the seeds of paralysis and antagonism are sown. What is true in one tradition may have little resemblance to what is true in another. Thus, for example, to accept the truth of science is to insulate one from the truth of religion;[23] to accept the truth of the Democrats is to render suspect the truth of the Republicans. To declare that "X is true" is effectively to silence all voices that speak otherwise, and thus to undermine the possibilities for collaborative action. The walls of tradition now become those of a prison.

From Erosion to Annihilation

Thus far I have touched on problems emerging from the bonding process. Relational suppression, internal subversion, and paralysis are all invited by close-knit relationships. Yet, there is another potential cost, possibly more

---

[23]The problem with the Christian embrace of intelligent design was not in the theory itself, but in its being championed as a scientific theory. Given the scientific tradition, the theory is of little merit. However, if one views intelligent design as a potential contributor to moral action in society, it is quite arguably superior to evolutionary theory.

dangerous to human well-being than these. Recall the ways in which the individualist invited alienation, competition, and disparagement of the other (Chapter 1). These tendencies are dramatically intensified in the case of bonded relations. Why is this so? In large part it is because bonded relations are extremely effective in creating, enchanting, and enforcing a singular account of the real and the good. Participants are in continuous communication, and through the co-active process give continuous support to "our way of life" and its attendant realities and values. Deviant voices are suppressed, and with them essential voices of doubt. In contrast, the lone individual may dwell in ambiguity. Because we are multi-beings, clarity of purpose is far more difficult to achieve. There is no one at hand to object, criticize or punish., Thus, for close-knit groups the boundaries of separation may be sturdy.

At this point we enter the familiar territory of inter-group hostility. As abundant research, and the death of millions attest, bonded groups of true believers are a potential danger to all those outside the boundary.[24] There is first the tendency toward self-congratulation. Whether we are speaking of couples, cliques, clubs, teams, organizations, religions, or nations, there are strong tendencies to create the reality of "we are better." With the glorification of *us*, there is an accompanying defamation of *them*. The invited result is mutual antipathy, physical avoidance, and the mutual creation of "the evil other." The path is now prepared for overt scorn, segregation, incarceration, and ultimately the obliteration of the undesirable. I am not speaking here only of the commonly recognized villainies—pogroms, invasions, genocides, terrorisms, and the like. Rather, I include here the walls that are every day erected around friendships, athletic teams, fraternities, communities, ethnicities, economic classes, political movements, religions, and nations. All may be cherished, but all harbor seeds of separation, defamation, and their sequelae.

> Prejudice, anger, and hatred are undesirable states primarily for
> the targets of scorn. For the actors they are sources of pleasure.
> There is comfort in disdain, delight in righteous indignation,
> and joy in eradicating the evil other. All are celebrations of
> bonded being.

[24]Illustrative of the many social science contributions to understanding inter-group hostility are Brewer, M. (2003). *Intergroup relations*. Buckingham: Open University Press; Ashmore, R. D., Jussim, L., and Wilder, D. (2001). *Social identity, intergroup conflict, and conflict reduction*. New York: Oxford University Press; Levy, S. R., and Melanie, K. (2008). *Intergroup attitudes and relations in childhood through adulthood*. New York: Oxford University Press.

Beyond the Barricades

We stand now at a critical juncture. The real, the rational, and the good are always in the making. And we are pleased when our efforts bring about the harmony, trust, satisfaction, and joy of bonded relationship. Yet, this same achievement of bonding also carries with it seeds of separation, self-eradication, antagonism, and mutual annihilation. In my view, there are forces at work today that dramatically increase the likelihood of global barricades and resultant bloodshed. Communication technologies increasingly permit otherwise scattered voices to locate each other, to unite, and to activate an agenda. For example, through radio and television a religious fundamentalist can find ideological and emotional support around the clock. Through the Internet a white supremacist can find dating and mating services to ensure a lifetime devotion to the cause. With cell phones and the Internet, terrorists may plan and execute global destruction. Banding and bonding are no longer limited geographically, and no circling of wagons can prevent alien intrusion.

I can scarcely offer a compelling slate of solutions to the emerging challenge. However, the vision of relational being does underscore the importance of one major resource: dialogue. If co-action is the source of inspiration and action within a group, this same resource can be mobilized to reduce conflict across groups. Yet, how is such dialogue to proceed? Parties in conflict are often loathe to speak with one another. After the president of a nation has branded other nations as an "axis of evil," how is dialogue possible? In the following section we take up this challenge from a relational perspective.

Hot Conflict and Transformative Dialogue

In later chapters we shall treat dialogic process within various professional contexts. Our concern here is with cases in which the borders of meaning have been sealed, visions of the evil other prevail, and the impulse toward mutual elimination is strong. Under such dangerous conditions, how do we go on? This is a vast and complex question, and my present aim is not synoptic. Rather, I wish to open discussion on peace building dialogue from a relational perspective.

As we inherit the problem of reducing conflict, the general consensus is that the primary gains are to be made through verbal interchange. There is wisdom in such investments, but to agree that "we must talk," sets a stage upon which a variety of dramas may play out. The possibilities are enormous and the outcomes can be disastrous. "Talking together" can also lead to exchanging blame, slander, and abuse; the barricades are only stren-thened. We must attend, then, to the forms of dialogue in use, to the scenarios of interchange and their outcomes. Scanning the existing terrain, we find four major orientations to dialogue:

Argumentation, in which participants try to convince one another of the acceptability or unacceptability of their position by means of compel-ling rhetoric. Primary examples include court proceedings, political deci-sion-making, and ethical debates.

Bargaining, in which parties to a conflict determine the costs and benefits of various outcomes, and negotiate trades to achieve the highest possible pay-off for themselves. Bargaining is most often used where there are intense conflicts in business or international relations.[25]

Negotiation, in which adversaries bargain, either to maximize their own gains or to locate a maximum joint reward. For example, in such best-sellers as *Getting to Yes* and *Getting Past No*, William Ury and Roger Fisher outline strategies by which parties generate "options for mutual gain."[26]

Mediation, in which participants traditionally depend on a neutral third party (the mediator) to intercede in resolving disputes. Mediation practices have ancient roots, and many contemporary variations. Divorce agreements are often settled through mediation, and increasing reliance is placed on mediators to settle legal disputes.

To be sure, all of these practices are preferable to mutually destructive combat, and all have a history of periodic success. However, there are also good reasons to press beyond the existing practices. First, each of these practices is premised on a conception of bounded being. That is, each presumes the existence of fundamentally independent parties, whether individuals, or groups. It is assumed that each party is driven by a desire for maximal gain and minimal loss. In addition, these traditional practices presume a fixed reality, one that is independent of co-active process. Money is money, and property is property. On the whole, traditional practices carry with them the sense that dialogue is essentially "war by other means." They sustain the reality of separation and ultimate conflict. Obscured are the potentials for restoring the relational flow.

•

[25]See, for example, Lebow, R. N. (1996). *The art of bargaining*. Baltimore, MD: Johns Hopkins University Press.

[26]Ury, W., Fisher, R., and Patton, B. (1991). *Getting to yes, Negotiating agreement without giving in* (Rev. 2nd ed.). New York: Penguin; Ury, W. (1993). *Getting past no: Negotiating your way from confrontation to cooperation*. New York: Bantam.

If it is necessary to share meaning and share truth, then we have to do something different.

—David Bohm

•

We are challenged, then, to explore forms of dialogue that do not carry with them the baggage of bounded being. Are there means of defusing hot conflict in such a way that boundaries are obscured, mutuality is revealed, multi-being is restored, and a consciousness of relational being encouraged? Here a range of recent developments is encouraging. Discontent with the capacities of large scale organizations to improve conditions of conflict, and a sense of urgency regarding the problems at hand, have stimulated various groups to forge new practices. Such practices are not generally dictated by philosophic background; they are often improvised reactions to hot conflict. While these newly emerging practices represent but fledgling steps, they do provide models of how we may re-direct the course of the future.[27]

I complete the present chapter, then, by briefly describing three of these innovative practices. I view them as contributions to what may be termed *transformative dialogue.* By this I mean forms of dialogue that attempt to cross the boundaries of meaning, that locate fissures in the taken-for-granted realities of the disputants, that restore the potentials for multi-being, and most importantly, that enable participants to generate a new and more promising domain of shared meaning. It is noteworthy that the included practices avoid headlong disputes over content. Rather than content, the chief emphasis is on the process of relational coordination. As these practices suggest, if the process of productive coordination can be achieved, commitments to content are softened. Softening the boundaries of meaning give ways to the development of new realities, rationalities, values, and practices.

The Public Conversations Project

In 1989, colleagues at the Public Conversations Project in Watertown, Massachusetts, began to apply skills developed in the context of family therapy to stalemated public controversies. Their practice has evolved over the years and with impressive results. Consider their attempt to bring together committed activists on opposing sides of the abortion conflict.

[27] For a more extended review of these developments see Bojer, M. M., Roehl, H., Knuth, M., and Magner, C. (2008). *Mapping dialogue, essential tools for social change.* Chagrin Falls, OH: Taos Institute Publications.

Here is a case in which debate has led nowhere, largely because the opponents construct reality and morality in entirely different ways. So fundamental are their disagreements about the "facts of the case," (e.g. what is a human being), and the values at stake (saving human life vs. human well-being), that none of the traditional forms of dialogue are very useful. Further, the stakes are high, there is enormous animosity, and the consequences can be lethal.

In the present case, activists who were willing to discuss the issues with their opponents were brought together in small groups. The Project guaranteed that they would not be required to participate in any activity they found uncomfortable. The meeting began with a buffet dinner, during which the participants were asked to share various aspects of their lives *other than* their stand on the abortion issue. As they talked about such matters as their children, jobs, neighborhoods, and the winnings of their local teams, the ground was prepared for transformative dialogue. One could see that what they shared in the way of realities and values was possibly more vast than the area of disagreement. After dinner the facilitator invited the participants into "a different kind of conversation." They were asked to speak as unique individuals about their personal experiences with abortion, to share their thoughts and feelings, and to ask questions about which they were curious. As the session unfolded, the participants were asked to respond— each in turn and without interruption—to three major questions:

1. How did you get involved with this issue? What's your personal relationship, or personal history with it?
2. Now we'd like to hear a little more about your particular beliefs and perspectives about the issues surrounding abortion. What is at the heart of the matter for you?
3. Many people we've talked to have told us that within their approach to this issue they find some gray areas, some dilemmas about their own beliefs, or even some conflicts ... Do you experience any pockets of uncertainty or lesser certainty, any concerns, value conflicts, or mixed feelings that you have and may wish to share?

Answers to the first two questions typically yielded a variety of personal experiences, often stories of great pain, loss, and suffering. Personal stories are far more successful means of crossing boundaries of meaning than arguing about abstract principles of morality. Personal stories invite the listener to imagine herself as the major protagonist of the adventure; the listener effectively becomes the actor. Participants also revealed many doubts, and found themselves surprised to learn that people on the other side had any uncertainties at all. In listening to the doubts, the participants heard those on the other side of the issue making statements that could lend support to their position. Again, boundaries of meaning were crossed.

After addressing the three questions, participants were given an opportunity to ask questions of each other. They were requested not to pose questions that "are challenges in disguise," but to ask questions "about which you are genuinely curious ... we'd like to learn about your own personal experiences and individual beliefs ... ." These discussions also served to illuminate the intelligibility of actions that were otherwise alien. Follow-up phone calls a few weeks after each session revealed lasting, positive effects. Participants felt they left with a more complex understanding of the struggle and a significantly re-humanized view of "the other." There was no apparent change in their fundamental views, but they no longer saw the issues in such black-and-white terms, nor those who disagreed as demons.[28]

Narrative Mediation

Practitioners have long sought means of settling disputes outside court. Bargaining and negotiation are frequent alternatives, but as noted, they continue to define the participants as bounded—fundamentally opposed, and seeking maximum self-gain. Mediation specialists have sought "kinder and gentler" ways of solving conflict, and in recent years have become sensitive to relational process. The most advanced of these practices is represented in narrative mediation.[29] At the outset, the narrative mediator understands that conflict is born within the co-active process. That is, people become antagonists largely because of the differing constructions of the world to which they are committed. They come with stories about how they are each deserving and the other is at fault. In effect, the conflict is between narrative constructions, and narratives can be transformed through dialogue. The mediator thus puts in motion forms of conversation that invite the parties to develop alternative and more mutually beneficial narratives. For example, disputants may be invited to speak about the conflict as if it were external to them, and getting in the way of their negotiations. They might come to say, "This problem is eating us up, *we* have to find a way to put it to rest." In this way they abandon the more familiar exercise of mutual blame (e.g. "This is all *your* fault."), and join together against a common threat.

[28]The work of the Public Conversations Project is indeed impressive and has led to many additional ventures and variants. See www.publicconversations.org.

[29]See Winslade, J., and Monk, G. (2001). *Narrative mediation.* San Francisco: Jossey-Bass.

Participants may also be asked to recall times in which their relations were successful. (e.g. "Tell me about a time when your relationship was working well.") In telling such stories the participants often find ways of praising each other, and realizing that their past relationship has been a valuable one. The result is not only a softening of the antagonism, but the generation of building material for constructing new narratives. The mediator may also invite others to participate—family, friends, and colleagues. Particularly helpful to the mediation process are people who have been hurt in some way by the conflict, people who are deeply invested in reaching resolution. They may spur the participants on, offering their support, and helping them to explore new ways of seeing each other and the situation. The outcome is the development of a new narrative or way of understanding the situation and the participants. Especially when this construction is shared by their family and friends, the conflict is replaced by productive coordination.[30]

•

We faced three days of collective hell. The conference had begun with a plenary session that was intended to contrast a social constructionist view of education with a cognitive constructivist view. To gain clarity on the differences, the planners arranged for a pair of plenary talks outlining the opposing positions. I was to take the constructionist position, and a revered colleague, Ernst von Glasersfeld, the constructivist. Further, however, two additional talks were invited, the first a critique of constructionism and the second a critique of constructivism. With the positions now polarized, the floor was open to the audience. Critical remarks soon gave way to hostile attacks, and these were followed by shouting and the waving of fists. Bedlam! How was the conference to proceed from there?

It did not. The planners had the good sense to postpone the formal program and to ask Karl Tomm, an eminent therapist present at the conference, to intercede. Tomm, as you may recall from the preceding discussion of multi-being, focuses on the voices of others we carry with us. On this occasion the conference audience watched as Tomm described a procedure in which he would first interview me role-playing Ernst, and then Ernst was to perform as me. Because we had known each other for many years, we could actually speak at length about our feelings for each other and each other's work.

[30]Closely related, is the work of the National Association for Community Mediation, which attempts to build networks of relationships to avoid destructive conflict between groups. See: www.nafcm.org

As this procedure began to make clear, von Glasersfeld and I were not independent and fundamentally antagonistic beings. Both of us carried each other with us. The results of the intervention were dramatic. Hostilities were terminated, and conferees attended the subsequent meetings with significant respect and curiosity for each other's work. Yes, there was continuing tensions between the positions, but these did not mean a termination of relationship.

Restorative Justice

In many situations of conflict—from domestic disputes and public assaults, to the abusive oppression of minorities—a system of justice will intervene. The system (including laws, police, courts, and prisons) functions to determine who has committed a crime, and to punish accordingly.[31] However, in terms of its impact on relational process, the justice system is significantly flawed. The ways in which imprisonment creates a culture of crime are well known. Less publicized, however, is the effect of imprisonment on the relationship between the criminal and his or her victim. Victims seldom have the satisfaction of an apology; offenders seldom have an opportunity to offer restitution. The relationship between the wrong-doer and those who have been wronged simply remains alienated, and the traditional scenario of apology, restitution, and forgiveness remains forever incomplete.

The international movement for restorative justice brings this relationship to the forefront, and generates dialogic means to achieve reconciliation.[32] Such dialogues are useful in many different contexts. Most obviously, they are used to bring about reconciliation between prisoners and those hurt by their crimes. Even for prisoners on death row, important healing can take place. They are also used in some communities as an alternative to standard judicial practices. For example, juvenile offenders may be brought face to face with victims of their crimes. In successful reconciliation, the participants locate alternatives to jail sentences. Such attempts have been especially important in nations such as South Africa, where massive segments of the population were brutalized for more than a century, and where the overturning of the government left deep residues of anger, fear, and guilt.

[31]I would like to replace "punish" with "correct" or "re-socialize" but such programs are increasingly rare.

[32]See for example, Umbreit, M. S., Vos, B., Coates, R. B., and Brown, K. A. (2003). *Facing violence: The path of restorative justice and dialogue.* Monsey, NY: Criminal Justice Press; Hopkins, B. (2005). *Just schools: A whole school approach to restorative justice.* Vancouver: University of British Columbia Press. Also see: http://www.restorativejustice.org/

Although there are many variations in practice, most attempts at restorative justice bring offenders and victims together to talk face to face. Victims typically have an opportunity to explain more fully their suffering, and offenders have an opportunity not only to explain their situation more fully, but to apologize and to offer means of repairing the harm. Steps are then taken to reintegrate both offenders and victims into the community. This process is most successful when family and friends participate in the dialogue. As in the case of narrative mediation, they lend vital support to the restoration and reintegration. In effect, successful restoration contributes to community vitality.

These three practices—public conversations, narrative mediation, and restorative justice—are only illustrative of the many creative developments in dialogic practice taking place today. It would have been equally illuminating to describe such initiatives as the Compassionate Listening Project, the Seeds for Peace Camp, the Deep Democracy Project, and dozens of other practices that now function around the world.[33] In my view, a broad and vital movement is taking place today. It is a movement concerned with the significance of dialogue in creating more promising futures. Receding is the emphasis on improving and strengthening individual entities— persons, organizations, or nations. Slowly we realize the preeminent significance of extended practices of relationship. My hope is that the next four chapters can illustrate the power and potential of this movement.

[33]See: www.compassionatelistening.org, www.seeds ofpeace.org, and www.democraticdialoguenetwork.

Three

Relational Being in Professional Practice

7

Knowledge as Co-Creation

It is one thing to realize the life-giving significance of relationship in our lives. It is another to give this insight a practical presence. For me this is the ultimate goal of this book—to stimulate transformation in our practices of living. My hope is that the vision of relational being can move beyond these pages to support, illustrate, and transform our lives together. It is to the flowering of relational practices in public institutions that the chapters in Part III are dedicated. In this chapter and the next, my concern is with the practices of establishing and disseminating knowledge. We shall move then to relational practices in therapy and organizational change. This will prepare us for Part IV, in which we take up issues in morality and spirituality.

•

Knowledge and *education* are the twin wonder-children of the Enlightenment. By the first we are set free from dogmas to secure a future of everlasting progress, and by the second we are to share the fruits of progress with future generations. Yet, as children of the Enlightenment, the concepts of knowledge and education are also wedded to the presumption of bounded being. In my view the result is indeed a rocky marriage in which the route both to progress and planetary well-being are impeded. Rather than freedom from dogma, we find claims to knowledge often functioning oppressively. Rather than progress, we often find degradation. In many respects, our traditional systems of education perpetuate and extend the effects. While I don't subscribe to utopias, I do believe that through a relational re-orientation of these concepts and the practices in which they are embedded, we can realize more fully the potentials for human and environmental well-being.

In this chapter and the next I shall consider both knowledge and education from a relational standpoint. In the present chapter, the traditional concept of knowledge is first placed under scrutiny. What are its shortcomings, and what is offered by a relational alternative? With this account in place, we are positioned to consider the practices of knowledge-making. Here I must be selective. However, given the concerns of the previous chapter with boundaries and barriers, I will focus on issues of division and relational recovery.

Knowledge as Communal Construction

We inherit a view of knowledge that is both individualist and realist. As commonly defined, knowledge is a "clear and certain perception of fact or truth." On this account we have the individual mind on the one side ("perception"), and the real world on the other ("fact"). Knowledge is attained when the mind accurately reflects or pictures the reality or truth of the world. In common parlance we ask, "Did *he* judge *it* accurately," "did *she* understand *him* correctly," or "is *his judgment* of *what happened* biased?" In most sciences we substitute various recording devices for direct experience (e.g. EKGs, photometers, radio telescopes, tachistoscopes), and we are more likely to ask, "does *this instrument* accurately record the *magnitude of the earthquake*," or "does *the EEG* indicate the presence of *a tumor*?" In the end, of course, it is the individual's reading of the measure that is at stake. In this sense, scientific measures are simply extensions or amplifications of individual experience.

•

In spite of its commonplace appeal, this separation of the knower from the known deposits enormous philosophical problems on our doorstep. From the ancient writings of Plato, through the Enlightenment attempts of Locke, Descartes, and Kant, and into the present-day philosophy of mind, no one has successfully solved these intellectual puzzles. For example, how are we justified in saying that people have "minds?" How could a mind know that it is a mind? And, if we are willing to say that we live within our minds, on what grounds are we justified in saying there is "a world *out there*?" How would we know what, if anything, exists outside of our own minds? And, if we simply suspend these problems as insoluble, we then face the difficulty of knowing how the "material stuff" of the world is related to the "mind stuff" inside our heads. Does the world-stuff stamp its impressions into the mind-stuff (e.g. Locke), or does the mind sift and sort to determine what exists out there (e.g. Kant)? And if the latter, then isn't it possible that no two people would experience the exact same world? And if people differ in what they perceive as the world, then who could we trust to rule on which is the correct perception? There is also the problem of brain structure. If what we perceive is limited by the structure and functioning of our nervous system, then aren't all our presumptions about the world ultimately byproducts of brain structure?

•

This is not the place for a blow-by-blow description of these philosophical debates. Problems in epistemology and the philosophy of mind have spanned centuries, and have yet to yield acceptable solutions. However, let us reflect: If these problems rest on the assumption of bounded being (the "knower" looking out to assess an independent world), then abandoning the assumption of boundedness may also eliminate these perennial conundrums. If the idea of bounded being is a construction that we have invented, then the philosophical problems of how mind and world are related are for the most part problems in discourse. They are not fundamental problems of human existence, but sophisticated games of language.[1]

•

It is to weakening the presumption of "the knower inside the head" to which earlier chapters of this work have been dedicated. As reasoned in Chapter 3, the idea of mind is born within relationship. That we speak of an "an inner world" at all—an originary source of action within the head, a "cogito" lying behind language—is a relational achievement. The discourse of the mind is not required by "what there is," but is derived from co-action.

The critic jumps in: "I can appreciate your arguments about the mind. Let's say for the moment that it is a human construction. But what about *the world*, that is, the "object" of knowledge? Doesn't the material world exist outside relationships? Surely you're not suggesting that there is no sun or moon, no rivers or trees, until there is relationship? And, isn't it true that with careful study we can know more about these? After all, we do know the world is not flat. And knowing this we can safely predict that ships at

[1]For more on epistemological problems as language games, see Rorty, R. (1979). *Philosophy and the mirror of nature*. Princeton: Princeton University Press.

sea will not fall off the edge of the world. Such knowledge is essential to our survival."

These are surely reasonable assertions, but let's look a little more closely. As I tried to make clear in early chapters, I may plausibly agree that "something exists" before co-action. But when we attempt to specify what this "something" is—animal, vegetable, or mineral—we draw from the resources of relationship. Depending on one's community we may call "this" a molecular composition, a female, a biological entity, a work of art, a child of god, an image in my head, or Mommie. However, outside *any* community of discourse, what would "this" be?

It is only when communal agreements are in place that we can begin to speak of knowledge. If we agree that "this" is a biological creature, we can compare its functioning and features with other such creatures. As a Mommie, we can know increasingly more about her practices of child rearing. If she is a child of god we can increase our knowledge of her spiritual condition. However, these are different kinds of knowledge, each issuing from a different community. Such knowledge clusters typically help such communities achieve goals they consider valuable. Thus, biological knowledge may be used to increase the lifespan of the organism. However, it is not particularly useful for knowing how to socialize your child or to live a virtuous life. In this sense, all forms of knowledge carry with them community values. To embrace the claims to knowledge is also to join the community.[2]

•

Let us then abandon the presumption of knowledge as a condition of individual minds in a privileged relationship to nature. Rather, let us view what we take to be *knowledge as an outcome of relational processes*. Through co-action people generate a world of the real. Within a tradition of relationship a particular discourse may be counted as "knowledge," certain people as "knowledgeable," and certain practices as "knowledge generating." Knowledge acquires its aura by virtue of its contribution to what is valued

---

[2]As Michel Foucault has argued, to embrace a given community's claims to knowledge is to become a "docile body," unthinkingly subject to the power this community. To accept biological knowledge, for example, would increase the hegemonic expansion of the biological definition of the human being (as opposed, let's say, to a humanistic or a spiritual view). On this account Foucault favors a general resistance to all knowledge-based institutions. The present account of knowledge is congenial with Foucault's view, except for the recommendation of general resistance. To resist all relational traditions would be to step outside meaning altogether, including the meaning of resistance. Resistance may properly be replaced with critically sensitive reflexivity. See Foucault, M. (1979). *Discipline and punish: The birth of the prison*. New York: Random House; and (1980). *Power/knowledge*. New York: Pantheon.

within the community. Western medical knowledge is not so much "true" as it is functional for those who share western beliefs and values. Western medicine represents *progress* primarily within this arena of consent.[3]

•

The scientist is an isolated individual, profoundly alone. Not evident in the picture are the props and crews that keep this man at center stage—his colleagues, his technicians, and graduate students, his secretaries and perhaps even his wife. Absent too are the patrons or politicians influencing the work.

—Linda Schiebinger

•

Approaching knowledge from a relational perspective, we can say goodbye to the thorny questions arising from mind/world dualism. We can also appreciate the many and varied claims to knowledge, for example, claims to empirical knowledge, intuitive knowledge, practical knowledge, spiritual knowledge, visual knowledge, musical knowledge, tacit knowledge, common sense knowledge, and so on. Further, we will find it unsurprising that the knowledge claims of one group may be discounted by another. We will understand that the reason the major universities of the land typically privilege empirical knowledge over artistic or athletic knowledge is not based on the intrinsic superiority of empirical research, but rather, it reflects the realities and values of particular people at a particular time in history.

•

What does a relational conception of knowledge mean for practices—scholarly, scientific, and educational? The potentials are enormous and the present account is necessarily selective. The remainder of the present chapter will amplify and extend the preceding chapter's discussion of bonds and barricades. I will focus in particular on three longstanding tendencies toward isolation and alienation in knowledge-making communities. These are cases in which traditional practices of research and writing break the flow of productive interchange, and contribute to corrosive conflict.

---

[3]This relational view of knowledge is now favored by broad-ranging scholarship demonstrating the dependency of scientific knowledge on communally shared discourse, practices, and values. Of particular significance is work in the history of science, the sociology of knowledge, social studies of science and technology, the rhetoric of science, and critical theory. For a summary of this work see Gergen, K. J. (1994). *Realities and relationships.* Cambridge: Harvard University Press; and (2009). *An invitation to social construction.* 2nd Edition, London: Sage.

First we take up the tendency for knowledge-making communities to isolate themselves, both from each other and the broader public. I will then turn to relations within these communities, with a particular focus on the alienating effects of traditional writing practices. In the third section I turn to the relationship of social science researchers to those they study. Here we find that traditional methods of study function as sources of alienation. In each case the challenge is that of developing more fully collaborative practices, forms of life in which relational well-being is the overarching goal.

Disturbing Disciplines

As I stroll about my campus I pass the biology building, then the engineering building, another structure that houses the English Department, and so on. Life within each of these edifices is comfortable enough. There are familiar colleagues, dedicated students, and computers that link the participants with colleagues around the world. Most important, there are shared assumptions about the nature of the world, and what is valuable to do. There is little need for visiting other departments; indeed, in many universities the distances between departmental buildings is so vast that one may never set foot in an alien territory. And, surrounding the entire complex is also a wall that protects the denizens from unwanted intruders. Sometimes the wall is perceptible—stone, brick, or steel mesh. However, the more important wall is invisible; it is erected within the practices that separate them from each other, higher learning from lower, and the university from the larger public.

•

The idea of separating disciplines of knowledge is significantly linked to the assumption of bounded being, and its emphasis on the mind as an accurate mirror of the world. From this standpoint, no one can observe everything at once. The task of accumulating knowledge must be distributed so that different observers can attend to different aspects of the world. Some may focus on growing plants, others on the firmament, others on economic practices, and so on. Each requires its own methodologies, logics, and instruments of measure. The ultimate attempt, as Stephen Toulmin points out, is the integration of all knowledge into an encompassing rationality.[4] In the meantime, however, it is important to nourish sophisticated specialties.

[4]Toulmin, S. (2001). *Return to reason.* Cambridge: Harvard University Press.

This is sound logic only if one accepts the traditional view that there are natural divisions in the world of nature, and that the description of these observations can yield a seamless theory of the whole. Yet, it is this very array of assumptions that is thrown into question by the argument for knowledge as co-creation. From a relational perspective, growing plants, the firmament, and the economy are not facts of nature; rather, they have come to be "objects of study" through one's relational participation. Through such participation these divisions became intelligible. Our departments of knowledge are not demanded by the contours of the world, but result from social agreements at a particular time in history in a particular culture. Likewise, these communal constructions of knowledge are not likely to converge. Given the disparate values and pragmatic ends to which these communities are committed, there is no reason to anticipate an integrated whole. In the world of the biologist, atoms play no role; for the atomic physicist there is no economic structure; for the economist there is no God. Indeed, from the perspective of any marginalized group, attempts at grand synthesis are dangerous. Inevitably, there will be silenced truths, a loss of pragmatic potential, and desecrated relationships.[5]

•

The question that demands attention, then, is whether the separation of disciplines serves humanity and its habitat in desirable ways. The obvious and most conventional answer is "yes." Biological study has led to forest management, physics has facilitated the development of atomic energy, demographic study has contributed to effective social policy, and so on. Such accomplishments were only possible through specialization. Yet, if knowledge is a relational achievement, we must be more cautious in our conclusion. The preceding discussion of bonds and barricades raises significant concerns about the impact of specialization. By dividing the world of knowledge into departments there are injurious consequences. Here I consider only four of the results.

Pervasive Antagonism

Departments are essentially constituted as competing species in a Darwinian world of survival. Laboratory space, new facilities, tenure track positions,

---

[5]This is also to call into question attempts to unify knowledge within or across disciplines, along with the coherence criterion of truth. It is to ask, in the case of E. O. Wilson's 1998 volume, *Consilience: The unity of knowledge* (New York: Knopf), who is carrying out such unification, with what assumptions, whose realities are absent from the overarching schema of knowledge, and on what grounds?

salary levels, teaching loads, and positions on top committees are all vital commodities. The game is zero-sum, with any department's gains representing losses for the remainder. The frequent result is acrimony, secrecy, anger, and humiliation. Department chairs step down, Deans lose their jobs, and faculty members quit in search of more welcome surrounds. Antagonistic tendencies may be found even within departments of knowledge. A professor of 20th-century literature is not likely to read journals on medieval literature, and should the department be asked to reduce the size of the teaching staff, suddenly the medievalists are potential threats. Departments have indeed been irrevocably split over such issues, and competing sides have moved to different locales on campus and taken different names. The goal is to see one's own area of study flourish; if others interfere or "rob" one of the potential, there is academic war.

•

Academic work ... is a heady mix of scholarly alienation and
disciplinary nationalism that shape the questions we ask and the way
in which we ask them. These scholarly values in turn foster—and
reward—alienation and aggression at all levels of academic life.
—David Damrosch

Discipline and Debilitation

The word "discipline" carries with it conflicting connotations. On the one hand we think of advances of knowledge as requiring the application of systematic, rigorous, and rational rules of conduct. Scorned are those who are "undisciplined" in their scholarship. It is through allegiance to a discipline that a community is formed, a position can be claimed within the universe of scholarship, and a defense mounted against any outsider who questions its adequacy. Further, by following the rules, the individual scholar is guaranteed the right to participate. Yet, the aura cast by this positive account of discipline is simultaneously accompanied by a less prominent view. Here discipline constitutes a form of suppression. Discipline functions to inflict punishment on those who fail to conform.[6] This latter view requires attention.

As I proposed in Chapter 5, when we develop common understandings within a group, we tend to limit what we can become. We enter academic institutions as multi-beings; we harbor many interests, talents, values, and ideas. However, because of common understandings within the

[6]See also, Foucault, *op cit.*

discipline, most of these are irrelevant or simply nuisances. In a broad sense, the effect of disciplining is the elimination of most of the potentials of its participants. An economist must be cautious in exploring literary theory; a physicist who turns to theology is suspect; a psychologist who fancies Marxist theory is looking for trouble. In disciplining there is a strong press toward eliminating all the voices of which one is capable, save one: the voice of the discipline. This not only means a loss of relationship between the discipline and the larger flow of relationships within the culture. It also means a closing down of the potentials of the discipline itself. To step outside the topics deemed worthy of study, the approved methods of research, the requirements for statistical support, the accepted forms of writing, the traditions of what may be said on the topic, or the proper channels of publication is to risk academic failure. Tenure decisions, salary, mobility, grant funds, and peer acceptance all hang in the balance. There are enormous forces at work to conserve the tradition.

•

It was jolly good fun. I was flushed with the romance of the experimental method in building laws of human social behavior, and my dexterous use of this core methodology had netted me my first academic position at Harvard. As Josh and I listened to the visiting speaker we soon began to exchange glances, then smirks, and then outright sniggering. The speaker had the audacity to rattle on about a phenomenon without a shred of empirical support! What arrogance; what silliness; how could he dare call himself a scientist? After the talk, we mimicked and satirized until we were rolling in laughter. I was a committed insider.

Because I had spent considerable time in "dabbling across disciplines" I also had some private doubts about this exuberant commitment. These doubts began to grow, and roughly a decade after rollicking with Josh, I shared these doubts with my colleagues in an article buried in the final pages of the discipline's flagship journal. I proposed, for one, that human social behavior was not fundamentally lawful, and that when apprised of the results of research, people might well change their behavior. This is especially true, I proposed, because when we psychologists label people's behavior as conformity, aggression, and prejudice, we are making value judgments. Thus, experimental research is not a neutral reading of universal patterns of conduct, but a form of social influence. And if we influence the culture, then we may undermine the very behavior under study. In effect, to teach about conformity, prejudice, obedience and the like could reduce people's tendencies to engage in these activities. The science of social psychology was not only recording history, I proposed, but changing it.

Publication of these views was akin to wounding a bull. Acrimonious defense was everywhere, and many wrote about a condition of crisis. The controversy continued until the flagship journal featured as its lead article a lengthy critique of my thesis, and thereupon refused to accept further debate. At the national meeting of experimental social psychology, the crisis was declared "over," and the field returned to business as usual. I was now an outsider.

•

If innovative scholarship is the outcome of hybridity, of impurity, or blurring the boundaries between disparate realms of reality, disciplining is its enemy. There is no "thinking outside the box" without risking banishment from the box.

The Elegant Sufficiency of Ignorance

When we presume that different forms of study are demanded by differences in the makeup of the world, the logic of dividing fields finds no limits. This is so because the world itself will place no limits on the divisions of knowledge; such divisions emerge from social interchange. Thus, knowledge-makers are forever free to declare a distinction in the world, develop a disciplining rationale, and create the institutional structures essential to continued flourishing. And, in a competitive market of scholarship, it is often more profitable to create a new discipline than to join the minions struggling for visibility in the old.[7] As disciplines divide, so there is a progressive diminution in what is important to know or care about. Sub-disciplines continue to multiply and domains of expertise are continuously narrowed. One may spend a lifetime of scholarship centered around a single text, event in history, or a particular species of bird. And there will be a small coterie of scholars for whom this cozy world is quite wonderful.

•

Kirsten was a graduate student in experimental psychology, assisting a senior researcher in the department. Their research focus was on language comprehension. In the summer Kirsten became curious

---

[7]Within the American Psychological Association there are currently 56 sub-divisions of knowledge.

about how scholars in literary study approached the problem understanding language. I suggested that she look to neighboring disciplines, and particularly the study of hermeneutics. For centuries hermeneutic scholars had hammered away at the challenging enigma of how we can reach valid conclusions in our interpretation of texts such as the Bible or early historical writing. For Kirsten the hermeneutic work wonderfully was illuminating. In the fall she addressed the professor's seminar on her summer's work. As she began to explain what she had learned, her professor broke in stonily: "Wait just a minute; who is this Herman guy? I don't think he's published anything in our field."

•

There are also risks for roaming. Scholars who are curious about another discipline are often viewed as alien interlopers by the denizens of the discipline. They are quickly dismissed for their failure in "truly grasping" the subject matter. Within their home disciplines the same scholars may be dismissed because their ideas are quirky or alien. For disciplinary defenders, the epithets "dilettante" and "dabbler" are ready at hand. Academic safety lies in knowing more and more about how to address an ever-smaller community of colleagues.

•

Monological forms of information produced in reductionistic disciplines are typically unconnected modes of knowledge alienated from other ways of knowing and being. An autistic epistemology is at work here that operates best when all parties work in isolation, within the closed boundaries of monolithic and self-sufficient disciplines.

—Joe. L. Kincheloe

Knowledge: For Whose Benefit?

Given tendencies toward the isolation of knowledge-making communities, we must again raise the question of "who benefits." This is a non-question for those within a community. Within a community there is a shared view of progress, and it is sufficient that one's work contributes to the shared goal. Within a discipline, the criteria of "what is worth doing" are robustly apparent. However, from a relational standpoint, benefits from *within* a given tradition are insufficient. More prominent is whether and to what extent knowledge-generating communities contribute to life outside their confines. The enormous investments in the sciences, for example, are lodged in the trust that there are broad benefits for society. Yet, as we develop isolated islands of meaning, so do the values of society become progressively muted. The traditional concepts of "pure knowledge" and "basic research" effectively dismiss the concerns of those beyond one's discipline. To embrace "pure knowledge" is to suggest that, "I don't know what you out there value, nor do I care." Simultaneously disparaged are those "impure" souls who truck in applied research. They merely follow the beck and call of industry or government, as opposed to following the higher path to pure knowledge.

•

This is not at all to discount the enormous contribution to society of research within the universities. For example, the contributions of chemistry to medical practice, of biology to sustaining undersea life, of physics to probing outer space, and of comparative literature to appreciating other cultures, of philosophy to deliberation on the human condition are laudable. Rather, the issues here are primarily those of priority and potential. If greater priority were placed on the contribution of research for the greater good, would the potential for societal contribution not be far greater?

•

For several years I served on the review panels of the National Science Foundation and the National Institute of Mental Health. The primary issues raised by those panels were whether the research methods were rigorous. Although applicants were required to add a section to their proposals on the contribution of the research to society, these were seldom read and never discussed. This was not viewed as a failure in oversight. Rather, everyone knew that the question of societal contribution was an afterthought, largely concocted as window dressing in the event of congressional curiosity.

•

A sample of PhD dissertation titles from Big Ten Universities in 2006:
- Dual electro/piezo property functionally graded piezocramics.
- Speaking beauties: Language use and linguistic ideologies in Tanzanian beauty pageants.
- Enhanced T lymphocyte function in young and old mice through changes in surface glycoproteins.
- Essays on optimal capacity and optimal regulation of interconnection infrastructures.
- Roots, rights and belonging: Garifuna indigenity and land rights on Honduras' north coast.

- Possible quantum behavior of classical Josephson junction arrays. But who is reading...

•

Confronted with this generalized disregard for the social good, the philosopher, Paul Feyerabend once proposed adding laypersons to granting panels.[8] If tax funds are largely used to support research in the universities, then taxation should be coupled to representation. I strongly concur in Feyerabend's recommendation.[9] In the meantime, I recommend to my colleagues a criterion of evaluation on which I have long relied: *the hairdresser test*. If I cannot make my research intelligible to the person cutting my hair in a way that sparks his or her curiosity, then I must reconsider its value.

•

As a cellist friend recently remarked, if their orchestra only played music composed after 1930, their audiences would be meager and the orchestra might collapse. Traditional symphonic music has broad appeal because of its roots with popular idioms. When composers in the 20th century began to experiment with music as a rationally based system, it ceased to speak meaningfully to anyone outside. Academic research confronts the same danger. When it ceases to be in dialogue with society more generally, the society will cease its support. State legislatures across the United States are often skeptical of the research contribution of their universities. Their skepticism leads them to ask why professors carry such small teaching loads. It also leads to meager allocation of tax funds to university education. For the public, there is also resentment over the billions spent on questionable explorations in space and atomic accelerators, while poverty, crime, and drug use remain unchecked.

Toward Transcending Disciplines

Communities of the like-minded are essential to generating knowledge of any kind. At the same time, we find a range of unfortunate consequences.

---

[8]Feyerabend, P. (1979). *Science in a free society.* London: Routledge.

[9]One might argue that such vetting is already carried out by Congress. However, from my experience there is little congressional oversight on specific matters of research content. Congressional interest is primarily piqued when speaking out on a given research initiative (e.g. stem cell research, cloning) can garner votes.

The development of disciplines erects barriers separating knowledge-making communities from each other and from the surrounding world. The result is antagonism, ignorance, a stifling of creativity, and a diminished contribution to general well-being. Yet, while these are common side-effects, they are not inevitable. Knowledge-making depends on discipline, but strong disciplining is neither essential nor welcoming of creative exploration. The challenge, then, is not to eliminate community, but to reduce the disciplinary stranglehold, and to blur the boundaries between the inside and the outside. From a relational standpoint, the goal is to replenish and enrich the free-flow of meaning. The presumption of permanent departments should give way to a view of community in continuous process of forming and dissolving as the dialogues of humanity move forward.

Such concerns are scarcely mine alone, and innovations are broadly apparent. It is in this context that we may draw inspiration from noteworthy attempts of forward-thinking scholars and administrators to challenge existing structures. I find myself attracted to the following four avenues of innovation.

Interweaving Disciplines

The problem of isolated disciplines has long been recognized, and the most common and conservative response is to require a broad or liberal education. Undergraduate students, in particular, are required to take courses over a broad spectrum. This form of "world tasting" does open new vistas for many students and prevents a premature freezing of interests. Yet, while a preparatory dip into multiple disciplines is required, it is not likely to make a difference once students enter the portals of a discipline. And too, this remedy relieves the teachers of responsibility for peering beyond the departmental doors. The disciplines themselves remain comfortably isolated.

More promising in their potential are inter-disciplinary or multi-disciplinary programs. I have been impressed with the growth of such programs of study over the years. They do seem to represent a growing consciousness of the problems just discussed. Virtually all colleges and universities now offer some means by which students can systematically combine work across two or more disciplines.[10] Yet, the vast share of such programs exists at the undergraduate level. Graduate programs are more fully invested in generating students who can contribute to the

---

[10]See also, the *Journal of Interdisciplinary Studies.*

respective disciplines. As noted by a committee of the National Academy of Science, "Despite the apparent benefits of [inter-disciplinary research] researchers interested in pursuing it often face daunting obstacles and disincentives."[11] To the extent that scholars are embedded within their disciplines, inter-disciplinary research has little promise. Disciplines can bestow value; inter-disciplines do not form a community in which achievements can be marked. Thus, while interdisciplinary programs may stimulate students to think about the connections among disciplines, there is no effort to inspire long-term professional investments.

•

My early experience teaching in a thoroughly inter-disciplinary program left me with both awe and disillusionment. The program was Harvard's Department of Social Relations. The Department, founded in 1946, combined the efforts of psychologists, anthropologists, and sociologists. Largely stimulated by Talcott Parson's integrative vision, there were hopes in the early years that the department could pave the way toward a fully integrated social science. By the time I took up my position there in 1964, this grand vision had succumbed. However, what did remain was a robust attempt to integrate the faculty in various teaching assignments. For me, as a new faculty member, the result was some of the most intellectually stimulating years I have ever experienced. For example, Thursday evening dinners took place at David Riesman's home. Riseman was nationally prominent for his sweeping work on contemporary cultural change. His popular course cut across virtually all the social science disciplines. On Thursday evening he met with eight of us, course assistants drawn from disparate fields, to discuss the major ideas to be addressed in the following week. There was also the legendary SocRel 120, a group dynamics course in which I participated with six other staff members, including a psychoanalyst and a statistician. Together with other jointly taught courses, these became aggregates of mutual stimulation and enlightenment.

Yet, when years later I departed for a teaching position at Swarthmore, the inter-disciplinary vitality at Harvard was beginning to wane. For the younger department members, the major alliances were not to the department's vision, but to their particular disciplines. This was scarcely surprising. It was their contribution to

[11]National Academy of Sciences (2005). *Facilitating interdisciplinary research* (p. 2). Washington: National Academy Press.

their disciplines on which depended their reputation, grant funds, research space, graduate assistants, and ability to publish. Within a few short years, these commitments brought the Department of Social Relations to an end. Disciplinary autonomy reigned again.

The Emerging Hybrids

Although departments of knowledge are social creations, once they are established as departments, strong survival motives are set in motion. On the one hand this means protecting one's traditions of study—including subject matter, methodology, and forms of expression. In spite of major changes in the global context, most departments of knowledge remain weighted by these traditions. Their practices were established long ago, and there is little room for challenges that fall outside the perimeter. And, as noted, there is also competition with other departments. Each demands its share of the economic pie. As a result, there is virtually no pie remaining for potential newcomers. In both respects, there is little room for new topics, concerns, or challenges to enter the establishment. If they do not fit within the established departments, they may go unaddressed. In a world where the speed of change is ever increasing, such resistance is debilitating.

•

Yet, there are promising signals of change. One source of change bears particular attention. A chief reason for the sustenance of isolated traditions can be traced to the inability of those within a discipline to subject its basic assumptions to critical assessment. One cannot question the logic of a discipline on its own terms. For example, you cannot sensibly question the validity of experimental evidence by using data from experiments. To question a discipline requires intellectual resources from outside the discipline itself. However, there is little pay-off in straying from one's discipline. As noted, to question the logics and practices of one's discipline invites the scorn of one's colleagues. Thus, disciplines seldom question their own premises, limits, or values.

It is in this context that we can appreciate the blooming of a new intellectual flower: *the scholarship of reflexive critique.* Its early roots may be traced to the philosophic writings of Kant and Hegel, and particularly the importance attached to negation and contradiction as opposed to harmony and unity. These concerns gained political significance in the 1930s, in the hands of talented philosophers and social researchers at the University of Frankfurt am Main.[12] Their aim was to advance Marxist thought and the

[12]For a review, see Wiggershaus, R. (1994). *The Frankfurt school: Its history, theories, and political significance.* Cambridge, Mass: MIT Press.

transformation of society. To do so required examining the contradictions inherent in both capitalism and its handmaiden, positivist science. While interest in the particular critiques of the "Frankfurt school" has diminished, their efforts did succeed in stimulating a new genre of scholarship. The genre, often called *critical study*, champions the process of critically reflecting on established doctrines and institutions. Through critical questioning of the taken for granted, it is reasoned, we are liberated from its grasp.

•

As the critical orientation takes root in the traditional disciplines, the results are catalytic. For example, critical theorists point to the Western biases that pervade anthropological research, find biology and physics rife with gender biases in their formulations and methods, challenge experimental psychology on the grounds of its individualist ideology, and so on. While such questioning seldom transforms the disciplines in question, it does create an atmosphere in which scholars are more cautious and sensitive in their claims.[13] And, as critically oriented scholars have united, new disciplines have begun to emerge. Feeling uncomfortable in their home discipline, critical scholars seek like-minded colleagues from across the disciplines, and with them, set out to create new forms of study. Thus, for example, we find the active development of women's studies, gender studies, African American studies, queer studies, and cultural studies. The critical impulse is also a uniting influence in many programs in film studies and rhetorical studies.

There is a second significant stimulus to hybridization of disciplines. It is economic in character. As the costs of university operations increase, and public funding withers, universities become threatened. They seek out new ways of generating income. Primary among them is the mounting of new programs of study, especially programs that can draw from professions that can pay full price. The radical expansion of business school programs is the most obvious exemplar. However, faculty members from across the disciplines are often challenged to generate new, income-producing programs of study. And, because such programs must appeal to the public market, they are typically linked to issues or topics not included in the traditional disciplines. Thus we find programs in dispute resolution, wildlife conservation, nanotechnology, evidence-based health care,

---

[13]There have also been vituperative reactions to such critique. One result is what we now in academia call the "science wars." See, for example, Gross, P., and Levitt, N. (1997). *Higher superstition: The academic left and its quarrels with science.* Baltimore, MD: The Johns Hopkins University Press; and Parsons, K. (Ed.) (2002). *The science wars: Debating scientific knowledge and technology.* Amherst: Prometheus.

software engineering, child care, advertising, construction management, sustainable development, globalization, climate change, tourism, labor studies, and more.[14] Further, because these are hybrid programs, they must necessarily draw from the multiple disciplines of the university. Increasingly, members of varied departments find themselves engaged in creative cross-talk. What can they draw from their respective disciplines that might generate a meaningful confluence? Traditional boundaries begin to evaporate.

•

I respond to these developments with both enthusiasm and reflective pause. I like to think that hybridization signals a major shift in the landscape of knowledge-making. With increasing frequency researchers may find ways to link their efforts to issues of global significance. However, there is also the danger in the tendency for hybrids to seek perpetual life. As they grow strong, they will also be attracted to visions of permanence. And here we have the building blocks for new walls of containment.[15] From a relational perspective, the ideal would be an open arena of participation, combined with organizational transience. That is, regardless of disciplinary background, scholars might at any time ally themselves with any knowledge-making group. At the same time, no enclave would have a permanent status. Peace studies, for example, might wax and wane with changes in the global context; new domains of study might be ushered in at any time (for example, global warming, inter-faith dialogue, nuclear proliferation, human rights), but not necessarily remain. Open intellectual exchange would be valued and curiosity stimulated, but without presumptions of permanence.

•

I have been inspired by my experience at Swarthmore College. Drawn by cutting edge issues in both the society and the academy, adventurous faculty members have sought ways to break from departments and form new alliances. They have sought like-minded colleagues from across the disciplines, and spearheaded the development of new programs of study. They have developed vibrant programs in such areas as black studies, environmental studies, film studies, cognitive science, media studies, interpretation theory,

[14]See also the Association for Integrative Studies (http://www.units.muohio.edu/aisorg/index.html).

[15]It is also in this sense that new programs such as women's studies, cultural studies, and queer studies run the risk of becoming ghettos, in which concerns of broad significance become limited to a beleaguered few.

peace and conflict, public policy, and women's studies. These programs are not housed within traditional departments. Indeed, they fall outside any of the existing departmental traditions. Nor are they intended to be permanent. They remain available to students as minor concentrations only so long as faculty and students remain enthusiastic. Members of different departments jointly teach many of the courses. I count my own experience in such courses as intellectual and pedagogical gems.

The Return of the Public Intellectual

In his book, *The Last Intellectuals*, Russell Jacoby documents the disappearance from the American cultural scene of scholars who can enter the public debates of the times.[16] Gone, for example, are Lionel Trilling, David Riesman, C. Wright Mills, Mary McCarthy, Daniel Bell, John Kenneth Galbraith, Lewis Mumford, Edmund Wilson, Betty Friedan, and Susan Sontag. Jacoby traces the disappearance of public scholars to the increasing specialization in the production of knowledge. Echoing the preceding discussion, he writes, "The professors share an idiom and a discipline. Gathering in annual conferences to compare notes, they constitute their own universe. A 'famous' sociologist or art historian means famous to other sociologists or art historians, not to anyone else. As intellectuals became academics, they had no need to write in a public prose; they did not, and finally they could not. (p. 7)"[17]

•

For several years Mary and I joined my brother David and his wife, Anne, to attend Renaissance Weekend in Hilton Head. These gatherings bring together over a thousand accomplished professionals, largely from politics, law, business, and the media, but includes as well a small number of scholars. During the weekend there are dozens of seminars offered by the attendees, largely on topics of their choosing, but typically related to issues of national significance. Lively dialogue prevails, with civility extended across professional and partisan lines. During these meetings I was particularly interested in the offerings of the academic contingent. How were they using their knowledge in speaking to issues of public

[16]New York: Basic books, 1987.
[17]For more on the travails of the public intellectual in the see Small, H. (Ed.) (2002). *The public intellectual.* Oxford: Blackwell; and Bowditch, A. (2006). *Public intellectuals: An endangered species.* Rowman and Littlefield.

concern? What forms of dialogue ensued? These experiences left me with two strong impressions. First, almost no one cared. That is, of all the seminars available, the academic offerings commanded the smallest audiences. Second, the dialogues were typically tense. The scholars seemed bent on establishing their authority, and the audience seemed caught between an inability to understand academic language and doubt regarding their own skills of expression.

•

Yet, there are movements of promise in motion. On the one hand, the insular disciplines have yielded up a spate of scholars who write effectively to the public about developments in their particular fields of study. There are widely popular books on such matters as the nature of time, brain and behavior, evolution, psychiatric disorders, the nature of happiness, and so on. Here the walls begin to crack…but insufficiently. Although these works do illuminate what are often engaging subjects within the academic sphere, they do not necessarily speak to issues of public origin. These scholars largely attempt to make their disciplinary work transparent to the public. The discipline comes first; the public should be educated. For Jacoby's generation, however, public concerns were often primary—issues of oppression, justice, genocide, ethics, and what it is to live a meaningful life. Academic knowledge was simply one input into the discussion. The public intellectual might thus relate history to current politics, personality study to organizational culture, technology to political domination, literary theory to physical illness, and so on. In these cases, the intellectual moves from a monological ("I know") to a dialogical position ("Let us explore.").

•

It is one of the paradoxes of our time that ideas capable of transforming our societies, full of insights about how the human animal actually behaves and thinks, are often presented in unreadable language.

—Doris Lessing

•

As the communal origins of knowledge have become increasingly clear, so has emerged a new group of scholars more fully immersed in issues of public concern. I believe Jacoby would find reason for celebration in various works of Edward Said, Noam Chomsky, Richard Rorty, Martha Nussbaum, Robert Bellah, Cornell West, Carol Gilligan, Stanley Fish, Robert Putnam, and Richard Sennett, among others. Many of these writers have been nurtured by the critical debates just described.[18] At the same time, their visibility has required the efforts of visionary administrators, adventurous publishers, supportive friends, and more. In the future we might hope to see academics in public office. Such is the case in many other nations of the world. Hollywood has been successful in generating highly influential politicians; should the groves of academe not be equally fruitful? Movements in this direction would benefit greatly by an inviting reward structure. Seldom are academics praised by their disciplines for public debate. It's as if a contribution to the greater society constitutes a loss for the discipline. College and university administrators may be the major key to the future. They are less captive to specific traditions, and have the capacity to establish meaningful incentives for scholars laboring for the public good.

Barricaded disciplines represent a difficult challenge to those who strive for more freely flowing and generative forms of relationship. More subtle in their alienating effects, however, are the forms of writing shared throughout much of the university. Let us explore.

Writing as Relationship

As I write these words I am not simply conveying content. I am also entering into a relationship with you the reader. As I select the topics, the genre of writing, the narrative, the metaphors, and the way in which I define myself as author, I invite a particular kind of relationship. If I write as an authority I will invite one kind of relationship; to cast myself as a humble explorer, will invite yet another. To rely on personal stories will create a different relationship than will abstract arguments. And so my writing could alienate, invite you closer, or even put you to sleep...horrors! Rhetoric and relationship walk hand in hand.

•

> Primary words do not signify things
> but intimate relations.
> —Martin Buber

•

[18]For more on the renewal of the public intellectual, see Michael, J. (2000). *Anxious intellects: Academic professionals, public intellectuals, and Enlightenment values.* Durham, NC: Duke University Press. For a critique of the current flowering of the public intellectual, see, Posner, R. A. (2003). *Public intellectuals: A study of decline.* Cambridge: Harvard University Press.

My concern here is in our traditions of scholarly writing. By and large, a scholar's success is determined by the quantity and quality of his or her writing. One's professional identity is primarily dependent on "contributions to the literature." If writing is also a way of creating relationships, we may rightfully ask about the relationships fostered by such efforts. In my view, our major traditions of scholarly writing contribute to a chilling ethos of alienation and antagonism both within the academy and between knowledge-makers and the public.

To appreciate how this is so, we must return again to the vision of bounded being, and the way in which this vision affects the character of academic writing. Above all, academic writing is prized to the extent that it is *well reasoned.* In terms of common convention, reasoning is the central ingredient of the mental world. Good writing, then, is equated with good thinking. But what is it to think or reason well? The answer depends, of course, on the myths we have constructed about the nature of effective thought. To appreciate the force of the traditional myth, consider some major criteria of excellence in scholarly writing: *verbal economy, logical coherence, clarity, dispassionate demeanor, comprehensiveness,* and *certainty.*[19] Such criteria can all be derived from a modernist construction of ideal reasoning. As Toulmin outlines, ideal reason in the modernist case, should approximate Euclidean mathematics and/or Newtonian physics.[20] When reason is given expression in writing, its quality should be judged on these criteria. And, to judge the writing is also to honor or condemn the mental capacity of the thinker.

This tradition places a heavy burden on the individual scholar. To step outside the accepted practices of writing is to risk being labeled, "a second rate mind." The pressure is not insubstantial: I have seen many colleagues write and rewrite a single manuscript a half dozen times, insecure in its acceptance as "well thought out." In contrast, to write without blemish is to display superior thought. To write without fault is a secular form of achieving purity of soul.

•

Consider, then, a single specimen of "excellence in writing" according to traditional criteria. As you read, consider the relationship with the author into which you are invited. This particular excerpt attempts to illuminate issues in moral responsibility:

> If it is A's job to Z, then his non-Z-in T (i.e. the fact that the relevant T contains some, different, X in place of Z) counts as an omission

[19]Although this account will be general in scope, the arguments play out quite differently across the various disciplines. Central to the present discussion is scholarship in the social sciences.
[20]*Op cit.*

even if it has no distinctive effects at all. Here the point lies just in the identification of the RRR: X-ing is identified as what was done at T instead of Z just because of the expectations on A, derived from his job.[21]

Putting aside its content, what are the effects of such writing on relationship? First, the author assumes the knowing position, with the reader cast into the position of ignorance. A hierarchy is thus implicit, with the reader cast as subservient. The flat formality also establishes a barrier. The reader is effectively informed, "I will reveal nothing personal to you, because ultimately, you mean little to me." Or more dramatically, "I am primarily interested in your admiration." Further, I am not invited to have a voice in the issues at hand. The logic is complete within itself; it strives to reach a conclusion that is so perfectly developed that the reader's admiration and sense of inferiority are sufficient to the day.[22]

•

It is not the metaphor of a "well wrought urn" that guides academic writing, but something more akin to the perfectly appointed gunboat—powerful in resources, flawless in operation, insistent on purpose, and beyond defeat by anyone.

•

Of course, few scholars are willing to be silenced and demeaned. They must defend their own rational powers. Thus, the primary response to most academic writing is critical; the challenge is to locate the hidden hand of unreason (unless there are ways one can use the writing to strengthen one's own position). When scholars publicly place their work before each other, they will often confront a phalanx of raised hands. The vast majority of these carry an invisible sword. This is academic life.[23] The primary result of most scholarly work, if it registers at all, is negation of relationship.

•

Is there a kind of violence at work in intellectual debates and discussions; in the university colloquium, seminar, or classroom; in academic texts? Is there something implicit in our very ways of

---

[21]Williams, B. (1995). *Making sense of humanity*. Cambridge: Cambridge University Press (p. 60).

[22]See also Pierre Bourdieu's discussion of symbolic capital, or the accumulation of honor, prestige, academic rewards and so on, that function as symbolic riches in the academic economy. Bourdieu, P. (1984). *Distinction: A social critique of the judgement of taste*. London: Routledge.

[23]See also, Krippendorf, K. (1993). Conversation or intellectual imperialism in comparing communication (theories). *Communication Theory*, 3, 252–266; and Tracy, K. (1996). *Colloquium: Dilemmas of academic discourse*. Greenwich, CT: Ablex.

relating ourselves to each other in academic life in present times that makes us fear each other? Is there something in our current circumstances that makes us (or at least some of us) anxious about owning certain of our own words, or taking a stand? Speaking from my own experience, I think there is.

—John Shotter

•

Consider as well the position of the writer. Typically an article published in journals in one's field will yield three reactions: First, a vast silence (most articles are read by only a fraction of one's colleagues); second, congratulations by those who are favored by the writing; and finally, critique. In effect, one enters a void of non-being. No one seems to care, and if they do, it is primarily in instrumental terms. You are liked if it helps them, chastised if you don't (or, if your work constitutes a target that allows them to gain publications through attack). The scholar confronts a condition of essential ambiguity: "Who am I, what is the value of what I do, is it all perhaps for nothing...?" There are few means of escaping the cocoon of isolation. Affirmation of one's scholarship may hang on the existence of a few close colleagues or students. They seldom recognize how significant they are. In graduate schools, senior professors will often surround themselves by an encampment of graduate students who confirm the significance of their activities together. The remainder of their colleagues are typically disinterested.

•

Public discourses of conflict, confrontation, and competition...
(have created) a culture of agonistic argument in which the university becomes more a war zone than a place of learning.

—Linda Hutcheon, MLA President

Writing in the Service of Relationship

In the current context of alienation, anxiety at professional meetings is especially acute. I know few scholars who are brave enough to present their work in anything less than written form; to stumble or falter would reveal less than perfect reasoning. I have indeed known colleagues who memorize entire papers for a 20-minute, one-time presentation at a scientific meeting. And of course, the somber drumming of text in monotone, soon has the audience either lost in fantasy or nodding off. Conference programs are replete with monologues that silence all but the speaker. The vitalizing communication is typically found in the hallways, the bars, and the dinner table—the venues of informal conversation.

•

> I recently overheard a senior colleague talking to a young scholar before their presentations at a professional conference. The senior colleague admitted to the junior, "You know, after 30 years in the profession, I am still nervous as hell before I read my paper."
> The junior colleague smiled and said, "Yeah, looking out on those serious faces gives me the creeps. I have been so freaked I paid $300 last summer for a coach to help calm me down before my talks." The senior colleague replied, "I suspect you are in good shape then." "No," said his protégé, "I'm petrified." "Thanks," said his superior, "you just saved me $300."

•

At least within the social sciences, I believe a sea change is taking place. As scholars become increasingly aware of the communal origins of knowledge, so are traditional "standards of scholarly and scientific writing" losing their aura. Traditional writing becomes simply, "one kind of writing," preferred by a certain group at certain times in history. There is no ultimately compelling reason to justify any form of writing. "Better reasoning" becomes simply "one kind of reasoning." Even rational coherence, a cornerstone of good writing, is suspect. As Jaques Derrida proposes, coherence is achieved only through the suppression of the fundamental ambiguity of all word meaning.[24] Given the divisive potentials of traditional writing, fresh alternatives are sought. Despite broad opposition, we find increasingly numerous experiments in expression. Scholars are increasingly willing to risk their careers to forge new ways of going on together. Here I consider only two significant departures and their relational implications.[25]

Writing as a Full Self

What if we abandon the formalisms of traditional academic writing, and attempt to "fully be there" for the reader? Here our writing might convey to the reader that "I am available to you, not as a partial, carefully

[24]Derrida, J. (1978). *Writing and difference.* (Trans. A. Bass.) Chicago: University of Chicago Press.
[25]For more extended discussion, see Gergen, K. J. (2007). Writing as relationship in academic culture. In M. Zachary and C. Thralls (Eds.) *Communicative practices in workplaces and the professions.* Amityville, NY: Baywood.

monitored façade, but as fully fragile and many-sided human being." Rather than positioning ourselves as fully rational agents, bounded, and superior, we might become more recognizably human and companionate. In contrast to the Enlightenment emphasis on transcendent reason, such writing could allow expression of desire, emotion, and bodily sensation.[26]

•

How, then, do we write ourselves into our texts with
intellectual and spiritual integrity? How do
we nurture our own voices, our own individualities,
and the same time lay claim to "knowing" something?
                                                —Laurel Richardson

•

Anthropologists are among the vanguard in humanizing their writings. In traditional ethnography the scientist reports on the lives of others (e.g. the Trobrianders, the Ifaluk, street gangs). However, the ethnographer as a person remains relatively obscure ("the silent, knowing one."). In the emerging experiments, the attempt is to remove the cloak of obscurity, and to write as a more fully embodied and culturally embedded researcher. The hope is to reveal oneself more fully in the work, as opposed to placing oneself in a god's eye position. To illustrate, consider Cleo Odzer's ethnographic study of the sex trade in the Pat Pong section of Bangkok.[27] To gain access to the site of study, Odzer became close friends with the prostitutes and their colleagues. At one point she became sexually involved with a young man who worked for a strip club. Here she depicts a few moments of their intimate life.

As I was about to fall asleep, he asked, "Do you get jealous easy?"
I wonder what he was thinking. "Yes, very."
"If we marry and I look at another woman, what do you do?"
"You wouldn't live long."
He laughed at the way I said that—"You don't have life a long time"
      —and repeated it a few times.
I pinched him. "Ow"
"Jeb luh" ("Hurts, huh?").
 "You don't have life a long time," he said again. "Very cutesy."

[26]See also, Sommer, R. (2006). Dual dissemination, Writing for colleagues and the public. *American Psychologist, 61*, 955–958; and Anderson, R. (2001). Embodied writing and reflections on embodiment. *Journal of Transpersonal Psychology, 33*, 83–99.
[27]Odzer, C. (1994). *Patpong sisters*. New York: Arcade.

"You're cutesy too" I said, putting my arm around his chest.

"What kind of man you like? Strong one?"

"Not with gross bulging muscles, no. Like you. Just like you."

"Oah!"

Big smile. Then he asked, "You like rich one? Thai woman only want
rich man. I think you find better man than me. You like man
with education."

*He did have a few points there. He wasn't exactly what I'd take home to
Momsy, but I said,* "No, no, you're perfect. There's no better
man. What kind of woman do you like? Beautiful one?"

"Beautiful not important. Someone with good heart."[28]

I feel very welcomed by this form of writing. As reader I am invited
to imagine myself as the writer, to live from inside her experience, to
feel and think *with* her and those "under study." The boundary between
us is diminished. Further, with the charged language of desire, jealousy,
fondness—I come to experience the writing not simply as an exercise in
reason, but as a fully embodied presence. And too, the sense of hierarchy
and competition induced by traditional writing is absent. Writing from
experience suggests a world of equality. We can all speak from our own
experience. Finally, with the admission of personal flaws, the posture of
authorial purity is abandoned.

•

To be able to dance with one's feet, with concepts with words: need I
still add that one must be able to do it with the pen too?

—Friedrich Nietzsche

•

Let us press the possibilities of personally present writing a little further.
There is a strong tendency in this genre to write as a singular person, open
and identifiable. Narrative writing of the above sort gives us the sense of a
knowable author. However, there remain here traces of the tradition of
bounded being, a sense of the author as a singular self, continuous and
unfragmented. Consider, in contrast, the earlier account of multi-being, of
persons embedded in a multiplicity of relations, and in possession of many
and conflicting ways of being. A more fully relational form of writing could
indeed reveal the facets of multi-being.

•

[28]p. 135, ibid.

I was first struck with the power of multiplicity in listening to a presentation by the social theorist Cornel West. His deft mixture of formal theory, middle class straight talk, and the argot of the black preacher was enthralling. Where one voice didn't reach me, another did. Rather than feeling that his words emanated from a singular being, somewhere inside, they seemed to reveal a history of relationship. In speaking he was giving me access to multiple traditions of which he was a part.

•

Michael Mulkay's 1985 volume, *The Word and the World*[29] was one of the earliest and most provocative adventures in writing as a multi-being. The work is particularly interesting, as it demonstrates how abstract theory can be rendered personal. For example, in the introductory chapter the voice of a querulous companion is interspersed throughout. The authoritative Mulkay speaks formally of "extending the range of analytical discourse to include forms not previously considered appropriate."[30] Mulkay as the impious interlocutor replies *"That sounds very attractive in principle, but it ignores the important distinction between fact and fiction..."*[31] Authoritative Mulkay goes on to explain to the interlocutor that even within science, "what is fact for one (scientist) is no more than fiction for the other." (p. 11)[32] His companion rebuts, *"Aren't we in danger of confusing two different meanings of fiction?"*... Later chapters include an exchange of correspondence between Mulkay, playing the role of department store magnates Marks and Spencer, and his role-playing a discussion among a group of inebriated participants at the Nobel Prize ceremonies.

•

I was recently privileged to participate in the examining committee of a PhD student, Catherine Maarie Amohia Love, from Massey University in New Zealand. Catherine's mother was British in origin, and her father was Maori. Her dissertation was on counseling practices used to assist the Maroi population.[33] Her particular concern was with the questionable use of British counseling practices with the Maori. Anglo assumptions about human behavior,

[29]London: George Allen and Unwin, 1985.
[30]Ibid, p. 10.
[31]Ibid, p. 10.
[32]Ibid, p. 11.
[33]Love, C. M. A. (1999). *Maori voices in the construction of indigenous models of counseling theory and practice. Unpublished doctoral dissertation.* Massey University.

she argued, were quite different than those shared by the Maori. Consequently the counseling practices were alien, clumsy, and counter-productive. Further, she reasoned, Anglo assumptions were also built into the writing practices embodied in the dissertation. Not only did the academic, Anglo language fail to speak to the Maori community, she argued, it functioned in a way that obliterated the indigenous traditions (for example, treating Maori metaphysics as so much folklore). Catherine thus developed an innovative and compelling form of writing. First, she introduced herself and much of the logic of the dissertation in what might be viewed as a personal style: direct, open, and passionate. At the same time there were large portions of the dissertation (marked by a particular font) that were written in traditional academic form. Yet, interspersed among these contrasting genres, Catherine also included sections written in a Maori–English style, a language often spoken among the Maori, but coded in such a way that it is opaque to those outside the tradition. At times the dissertation also demanded of her readers that they master a Maori vocabulary. Catherine wanted her family and friends to understand her writing. With each move in her identity as a writer, I was also invited to experience another facet of her complex network of relationships.

Scholarship as Performance

More radical in their departure from traditional forms of academic expression are adventures in performance. Traditional writing carries with it a hierarchical division, with the private and highly valued act of research given primacy over the secondary, social act of reporting the "findings." First it is important that "I know," and then it might also be helpful if "I would tell others." From the standpoint of relational being, we may properly reverse the hierarchy. That is, knowing comes into existence only through social participation. Acts of research only become intelligible and worth doing through a relationship that precedes the acts themselves. In effect, "I speak with others, and therefore I can know."

For many scholars this means that "speaking with others" takes precedence over research. As they reason, when we come into new ways of speaking, understandings are altered and new forms of action invited. Yet, academic discourse typically fails to be intelligible or commanding to anyone who is not a member of the academic guild. As often said, it is "elitist" in character. Rather, if the scholar wishes to reach a general audience, it is essential to expand the range of expression. From this standpoint, virtually all forms of human expression now register as possibilities: poetry, music, dance, theater, multi-media, and more. The scholar may draw from all the potentials of multi-being to explore useful forms of engagement.

•

> I tell stories about my life in order to illuminate the stories which form our culture—the stories by which we organize ourselves, often without really knowing it. These are stories about the human experience, told from the perspective of a woman, a parent, and a queer... .We have to be able to relate to one another before our culturally patterned circumstances become real to us. When we see ourselves and each other in the complexity of our experiences, we start to see how we fit together—who has privilege, who is oppressed or marginalized, who seems worthy of love.
> —Kimberly Dark, Artist/Activist

•

Such options are not wholly new to the academic scene. Anthropologists and sociologists have long used photography to supplement their verbal texts.[34] However, as professional photographers expanded their view of photography as an art, to include photography as political commentary, new vistas of social science expression have opened.[35] The work of independent filmmakers has also been important in stimulating academic expression. Central to many has been the inspiring work of documentary filmmaker Fred Wiseman. His depiction of the dehumanizing effects of bureaucracy, in such films as *Titicut Follies, Juvenile Court,* and *High School,* paved the way for socially conscious academics to experiment in film expression. Jennie Livingston's work is exemplary. Livingston received her PhD from Cornell University. Her early film, *Paris is Burning,* is essentially a documentary depiction of the competitive "balls" staged by impoverished gay and transgendered blacks and Latinos in New York. The enormous success of this film helped to launch Livingston's career as a commercial filmmaker.

•

If photography and film, then why not poetry and music? As these questions are asked the repertoire of possibilities expands. For example, here is

[34]In sociology, see the journal, *Visual Studies* (London: Routledge), and in anthropology, the *Visual Anthropology Review* (Berkeley, CA: University of California Press).
[35]See, for example, Hall, J. R., Becker, L. T., and Stimson, B. (Eds.) (2006). *Visual worlds.* London: Routledge; Pink, S. (2001). *Doing visual ethnography: Images, media and representation in research.* London: Sage.

an excerpt from a poem, co-constructed by Deborah Austin (a researcher) and a participant in the Million Man March of African Americans in Washington, DC:[36]

> Africans are the same
> wherever we are, she says to me
> matter-of-factly
> I look at her and smile
> and ask
> like a good researcher should
> How so?
> I can't explain, she says
> with that voice that sounds
> like the rush of many rivers.

•

Music also becomes a relevant medium of expression. For example, feminist scholar Glenda Russell was chagrined by the passage of Amendment 2 to the Colorado State Constitution. The amendment effectively removed legal rights from those encountering discrimination based on sexual orientation. Using themes and statements taken from the transcripts of interviews with those opposed to the legislation, Russell helped to create two highly sophisticated and complex artistic projects. The first was a five-part oratorio, *Fire*, written by a professional composer and sung by a highly skilled choir at a national competition. The second was a professionally produced television documentary aired on PBS. In this work one senses the blurring of many boundaries, between insider and outsider, researcher and researched, performer and audience.

•

For many, the theatrical performance represents the most fully embodied means of relating to one's audience. The actor may give full-blown bodily expression to ideas of importance. Acts of passion, humor, pathos, irony, logic are all available, and more. The audience, in turn, is invited to silently play out the part of the actor, metaphorically living in his or her shoes. No longer is the scholar passively speaking about an issue that is located

---

[36]Austin, D. (1996). Kaleidoscope: The same and different. In C. Ellis and A. Bochner (Eds.) *Composing ethnography: Alternative forms of qualitative writing* (pp. 207–208). Walnut Creek, CA: AltaMira.

Here I share one of my favorite works from a visually oriented scholar. In his volume, *Incurably Romantic*, Bernard Stehle explores the love between people otherwise severely disabled. As Buddy says, "I love her figure, her beautiful hair, and her heart." Gina responds, "Love most about him? His sweetness, his smiling, his happy-go-lucky kind of way." The scenarios of love are resources available to all.

Courtesy: Bernard F. Stehle, from *Incurably Romantic*. Temple University Press, 1985.

somewhere else; he or she is living the issue in the moment before others, and if successful, with them.[37]

•

The concrete language of the theater can fascinate and ensnare the organs... It ultimately breaks away from the intellectual subjugation of language.

—Anton Artaud

•

[37]See Victor Turner's 1982 volume, *From ritual to theater: The human seriousness of play.* (Baltimore, MD: PAJ Books), for an account of the significance of performance in educational practice.

Preeminent in stimulating the move toward theatrical performance is the work of Brazilian political theorist and theatrical director Augusto Boal.[38] Influenced by Marxist theory, Boal viewed the economic system as oppressive and racist. Further, the masses were sufficiently mystified by this system that they had no obvious reason to rise up in rejection. As Boal reasoned, the mystification was largely sustained by policies and practices that approximate theatrical drama (e.g. the staging of political extravaganzas, controlled news reporting). Thus, to stimulate protest, practices of anti-theater were required. Such practices included invitation to the audience to join in the performance, to become "spect-actors." While watching the play, for example, audience members were free to break in and reject the script that was being played out. They could step onto the stage and supply alternative and potentially more liberating lines. Experiments in performance are now evident across the social sciences.[39] Critics see these attempts as dangerous; they believe theatrics will rob the social sciences of authority and erode its standards of rigor. Such are the criticisms of those who would sustain the walls between "us and them," who wish to claim superiority of voice, and for whom alienated relationships are simply "normal life."

In the preceding sections, we have confronted the erosion of relationship generated by departmental structures, and by the form of writing common to contemporary scholarship. In each case the challenge was to bring forward practices that might restore the generative relationships. In this final section, we turn, to the relationship between scientists and those they study.

Research as Relationship

Nowhere is the individualist view of knowledge so fully embodied as in traditional methods of scientific research. Such research is based on the assumption of a strict separation between the scientist and the object of study. "*We* study *it*." Methods of research solidify this separation. Relations between the scientist and the object are carefully controlled so that the scientist's objectivity is not undermined by his or her values, desires, ideology, and the like. Standardized instruments or measures also insure that the distance between subject and object remains inviolate. Further, most methods of research typically presume a causal relationship between the entities

[38]See especially, Boal, A. (1979). *Theater of the oppressed*. London: Pluto Press.

[39]See, for example, Carlson, M. (1996). *Performance: A critical introduction*. London: Routledge; Case, S., Brett, P., and Foster, S. L. (1995). *Cruising the performative*. Bloomington: Indiana University Press; Richardson, L. (1997). *Fields of play*. New Brunswick, NJ: Rutgers University Press.

under study. In experimental psychology, for example, the individual is typically viewed as a bounded entity, whose actions are essentially the effects of impinging forces. In the standard experiment the attempt is to compare the impact of various causal conditions (e.g. an experimental vs. a control condition) on the behavior of the person. The traditional science experiment isolates the "subject" insofar as possible so that the conditions can be manipulated and behavior recorded without the presence of the investigator. Experimental methods are prized, in particular, for their capacity to "trace cause and effect" sequences.

•

Methods of research are scarcely value-neutral. They are saturated with assumptions about what is real and what is valuable, and methods of research realize these assumptions in action. Research methods do not reveal the contours of an independent phenomenon but create the phenomenon in their terms. Intelligence tests create people we deem to be intelligent or not; tests of memory create what we take to be good and bad memory. In the social sciences such methods typically reinforce the prevailing ideology of bounded being, and create a hierarchy that favors the knowledge of the scientist (the knower) over the "objects of research" (the known). The claim to objectivity in method permits the researcher to dismiss the knowledge claims of the "objects of research" as biased and ignorant.

The effects of such silencing have become increasingly visible in recent decades, as numerous groups have voiced anger at the scientific characterizations of their lives. The psychiatric establishment was among the first professional group to be attacked, when it was forced by 1960s gay activists to withdraw homosexuality from the categories of mental illness. This same message of resistance has also been delivered by African Americans, women, and the elderly, all of whom have been depicted by professionals as less than adequate in psychological functioning. These gathering voices now join the vast numbers of the so-called "disabled," who demand with increasing intensity, "Nothing about us without us."[40]

•

Research methods also deliver a subtler message to society concerning human nature. As noted, traditional research constructs a world in which there are separate entities, typically related to each other through cause and effect. If we presume the social world is composed of separate individuals,

---

[40]See Charlton, J. I. (2000). *Nothing about us without us: Disability oppression and empowerment*. Berkeley, CA: University of California Press.

and employ methods consistent with this view, we shall find (lo and behold!) a world of starkly separated selves. Simultaneously such research informs us about the best way to acquire knowledge of others. It suggests that if we wish to have accurate and objective knowledge of those we hold dear, we must observe carefully from a distance, remove our passions from the table, and carefully analyze the "necessary and sufficient conditions" producing their behavior. "To know you" would mean calculating the conditions causing your behavior and testing out my hunches by observing you in subsequent settings. I shall do this secretly, for if you knew I was examining you, you might not reveal the truth about your behavior. The result of this orientation to knowledge is a world of alienation, suspicion, and dispassion.[41]

•

I am not at all arguing for abandoning the individualist tradition of research. As stated at the outset of this book, my aim is not to exterminate tradition. In many contexts the individualist tradition can make important practical contributions to society. However, it is important to explore its limitations, and add resources for alternative futures. Specifically, the challenge is to generate alternatives that breathe life into the promise of relational being.

Relational Alternatives in Human Research

Particularly within the social sciences, discontent with the alienating conception of scientific research is widespread. Feminist researchers have been especially active in pointing out the manipulative and divisive character of traditional research methods.[42] As a result, adventurous researchers everywhere have begun to create and nurture alternatives. So vibrantly productive are these efforts—often falling under the broad label of *qualitative inquiry*—that the past decade can properly be viewed as a renaissance in research practice.[43] Many of these innovations are specifically dedicated to reducing distance between the scientist and those under study. Or, more properly, the move is away from research *about* others to

---

[41]I recommend the dramatic illustration provided by Bent Hamer's 2003 film, *Kitchen stories*.

[42]See for example, Gergen, M. (2000). *Feminist reconstructions in psychology: Narrative, gender and performance.* Thousand Oaks, CA: Sage.

[43]An excellent review of these developments is contained in Denzin, N., and Lincoln, E. (2005). *The Sage handbook of qualitative research.* Newbury Park, CA: Sage. See also the print journal, *Qualitative Inquiry*, along with the on-line journals.

research *with* them. For purposes of illustration and invitation, I touch on only two of the more significant ventures.

Narrative Inquiry: Entry into Otherness

Traditional practices of research encourage an *instrumental* orientation toward those under study (See Chapter 1). Investigators examine the subject's behavior so that they can speak to their discipline. There is a strategic search for evidence that can be used for professional purposes. In the extreme, it is to say, "It is neither you nor our relationship that interests me; my aim is to use what you do or say to gain the esteem of my peers." Virtually all experimental research in the social sciences functions in the instrumental mode, along with standardized interviews and data analysis programs. In contrast, consider what can be described as a *mimetic encountering* of the other. This orientation is more prominent in friendships. One does not consciously scan the other for useful information to be used elsewhere, but absorbs the other's actions in such a way that they can be reproduced (or mimed). It is silently and partially to participate in the other's life world. This process is essential to the creation of multi-being (Chapter 5), in which we absorb other ways of speaking, the styles, mannerisms, cadences, and so on. We emerge from such relationships with residues of the other, now readied for further relationships.[44]

•

Mimetic encountering is facilitated by a range of research methods, not so much new to the scene as rapidly expanding in scope and potential. Most notable in this case is the narrative movement in the social sciences.[45] Here researchers often give voice to the lives of the otherwise unheard. For example, such research may bring us into an "experience near" state with Holocaust survivors, immigrants, back-packers, mothers on drugs, and so on. Dan McAdams illuminates the world of middle-aged Americans whose

[44]The instrumental orientation is similar to what Martin Buber terms an I–It relationship. The mimetic orientation is resonant with (but not identical to) his more favored I–Thou relationship. See Buber, M., *op cit.*

[45]The literature here is enormous and cuts across many disciplines. See discussions by Clandinen, D. J., and Conneley, F. M. (2004). *Narrative inquiry: Experience and story in qualitative research*. San Francisco: Jossey-Bass; Czarniawska, B. (2004). *Narratives in social science research*. London: Sage; Lieblich, A., Zilber, R., Tuval-Mashiach, R. (2003). *Narrative research: Reading, analysis, and interpretation*. London: Sage; and Josselson, R., Lieblich, A., and McAdams, D. P. (2007). *The meaning of others: Narrative studies of relationships*. Washington, DC: APA Books. For a "state of the art" report, see *Narrative Inquiry*, V. 16, 1, 2006.

lives are enriched by redemption narratives.[46] These stories, told to self and others, are about ways in which negative circumstances (failures, loss, disease, tragedy, etc.) have been transformed into something positive. This understanding of one's life (i.e. "how I learned," "how I overcame," "how this has helped me to become...") is not only a significant way of giving value to one's life, but as well, a sense that one can make a lasting contribution to the future. We, as readers, are positioned by such research to listen mimetically, and to create such stories for ourselves.

•

From a relational standpoint, one of the shortcomings of most narrative research is that the subjects don't *fully* speak for themselves. Rather, the researcher is placed between the reader and the narrating individual. In this sense, the narrative is "managed" by the researcher, at times for academically instrumental purposes (e.g. "to demonstrate my point"). In any case, the reader is often left asking, "Whose story is this, anyway?" Such concerns inspire still further innovation. Some researchers experiment with what might be called *conjoint narration*. In this case both the subject of the research and the researcher each take control over their own narratives. For example, in their work *Troubling the Angels, Women living with HIV/AIDS*, Patti Lather and Chris Smythies give significant portions of the book over to the women themselves.[47] They also supplement these narrations with their own commentaries, and ask the women to comment on them.

•

Most radical in its enabling people to speak for themselves are experiments in *autoethnography*. Here the researcher also serves as the subject of research.[48] Rather than reporting on *other* people, researchers use themselves as case studies. To illustrate, here Carol Ronai details what it is like to be parented by a mentally retarded mother:

> I resent the imperative to pretend that all is normal with my family, an imperative that is enforced by silence, secrecy, and "you don't talk about this to anyone" rhetoric. Our pretense is designed to make events flow smoothly, but it doesn't work. Everyone is plastic and

[46]McAdams, D. (2006). *The redemptive self: Stories Americans live by.* New York: Oxford University Press.

[47]Lather, P. A., and Smythies, C. (2001). *Troubling the Angels, Women living with HIV/AIDS.* Boulder, CO: Westview.

[48]For more on autoethnography, see Ellis, C., and Bochner, A. P. (Eds.) (1996). *Composing ethnography.* Walnut Creek, CA: AltaMira; Ellis, C., and Bochner, A. (2002). *Ethnographically speaking: Autoethnography, literature and aesthetics.* Walnut Creek, CA: AltaMira.

fake around my mother, including me. Why? Because no one has told her to her face that she is retarded. We say we don't want to upset her. I don't think we are ready to deal with her reaction to the truth... .Because of (my mother) and because of how the family as a unit has chosen to deal with the problem, I have compartmentalized a whole segment of my life into a lie. (p. 115)[49]

In this sample, the mimetic encounter is most fully realized. The frontal openness, the vulnerability, and the passion all invite the reader into a mimetic state of becoming the story-teller. One begins to "feel with" the author, blurring the distinction between author and reader.

Action Research: Knowing With

Scientific research is not principally a matter of revealing The Truth, but of participating in a community of meaning makers to achieve goals valued by this community. Sensitive to this view, many researchers now abandon the goals of the academic guild, and ally themselves directly with the public they wish to serve. They give up the attempt to know about others in favor of helping them to know them. In these endeavors, called *action research*, researchers typically offer their skills and resources to enable or empower groups to achieve ends that are important to them. Such research also removes the misleading guise of scientific neutrality. Researchers join in efforts to achieve ends they see as politically and socially valuable. Thus, to name but a few, action researchers have been involved in helping :

- women in prisons create educational opportunities
- poor neighborhoods organize to control drugs and lift themselves up educationally and economically
- school children to develop decision-making practices
- women in Nepal to develop grass-roots businesses
- Mayan villagers to develop health care programs
- parents and teachers in East Timor to develop better relations
- Protestants and Catholics in Northern Ireland to bridge differences
- diabetes patients and physicians to work more productively together
- the elderly in the Netherlands to work toward better care
- teachers in Zimbabwe to develop more dialogic teaching strategies
- agricultural workers in Iran to develop more collaborative practices.

•

[49]Ronai, C. R. (1996). My mother is mentally retarded. In C. Ellis and A. P. Bochner (Eds.) *Composing ethnography.* Walnut Creek, CA: AltaMira.

The range of contemporary action research is enormous, and there are ample resources available to the interested reader.[50] However, the work of Brinton Lykes effectively illustrates the ingenuity of such researchers.[51] For many years Lykes had been working with women in the mountainous regions of Guatemala. These women had suffered greatly as a result of the civil wars raging over their lands, and their villages and families had been ravaged by enemy troops. Both as a research endeavor, and as a means to heal and create solidarity among the women, Lykes gave each of the women cameras. They were asked if they would join in sharing photos of the destruction and violence in their areas. She then arranged for the women to share the photographs with each other and to talk about the implications for their lives. Conversations about the photographs lead to a deeper, more complex understanding of events. Women who would not ordinarily have a chance to express their visions of life and the future were able to do so as a result of the photographs. This sharing helped to develop the solidarity and inspiration to rebuild community together.

Courtesy: M. Brinton Lykes

[50]See, for example, Reason, P., and Bradbury, H. (2008). *Handbook of action research* (2nd ed.). London: Sage.

[51]Lykes, M. B., and Coquillon, E. (2007). Participatory action research and feminisms: Towards transformative praxis. In S. Hesse-Biber (Ed.) *Handbook of feminist research: Theory and praxis*. Thousand Oaks, CA: Sage.

8

Education in a Relational Key

Sometimes I think I inherited my occupation. My father was also a professor. I was transfixed by his teaching. In part it was the fascination of irony. As a growing boy I had experienced him as a stern and demanding authoritarian. My friends called him "the bear." Only slowly did I realize that we—his four sons—might be responsible for his Prussian personality. It was his best option for controlling and channeling the ever-impending chaos. My father, "the mathematics professor," was an altogether different man. In the classroom his animated movements were coupled with a spontaneous wit, and as words and chalk-dust filled the air, his students were enchanted. So was I.

Although drawn by his classroom performance, I could never emulate my father's style. That was his alone. However, in my first years of teaching I did detect a certain resonance. Like him, I was the master of the classroom: I designed our routes, ordered the intellectual provisions, delivered commanding lectures, and evaluated performance with an impartial hand. In these respects, I also resembled most of my colleagues.

•

I no longer teach in this way. The classroom is no longer my ship; I am no longer its commander. I have shed the traditional vision of individual minds, of the knowing teacher and ignorant student, of teaching as a cause of learning. I find it difficult to think of my actions in the classroom independent from the students I teach, and student performance as issuing from an internal well-spring of intelligence. What takes place in the classroom is our achievement *together*. I scarcely think I am alone in this increased sensitivity to relationship. Today, new practices are everywhere in motion, slowly leaving behind the myth of individuals who succeed or fail by virtue of individual talents.

•

In the present chapter I explore these emerging practices and their potentials. I begin by reconsidering the aims of education. If we dispense with the presumption that education is about improving individual minds, how are we to conceptualize its function? Here I propose that because all knowledge is a communal creation, education is more fruitfully conceived as a process for enhancing participation in relational process. With this view in place, I turn to the central concern of the chapter, namely educational practices that reflect, sustain, and advance productive forms of relational being. Here I shall take up a range of relationships—between teachers and students, among students, between the classroom and the world outside, and more. In each case we shall explore practices that link excellence in education with excellence in relationship.

Aims of Education Revisited

Western culture has long been enamored with the vision of the individual as the origin of reason. We marvel at the idea of the lone genius, the Galileo, Newton, or Einstein, all symbolically embodied in Rodin's classic pose of The Thinker. Likewise the educational establishment has long flown the Cartesian banner of *cogito*. We spend long hours developing curricula to help students "think for themselves." We also hold that thinking takes place prior to, and separate from, speaking or writing. Thinking is a private act, and words are merely the vehicles by which we make our thoughts known to others. The individual mind is primary; relations are secondary and optional. In this tradition we draw a clear distinction between the knowing teacher and the ignorant pupil; we believe the purpose of education is to fill the minds of individual students; and we presume that a knowing mind is good preparation for a successful future. All of these presumptions derive from the tradition of bounded beings—separate and independent minds. But, why should we suppose that knowledge is an individual possession, or that education is about "filling" or "fashioning minds?"

•

Early in the 20th century the philosopher John Dewey raised much the same questions. For Dewey the cultivated mind was essentially a social mind. "All education proceeds by the participation of the individual in the social consciousness" (p. 77).[1] In this sense, Dewey foreshadows themes central to relational being. If raised in social isolation, what would an individual think about? There would be no capacity to think about science, literature, or art; no deliberation on good and evil; no concern with family, community, or global well-being. These "objects of thought" all develop through our relationships with others. To deliberate at all about such matters first requires language, and language by its nature can only be generated within relationships. A language spoken by one person alone is nonsense.[2]

•

What is "rational thought" outside relationship? To think rationally is to participate in a cultural tradition. For example, that $14 \times 24 = 336$ is rational only if one agrees to play within the conventions of a number system with the base of 10. The same may be said of memory. To remember what has been taught is not to consult a recording in the brain. Rather, it is to engage in a cultural convention concerning what counts as an acceptable performance of memory. If a teacher asks a student what he remembered from class the day before, and the student perfectly mimed the bodily movements of the teacher, he would be chastened. These were among the proposals of Chapter 3.

•

All the knowledge we dispense in our classes—from history to literature, biology to calculus, geography to psychology—is invariably a community achievement. Without a community to agree about the objects of study, the methods of research, the terms by which the world is described, and the value of inquiry, there would be virtually no bodies of knowledge available. To put it broadly, knowledge is not lodged somewhere within the minds of individual scientists or scholars. These were the arguments of the preceding chapter.

•

[1] Dewey, J. (1897). My pedagogic creed. *The School Journal.* LIV, 4, 77–80.
[2] See Wittgenstein, L. (1953). *Philosophical investigations.* (G. E. M. Anscombe, Trans.) Oxford: Blackwell. Section 243.

If knowledge and reason are relational achievements, we must reconsider the question of educational goals. If relations are primary, what then is the aim of education; what do we hope to achieve from our practices? If what we call mental functioning is relational functioning, we must begin to ask questions about the relationships in which students are, or will be, participating and the outcome of such participation. From this standpoint I propose that *the primary aim of education is to enhance the potentials for participating in relational processes—from the local to the global.* The aim, then, is not that of producing independent, autonomous thinkers— mythological creatures at best—but of facilitating relational processes that can ultimately contribute to the continuing and expanding flow of relationships within the world more broadly.[3]

What would it be to place relationship prior to the individual in education? First, the focus would be directed to relations between teachers and students, and among students. Who is participating and in what manner? In the long run, the character of these relationships may prove more significant than the subject matter under study. Second, we would move beyond the classroom. The classroom should give voice to the webs of relationship in which students and teachers are engaged. Relations between the classroom and its environment should also be extended from the local to the global context. The classroom would ideally be a meeting ground for the concerns of the world. And finally, there are the relationships of the future. With what skills are students prepared to enter the relationships on which global life will depend? Most obvious are entries into the prevailing communities of practice: law, medicine, teaching, business, government, the helping professions, the military, and so on. A relationally effective education would also consider the potentials for productive participation in families, communities, the political process, the arts, diverse cultural traditions, nature, and more. Education is not, then, a process of *producing* effective individuals; it is one of fostering processes that indefinitely extend the potentials of relationship.

•

In my view, education in a relational key is critical to the global future. Owing to the profound technological transformations of the past century, we confront increasing numbers of people, from differing locales, for differing purposes. Everywhere there is a need for collaboration, teamwork,

[3] There are also similarities here to Bruner's vision of educational process serving the needs of the culture. See Bruner, J. S. (1996). *The culture of education.* Cambridge: Harvard University Press. However, there are notable differences as well, especially in terms of Bruner's emphasis on education dedicated to affirming individual minds and esteem.

networks, and negotiation. Required are continuous adjustments to a continuously changing sea of meaning and material. In the organizational sphere, for example, this reliance on relationship is reflected in moves from hierarchical to flattened structures and increased reliance on cross-functional teams for vital decisions. Successful collaboration is also pivotal for the dramatic billowing of virtual organizations and international voluntary moments (NGOs).[4] And it is in just such capacities for coordinated relationship that ecumenical movements, geopolitical organizations, and scientific research teams depend.[5] The tradition of individual-centered education is ill-suited for participation in such ventures.

There is more: Contemporary communication technologies also feed the flames of conflict. Through the Web, the Internet, cell phones, and the like, it is possible in short order to assemble enclaves of the ideologically committed. Each ordering is also a disordering; an antagonistic gap is created between *us* and *them*. And, as the control of violence shifts from large military regimes to small bands of "terrorists," every antagonism is lethal in its potential. In this context of the global powder keg, contributions to productive relational process are essential.[6] Here we must consider that educational institutions are virtually alone in their capacities for building the vocabularies of effective relationship. Most institutions are bent on self-enhancement; in contrast, education in relational process can serve the good of all.

•

The implications of education for relational ends are profound. Our attention first shifts from the mind of individual students to the kinds of relationships out of which mutual knowing can emerge. As noted, we focus on relational processes within the classroom, between the classroom and community, and educational systems throughout the world. Further, we become sensitized to community differences and the ways in which knowledge in one may be dysfunctional within another. We begin to ask whose voices are present in the educational process and whose are absent or silenced. In all these contexts, interest shifts from the excellence of a bounded unit, to the potentials inherent in coordination. Isolation, hierarchy, and antagonism give way to co-creation.

[4]On the significance of multinational work teams, for example, see Earley, P. C., and Gibson, C. B. (2002). *Multinational work teams: A new perspective*. Mawhah, NJ: Erlbaum.

[5]See Earley, P. C. and Gibson, C. B. (2002). *Multinational work teams: A new perspective*. Mahwah, NJ: Earlbaum.

[6]See especially the Chapter 6 discussion of conflict and dialogue.

Circles of Participation

At present most educational practices and policies are individualist in character. The educational system is designed to bring about lasting changes in the condition of the individual mind. In metaphoric terms, the school functions as a factory for turning the raw stuff of the mind into a finely functioning machine. In today's vernaculars the machine product is a computer into which the educational system has installed durable software. The factory metaphor is often linked, as well, with an economic one. In this case we are inclined to judge schools in business terms, such as cost effectiveness and product quality. There are numerous critics of this tradition, and many attempts to avoid its strangulating grip.[7] My attempt here is not to review these many important resistances. Rather, what horizons are now opened if we replace the individual with the relationship as the fundamental unit of education? What practices and policies are invited?

•

To prepare for this discussion, further scaffolding is useful: Consider first that within the existing tradition we largely view the student's state of knowledge as an effect for which the educational system is the cause. The system *teaches* and the student *learns*; the factory grinds out its product. On this view, we have no easy way of asking about the effects of the student on the system; we don't ask about the effects of computer software on the factory that produced it. But what if we view the student and the teacher as participants in a relationship? I am not speaking here of a relationship of bounded units, causing each other's movements like so many billiard balls. Rather, they are engaged in a relationship in which they are mutually creating meaning, reason, and value. The student does not possess meaning until granted by the teacher; the teacher speaks nonsense until the student affirms that sense has been made. Without co-action, there is no communication and no education. With mutual engagement the student and teacher actively participate in a mutual process of teaching/learning.

But the teacher and student are scarcely alone. Each is a participant in an extended array of relationships. Thus, the student arrives in class as a multi-being, already participating in relations with family, friends, and

---

[7]Pivotal in such critiques is the writing of Paulo Freire, who has characterized the existing tradition as *nutrutionist* or a *banking* model. Education, on this view, is an instrument of the powerful, implanting knowledge or investing in the student, with a view toward a future harvest or profit. See his 1970 volume, *Pedagogy of the oppressed*. London: Continuum.

neighbors, along with a host of fantasy figures from television, videogames, and the like (Chapter 5). Following the earlier analysis, let us view each of the student's relationships as a *circle of participation*. Thus the student arrives embedded within multiple circles, with mother, father, siblings, friends, and so on. Further, let us recognize that each of these circles is also educational. That is, participation in any relationship will bring with it an increase in one's capacities, sensitivities, and skills for relating. Each fosters a way of being with others, favoring certain ways of talking, values, fears, enthusiasms, and so on. Each generates its own limitations as well. In effect, each establishes its own ways of "doing knowledge."

We further recognize that the teacher arrives in the classroom as a multi-being, embedded in a similar matrix of connection, along with relations with other teachers, administrators, and more. Each of these relations leaves the teacher with a residue of potentials. When teacher and student meet, each is embedded within a multiplicity of relationships, and each is replete with multiple skills (and potential deficiencies) in relating. In this sense, the meeting of the student and teacher brings about a new circle of relationship, one that could link each of them to an expanded sea of potentials—or not.

Yet, we also recognize that a student's achievements depend on his or her circle of relations with classmates. Not only do these relationships harbor significant educational potential, but they will also insinuate themselves into the relationship between teacher and student. Effective teachers, then, will attend not only to their personal relations with their students, but will develop practices that draw into the circle the relations of students among themselves. In effect, we expand the potentials of the educational process by broadening the range of circles taken into account.[8]

Let us again expand the relational realm: In recent years educators have become increasingly concerned with the relationship of students to their families. What takes place within the teacher/student relationship can be significantly influenced by the student's home-life. Effective pedagogy should take this circle into account. Further, it is useful to expand the focus on relationship to include the surrounding institutions of business, government, industry, and so on. If education is to be successful, these circles should also be drawn into the classroom proceedings. Finally, we may inquire into the relationship within the classroom to the world more

[8]Useful here is Bruner's view of education as issuing from a "sub-community in interaction." Bruner, J. S. (*op cit.*)

generally. If schooling is to prepare students to become world citizens, then global relations are to be prized.

Relational Pedagogy in Action

My concern in the remainder of this chapter is with educational practice. What does a relational orientation invite in the way of specific practices? There is much to be said here—on practices of curriculum development standardization, educational policy, and the like. However, for illustrative purposes I will focus on pedagogy. To keep the discussion manageable, I will also limit the focus to four specific circles of relationship. We will consider practices in the relationship between teacher and student, among students, between the classroom and the community, and between the classroom and the world. Each discussion will constitute a lens through which certain issues and potentials will become prominent. When we focus on the circle uniting teacher and student, certain practices will become salient; through a lens in which student relations are focal, further practices emerge. As each lens brings a relational circle into visibility, so do our sensitivities and creative potentials expand. Throughout these discussions, I will illustrate with a variety of innovative practices from contemporary classrooms. The multiple sites in which these innovations emerged suggests that a broad movement is in the making.

Circle 1: Teacher and Student

Educators have long pondered the question of what makes a good teacher: which personality traits and practices are most effective. In recent years attention has also centered on the student: his or her stage of cognitive development, personal needs, self-esteem, and so on. The concern with teacher characteristics traditionally lends itself to *curriculum-centered* education (drawing from the teacher's knowledge base), while concern with student capabilities lends strong support to a *student-centered* curriculum. However, each of these traditions is typically focused on the bounded individual—*either* the teacher *or* the student. A relational orientation asks us to consider them together. A teacher may demand classroom order, but such demands will go unnoticed if students disrespect the teacher. Teaching cannot be separated from learning; without one the other fails to exist.

•

When a student fails a course, there are ways in which the teacher has also failed; a teacher receiving a "best teaching award" should share it with his or her students. Parents rewarding their children for good marks, should also congratulate the teacher.

•

In this light consider the traditional relationship between teacher and student. The teacher stands in the front of the classroom with students seated about; the teacher describes, explains, and demonstrates a subject matter while the students listen and possibly take notes. Here we notice, first, that the teacher controls the classroom, including who can speak, when, and about what. Second, we notice the dependence of the relationship on *monologue* (the teacher does most of the talking). In my view, these conditions vastly reduce the potentials of relationship, and in doing so markedly limit the educational outcomes.

When the relationship is dominated by the teacher's monologue, students are not only denied full participation, but as well the capacity to draw from the multiple relationships of which they are a part. Rich potentials remain unused or suppressed. When teachers alone generate the order of the classroom, students often find it an alien one. It is not their order; it makes little sense within their relational histories. For older students, teacher control can often invite resentment and a resistance. Ideally, the order of the classroom should emerge through collaboration. In significant degree, this can be accomplished by shifting from monologue to dialogue as the primary form of teaching. Here students have greater opportunity to give expression to their outside relationships, and to weave them into the classroom order. In effect, students bring their extended network of relationships into the classroom. One student might relate the course material to her personal life; another might inject humor, and another amplify with a relevant story. Their lives are brought more fully into contact with the teacher, with their fellow students, and with the course material itself. To be sure, there might be less "coverage of the course material," but the outcome enriches the potentials for relational participation.

•

As a teacher, I love having extensive knowledge at my fingertips and bringing it to life with my words, creating interest and admiration among my students. I am the center of their attention, the font of knowledge, the wise and giving father. Yet, I have also come to realize that this same romance with myself as teacher may also be more self-serving than educational. The students essentially witness a performance. They are scarcely aware of the years of effort required for me to speak with ease; they have not seen the hours I have spent in organizing, brushing up, and thinking through the trajectory of the appointed hour. What I say appears to spring spontaneously from my powers of reasoning. Not only is this misleading, but the students are minimally prepared by my performance for action in the world. They are primarily prepared to observe, appreciate, take a few notes, and in some form to repeat my words when later quizzed. They are minimally prepared to enter later relationships as effective dialogic partners. They have no experience in offering ideas, responding sensitively to others, or joining with others in creating visions that none could have imagined alone.

•

Many teachers are sensitive to these issues. The emphasis on narrative writing and reporting, requests for students to bring artifacts from home into the class, and assignments that link class and neighborhood move in this direction. However, there is also a family of metaphors springing to life within recent years, each offering a more inclusive alternative to the monologic orientation, and a richer vision of the relationship between teacher and students. I find the following among the most promising of these metaphors:

The Dialogic Classroom. In the co-active creation of the real and the good, dialogue is the preferred form of pedagogy. But dialogue comes in many forms. The most popular is that of *debate*: one side versus the other. In earlier years I often used debate as a means of stirring interest and engagement, and in demonstrating the intelligibility of both sides of an issue. Over the years, however, my enthusiasm waned. Debate has a way of closing the focus. When it is "one side versus another," the broader context is seldom considered. Further, debate tends to polarize the class. Once committed to a given side, students can see little of value in "the opposition." The participants are now combatants, and relationships are threatened. In how many debates do we find one side congratulating the other on making a good point, or adding their insights to the ideas offered by the other? Argument is effectively an invitation to mutual negation.[9]

---

[9]For further discussion see the essay, "The limits of pure critique," in Gergen, K. J. (2001). *Social construction in context.* London: Sage.

Many teachers forego debate in favor of Socratic dialogue. Here the teacher employs conversation as the means to bring students into a state of knowledge. However, while an important contribution to collaborative learning, the Socratic method is implicitly monologic. That is, the teacher knows in advance the desired conclusion of the interchange, and fashions his or her questions accordingly.

In contrast, more recent contributions to the concept of the dialogic classroom emphasize fully participatory forms of exchange.[10] In particular, they seek means of (1) expanding participation to include all students, while preventing a few opinionated or articulate students from dominating discussion, (2) reducing control over the direction of discussion, so that student concerns more easily determine the topics, (3) crediting students with intelligibility as opposed to correcting them, and (4) replacing the goal of Truth with that of expanding the range of intelligible realities. The dialogic orientation discourages "canned lectures" and lock-step power-point presentations; it also encourages teachers to risk their status as ultimate knowers. Teachers are invited to thrust themselves into the collective process, and to make whatever they bring to the table relevant to the unfolding conversation.[11] The results of such practices are a more intense level of engagement, a flourishing of ideas and insights, affirming and supportive relationships, and a reduction in alienation and resistance. Scholars also praise these developments for the ways in which they prepare students for democratic participation, enable them to master multiple points of view, and invite a deeper probing of moral issues.

•

Life by its very nature is dialogic. To live means to participate in
dialogue: To ask questions, to heed, to respond, to agree... In this
dialogue a person participates wholly and throughout his whole life:
with his eyes, lips, hands, soul, spirit, with his whole body and deeds.

---

[10]Highly influential in placing dialogue in the educational forefront was Theodore Sizer's 1984 book, *Horace's compromise*. (Boston: Houghton Mifflin). See also Wells, G. (1999). *Dialogic inquiry: Towards a sociocultural practice and theory of education*. Cambridge: Cambridge University Press; Vella, J. K. (2002). *Learning to listen, learning to teach: The power of dialogue in educating adults*. San Francisco, CA: Jossey-Bass; Applebee, A. (1996). *Curriculum as conversation: Transforming traditions of teaching and learning*. Chicago: University of Chicago Press; Brookfield, S. D., and Preskill, S. (1999). *Discussion as a way of teaching: Tools and techniques for democratic classrooms*. San Francisco: Jossey-Bass; Simon, K. (2003). *Moral questions in the classroom*. New Haven: Yale University Press.

[11]For a refreshing argument for dialogue over power-point, see Bowen, J. (2006). Teaching naked: Why removing technology from your classroom will improve student learning. *National Teaching and Learning Forum Newsletter*, vol.16, no.1.

He invests his entire self in discourse, and this discourse enters into the dialogic fabric of human life, into the world symposium.

—Mikail Bakhtin

Cognitive Apprenticeship. Stimulated by Vygotsky's views on development, educational specialists have developed a vision of the relationship between teacher and student as an *apprenticeship.*[12] As Vygotsky reasoned, human thought is largely a reflection of social dialogue. Thus, the major key to development in thinking is immersion in social interchange. In this vein, educators came to see the relationship between teacher and student as the fundamental source of learning. Most effective is the teacher who shares and cares. The teacher must share not only his or her knowledge of content with the student, but the heuristics (or know-how) vital to using such knowledge in practice. (It is one thing to master the multiplication tables, but another to know the various "tricks" for solving complex problems in multiplication.) And this sharing must take place in a context in which the teacher is invested in the student's mastery. In effect, the student becomes an apprentice to the teacher.

Many educators believe apprenticeship education is most effective in practical contexts. Instead of the student embracing abstractions cut away from their contexts of usage, knowledge development is tied to action. For many teachers this means moving the educational experience from the classroom to the community. In such activities as planting a collective garden, developing a re-cycling program, or participating in a national engineering competition, the student eagerly searches for the kind of useful information and know-how that the teacher may provide. More broadly, many draw from Vygotsky a view of ideal educational practice as situated within the conditions of application.[13]

Liberation/Empowerment. More overtly political in its aims is the *liberation and empowerment* vision of teaching, inspired by Paulo Freire.[14] Freire was deeply concerned with the conditions of the illiterate poor in Brazil.

---

[12]See Collins, A., Brown, J. S., and Newman, S. E. (1989). Cognitive apprenticeship: Teaching the crafts of reading, writing, and mathematics. In L. B. Resnick (Ed.) *Knowing, learning, and instruction: Essays in honor of Robert Glaser.* Hillsdale, NJ: Erlbaum; Rogoff, B. (1990). *Apprenticeship in thinking.* New York: Oxford University Press. For excellent case examples of a Vygotskian approach to education and its emphasis on relationship, see Holzman, L. (1997). *Schools for growth: Radical alternatives to current educational models.* Mahwah, NJ: Erlbaum.

[13]See also research and theory on situated learning or cognition, including Lave, J. (1988). *Cognition in practice.* New York: Cambridge University Press; Kirschner, D., and Whitson, J. (Eds.) (1995). *Situated cognition: Social, semiotic, and psychological perspectives.* Mahwah, NJ: Erlbaum.

[14]Freire, P. (1970). *op cit.*

As he saw it, this population was not only unaware of the oppressive forces responsible for their impoverished state, but they had little means of effecting change. The educational process, as he reasoned, should foster a critical consciousness ("conscientization") of their economic and political condition. It must furnish them with the tools for transforming the economic and political conditions. In short, they should be liberated and empowered.

In this context Freire argued for eradicating the traditional, hierarchical teacher/student distinction. That is, teachers should also be learners, and students should function as teachers. Abandoned is the traditional view of the student as a passive recipient of knowledge (as defined by those in power), and favored instead is a view of the student as an active agent. As students come to see themselves as agents of the future, reasoned Freire, they will also be encouraged to join in movements for social change. The importance of the phrase "to join" should be underscored in this case, as Freire believed that change can emerge only from collective action.[15]

•

To study is not to consume ideas, but to create and re-create them.
—Paulo Freire

•

The liberation movement has played a powerful role in stimulating critical reflection on traditional educational practice, and made quite clear the fact that there is no politically neutral education. However, from a relational standpoint, further developments are needed. In particular, the critical movement tends to intensify political tensions and to generate a backlash among the targets of critique. Much needed are practices that bring people together from otherwise disparate camps, and enable them to engage in collective action for the collective good. From a relational perspective, one must handle critique with care.[16]

Facilitation/Coaching. Less radical, but widely shared in many schools, is the metaphor of the teacher as *facilitator* of student development, or a *coach*.[17] Ideally the teacher shares his or her knowledge base, but not so

---

[15]Liberatory classrooms are not without their critics, even those who champion their aims. See Patti Lather's volume *Getting smart: Feminist research and pedagogy with/in the postmodern* (1991, New York: Routledge), for an excellent analysis of resistance to liberation pedagogy and useful means of sustaining the critical impulse while avoiding its potentials for domination.

[16]For further discussion of the limits of critique, see Gergen, K. (2001). *Op cit.*

[17]For more on teacher as coach, see Sizer, *op cit.*

much in order to direct students as to offer resources enabling them to reach goals in which they are personally invested. As a facilitator/coach, special attention is given to the life circumstances of the student. Yet, the facilitator/coach role is also controversial. It is a view invited by the tradition of student-centered curricula, in which students are conceptualized as intrinsically motivated. Much like growing flowers, it is assumed they have their own internal callings (intrinsic motivation), and if they follow their impulses they will blossom forth. From a relational standpoint, this view requires modification. Whatever students are invested in, whatever they find exhilarating, will owe its existence to relationship—including the relationship with the teacher.

Many teachers adopt the facilitation/coach model are indeed sensitive to their role in injecting value into action. They do see that dialogue may be essential to creating the worth of a given undertaking. Indeed, for many who approach teaching in this way, an appreciative approach to the student replaces the more traditional emphasis on evaluative judgment. In effect, the teacher becomes an important aid to the student's sense of worth. As many teachers find, when they place appreciation as opposed to judgment in the forefront of their relations, students are far more motivated; their participation in classroom discussion is sparked.[18] Students who fear critical appraisal often resist speaking out. They may feel they have something to say…but are unsure. By the time they have the courage to speak, the conversation has often passed. They remain quiet, now bearing the additional burden of shame at their lack of courage.[19]

Friendship. The teacher–student relationship may also be viewed as a *friendship*. When education is lodged in a tradition of bounded being, teachers are invited to take an instrumental attitude toward students. Prominent questions include, "How can I get their interest," "How can I bring the classroom under control," "How can I boost their scores on a national test?" In this sense, there is always an "I" as a causal agent *working on* "them." Not only is such an orientation distancing and manipulative, it also creates the student as "other." Refreshing in this respect is William Rawlins' proposal that the most effective education emerges from a

---

[18]Some teachers extend the appreciative approach into the students' orientation to their work. For example, in her book, *Writing from the heart* (Berkeley, CA: Crossing Press, 1998), Nancy Aronie recommends that students be asked to write about what they loved about their reading, what they found valuable, what it offered to their personal lives.

[19]This emphasis on appreciation should not be confused with the movement to build student self-esteem. In certain respects, the latter sustains the conception of students as bounded beings on whom the program of study has *an effect*.

friendship relationship between teacher and student.[20] This concept recognizes the potentials of mutual regard and caring in the educational process. The attempt is to create a bond of mutual trust, one in which the teacher can evaluate the student's work in the way a good friend might share a helpful opinion. When mutual regard is established, the student is also more likely to absorb the teacher's actions into his or her ways of being. The teacher is more likely to become a resource for multi-being. At the same time, Rawlins recognizes that friendships are not without tensions. One must avoid the danger of "caring too much," for example, lest issues of favoritism or jealousy arise.

•

Teaching is friendship.
—Kurt Vonnegut

•

We find, then, a rich variety of ways to enrich relations between teacher and students. Should we now set out to contrast and compare, hoping to locate the superior practice? I think not. In moving away from the mechanistic form of teacher/student relationship, we should be wary of replacing it with yet another frozen form. Like a good conversation, one's lines should not be prepared in advance. In an open process of co-creation, relationships are ever in motion. As in daily life, there will be unpredictable twists and turns. A humorous word here, an angry tone there, a surprising revelation—all may suddenly thrust the relationship in a different direction. Thus, the best option is flexibility. Drawing from one's resources as a multi-being, one should be readied to access many different voices, to move fluidly with the shifting tides of dialogue. Drawing from this family of metaphors, one should be able to engage in collaborative dialogue in one situation, serve as a mentor in another, or variously act as a facilitator, an agent of empowerment, or a friend.

Finally, it is important to underscore that this move toward richer relationships is not intended to obliterate the traditional role of monologic knower and disciplinarian. It is not that the traditional relationship is bankrupt; it is simply limited. In various contexts—for example, in a large lecture hall—it may be optimal. In many ways, the vision of the effective teacher here is that of a good family member. As effective participants in family relationships, we are called on to play many different roles—nurturing,

[20]Rawlins, W. (2000). Teaching as a mode of friendship. *Communication Theory, 10,* 5–26.

informing, facilitating, commiserating, and so on. In my view, the relationship between teacher and student should be no less rich in potential.

•

> There were teachers in my early years in whose presence I experienced something akin to spiritual ecstasy. Their words, gestures, tone of voice, clothing, mannerisms—all worked together to open worlds beyond my dreams. I was a willing and grateful supplicant participating in an ancient ritual of illumination. The aim here is not to eradicate traditions of relationship. Clearly we should retain remnants of this tradition, but without letting them bind us to ancient pillars.

Circle 2: Relations Among Students

We move now from the teacher/student relationship to a second circle: relations among students. Teaching practices that focus on the individual mind invite a classroom in which every student is out for him or herself. The top students are a teacher's joy; the slow and unmotivated are drudges. The result is alienation, insecurity, and conflict. To nourish relational process among students is to bring multiple worlds into coordination, and to replace divisive hierarchies with mutual appreciation. Students also acquire potentials to become border-crossers in an ever-splintering world of meaning. Thanks to a number of forward thinking educators, it is just such ends that are favored by an emerging array of practices. I focus here on three of my favorites.

Collaborative Classrooms

An educational focus on individual excellence favors the development of hierarchical structures. It is in this context that Edwin Mason concluded, "We are directly teaching mistrust of humanity wherever we make the young compete for esteem" (p.33).[21] And it is in this context that Kenneth Bruffee has stimulated a movement toward collaborative learning.[22] As Bruffee characterizes it, in the collaborative classroom an emphasis is placed on *sharing knowledge among students*. From a relational standpoint, such sharing enables students to absorb characteristics of each other,

[21]Mason, E. (1971). *Collaborative learning*. New York: Agathon.
[22]Bruffee, K. A. (1993). *Collaborative learning: Higher education, interdependence, and the authority of knowledge*. Baltimore: Johns Hopkins University Press.

to model their ways of acting and relating (Chapter 5). As they "become the other," so are they enabled to participate in a new range of relationships. To relate with someone who participates in an unfamiliar religion, or who is an athlete, an intellectual, an artist, or a political activist, and so on, is to absorb a way of being. These ways of being, in turn, enable one to relate to groups or traditions in which such characteristics are honored.

Further, student sharing enables one to develop new identities, to forge a way of being adequate to the other. One may learn how to be a helper, a competitor, a nurturer, a jokester, and so on. Finally, there is the newly developed choreography of relating to others, a choreography that may itself enrich future relationship. For example, one may learn how to complement another's behavior in some situations, to challenge it in others, and to react with irony, evaluative judgment, and the like. In effect, student sharing is a major contributor to multi-being.

•

The very structuring of our graduate training emphasizes an increasing isolation, as students go from working in courses to working with a few professors for their doctoral orals, and then working alone in the library to complete a dissertation, often under the guidance of a single sponsor. So natural does this progression seem that we rarely take note of the cultural adjustment we require students to make in the process.

——David Damrosch

•

Informal relations at school—at lunch, in the gym, after school, and so on—permit students to remain in familiar and comfortable relationships, thus fostering thick friendships, cliques, and ethnic enclaves. All too often the result is in-group/out-group conflict, along with its distancing and antipathies.[23] In contrast, a teacher can organize the classroom in such a way that more generative relations are achieved. Classroom discussion groups, working partners, laboratory research groups, and the like can cut across these informal boundaries. Further, specific kinds of dialogues can be invited. With effective planning, for example, groups will find it useful to affirm and build on disparate or unfamiliar ideas, express curiosity, admit doubts, share personal stories, etc.[24] As Lois Holzman proposes, it is

---

[23]See, for example, Willis, P. (1977). *Learning to labour*. London: Avebury.

[24]Practical details on bringing about lively dialogue in the classroom are contained in Oldfather, P., West, J., White, J., and Wilmarth, J. (1999). *Learning through children's eyes: Social constructivism and the desire to learn*. Washington, DC: APA Press; Fosnot, K. (1989). *Enquiring*

as important for students to learn how to develop and sustain emotionally significant relationships as it is those which are practically effective.[25] In each of these contexts, participation nourishes collaborative skills for worlds to come.

●

Enormously important in its contribution to student collaboration is the establishment of computer-based learning. The computer provides means of linking small groups of students to work on common goals. As a vast range of research suggests, such practices can lead to (1) a reduction in the teacher's control over class discussion and outcomes, (2) greater student participation in dialogue, (3) more evenly spread contributions to ongoing discussion, and (4) increased instances in which students help each other.[26] Careful preparation is required to achieve these ends, but they are within relatively easy reach.

●

Computer-aided collaboration has been an important teaching adventure for me. In one of the most successful experiments, I abandon individual exams and term papers in favor of group dialogue. I arrange for small groups of students to work together on a given problem or topic. They are challenged to carry out a week-long dialogue on e-mail. Prior to the event, I have the students work together to generate what they feel are the criteria of good dialogue. Here it is interesting to note that these criteria are quite different from those valued in the monologic essay. Where the good essay, for example, is one that is logically coherent and leads to a single best conclusion, the effective dialogue is one that entertains multiple ideas and does not close down voices of possibility. As my students also tell me, in a good dialogue the participants care for each other. In contrast, the individual essay, as described in the preceding chapter, is typically built around a logic of self-protection. The entire transcript of the dialogue is turned in to me at the end of the week. Individual grades (required by the Registrar) are a combination of my

teachers, enquiring learners: A constructivist approach to teaching. New York: Teachers College Press; Stein, R. F., and Hurd, S. (2000). *Using student teams in the classroom: A faculty guide.* San Francisco: Anker; and Barkley, E. F., Cross, K. P., and Major, C. H. (2005). *Collaborative learning techniques: A handbook for college faculty.* San Francisco, Wiley.

[25]Holzman, L. (2009). *Vygotsky at work and play.* London: Routledge.

[26]For an early compilation of this research, see Schofield, J. W. (1995). *Computers and classroom culture.* New York: Cambridge University Press.

evaluation of the dialogue as a whole (based on their criteria), in addition to individual efforts.

Most students find these dialogues wonderfully energizing and intellectually stimulating. They are also enthusiastic about the form of interchange. There is no pecking order; no one dominates the conversation; all contribute. All feel welcome, and at the close of the conversation, they will often congratulate or thank each other for their contributions. They are also eager for me to read their work, as they believe they have very interesting things to say. And they do... .

You can appreciate the flavor of such dialogue, and perhaps the reason for my enthusiasm, from the following excerpt. The case is particularly relevant, as the students were challenged to address the possibilities of replacing an individualist with a relational orientation to educational practices. Mike was assigned the task of opening the conversation:

MIKE:...I figured that we should start...with the idea of how relationships and the meaning derived from them would change our system of education. Feel free to comment on other ideas. Maybe we should give pros and cons for how this would affect student/teacher relationships, or relations among students.
I think we should also keep in mind ways that the current system enforces competition and separation.

KATIE: Hey guys, hope everyone's day is going well. Thanks for starting, Mike. In the past 24 hours it has really hit me just how closely tied to a tradition of individual responsibility our educational system is!
But students are supposed to learn information...what is the significance of education if material isn't learned... . I suppose we could just assume that students are learning without testing or confirming this, but if educators don't have any sense of results of the educational process, how can it be tweaked and improved...?
Because, I mean, even an assignment like this which is trying to break away from individual responsibility by having us conduct a group dialogue...what we produce is still being critiqued and we as a group are still being held collectively responsible for what we do or do not produce. Seems to me the situation should be pushed further still...would it help if the professor were continually involved in the dialogue as opposed to evaluating a record of it externally at the end?...

SANDRA: I believe that the current system of education is unidirectional in the creation of meaning... The teacher tries to present the material in such a way that the meaning gets created in the student's mind...yet the student doesn't get to share in the process. The meaning has already been created in the teacher's mind...

This could be a reason why some students have a hard time transitioning to a college like ours. I know in my experience in high school, we didn't have very much dialogue such as this. My education focused intently on memorizing facts and ways to accomplish certain goals with the hope of scoring well on tests.

ROBBIE: I admit, up front, that I am a biology major and so at times my views on education may seem not to fit your experiences in the humanities or social science... We might compare my thoughts on education and what role dialogue currently plays in it... I hate to add yet another proposal...but hopefully we can inspire each other to speak up. (Robbie goes on to write about dialogue in the context of laboratory work.)

I hang on their words...perhaps they are also reflected in the pages of this book. I turn now to a second adventure.

Collaborative Writing

In the tradition of bounded being, public language is an outward expression of an inner world. In the educational sphere this assumption is realized in the stress we place on individual writing. As described in the preceding chapter, we look at incoherent writing as a sign of "poor thought." In this vein, the strong sanctions against plagiarism exist primarily to ensure that the writing reflects the mind of its author, and not someone else's. The writer is the well-spring of thought. This conception of writing is but one further contribution to our viewing ourselves as fundamentally separated from each other. Alternatively, as the present work emphasizes, all intelligibility emerges from relationship. In this sense, writing does not reflect an independent mind, but a history of relationship.[27]

●

"Independent scholarship" is essentially
a contradiction in terms.
　　　　　—Patricia A. Sullivan

●

[27]Interestingly, novels in the United States were not always the product of individual authors. As Susanna Ashton describes, between 1870 and 1920 there were several hundred novels authored by people working together. See Ashton, S. (2006). *Literary collaborators in America: 1870–1920.* New York: Palgrave.

Reflecting this view, forward-looking scholars have sought means of teaching writing as a social activity, one in which the individual is not only sensitive to the traditions of relationship from which he or she is drawing, but takes into account the reader for whom the writing is intended.[28] For example, students may be asked to write about their lives, and especially to share with their classmates events relevant to their studies. In this vein, a friend who teaches in an inner-city junior college related to me his success in having students in a multi-cultural class write about times they felt they were the victims of prejudice. The narratives revealed that all groups, regardless of race, ethnicity, religion or gender, shared the anguish and anger. In a later variation on this assignment, he asked them to write about times in which relations with someone from "another group" had added significantly to their lives. As he reported, the effects on classroom solidarity were stunning.

Other scholars have taken a more radical step by creating collaborative writing practices.[29] Rather than viewing students as lone authors, the attempt is to generate a pooling of talents and resources. Students can offer complementary information, perspectives, and opinions, thus teaching each other and contributing to a richer and more informed product. Students may participate in brainstorming, information gathering, organizing, drafting, revising, and editing the work. Where one student may be good at conceptualizing the project, another may have innovative insights or a fluid writing style. Others may excel at injecting humor or self-reflection into the group discussions. And through such collaboration, students become models for each other. The potentials for multi-being are again expanded.

There is an important point to be made here for those who treasure the educational goal of critical thinking. There are many definitions of critical thinking, ranging from basic skills in writing, math, and science, to the capacity to subject assumptions to critical analysis. From the present standpoint, however, whichever definition we select, we are speaking of the result of an individual's participation in relationship. Most important in the present context, the capacity to subject assumptions to critical

---

[28]See, for example, Cooper, M. M. (1989). *Writings as social action*. Portsmouth, NH: Boynton/Cook.

[29]See, for example, Forman, J. (Ed.) (1992). *New visions of collaborative writing*. Portsmouth: Boynton/Cook; Reagan, S. B., Fox, T., and Bleich, D. (1994). *Writing with: New directions in collaborative teaching, learning, and research*. Albany: State University of New York Press; Ede, L., and Lunsford, A. (1990). *Singular texts/plural authors: Perspectives on collaborative writing*. Carbondale: Southern Illinois University Press; Topping, K. J. (1995). *Paired reading, spelling and writing: The handbook for teachers and parents*. London: Cassell.

reflection demands that one participates in more than one tradition. If there is only one account of reality, one cannot step outside to assess its limitations. (See Chapter 7). A committed scientist cannot easily or convincingly evaluate science from a sociological standpoint. Thus, practices like collaborative writing are to be cherished. Students writing an essay on the value of democracy, for example, may well find classmates who find democracy problematic; a term paper on the origins of human life may bring forth highly diverse opinions. Here the seeds can be planted for liberating reflection.

•

> To think critically is essentially to deliberate on one tradition
> through the discourse of another. The advantage of the critical
> thinker is not in having the superior tradition, but in being capable
> of seeing the advantages and disadvantages of both traditions.
> The critical thinker who claims superiority of perspective, not only
> loses this advantage, but strangulates the potential for action.

•

In terms of the global future, the significance of collaborative education cannot be overestimated. Increasingly, work takes place in the context of networks—whether speaking of business, government, private sector activities, or scientific research. As Brian Connery and John Vohs put it in their work on collaborative writing:

> While we give lip service to the value of the rugged individual,
> admiring ground-breaking geniuses like Newton, Woolf, Einstein,
> and McClintock, or yearning for the self-sufficiency of the early
> settlers. The social reality is that, for most of us, the bulk of our
> professional lives will be spent working in cooperation and
> collaboration with others within committees, research teams, boards,
> departments, professional societies, or corporations. Self-sufficiency is
> arguably a noble ideal but also arguably an obsolete one. A visit to
> your local survivalist's cave in the hills will quickly demonstrate that
> absolute independence most often results in a primitive crudity,
> which few of us are willing to accept as the price for uncompromising
> self-sufficiency.[30]

[30]Connery, B. A., and Vohs, J. L. (2004). *Group work and collaborative writing*. Davis, CA: University of California, Davis. See: http://dhc.ucdavis.edu/vohs/index.html

Circle 3: Classroom and Community

> I believe that the school is primarily a social institution. Education being a social process, the school is simply that form of community life in which all those agencies are concentrated that will be most effective in bringing the child to share the inherited resources of the [society].
>
> —John Dewey

•

The walls of the school are misleading. They suggest a separation between the school and its surrounds; they suggest that the success of the educational process depends on what takes place within the walls. Yet, as increasingly clear, what takes place in the classroom can never be separated from the family life of the students, local politics, the economy, and so on. The result of such sensitivity has provoked scattered efforts to change the external conditions with the hope that schools will benefit. For example, forward-looking schools in economically depressed areas establish programs to insure that not only their students have enough to eat, but also their families. Yet, while commendable, there is reason for further blurring the boundaries between classroom and community.

Stimulated by John Dewey's writings, many educators stress the function of the schools in preparing students for participating in democratic society. As reasoned, this end is most fully served by learning within the community itself. As Lave and Wenger emphasize, by participating in the community, one becomes a collaborating member of an ongoing practice.[31] The learner comes to *know how* things are done within the community, and how its local realities and values function. Echoing the earlier discussion of situated learning, education in context is also valued. The student participates in the actual practices, as opposed to memorizing general principles of ambiguous relevance to concrete circumstance.[32] Community-based learning also opens students up to multiple realities and values. Students might be challenged, for example, to plan a new transportation system that would help the poor of the inner-city find new jobs. In this case students would face the challenge of avoiding the destruction of neighborhoods, allocating tax monies, and establishing job training. When students are confronted with such multiple challenges, they are more likely

[31]Lave, J., and Wenger, E. (1991). *Situated learning: Legitimate peripheral participation.* Cambridge: Cambridge University Press.

[32]See also Lave, J. (1988). *Cognition in practice: Mind, mathematics, and culture in everyday life.* Cambridge: Cambridge University Press.

to seek out opinions. They will realize the value of working together. Although community-based learning takes many forms, three initiatives are particularly visible.

Community Collaboration

Associations between parents and teachers have long been encouraged. However, such programs are also limited, as students are not so much participants as objects of conversation. Further, the form of the relationship can also be threatening. Many teachers feel that parents are advocates for their child alone, and often meddle in the school programs. Schools do take steps to overcome these barriers. For example, parents are invited to observe classes, class performances are put on for parents, parents contribute to classes, and so on. However, there is also enormous room for further exploration. Exemplary are programs emphasizing *distributed leadership,* that is, practices that attempt to bring multiple participants into sharing leadership in school development and change.[33] Distributed leadership may be small, as in the case of a school principal who initiated a breakfast gatherings with his teachers, or large, as in the San Francisco Bay Area School Reform project in which 86 schools participated in experiments in "whole school reform."[34]

The work of Barabara Rogoff and her colleagues nicely illustrates community collaboration at work. Together they developed a program bringing together students, teachers, and adults from the community.[35] Their belief was that learning occurs most effectively through the interested participation of learners together. Thus, teachers joined with both parents and students to plan the curriculum and classroom activities. Even the youngest students were brought into the discussions. Parents also served periodically as co-teachers. On occasion, students from different grades were brought together for co-learning sessions. The result was the successful creation of a broad community of learners, all drawing from the adventure in collaboration.[36]

---

[33]See, for example, Donaldson, G. A. (2006). *Cultivating leadership in schools: Connecting people, purpose, and practice.* Williston, VT: Teachers College Press; Rubin, H. (2002). *Collaborative leadership: Developing effective partnerships in communities and schools.* Thousand Oaks: Corwin.

[34]Copland, M. A. (2003). The Bay Area School Reform Collaborative: Building the capacity to lead. In J. M. Murphy and A. Datnow (Eds.) *Leadership lessons from comprehensive school reforms.* Thousand Oaks: Corwin.

[35]Rogoff, B., Turkanis, C. G., and Bartlett, L. (Eds.) (2001). *Learning together: Children and adults in a school community.* Oxford: Oxford University Press.

[36]For more on ways in which teachers involve the community in the educational process, see Weiss, H. B., Kreider, H., and Lopez, M. E. (2005). *Preparing educators to involve families: From theory to practice.* Thousand Oaks, CA: Sage.

A further illustration is furnished by the work of the Study Circle Program.[37] This program facilitates community-wide dialogue on issues of common concern. Such practices are highly effective in bringing schools and communities together. For example, in the Montgomery County Public School district, outside Washington, D.C., there was a distinct gap in grades between the racial and ethnic minority students and the white majority. Study circles were developed that included over 350 parents, teachers, and students. They met together for six, 2-hour sessions, and talked about a range of relevant and often provocative topics, including trust, diversity, and barriers to communication. They also took up questions of common ground, friendship, and steps for narrowing the gap. The result was not only a bridging of otherwise alienated groups, but the development of community-supported programs for improving the school.[38]

Cooperative Education

The preceding programs are devoted primarily to classroom welfare. The major aim is to improve the educational process, with community a secondary consideration. However, it is also important to reverse the priorities, to consider ways in which schools may serve the community while simultaneously stimulating the educational process. Cooperative education is an important step in this direction. The idea can be traced to the early 1900s. At that time, many potential students lacked the financial means for attending university on a full time basis. Many university courses were also irrelevant to the professions they wanted to pursue. As a result, a number of enterprising universities began to consider a new site for learning: the workplace. Ideally, students would draw both from the workplace and the classroom, generating combinations of unusual promise. For example, Antioch College and Northeastern University developed impressive co-op or work-study models of education. Corporations also took an increasing interest in such programs, as they provided training

[37]See www.studycircles.org

[38]I have also been impressed with the work of the Intergenerational School in Cleveland Ohio. Inspired by the husband and wife team of Catherine and Peter Whitehouse, the school brings together children from K-8, largely African American, with the elderly population. Elders serve as mentors and tutors and simultaneously participate in lifelong learning. In spite of the fact that student work in school is ungraded, students participating in the program score significantly higher in the yearly tests of reading and math than both the Municipal and State averages.

grounds for future employees. There are now over a thousand such programs in operation, spanning over 40 nations.[39]

Although there are exceptions, in my view the cooperative education movement has yet to reap the full benefits of relational thinking. In most cases both the university and the workplace remain relatively intact. The student participates in the workplace and in the classroom, and is expected to learn what each has to offer. Not only is the student voice often ignored, but the linkages between the class and the workplace are frequently unexplored. Conversation between scholars and employers can also be infrequent. In effect, there is too little in the way of cross-talk and conjoint meaning-making. One can only imagine the potentially rich outcomes resulting from dialogue among students, faculty, and firms on how they might collaborate for the common good.

Service Learning

One of the most exciting community outreach initiatives of recent years is the service learning movement. Inheriting the view that one learns best by doing, many schools foster programs in which students learn by working outside the institution. In the case of service learning, however, such education has a humanitarian twist. Education takes place through contributions to community well-being. Thus, students gain academic credit for helping to collect food for the homeless, growing vegetables for a school cafeteria, tutoring the inner-city teens, working in half-way houses, installing drywall for Habitat for Humanity, and much, much more. In all cases, service learning gives students more voice than traditional forms of learning provide, thus representing a shift from passive, hierarchical models of learning to active participation in the community. Further, in many cases, schools place both students and community dwellers in learning/teaching roles. Here the relational potentials are maximized.[40]

Yet, from a relational standpoint, service learning programs often tend to sustain the tradition of bounded units. That is, built into such programs is typically a view of intact communities: the school on the one hand, the community on the other. Students typically "go out" into the community,

---

[39]See the World Association of Cooperative Education (www.waceinc.org). For useful reflection on the cooperative movement, see *The Journal of Cooperative Education*.

[40]For more on service learning see Jacoby, B. & Associates. (1996). *Service learning in higher education: Concepts and practices*. San Francisco: Jossey-Bass Publishers; also www.servicelearning. org.; Campus Compact, http://www.compact.org/; and 101 Ideas for Combining Service and Learning, http://www.fiu.edu/%7etime4chg/Library/ideas.html

and return to reflect on what they have learned. Much needed are creative models that more fully integrate class and community.

•

For me, the work of Swarthmore College professor John Alston with the Chester Children's Chorus approximates the creative ideal. Alston developed a program for young students in Chester, a nearby town in severe economic depression. Children may enter the program as young as 8 years old, and they can remain until high school graduation. The chorus rehearses twice a week during the school year, and in the summer they attend a 4-week summer camp at Swarthmore College. The regimen for the students is demanding, but the result is a very proud and committed group of almost 50 singers. So impressive is their music that they perform in numerous locations in the area, including standing-room-only performances at Swarthmore College each year. The program has also been effective in encouraging the participants to go on to college from high school.

The Chester Children's Chorus in concert at Lang Music Hall, Swarthmore College. The chorus is led by Dr. John Alston who teaches at Swarthmore and who founded the chorus in 1994.

Courtesy: Jonathan Hodgson.

We should not conclude from this discussion that community-based learning must necessarily take place outside the school itself. The classroom itself may be a source of such learning. For example, energized classes may also take on issues facing the community (or the nation as a whole), generate relevant information, and communicate to public officials about their concerns. I was most impressed by a recent initiative in Italy that promoted "newspapers in the classroom." Students in some 29,000 schools throughout the country devoted an hour a week comparing how different daily newspapers covered the news. This initiative not only revealed how news-writing creates the realities it reports, but also demonstrated how differently the "same" event can be constructed. Such study not only provoked lively discussion, but significantly advanced the level of media literacy.

Circle 4: The Classroom and the World

The concept of community should scarcely be limited to the local sphere. Rather we must extend the participatory circle to the global sphere. Western educational thought has long favored the idea of learning about distant lands and other peoples. However, there are two distinct features of the traditional orientation. First, the subject matter is bounded; that is, the lands and the peoples are observed and analyzed as *the other*. The underlying message is, in effect, "*we* learn about *you*." The worldview of fundamental separation is sustained. One does not transcend barriers of meaning so much as extend local understanding so as to incorporate the other. And, too, much traditional study of "foreigners" is dependent on verbal representation. In reading books alone, representation is highly constrained. There is little in the way of sound, touch, smell, or taste—in short, little immersion in the full dance of relationship.

Today these traditional limitations are no longer binding. Opportunities for broad relational immersion are copious. The major engine of innovation is, of course, technology. Through the Internet, one can connect within seconds to people, images, and sources of information from virtually any nation around the world—and at little if any cost. These developments open up exciting vistas of relationally rich education.[41] No longer are students limited to learning *about* others, but can begin to learn *with* them. The development of the Gardiner Symonds Teaching Laboratory at Rice University was groundbreaking in its linking classroom and world.

[41]For useful resources, see http://lap.umd.edu/SOC/sochome.html

The classroom provides no lectern or desk for the teacher, only a mobile chair. Multiple computers, and similarly mobile chairs enable small groups of students to organize themselves at any time in any part of the room. There are three walls with multiple screens onto which any computer can beam its contents, or onto which video and power-point materials may be displayed. Through the Internet groups within the class can travel virtually anywhere in the world, and bring back materials for discussion. Further, their own efforts can be sent to remote stations outside the room, and indeed, outside the university. Most universities now feature computer classrooms with global links, but teachers are only slowly realizing the potentials.

Such explorations in education become increasingly dialogical. In one early experiment, philosophers Mark Taylor and Esa Saarinen[42] used satellite transmission to add an audio–visual component to dialogue between American and Finnish students.[43] More common now are distance learning programs, in which faculty and students from around the globe can converse.

> My first experience in this medium was sponsored by the Collaborative Learning Program at the University of Tennessee. They arranged for seminar students at their university to join with students in Australia, along with faculty from other continents, to meet for weekly dialogue on the net.[44] The subject matter was common to all of us, but the ways in which we approached the materials were dramatically different. I learned as much as I taught. In another such venture, students from New Zealand join in dialogue with teachers from around the world (www.virtualfaculty). I found the bi-weekly dialogues both intense and engaging. Students asked questions of me that I had never encountered. The reverse was also the case. And, though we never met face-to-face, some of these on-line relations continue to the present.

•

Such boundary-crossing adventures are not limited to older students or to those who are proficient in multiple languages. In one inspiring case, an American school teacher linked her class of children via the Internet to students in Japan. While they did not share a common written language, they could exchange drawings and photos. They shared photos of their parents, friends, and pets; they exchanged pictures of their school, their neighborhood, and their favorite meals. They also drew pictures to illustrate their favorite activities. With the current development in transmitting

[42]Taylor, M., and Saarinen, E. (1994). *Imagologies: Mediaphilosophy*. New York: Routledge.

[43]An extensive bibliography on collaborative practices may be found at www.psu.edu/celt/clbib. html. The publishing company, Houghton Mifflin, also makes available through its Project Center a range of on-line practices enabling students to collaborate via e-mail with others around the world.

[44]See http://web.utk.edu/~edpsych/grad/collab_learning/

music and videos, the opportunities for immersion in the global community are enormous.[45]

•

The rates of social change, the movements of the world's people, industrialization, globalization, and militarization continue to escalate at an ever-accelerating pace. Educators face an unprecedented task. They must support people to become highly creative, collaborative, problem-solvers, and critical thinkers. They must cultivate people's capacities to see the world from profoundly different perspectives. They must nourish people's capacities for connection and caring in a fragmented and divisive world.

—Mary Field Belenky

Circles Unceasing

In the preceding pages I have touched briefly on four domains of relationship: the teacher and student, relations among classmates, and the relation of the class both to the immediate environment and to the global context. Yet, this is but a sampling. Attention could have as easily been directed, for example, to relations among teachers,[46] between teachers and administrators, between administrators and the government, and more. Further, there is much to be gained in multi-party circles, with teachers, students, parents and administrators, for example, all in dialogue. With each new configuration, we could again re-evaluate our inheritances and open new vistas of practice. How could collaborative activities among teachers, for example, be used to enhance the relational process within classrooms, or between classrooms and the world outside? With a conscious focus on relational practices, we would also find a sharing across the circles. The classroom practices of dialogue, for example, might be used to bring teachers and administrators into synchrony, and vice versa.

When education focuses on relationships as opposed to individuals, we enter a new world of possibility. Our concern shifts from what is taking place "within minds," to our life together. And within this space of collaborative meaning-making, we can appreciate our multiple traditions and their various potentials. Further, we can ask about the kind of world we wish to create for the future—both locally and globally. When education is sensitive to relationship, we realize that in terms of future well-being, "we are all in it together."

[45]Useful resources for integrating multimedia and the internet, and for expanding global relations may be found at: http://ss.uno.edu/SS/homePages/TechClass.html.

[46]Relevant here are works enabling teachers to share their experiences with each other. See, for example, Miller, C. M. (Ed). (2005). *Narratives from the classroom.* Thousand Oaks, CA: Sage.

9

Therapy as Relational Recovery

Psychotherapy is a fascinating practice. A close friend drops out of his busy life for some 50 minutes a week to reveal his most secret longings, doubts, hatreds, and failures to someone he scarcely knows. Like thousands of others, he departs these brief encounters with a strong sense that he is better fit to go on with life. He, like others, feels he is in a better space of being. I fully believe that he is. But there are others who have responded to therapy with indifference, frustration, and anger.

It is when we realize the enormous range of reactions to the therapeutic process that we most vividly see that therapy is not therapy—that is, there is no process of therapy *in itself*. Therapy comes to be what it is—for good or ill—within a matrix of relationship. Therapists have nothing significant to say unless there are clients who grant them significance, and clients vary dramatically in their interpretive habits. At the same time, the client's words and actions are granted significance—or not—through the therapist's responses. A client's "problem" must be granted the privilege of being a problem. We are dealing, then, not with therapists *and* clients but with coordinated action.

The client–therapist relationship is the focal subject of this chapter. My chief concern is with extending the implications of relational being to this site of practice. However, this relationship cannot be considered alone, cut away from other relationships. Whatever problems an individual confronts find their origins in a context of socially engendered meaning. Thus, therapy is a matter of restoring viable relations—for the client(s) and the sea of relations in which they are immersed—both present and past. Ultimately, however, one must think of this sea of relations as extending from the local to the global milieu. To appreciate the force of this proposal, I want to first take up the the broad relational context in which the very possibility of therapy—along with its potentials for human change—comes into being. I then turn to the relational process in therapy itself. As therapist and client enter a process of co-action, what kinds of practices are invited; what are the potentials and limitations of existing practices? Here I open discussion on three major ways in which therapy can function in the restoration of relationship. I complete the chapter with a discussion of new therapeutic horizons that emerge from a relational perspective.

Therapy in Relational Context

The relationship between therapist and client is scarcely isolated. What takes place within the therapeutic encounter is first linked to the relational histories of the participants. Here is a meeting of multi-beings. Further, these relationships are embedded within an expanded array of relations— ethnic, religious, professional, and so on. Therapy is but a single relationship nested within a potentially limitless and dynamic complex. There is no personal problem, mental illness, or family dysfunction *in itself*, but only within this complex. In many ways the limits and potentials of the therapeutic encounter are established before the participants utter the first word. They come together because it "makes sense" within the expanded arena of relationship at a particular time in history. And whatever they do together, along with whatever they consider "progress," will carry the imprint of this broader matrix of meaning.

The cultural and historical context of the therapeutic encounter has been a subject of long and lively debate.[1] Here I want to draw attention to three significant vistas, those specifically bearing on therapy as relational recovery. First I address the relationship between the socio-cultural context and the construction of personal problems, and then to the concept of cure. Then I turn to the impact of therapeutic practice on the cultural surrounds. By way of illustration, I will also take up a specific case: the now burgeoning neuro/pharma movement in therapy. I focus on this topic not only because of its increasing dominance, but because of its gross insensitivity to issues of relationship.

---

[1] See, for example, Cushman, P. (1996). *Constructing the self, constructing America: A cultural history of psychotherapy.* Don Mills, Ontario: Addison Wesley Publishing Company.

The Social Genesis of "the Problem"

All of us suffer from time to time; we all confront people who are strange or baffling in their behavior. Many of us have confronted problems of such severity that we have urgently sought help. Such is life. Yet, immersion in the tribulations of daily life is also blinding. We encounter the problem before us, without seeing the culturally "thrown" character of such problems, and the extent to which we participate in their very existence.

As outlined in preceding chapters, virtually all enduring relationships will bring into being a relatively stable definition of "the way the world is," along with an associated array of values. By the same token, relational process will tend to create a domain of undesirable deviation, and a dishonoring of people who are "out of line," "stupid," "ridiculous," or otherwise evil.[2] Thus, whether an event or behavior constitutes "a problem," and warrants "suffering," depends on the configuration of our relationships. No one is weird, neurotic, psychotic, or pathological outside a tradition in which certain acts are defined both as "unusual" and "unwanted." One is only "disordered" by virtue of social convention. The individual who starves himself in the service of a passionate political cause will not see his behavior as a problem, but as a solution to a problem. If a teenager starves herself for no obvious reason, it is commonly defined as a problem (even if the teenager herself does not.)[3] Similarly, one suffers largely because it is culturally intelligible to do so. One does not "suffer failure" outside a tradition in which success is valued. There is no anguish over "losing" outside of a tradition that values "winning." Unhappiness is not a problem in itself; in many relationships it may be an honor. Grieving for a loved one is an obvious case in point.[4]

•

If you are not depressed, you are stupid.
——Eastern Europe Cold War saying

•

It follows that a problem in one subculture may not figure as such in another. With the existence of innumerable subcultures in society, the stage is set for interminable conflict in what constitutes "a problem to

[2]See also Link, B. G., and Phelan, J. C. (1999). The labeling theory of mental disorder. *A handbook for the study of mental health* (pp. 139–150). Cambridge: Cambridge University Press.
[3]See Hepworth, J. (1999). *The social construction of anorexia nervosa.* Thousand Oaks, CA: Sage.
[4] Stroebe, M., Gergen, K. J., Gergen, M. M., and Stroebe, W. (1992). Broken hearts or broken bonds: Love and death in historical perspective. *American Psychologist, 47,* 1205–1212.

In the same way we distinguish between the normal and the pathologic person, we also distinguish between dancers and the disabled. Here the revolutionary Axis Dance Company challenges such conventions. In the Fantasy in C Major choreographed by Bill T. Jones, the "disabled" become dancers. Depending on the co-active process, individual inadequacy dissolves. Potentials and weaknesses are brought into being through relationship.

Photo by Margot Hartford.

be treated." There are thousands of people in the U.S. classified as criminals and locked in prison cells, otherwise defined by one or another mental health community as mentally ill. Vast segments of the population find abortion, marijuana, and homosexuality unproblematic; for others, such behaviors are illegal or sinful.

•

My friend Mac took my breath away. His energies were effervescent, his passions intense, and his words were a wondrous waterfall of imaginative images, ironies, and quips. In my junior year at Yale, it was Mac and not my teachers who most fully captured my attention. No, I could not depend on his continued presence at the university. He possessed an infectious spontaneity that rendered his actions unpredictable. The year prior he had seen a compelling film on the Everglades of southern Florida and left college in mid-semester. Six months later he was an Everglades guide.

In my senior year I had an opportunity to serve as a conference assistant at the annual meeting of the Young Presidents Organization, an exclusive group of individuals who had achieved presidency of a corporation before the age of 40. The meetings were to take place at the elegant Greenbrier resort in White Sulfur Springs, and I invited Mac to join our group. The two of us had a rollicking time, privately treating the affair as a hilarious game. However, one noon I returned to my room to find an armed guard in front of Mac's room. I asked if he could tell me what was going on, and he grunted a refusal. I entered my room and tried to call Mac; the line was continuously busy. A few minutes later I looked out of the window to see Mac in a straight jacket, being whisked away by a retinue of guards. Rushing to confer with the conference director, I was told that there was a consensus that Mac was mentally disturbed, was a threat to the guests, and had to be forcibly removed.

I did not see Mac again for five years. He had been confined to a mental hospital, treated with electroshock, and finally released under a heavy dose of drugs. The result, for me, was the death of Mac, or at least the wondrous Mac I had known. He was now lethargic, plump, and dull-witted. I had lost a friend, and have never ceased to ask why this treatment was either necessary or good.

•

Given multiple conceptions of "the problem," we confront the question of conflict. In the case of Mac, the two of us were at odds with the established culture around us. We lost. From a relational standpoint, the existence of conflict should not mean the loss of voices. Such losses not only reduce our options for action, but represent a rupture in the flow of meaning-making. In this sense, there is significant reason to resist the way in which the mental health professions are becoming singularly important professions in terms of defining disorder. Drawing from the prestige of medical science, and with the support of the insurance and pharmaceutical industry, the psychiatric community has generated a taxonomy of mental illness, disseminated widely in the *Diagnostic and statistical manual of mental disorders* (now in its fourth edition). The taxonomy functions as the bible of the mental health professions, and is purported to be objective and universal in application. At the same time, it is clear that the categories of "illness" are those of a particular group at a particular time in history. For many others it is highly suspect.[5] Further, the categories function as value positions

---

[5]Illustrative of of the critique are Kutchins, H., and Kirk, S. A. (1997). *Making us crazy: DSM: The psychiatric bible and the creation of mental disorders.* New York: Free Press; Gergen, K. J. (2006).

regarding what is appropriate, tolerable, or proper behavior in contemporary life.[6] As the categories suggest, the "good person" should neither be too happy nor too sad, too energetic nor too lethargic, eat too much nor too little, indulge too much in alcohol, gambling, or sex, and so on. To be sure, the categories often represent common agreements in society as to desirable behavior.[7] However, the result of the way in which the mental health professions have defined the categories, that which is undesirable is transformed into the pathological.[8] In this sense, there is much to be said for various anti-psychiatry, ex-mental patients, and other politically active groups that resist the taxonomy. The homosexual community pulled together to remove homosexual behavior from the list of "disorders." Why shouldn't those who hear voices, are highly energetic, or live in silence, do likewise? Ultimately, however, it is dialogue among those with competing conceptions that is most required.

•

In a world where all hear voices,
beware the one who fails to do so.

The Origins of Therapeutic Solutions

If behavioral problems are the byproduct of collaborative process, so are the forms of treatment. In courts of law, for example, the optimal "treatment" of deviance is typically punishment. For religious institutions there may be rituals of redemption. It makes sense within many business organizations simply to expel the deviant. In closely-knit communities, such as the Amish, shunning is a meaningful corrective device. In more loosely knit communities people may simply avoid the deviant. In this latter context, one might be pleased with the spectacular growth of the mental health professions over the past century. These professions are virtually unique in responding to undesirable actions with care instead of punishment. If we

---

Therapeutic realities: Collaboration, oppression and relational flow. Chagrin Falls, OH: Taos Institute Publications; Wakefield, J. (1991). Disorder as harmful dysfunction: A conceptual critique of DSM-III-R's definition of mental disorder. *Psychological Review,* 99, 232–247. See also: www.drzur.com/dsmcritique.html.

[6]See, for example, Mathews, M. (1999). Moral vision and the idea of mental illness: *Philosophy, psychiatry, and psychology,* 6, 299–310.

[7]For more on the moral judgments implicit in diagnostic categories, see Sadler, J. Z. (2004). *Values and psychiatric diagnosis.* New York: Oxford University Press.

[8]See, for example, Horwitz, A. V., and Wakefield, J. C. (2007). *The loss of sadness: How psychiatry transformed normal sorrow into depressive disorder.* New York: Oxford University Press; Lane, C. (2007). *Shyness: How normal behavior became a sickness.* New Haven: Yale University Press.

put aside the penchant for equating deviance with disease, one can credit the mental health professions with a significantly advancing the humane treatment of deviance.

At the same time, what counts as good treatment is not determined by the professions alone. In terms of its success, the therapeutic community is dependent as well on the surrounding culture. Without recognition by the medical profession, courts of law, insurance companies, and the media, therapists could scarcely claim to be "offering help." All these institutions grant to the therapeutic community their legitimacy as "healers," and invite the public to respond positively to therapeutic practice. In effect, the therapist's words carry the enormous symbolic weight of the cultural surrounds. It is this very weight that permits the therapist to ask probing questions about a client's private life, to discuss matters of greatest sensitivity to the client, and to provide insights and advice. And it is this same weight that pulls the client into a collaborative posture, and enables the client to depart from an anguished hour in therapy with a sense of accomplishment. The therapist thrives in a specific climate of meaning. In this sense, contemporary therapeutic practice in itself—cut away from a context of meaning— is no more or less effective than shamanism, astrology, or voodoo. It is our cultural understanding and appreciation of therapy that grants it the potential to be effective. In the contemporary, educated mainstream shamanism, astrology, and voodoo lack the legitimacy that would render them effective either in defining human problems or treating them. By the same token, drug treatments owe their efficacy not only to the physiological changes they bring about, but to the cultural interpretations of both drugs and their outcomes. Some people view Ritalin as a cure for Attention Deficit Disorder; for others, however, accelerated activity is not a disease and Ritalin is a soporific.

•

Let us return to the issue of conflict, this time in terms of conceptions of treatment. For the past 30 years I have worked with therapists from many different schools—psychoanalytic, Rogerian, cognitive, Jungian, constructivist, systemic, narrative, Buddhist, and postmodern among them. While similar in many respects, each invites a different form of therapist/client coordination. Unfortunately, however, the relationship among many of the therapeutic sub-cultures is contentious. In part it is a contention fostered by the widely shared belief that the Truth about therapeutic efficacy can be established. Embracing a realist vision of Truth, the attempt is to establish a foundation for therapy that does not depend upon the negotiations of people in relationship. Thus, within various schools of therapy, bonds are developed, realities created, values shared, and barriers then erected between the "truth within" and "the ignorance without" (see Chapter 6). The unfortunate result is freezing of the discourse within the circles, and a resistance to that which lies beyond. With this stabilizing of intelligibility, therapeutic schools become progressively removed from the surrounding context of meaning. As they do so, their capacity to move effectively in the cultural currents of meaning is diminished. One cannot practice psychoanalysis if people no longer believe in the reality of unconscious desires; Rogerians are rendered inept in a culture that judges positive regard as manipulative; and so on.

•

The search for evidenced-based anchors for effective therapy further fuels the competition among schools of therapy. As it is commonly reasoned, "Let us honor those therapies most likely to guarantee us something for our money." Yet, such reasoning is blind to the relational context that grants to therapy its efficacy. Therapeutic camps differ significantly in their conception of positive outcomes. What counts as progress for a cognitive behavioral therapist may not be considered so for a psychoanalyst or a family therapist. And none of them may agree with the views of clients and their families. That there are innumerable points of view on causes, and cures should not send us scuttling for proof of pedigree. To live effectively in a richly variegated world, where meaning is everywhere in motion and traditions everywhere eroding and reforming, multiple resources are essential. To reduce the range of reimbursable practices to a handful—as therapists and policy makers are wont to do—is not to render therapy more effective. It is to withdraw valuable assistance to those seeking help.

Relational Consequences of Therapy

From the present standpoint the primary concern of therapy should be the viability of the client's participation in relationships, past, present, and future. In effect, this is to bracket the view of therapy as specifically *psychological* in its focus. It is not mind-repair that is ultimately at stake, from a relational perspective, but relational transformation. This is not at all to abandon talk about mental states (e.g. emotions, memories, fantasies), but to remove "mental states" as the object of major concern. As outlined in Chapters 3 and 4, talk about mental states is a form of relational action. The question is not whether such talk "gets it right," but how it functions within relationships. In this focus on relational change, there are two major fields of concern. The first and most obvious is the cast of daily relationships to which clients return. To what degree is the client's participation in these patterns of relationship enhanced? This concern with daily relationships will be our primary focus as the chapter proceeds.

However, before completing this discussion I wish to underscore the importance of a second, and less obvious way in which the therapeutic process affects relationships outside. Specifically, we may view all therapists as social activists. For better or worse, their assumptions and practices enter society in such a way that meanings are altered or sustained. We glimpsed this possibility in the earlier discussion of diagnostic categories. As such categories are disseminated throughout the society and sealed with a professional stamp of approval, people come to understand themselves in just these ways. Common meanings are displaced. "The blues" becomes "depression," the "moody child" becomes "bipolar," an "intense dedication to work" becomes an "addiction," and so on. It is interesting that as the mental health professions have grown, so have the number of diagnostic categories, along with the number of therapeutic patients, and the annual expenditures on mental health.[9] While diagnostic categories may have utility within the profession, there are important respects in which their dissemination within the society more generally is crippling.

•

There are many therapists who understand their function as social activists. Thus, for example, therapists challenge the diagnostic categories, actively participate in resistance against dehumanizing treatments, and resist expansion of pharmaceutical "cures." These are not mere troublemakers. They function to unfreeze the taken-for-granted realities. They open alternatives that may accommodate the vast variations in society and can lead to more open dialogue.

This view of the therapist as social activist also means that the profession should give more concerted attention to the social conditions from which anguish emerges. For example, probing the injurious consequences of competitive practices in school and work, the ethos of materialism, and the technological landscape seems imperative. One may also question the willingness of people to accept the invitations to anguish currently favored by society. We are not biologically obliged to respond to criticism, failure, or loss with suffering. With the compelling words of the therapeutic community, we might replace this naturalized response with indifference,

[9]For further discussion of this point, see Gergen, K. J. (2006). *Therapeutic realities.* Chagrin Falls, OH: Taos Institute Publications.

or even resistance. Societal concerns were central to early therapists, such as Freud, Fromm, and Horney. They should be no less so today.

A Contemporary Case: Mind and Meds

To illustrate these concerns with the cultural context of therapeutic practice let's focus on a major issue of the day. There is a rapidly growing romance with a biological view of behavior disorders and pharmacological treatment. This romance is fed in part by the development of brain scanning technology, and its invitation to see human behavior as a byproduct of cortical activity (See Chapter 4). In arguing for a biological basis for behavior problems, psychiatry can also claim itself as a *medical* profession. The movement is also supported by pharmaceutical industries invested in a broad range of drugs specifically pegged to diagnostic categories. To underscore the impact of this movement, 30 years ago there were relatively few antipsychotic drugs available, and drug treatments were typically limited to the severely impaired. In 1970 there were approximately 150,000 mental health cases treated pharmacologically in the U.S. By the year 2,000 the number jumped to between 9 and 10 million. Further, and most alarming, more than half the cases treated by psychotropic drugs were school children. At the publication of the present volume, Amazon.com lists almost 8,000 volumes treating the subject of psychopharmacology. The browser of this list will also have a difficult time locating more than a handful of books critical—or even cautious—about the use of drugs in psychiatric practice.

•

> A 60-year-old divorced female was referred to me by a fellow psychiatrist who was leaving private practice. The frazzled looking woman informed me that she is diagnosed as a rapid-cycling bipolar and then presented me with a list of her current medications. She was being treated with Lamictal (an anticonvulsant) 100 mg three times a day, Alpazolam (a tranquilizer) 1 mg three times a day, Celexa (an antidepressant) 40 mg per day, Wellbutrin (an antidepressant) 150 mg twice a day, Seroquel (an antipsychotic) 300 mg at bedtime, Fiorinol (a barbiturate containing pain pill) up to 4 a day, and finally Ritalin (an amphetamine stimulant) 20 mg three times a day. That is 17 pills a day! Asked about her current supply of medications, she didn't know what she had or needed. All she knew for certain was that she was out of Ritalin and needed a refill. By that time, the hour allotted for her intake was up. So, do I give her a refill and further legitimize what I view as an irrational and dangerous diagnostic

conceptualization and treatment plan by her previous psychiatrist? And if I choose not to, what do I do?

—Phillip Sinaikin, MD

•

The interest of pharmaceutical companies in the biologizing of behavior problems is debatably humanitarian. Consider, for example, the profit from the growth of the antidepressant drug, Prozac. According to a *Newsweek* report (March 26, 1990), a year after the drug was introduced to the market sales reached $125 million. One year later the sales had almost tripled to $350 million. By 2002, Prozac was a $12 billion industry, and there were over 25 million prescriptions for Prozac (or its generic equivalent) in the U.S. alone. A similar number of prescriptions are written for Zoloft, a close cousin, and another 25 million for a combination of other competitors.[10] Consider that at the turn of the 20th century, depression was virtually non-existent as a cultural concern. Through the intensive efforts of psychiatrists, the pharmaceutical industry, and the mass media, over a tenth of the population today is said to be depressed, and there are over 88 million websites discussing depression.

•

One may read such figures in three equally unsettling ways. In the first instance, they represent increased expenditures on mental health. Given the problematic practice of diagnosis, we must confront the possibility that as a culture we are needlessly constructing the population in ways that increasingly raise public expenditures. In this sense, drug cures do not help managed care programs to reduce health-care costs. Rather, with the cooperative efforts of psychiatrists and the pharmaceutical companies, there is an exponential increase in expenditures.

One may also read these economic figures in terms of the future condition of the society. Given the unfettered expansion of psychodiagnostic categories and the willingness of the society to "trust the experts," future profits are almost guaranteed. The availability of profit also means the launching of still further drugs, and the marketing of these drugs to both mental health professionals and the public. We confront an unending spiral of diagnosis and drugging. Further, because of their economic power, the industries may be able to discourage or block any legislation that would threaten profitability.

•

[10]*New York Times*, June 30, 2002.

There is a final concern: the message that is sent to the culture at large. In effect, the culture is informed that drugs are the answer to common problems of human living. If one is deeply grieving, anxious about work, distressed by failure, frightened of social life, worried about homoerotic tendencies, or is growing too thin, drugs are the favored answer.[11] We are approaching a condition in which we will turn to the medicine cabinet in order to "get through" a normal day. And, given the prevailing view that one's problems are biologically based, there is little incentive to remove oneself from the drugs.

This is not to argue against the cautious use of psychotropic drugs; there are many instances in which a strong case can be made for their use. However, at this point the culture is endangered by the spread of a singular discourse, and the resultant silencing of alternatives. Silenced is discussion of the historical and cultural processes of meaning-making, processes that define what counts as a problem and a solution. Attention is removed from the cultural surrounds contributing to states of anguish. We cease to focus on the co-active process from which the meaning of life events is derived. Minority voices go unheard, and the capacities of people together to foster resiliency are undermined. The need for broad-ranging dialogue is essential.

•

"Early on the morning of Dec. 13, police officers responding to
a 911 call arrived at a house in Hull, Mass., a seaside town near
Boston, and found a 4-year-old girl (Rebecca) on the floor of her
parents' bedroom, dead... The police said the girl had been taking a
potent cocktail of psychiatric drugs since age 2, when she was
given a diagnosis of attention deficit disorder and bipolar disorder,
which is characterized by mood swings... Indeed, the practice of
aggressive drug treatment for young children labeled bipolar has
become common across the country. In just the last decade, the
rate of bipolar diagnosis in children under 13 has increased
almost sevenfold... And a typical treatment includes multiple
medications. Rebecca was taking Seroquel, the antipsychotic
drug; Depakote, an equally powerful medication; and Clonidine,
a blood pressure drug often prescribed to calm children.
—*New York Times*, Feb. 15, 2007

[11] A recent cartoon featured a little league baseball player asking the local pharmacist if he had a drug that would help him hit home runs.

Therapy: The Power of Coordinated Action

We now turn to the therapeutic relationship itself. From the present standpoint, how are we to understand the relationship between therapist and
client, its potentials, and its efficacy? In responding to this question, we are
invited to think beyond the tradition of bounded being in which the aim
of therapy is to "cure" the mind of the individual client. The metaphors of
the therapist as one who "plumbs the depths," or serves as a mechanic of
the cognitive machinery must be bracketed. We also set aside the causal
model in which the therapist acts *upon* the client to produce change.
Rather, we are invited to view the therapist and client as engaged in a subtle
and complex dance of co-action, a dance in which meaning is continuously
in motion, and the outcomes of which may transform the relational life of
the client.

•

Consider the situation: Both therapist and client enter the therapeutic relationship as multi-beings. Both carry with them the residues of multiple relationships. Therapists bring not only a repertoire of actions garnered from
their history of therapeutic relations; they also carry potentials from myriad
relations stretching from childhood to the present. Likewise, clients enter
carrying a repertoire of actions, some deemed problematic, but alongside a
trove of less obvious alternatives. The primary question, then, is whether the
process of client/therapist coordination can contribute to a transformation
in relationships of extended consequence. Can their dance together rever-
berate across the client's relational plane in such a way that more viable
coordination results? This is no small challenge, for the client's plane of
relationships is complex and fluid. How, then, is this single circumscribed
relationship between therapist and client to achieve significant change?[12]

There is much to be said about therapy from a relational standpoint,
and in the present context I must be selective. My focus, then, will be on
three specific challenges to effective therapy: affirmation, reality suspension, and reality replacement. I believe that in one respect or another all
therapeutic practices offer resources for meeting these challenges. At the
same time, a new array of practices has sprung forth over recent decades.
This genre is acutely sensitive to relational process and to the creation of
meaning. Within this genre I would include practices currently found in

---

[12]The focus on this particular relationship is clearly insufficient. If therapy is devoted to
relational recovery, the invitation is to expand the range of those engaged in the therapeutic process. For a recent illustration of how the therapist can marshall the larger community for therapeutic ends, see Fredman, G., Anderson, E., and Stott, J. (2009) *Being with older people: A systemic
approach.* London: Karnac.

systemic therapy, narrative therapy, strength-based therapy, brief therapies, collaborative therapy, neo-analytic therapy, constructive therapies, post-modern therapy, social therapy, and the meditative practices inspired by Buddhist practitioners.[13] These practices will receive particular attention. This discussion will also set the stage for exploring ways to augment the current repertoire of practices.

Rejection and Affirmation

Consider my situation: I sit here typing these words under the presumption that I have something important to say. But why do I presume these words have any importance? If left strictly on my own, I couldn't reach such a conclusion. Significance doesn't leap from the page. What gives me courage is that I draw support from continuous connection with colleagues; they affirm the value of what I am doing. If their support were to drop away, and if journals and publishers no longer accepted my work, how long would I persist? I might draw nourishment from distant memories; I might also dwell on stories of lonely heroes recognized after their demise; and I might also begin to develop fantasies. I might begin to believe that I dwell in a world of fools, possibly jealous, and possibly pleased to see me fail. With selective attention I am sure to find support for such a view. Leave me utterly alone for a year, and I might begin to write only for myself—the only genius who can truly understand my work.

•

If all that we hold to be real and good finds its origins in relationships, the removal of relationship is an invitation to agony. No longer can I sustain a sense of a stable reality and valued goals. When we move out of the ongoing conversations of daily life, the doubts begin:

> Am I unreasonable?
> Why can't I shake these feelings loose?
> Why can't I get it together?
> Why am I so low in self-confidence?
> Why can't I stop being a schmuck?
> Am I crazy?

•

[13]Much of this work will be referenced later in this chapter. For more general accounts, see for example, Mitchell, S. A. (1988). *Relational concepts in psychoanalysis.* Cambridge: Harvard University Press; Gutterman, J.T. (2006). *Mastering the art of solution focused counseling.* Alexandria, VA: American Counseling Association; Strong, T., and Paré, D. (2004). *Furthering talk: Advances in the discursive therapies.* New York: Kluwer; Monk, G., Winslade, J., and Sinclair, S. (2008). *New horizons in multicultural counseling.* Thousand Oaks, CA: Sage.

In one way or another, virtually all of us dwell at the borders of the unacceptable. Most all of us labor with questions of being too fat or too thin, too short or too tall, too quick or too slow, too talkative or too silent, too ambitious or too lazy, too emotional or too rational, and the like. When we live in a world of bounded being, individual evaluation is pervasive; this was the concern of Chapter 1. Typically, however, we find ways of escaping criticism and not stepping on too many toes. Most importantly we overcome doubt and sustain our sense of being "OK" through our relations with others. We draw continued nurturance from the subtle affirmations of daily interchange. Energetic greetings, the unselfconscious sharing of conversation, congenial laughter, making plans together, and the like, all affirm one's membership within the walls of the acceptable. For most, these commonplace scenarios are sufficient; for others they are not.

•

Any visible marker of deviance risks a slide into *progressive rejection*. By this I mean a circular, self-sustaining trajectory in which a minor form of deviance and doubt invites others' avoidance, which in turn triggers further doubt and deviation, with the result of once again increasing social rejection. To expand, in the common hustle-bustle of life we tend to avoid anyone who is too loud, aggressive, silent, incoherent, critical, slow, unpredictable, or otherwise bothersome. In a world of bounded being we understand that we must take care of the self first, that everyone is responsible for their own behavior, and that the deviant stands in the way of our progress. Confrontation is unpleasant and time consuming; avoidance is the best option. Now consider the situation from the standpoint of the offending one. Here uncertainty creeps in. "Have I done something wrong; I was only doing my best; I am only reasonable; why is that so bad; what is it about me; why can't I have a break?" Such doubts can first give way to rejecting others ("They don't understand anything," "Jerks," "I don't care what they think.") and then to avoiding them ("They don't like me, so why hang with them?" "They don't appreciate me, so what's the point?") At the same time, by avoiding contact with others, one further reduces the possibility of being affirmed. Self-questioning intensifies, often leading to uncontrollable rumination.

To combat the whirl of self-defeating suspicions, one may seek sustenance from the repertoire of multi-being: "I am a person of especially deep feelings." "I am just smarter...more creative...more insightful..." Again affirmation is lacking, opening the way to actions one may find appropriate to his or her private reality, but nowhere else. For example, one may punish oneself in order to confirm one is indeed loathsome. Cutting one's body, binge eating, and starving oneself all function in this way. Alcohol and drug addiction are especially invited, as they allow moments of ecstatic forgetting, while simultaneously affirming one's sorry state. One may also take action to punish those held responsible for the rejection. For example, one can adopt more extreme form of deviance, understanding full well that others will be anxious, frightened, or irritated. Disrupting conventions yields a satisfying revenge. Offensive clothing, slovenly or menacing actions, screaming uncontrollably, and muttering incessantly to oneself are all effective options. As others' avoidance is further increased, there are no limits to one's imagination. And this may include inclinations to eliminate the arrogant abusers.

•

Several years ago I was approached by a company that supplied protection to celebrities. It happens that if you are popularly featured in the national media you will receive each year a substantial volume of "hate mail." Unknown persons may wish to break your bones, dismember you, or escort you to hell. Even the "love mail" may turn ominous, as you become the target of intense jealousy, or are invited to depart the earth with an admirer.

The task posed for me as a consultant was to generate a set of criteria by which the company might judge the likelihood that an ominous writer might actually arrive on the scene with weapon in hand. The numerous cases of celebrity stalking fortified their desires. A substantial number of cases in which celebrities had been attacked, injured, and even killed by stalkers made the search imperative.

In the process of creating criteria, I studied the files of individuals convicted for stalking crimes. Only one factor characterized the group as a whole: They were all "loners." There was little indication of significant personal ties with anyone—parents, spouses, lovers, children, friends, or even neighbors. In most cases they seemed to live in a fantasy world where they largely carried out imaginary relations with figures generated by the media. With these figures they could love and hate without limits. Outside the media there were no significant relationships in which common reason was nurtured, no one about whom they cared, no one who could help them participate in the surrounding moral community. In this private world, taking a life could easily become sensible.

•

Cho Seung-Hui's massacre of 32 people at Virginia Tech University is a vivid illustration of progressive rejection. Cho had experienced widespread rejection by his classmates, including women to whom he was attracted.

As he characterized his classmates in a manifesto, they were "debauched and deceitful charlatans." As surmised from the Columbine massacre of 1999, the process of progressive rejection may target not only the lone individual but bonded pairs. In this case two high school seniors, Dylan Klebold and Eric Harris slowly became "outsiders"—avoided and ridiculed by their classmates. The result was their decision to take revenge by killing as many classmates as possible. Twelve were murdered in the subsequent melee, along with Klebold and Harris themselves. In suicide an outsider ultimately and ironically achieves what he or she believes is the "will of the group."

•

He who is unable to live in society, or who has no need
because he is sufficient for himself, must be beast or god.

——Aristotle

•

In my view, recent decades have multiplied the potential for progressive rejection. This is so for two reasons, both related to 20th-century technologies. On the one hand technologies of communication contribute to the multiplication of *oughts*. We are bombarded, for example, with advertisements regarding the most desirable body shape, clothing styles, color of the teeth, texture of the hair, and so on.[14] The media inform us of what is "in" in the way of music, books, restaurants, film, and wine. Everywhere we encounter the "top 100," "the top ten," and "number one." Rapidly the standards are multiplied and proliferated, so "every savvy person" knows the rules of acceptability on the club scene, at the beach, in the classroom, and so on. When oughts are multiplied, so is deviance.

Further, there is a dwindling number of people who can provide the needed affirmation. The 20th-century technologies have quickened the pace of life. With increased capacities to move about the globe—both physically and electronically—we find ourselves with more opportunities, more invitations, more information to process, more open vistas, and more things that we "must do."[15] Most of us find ourselves continuously under pressure—so many demands, so little time. Work on the job is extended into the home; home life is interrupted by travel requirements, lessons, meetings, and children's activities. Extended time together is reduced to "quality time," and relationships in depth are replaced by an extended and superficial network of acquaintances. Under these conditions it is difficult

---

[14]Anorexia and obesity would be non-existent if there were not commonly imposed standards for the properly proportioned body.

[15]Gergen, K. J. (2001). *Op cit.*

to find others to trust with one's secret doubts and yearnings; it is equally difficult to locate others who have the time to listen, probe, and understand. There is simply no time for "deviants."

•

The most important vehicle of reality maintenance is conversation.
—Peter Berger and Thomas Luckmann

•

In my view, therapists from virtually any school—from psychoanalysis to Buddhist meditation—can provide important resources for enabling clients to escape isolated self-torment. All can affirm the individual as a valid participant in the social world as opposed to treating him or her with disbelief or disregard. All may establish a relationship of care, thus contributing to the special advantage of therapy over other forms of responding to deviance. At the same time, there are great variations in how much of the client's private wandering will be affirmed and legitimated within the conversation. In many respects, Carl Rogers' non-directive orientation sets a standard for practices that are maximally affirming.[16] For Rogers, all self-doubts, private fantasies, or hidden loathings are invitations to the therapist's unconditional regard. As many contemporary therapists would say, Rogers was *fully present* to his clients. Yet, Rogers was also committed to his own particular theory of dysfunction and cure. He knew the source and cure for clients' problems before they entered the room. While he listened fully and affirmingly, his responses were virtually scripted before the client spoke the first word.

In this respect I am drawn to Harlene Anderson's proposals for bracketing the demands of theory in favor of full attention to the client's accounts.[17] It is not simply that the "knowing" therapist may shape the client's account so that it confirms the therapist's pre-established theory. Strong theoretical commitments also encourage selective listening. Especially for the diagnostically oriented therapist, there is the danger of questions that position him or her judge of the client's sanity. As one of Anderson's clients reported, when his previous therapist asked him "Is this an ashtray," he was thrown into a panic. He needed to talk about his fears, and not to be placed under evaluation. Anderson proposes, instead, a form of curious and responsive listening in which one treats the

---

[16]See, for example, Rogers, C. (2004). *On becoming a person: A therapist's view of psychotherapy.* London: Constable and Robinson.

[17]Anderson, H. (1997). *Conversation, language and possibilities: A postmodern approach.* New York: Basic Books.

client's story as a trustworthy and legitimate reality. The client's reports are not treated as an indication of something "behind" the words—a hidden, unconscious problem, for example—but as one might treat the words of a close friend. One responds "into" the client's story world, accepting the language, vocabulary, and metaphors. Therapy, in this sense, is a collaborative relationship in which responsibility is shared for the outcome.[18]

•

In the case of affirmation, important resources are also available outside the therapeutic chamber. Here I refer to the many groups resisting the stigmatizing practice of mental illness labeling.[19] The same explosion in communication technologies lending itself to progressive rejection also provides outlets for marginalized individuals to locate others in kind. Thus, networks such as the hearing voices movement, and the Anti-psychiatry Coalition offer numerous outlets and information (in 11 languages to date) enabling those feeling abused by cultural traditions and diagnostic labeling to build communal support.[20] This is not to conclude that affirmative support for culturally deviant behavior is an end in itself. From a relational standpoint, the aim of therapy should not be to create separate and alienated enclaves, with those occupying these separate worlds sufficient unto themselves. There is ultimately the challenge of living viably in multiple worlds, a topic to which we will return later in the chapter. We now turn to a second major focus of relationally sensitive therapy.

•

Suspending Realities

For many anguished people, the affirming voice of a therapist may remove plaguing doubts and restore a sense of a secure reality. With potentials restored, they may also move more effectively in the extended dances of relationship. Yet, for many therapeutic clients, it is not a sense of spinning into a vortex of doubt that is troubling; rather it is an altogether compelling reality that crushes them in its grip. We are not dealing here with people who writhe in ambiguity, but with those locked within debilitating patterns of relationship from which there is no apparent exit.

[18]Anderson, H., and Gehart, D. (Eds.) (2007). *Collaborative therapy: Relationships and conversations that make a difference.* London: Routledge.

[19]www.antipsychiatry.org, www.hearing-voices.org. Farber, S. (1999). *Madness, heresy, and the rumor of angels: The revolt against the mental health system.* New York: Carus; Smith, C. (1999). *Escape from psychiatry: The autobiography of Clover.* Ignacio, CO: Rainbow Pots and Press.

[20]See www.antipsychiatry.org

How do people become so inflexibly committed to self-defeating ways of being? Let us place this question in the context of multi-being. As outlined earlier, normal life equips us with innumerable potentials for relating. However, we often confront people whose patterns of action are narrowly constrained. Rich potentials remain unrealized. We often view such persons as problematic personalities: "Jack is aggressive; Jill is a chronic depressive." This is to mistake the self of the moment for the potentials in waiting.[21]

If our potentials for action originate in relationship, so must we turn to relationship to understand the origins of constriction. There are two major forces at work in such cases. The first may be located in ongoing relations and the second in the past history of relationships. Each requires special therapeutic attention. With respect to ongoing relations, let's return to the earlier account of relational scenarios (Chapter 4), that is, the extended and more or less reliable patterns of co-action. There are the conventional scenarios, such as playing games, gossiping, and exchanging gifts. There are also scenarios that are degenerative in their effects on the participants. Among the most common are arguing, exchanging criticisms, and mutual blaming. The relational drift is toward mutual rejection and alienation. As communication specialists Pearce and Cronen point out, such patterns may become so well practiced that they seem "just natural."[22] If attacked by another, it is only natural to counter-attack. And, even when the participants recognize the harmful effects of participation, they continue to repeat the pattern. They don't know what else to do. In effect, we become locked within locally created forms of hell, and can scarcely envision an alternative.

•

It was an idyllic day at the beach, and our conversation with Laurie and Jon played in counterpoint to the breaking waves. Laurie had also brought along her parents, now in their 80s. Laurie's mother was a large and ebullient woman and her husband, thin, silent, and suffering from chronic depression. Tired of sitting, Mary and I asked our friends if they would like to stroll the beach. They were keen for a walk, but Laurie thought it might be good for her father to join us. Reluctantly he rose, his brittle frame creaking at the effort. As we

[21]The common use of personality tests and trait measures in both professional and pop psychology serves to recreate this mistake as an "official reality."

[22]Cronen, V., and Pearce, W. B. (1982). The Coordinated Management of Meaning: A theory of communication. In F. E. X. Dance (Ed.) *Human communication theory* (pp. 61–89). New York: Harper & Row.

strolled, our discussion resumed, and soon we were chattering away happily in the sun. Laurie's father, however, dragged his sagging body along in silence. After some time we realized we were approaching a nudist beach. As we continued strolling toward the naked figures, we noticed that Laurie's father began to straighten up and his gait quickened. As we entered the nudist area, he joined our conversation. Soon we were all bubbling along together. Finally, however, the time arrived when it was necessary to reverse our direction and return to our encampment. As we made our way back, Laurie's father slowly returned to a silent slump. When we arrived at our station on the beach, he fell into a heap on his towel, once again "chronically" depressed.

•

Almost all schools of therapy offer resources for challenging the client's life-world. This is so in large part because most schools are committed to an unconventional view of human functioning. Thus, whenever the therapist asks a question dictated by his or her theoretical background, it will typically unsettle the presented reality of the client. The client wants to talk about family problems, and the humanist therapist asks about his feelings; the client talks about how everyone is laughing at her, and the cognitive therapist asks her if they could be laughing at something else; the client talks about problems of sexual perversion, and the psychoanalyst shifts the discussion to childhood experiences. All such questions move toward dislodging the taken-for-granted.[23] They all inform the client, "you thought it was this, but it is that."

On the problematic side, however, such schools approach clients with a "one size fits all" orientation. Regardless of the particularities of the client's life circumstances, for example, a Freudian will reconstruct the client's problems in terms of an early family romance. Such dedicated dislodgement may also direct the client toward a relational view. Classic is the work of the Milan school of therapy, and the development of *circular questioning*.[24] Although there are many forms of circular questioning, one of the most prominent shifts the emphasis away from the individual to the circle of relationships of which the individual is a part. For example, in a family with an angry and rebellious adolescent, an individualist therapist might

---

[23]For a detailed account of how psychoanalytic questions help to foster the reality of the analytic world-view, see Spence, D. (1984). *Narrative truth and historical truth: Meaning and interpretation in psychoanalysis*. New York: W.W Norton & Company.

[24]Becvar, R. J., and Becvar, D. S. (1999). *Systems theory and family therapy: A primer* (2nd ed.). Lanham, MD: University Press of America.

ask her to talk about why she feels so angry. Such a question not only affirms the existence of anger, but creates the individual as an independent center of gravity. In contrast, a circular question might be directed to the father; he might be asked, for example, "How does your daughter show her love for her mother?" Not only does the question generate a positive alternative to the reality of anger, but focuses on the links between daughter and mother and his relationship to them. Or, in couples therapy, rather than asking each individual about their personal feelings, each might be asked, for example, "What do you think is the most important thing you should be working on in your relationship," "What goals do you share in your relationship," or, "Are there outside forces that are hurting your relationship?" In the new conversational object—the relationship—may lie seeds for new growth.

•

> In each new way of talking lies the potential
> for a new way of relating.

•

Yet, the dislodging of long-term patterns may also be more tailor-made to the client. Highly influential, for example, were the early paradoxical practices of Milton Erickson.[25] If a client was suffering from obesity, for example, Erickson might suggest eating more food; if suffering from a fear of failure, he might advise the client to seek failure. In resisting the therapist, discussion is invited on the client's resistance to change. This approach reaches its extreme in provocative therapy, in which the therapist plays devil's advocate with the client. If the client worries about her anger toward her husband, the therapist might show the client how she actually wishes to murder him.[26]

Because such forms of dislodgement may also be both insulting and assaulting to clients, therapists turn elsewhere for inspiration. It is here that I am particularly impressed with reflecting team practices, as developed by Tom Andersen and his colleagues.[27] Especially useful with couples and families the therapist is joined by a team of colleagues who observe the therapeutic proceedings. As envisioned by Andersen, each member of the

---

[25]See Haley, J. (1993). *Uncommon therapy: Psychiatric techniques of Milton H. Erickson, M.D.* New York: Norton.

[26]www.provocativetherapy.info

[27]See Andersen, T. (Ed.) (1991). *The reflecting team: Dialogues and dialogues about dialogues.* New York: Norton. Also, Friedman, S. (1995). *Reflecting team in action: Collaborative practice in family therapy.* New York: Guilford.

team offers a commentary or interpretation that is at once supportive, but simultaneously different from all the other interpretations. Where one reflector may see a husband and wife in competition with each other, another may see them feeling hurt, but unable to express their feelings. The reflectors speak in an understandable or jargon-free language, and try not to offer interpretations so radical that they would be implausible. To enhance the sense of authentic relationship, and to reduce the power difference between therapist and client, reflecting team members tend to sit in the therapy room (as opposed to observing from behind a one-way mirror), and to use their own personal experiences to flesh out their insights. The discussions that follow their comments are used to stimulate a new range of dialogues. The presented reality is softened, and new possibilities are opened.

•

So far we have focused on unsettling constraining patterns of action in on-going relations. However, as multi-beings we also carry with us the residues of the past. Most of these residues are valuable resources, available to enrich the present. At the same time, some inheritances from past relationships may be strangulating. They become so hardened that we are insensitive to the changing situation; they are knee-jerk responses that disrupt and destroy on-going relations. For example, one may be quite convinced of his or her inferiority, failure, or undesirability; or one may be overwhelmed by an unstinting sense of injustice or jealousy. Other people find the world all too dangerous, threatening, or replete with forces beyond their control. Here we are also dealing with people whose relational partners may find themselves in despair. Nothing they do seems to invite change. They want their wafer-thin daughter to eat more, their mate to be less sullen, their father to be less aggressive, and so on. How, then, do we to account for the continuation of such inflexible patterns of being?[28]

•

I think here of a neighbor, Alice, whose marriage seemed quite successful. She and her husband lived a prosperous life, were pillars of the community, and had three lovely children. However, after 16 years of marriage Alice discovered that Jim was having an affair with an old friend of hers. Alice exploded into a mixture of rage, grief, and self-pity.

---

[28]It is also possible that others' unfavorable responses may sometimes serve as the critical supports for undesirable actions. Depression, hostility, passivity, and the like may be used to punish those who are close. Their disappointment, frustration, and irritation are the sweet fruits of one's efforts.

Jim was thrown into a state of deep remorse and guilt, and immediately ended the affair. However, in spite of their continuous attempts to work through the event, Alice could not shake her feelings of rage. She found herself attacking Jim at every opportunity, and could not bear the idea of his "sleeping with the enemy." As she told her therapist, she and Jim both wanted to restore their relationship, but she simply couldn't shake off her anger and desire for revenge. This was

The eternal sounds of the internal voices...
Mother...father...brothers...sisters...

Listen carefully when I speak
and you shall hear them.

And when they speak, their words will carry countenances
Of mothers...fathers...brothers...sisters...

As I speak with you now
You will hear the echoes of distant times.

Courtesty: Regine Walter, Artist

20 years ago. Today the two of them indeed remain together, but occupying separate bedrooms.

•

Being locked in the past is to remain bound in some form of relationship. It is to participate in a scenario that privately sustains itself. The reasons for sustaining such debilitating scenarios may be many. Often they sustain themselves because they remain unfinished; a drama has unfolded, and one continuously returns in search of a satisfactory conclusion. For example, one may have been rejected without a satisfactory reason, unjustly, attacked without an opportunity to retaliate, or sexually abused without any reconciliation. The story is suspended; its awful drama holds one in its grip. A common form of the "unfinished story" leaves us with a residue of self-recrimination. Here is the "negative voice," a voice that reminds us all too often that we are unworthy, unlovable, or inferior.[29] Typically this is the voice of authority (e.g. parents, teachers, older siblings). In effect, these are people to whom one could never offer an adequate reply, a refusal, or a counter-attack. The story is unfinished; the voice remains unanswered and unanswerable.

•

I was riding a crest. My book *The Saturated Self,* had just been glowingly reviewed in the *Washington Post*'s Sunday Book Review. "This book has the power to change the way we think about ourselves," they said. I now looked forward to the following week, when a review was to appear in the Sunday edition of the *New York Times*. When I greeted the arrival of the paper that Sunday I was devastated. The review was a disaster. The reviewer, a conservative philosopher, could find no redeeming qualities. I was enraged and humiliated. I did receive numerous letters of support, and the review didn't seem to deter the potential readers (the book remained popular enough to merit a second edition a decade later). However, for over 10 years the thorny residues of the review disturbed my reveries. Privately I composed countless letters of bitter retaliation. Sometimes I would wake from my slumber with a half-formed letter of contempt to the reviewer endlessly repeating itself. It was only when I learned of the reviewer's death that the flame of reprisal was extinguished.

•

[29]See, for example, Claude-Pierre, P. (1998). *The secret language of eating disorders.* New York: Vintage.

In the case of these privately repeating scenarios, the challenge for the therapist may be formidable. In the most extreme cases, the whirring of the private world may reject all who would attempt to enter. The resentment, hostility, or sense of self-righteousness may function as a fortress. No one can truly understand, no one is sufficiently worthy, and those who attempt to do so may seem condescending or manipulative. How is one to enter the conversation?

•

My friend Edgardo tells the story of his early days as a therapist. He was given a highly difficult case to treat, a young woman with a history of drugs and anti-social behavior. Her stormy disposition had lead to her hospitalization. When she was brought to his office, she sat sullenly before him, her stony face set off with dagger eyes. Edgardo began with a congenial greeting, and gently outlined how talking together might be helpful to her. She stared silently. After more false starts, Edgardo recalled that she had owned a white cat. Abandoning the therapeutic protocol, he asked about the cat. Although the stare was never broken, Edgardo did notice a slight movement of her mouth, as if she were almost ready to respond. With this, Edgardo proceeded to tell her that he, too, owned a white cat. But, he said, his cat was very naughty. Edgardo then sat himself behind his desk and began to tell the young woman that at night when he was working at his desk, the cat became jealous. He wanted attention. Then, role playing the cat, Edgardo climbed on top of the desk and stood up. Suddenly, with a loud MEOW, he pounced with all fours on the desk top. The patient suddenly screamed out, "You are crazy!" Edgardo responded, "Yes, but I get paid for it." The girl burst into laughter, and with that, their conversation began.

•

I have been especially impressed with Peggy Penn's innovative ways of disrupting a client's self-sustaining scenarios.[30] If the offending other cannot be addressed in person, she asks, are there other ways of "finishing old business"? Specifically, Penn has made extensive use of letter writing to generate dialogue with the unavailable participant in the debilitating relationship. Consider a woman who has suffered abuse from a now-deceased stepfather. She cannot rid herself of the humiliating experience; normal sexual relations are now beyond her grasp. Penn might have her compose a letter

[30]Penn, P. (2009). *Joined imaginations: Writing and language in therapy.* Chagrin Falls, OH: Taos Institute Publications.

to her step-father. There she could quietly and articulately spell out the full range of her feelings, her anger, anguish, self-blame, and possibly even her love. With the private brooding now in the open, Penn can be brought more fully into the conversation. The private scenario is now open to another conversational partner. However, the process does not necessarily terminate at this point. Rather, Penn might then invite the woman to compose a letter in which she takes the part of the step-father. What can she imagine her step-father saying to her? How would he explain his actions; what would he be feeling? Now the scenario approaches conclusion. And with Penn as a collaborator, its grip is released.

•

In my view, Buddhist practices now represent an enormously important addition to the therapist's resources. In many respects, such practices are also allied with the present view of relational being. The Buddhist tradition recognizes that the source of human anguish is located in socially shared constructions. Further, such anguish is particularly derived from the value placed on the self. In this sense, many Buddhist practices of meditation or mindfulness have the effect of calling into question the naturalized meanings responsible for one's torment. Through meditation in particular, the meanings are suspended; one escapes into an open space of what Zen masters characterize as "no mind." Through careful focusing, one may break the stranglehold of accepted realities.[31]

Speaking directly to the challenge of private scenarios is a Buddhist practice called Shikanho.[32] In one variation, clients are asked to think of the unpleasant occurrence that unsettles them, and to summon forth the feelings that it evoked. Once the image is in focus, they are asked to envision the situation without making any evaluations or judgments. They are to allow the scenario to play itself out without judging, for example, that it was humiliating or disastrous. After suspending judgment of the scenario, the clients are challenged with a new task: Imagine looking at the situation from various angles of vision. How would it appear from above or below, from near or far? With the help of the therapist, clients move through these angles of vision every 2 seconds. After 30 seconds, however, they are allowed to pause for 30 seconds to take a deep breath before continuing. Through this form of concentration, the unpleasant occurrence ceases to be commanding.

[31]For a discussion of current practices and their theoretical base, see Kwee, M., Gergen, K. J., and Koshikawa, F. (Eds.) (2006). *Horizons in Buddhist psychology.* Chagrin Falls, OH: Taos Institute Publications.

[32]Koshikawa, F., Kuboki, A., and Ishii, Y. (2006). Shikanho: A Zen-based cognitive-behavioral approach. In M. Kwee, K. J. Gergen, and F. Koshikawa (Eds.) *Horizons in Buddhist psychology.* (pp. 185–195). Chagrin Falls, OH: Taos Institute Press.

One increasingly approaches the memory as simply "something that happened," but with its emotional significance now optional.

We turn now to the third major challenge for a relationally sensitive therapy.

Realities Replaced

Through the preceding practices there is an erosion of the realities, the logics, and the values that thrust people's actions into the register of dysfunction. And, with this softening a space opens for exploring new dances in the relational complex of daily life. However, in many cases a release from dysfunctional patterns is insufficient. To remove the shackles is one thing; to have a new direction for the future is another. For many, therapy is more fully effective when compelling alternatives are made visible. Consider: If I were fired from my job because I flew into a rage at my boss, and then my wife took the children and left me, and I was forced to move into a homeless shelter, and I had to beg on the streets for money, I suspect that my friends and acquaintances would soon begin to treat me as a failure. Indeed, I would probably agree with them. And because of my humiliation I would probably not wish to see them. Why should they want to hang out with the likes of me? When I did see them, I would be in anguish over my inferiority. Better to remain alone...or possibly, to end it all.

Under these conditions, the softening of the reality is only a beginning. I may indeed realize that the conventional views that sustain my life of isolation and dejection are simply constructions. By reducing the relevance of these constructions, placing them at a distance, and realizing that there are many other ways to understand my situation, I might cautiously search out my old friends. But now to the important point: If I had another way of talking, another compelling story of what happened, or another characterization of myself at hand, I might be prepared for new courses of action. Freedom from a convention opens the gate, but new visions of reality may be necessary for future building.

•

Most forms of therapy are capable of furnishing the client with alternative realities. In classic psychoanalysis, for example, I might well learn that my office rage had its roots in my relationship with my father. He was the symbolic target of my attack. With the Rogerian I will likely find that my explosion was the outcome of a long history of conditional positive regard. With the cognitive therapist, I may learn that I wasn't processing information realistically, and so on. I do believe that many people benefit from these new forms of understanding. For one, each removes the burden of guilt I might otherwise feel; each tells me I was suffering from something beyond my control at the time, and that I can successfully regain control. However, that these ways of seeing my life were not specific to me; they were all in place before I entered therapy.

•

From a relational perspective, the most important seeds for building a new future are supplied by past relationships. As a multi-being one possesses enormous resources, often suppressed by current life circumstances. The therapist may help the client to draw from these in charting a new life direction. In one form or another, many therapists have developed practices congenial with this view. They specifically center conversation on client strengths, solutions, and positive prospects.[33] The following practices are especially useful—both within therapy and daily life:

- Search for exceptions to the problem: Rather than reifying the problem by continuous exploration, ask about exceptional experiences, situations in which the problem did not exist. For a client who is fearful of heights or open spaces, for example, are there instances in which he or she had no fear? Build a vision of the future based on these.
- Inquire into achievements: When exceptions are located, inquire into how the client achieved success. For example, if a man is generally impotent, with occasional exceptions, how did he manage this success? In constructing a response, not only do potentially useful practices become salient, but the client also realizes a sense of competence.
- Explore resources: Rather than focusing on the client's inabilities, inquire into resources. What has been achieved in life, what resources were necessary for such achievement, where are the interpersonal strengths, what are the capacities for resilience? The realization of resources generates confidence in entertaining alternatives.
- Imagine positive futures: In generating conversation about possible improvements and new alternatives, the weight of failure or loss is replaced by active planning.

•

[33]See, for example, de Shazer, S. (1985). *Keys to solution in brief therapy.* New York: Norton; de Shazer, S. (1994). *Words were originally magic.* New York: Norton; O'Hanlon, W., and Weiner-Davis, M. (1989). *In search of solutions: A new direction in psychotherapy.* New York: Norton; O'Hanlon. W. (2003). *Solution-oriented therapy for chronic and severe mental illness.* New York: Norton; Bertolino, R., and O'Hanlon, B. (2001). *Collaborative, competency-based counseling and therapy.* New York: Pearson, Allyn and Bacon.

Generally, these invitations into alternative worlds are used in therapies of brief duration. The attempt is to open possibilities that the client may subsequently pursue. In more severe cases, many therapists are drawn to what Michael White and David Epston view as "narrative means to therapeutic ends."[34] Here the focus is primarily on the narrative construction within which the individual understands his or her life (see Chapter 5). Problems are not possessions of the person, it is reasoned, but are generated within a narrative that the person has come to embrace. Depression over a failed marriage is only a problem when one is committed to a narrative of happily ever after. As it is said, the way one understands the problem is itself a problem. Thus, therapy is dedicated to a process of re-storying one's life. Typically, the attempt is first to challenge or de-construct the dominant story. In this stage of therapy, discussions often turn to the cultural basis of the story. Many narrative therapists are critical of the dominant discourses of the culture and the way in which people's life stories become centered around such values as being thin, financially successful, heterosexual, or superior to others. In this respect narrative therapists often take seriously their role as social activists.

Once the client's resistance to such narratives has been established, the way is open to develop an alternative. Here the search is for elements of marginalized self-narratives, or in terms of multi-being, the residues of relations that have been suppressed by the dominating and dysfunctional narrative. Most useful are residues that are unique in their opposition to the dominant narrative. For example, if one feels his life has been a failure, can suppressed stories of success be located? If one no longer feels in control of her life, can latent stories of autonomy be found? These "lost events" form a scaffold for re-storying. Therapy is used to help the client mold these into a new, richer, and more viable narrative.[35]

•

A recently related story of one who took re-storying into her own hands: Francine struggled for years with a body that seemed destined for obesity. Relentlessly she toiled with diets, joined weight-reduction programs, took exercise classes... all to no avail. Francine finally hit on a solution: She threw out all her clothing that revealed her hefty body, and replaced it with Polynesian muumuus—vast and colorful

---

[34]White, M., and Epston, D. (1990). *Narrative means to therapeutic ends.* New York: Norton.

[35]For more on narrative therapy see Freedman, J., and Combs, G. (1996). *Narrative therapy: The social construction of preferred realities.* New York: Norton; Angus, L. W., and McLeod, J. (Eds.) (2004). *The handbook of narrative and psychotherapy.* London: Sage; White, M. (2007). *Maps of narrative practice.* New York: Norton.

tent-like dresses. She then pinned a large button on the muumuu of the day, that announced, "I survived anorexia."

•

Narrative therapy is outstanding in its sensitivity to the way in which meaning is molded in relationship. Therapists understand that life narratives are born within relationships, and that such relationships may be lodged within institutions and the mass media. Ultimately, however, the significant question is that of *carry-over*. By this I mean the capacity of the exchange within therapy to enter effectively into relationships outside. It is insufficient that the client and therapist negotiate a new form of self-understanding that seems realistic, promising, and coherent. They may appreciate their handy-work, and even enjoy each other's company. The important question is whether the new-formed realities contribute to relational recovery outside the therapy room. Here narrative therapists make a significant contribution in the form of *definitional ceremonies*. The therapist and client invite a group of carefully chosen witnesses from outside. These may be, for example, family members or close friends of the client. After hearing the client tell his or her newly emerging story, the witnesses are asked to talk about what in the story they were drawn to, what images were evoked, what personal experiences resonated with the story, and how their lives were touched by it. In effect, the re-storying now enters directly into the client's outside relationships.

More radical in moving therapy into the public arena is the practice of *dialogic meeting*. Developed by Jaakko Seikkula and his Finnish colleagues,[36] dialogic meetings were developed in response to an expanding number of psychiatric hospitalizations. Not only were the number of occupied beds in the hospital increasing, but prescriptions for medication were skyrocketing. Realizing that definitions of mental illness and cure depend on community relations, and that the voice of the psychiatric community favored hospitalization and drugs, an alternative practice was sought. Thus, Seikkula and his group developed teams for each new case. Teams might be composed of several professionals, representing different points of view, along with family members, close friends, colleagues from work, and other stake-holders. The designated "psychotic" also participated in conversations with the team. The meetings encouraged a full expression of opinion and insight, and ultimately a commitment from the group to work together for change. Meetings of the group might be daily in the case of severe

[36]See Seikkula, J., and Arnkil, T. E. (2006). *Dialogic meetings in social networks*. London: Karnac.

episodes, but tapered off over time. The group also remained flexible, with conversations shifting in emphasis, along with views of what courses of action should be taken. There was no attempt to "pin down" the problem, to get to the bottom of it. Rather, the point was to sustain the process of dialogue across shifting circumstances. The results of such dialogic meetings proved dramatic: Over the next two years there was a significant reduction in the number of diagnosed schizophrenics, a decrease in hospitalization, and a lowered number of drug prescriptions.

•

To meet the challenge of carry-over, a premium can be placed on practices that expand the range of voices included in the change process. I have been struck by three additional practices that move effectively in this direction:

– Harlene Anderson and her colleagues brought together homeless women, many of whom suffered from drug abuse and domestic violence.[37] The women were encouraged to talk about their experiences, to share stories about success and failure, and more generally to talk about their lives. Over time, the group grew into a small and caring community. By seeing themselves as a community, they also acquired the ability to look ahead with determination to change their conditions. With the help of the therapists, they ultimately issued a manifesto. As evidenced in the following excerpt, these women collectively created a pact on which to build a future: "We the participants of Building Safer Families, agree to be responsible for building better lives for ourselves and our families. We will do this through prioritization, acceptance, and respect for our uniqueness, with unconditional love, lack of judgment or criticism, and living our values for our families and ourselves… We hope to maintain independence and interdependence through this group."

– Self-starvation among adolescents (diagnosed as anorexia) can be difficult to treat, and deeply unsettling to family relationships. Rather than focusing on the anorexic individual, London practitioners have developed a multi-family program of participation. Families with a designated anorexic meet together and talk over problems, issues,

[37]Feinsilver, D., Murphy, E., and Anderson, H. (2007). Women at a turning point: A transformational feast. In H. Anderson and D. Gehart (Eds.) *Collaborative therapy: Relationships and conversations that make a difference.* New York: Routledge. Consult this volume for many additional cases of collaborative work outside the therapy room. Also see Paré, D.A., and Larner, G. (Eds.) (2004). *Collaborative practice in psychology and therapy.* New York: Haworth.

and successes in dealing with eating problems. In this way, both the families and the diagnosed individuals find themselves with others who "understand" and lend support. Moreover, by exchanging stories of what works and what doesn't, the participants gain new insights into practices they might try in their own families. These meetings are often removed from the antiseptic and largely irrelevant context of the hospital, and take place within family homes.[38]
– In their work, Carina Hakansson and her colleagues at the Family Care Foundation in Sweden reject both diagnostic categories and drug "cures."[39] Rather, they place troubled individuals into "ordinary" family homes where they are treated with care and respect, and where they are allowed to adjust slowly, over time, to the life of the family. In addition, each week the client goes to therapy, sometimes with other family members, as well. The "clients" are of all ages; they may be suffering from battering, drug addiction, self-mutilation, abandonment, sex abuse, feelings of terror—often problems of long duration. The family homes are supported by a team, including supervisors of the family home and therapists. The attempt is to treat the client not as "an illness" but as a multi-faceted individual whose views should be taken seriously. One might say of a client, "He has his crazy moments, but sometimes he is wiser than me." The therapists also meet with the family of the client, and periodically there are festive gatherings of all the members of the family homes, the foundation staff, and their families.

Expanding the Therapeutic Repertoire

In the preceding section I addressed three major challenges to therapy from a relational standpoint. Specific attention was directed to the challenges of progressive rejection, suspending debilitating realities, and the building of new realities. Yet, through the lens of relational being we are also invited into further exploration. In the preceding account it was easy enough to illustrate the proposals with many existing practices.

[38]Honig, P. (2005). A multi-family group programme as part of an inpatient service for adolescents with diagnosis of Anorexia Nervosa. *Clinical Child Psychology and Psychiatry, 10*, 465–475; Asen, E., Dawson, N., and McHugh, B. (2002). *Multiple family therapy: The Marlborough model and its wider applications.* London: Karnac.
[39]See Håkansson, C. (2009). *Solidarity, dreams and therapy, experiences from a collaborative systemic practice.* Chagrin Falls, OH: Taos Institute Publications.

However, what is on the horizon? How might we enrich the potential? To conclude this chapter, I wish to focus on what I see as two of the most promising challenges.

From Fixed Reality to Relational Flow

From the present standpoint, successful therapy should facilitate relational recovery. In this context, however, it is interesting to consider the traditional view of therapeutic change. The view borrows heavily from the medical metaphor: The aim is to replace a state of disease with a state of health. The hope, then, is for a fixed outcome. For Freud, this was the replacement of repression by ego control, for Jungians the realization of self-hood, for cognitive therapists the replacement of dysfunctional cognition with reality-based thought, and so on. Even for some relationally oriented therapists, vestiges of the early tradition may be found. As various therapists might put it, successful therapy generates a new narrative, a solution, more serviceable self-understanding, more accurate cognition, insight into family functioning, and so on. When they are successful, the new realities replace the dysfunctional orientations existing prior to therapy. In effect, successful therapy has a fixed end.

But why should we be optimistic about the serviceability of a newly-fixed, or "cured" state of being? After all, the sea of relationships is never calm; the co-active process is continuously transforming meaning; the confluence is ever shifting. In conditions of continuous flux, is a firm sense of self or world an advantage? To illuminate, consider first a narrative of failure—how you tried your very best to pass an important professional exam, but failed. As we have seen, this reality is simply one construction of events among many. However, as this story is inserted into various forms of relationship—into the varied games or dances of the culture—its implications are strikingly varied. If a friend just related a story of great personal achievement, your story of failure might not be welcome. The friend anticipates congratulations, and you have changed the subject of the conversation in a way that makes you the center of attention. Similarly, to obsess about your failure with your wife who worries each month over making ends meet may produce both frustration and anger. In these contexts it is dysfunctional. In contrast, if your friend had just revealed a personal failure, sharing your own failings is likely to be reassuring and to solidify the friendship. Similarly, to relate your story of failure to your mother might elicit a warm and sympathetic reaction—in effect, enabling her to sustain her role as "mother."

•

"The real" and restriction walk hand in hand.

•

To put it otherwise, a story is never simply a story. It is a situated action, a performance that gains its significance through the co-active process. A given story may variously contribute to creating, sustaining, or destroying worlds of relationship. Accounts of self and world are significant entries into ongoing relationships—essential for maintaining the intelligibility and coherence of social life, useful in drawing people together, creating distance, and so on. Stories of the self enable public identities to be established, the past rendered acceptable, and the rituals of relationship to unfold with ease. The utility of these stories derives from their success as moves within these various relational arenas.

•

Think of the tools in a tool-box: there is a hammer, pliers, a saw, a screw-driver, a rule, a glue-pot, glue, nails, and screws. The functions of words are as diverse as the functions of these objects.
—Ludwig Wittgenstein

•

Now we must ask, would it not be more functional for an individual to have a repertoire of available selves than a single, "true" understanding? Would it not be better to have multiple "lenses" for comprehending the world than a single lens, a *multiplicity of plausible narratives* than a singular "narrative truth?" The challenge, then, is to expand the range of therapeutic practices that facilitate access to the full range of multi-being, and an openness to the world that is ever responsive to the unfolding invitations of co-action. In this space of relational being, we transcend all fixed belief, all necessary truth, and all compelling reality. We begin to recognize the intelligibility of multiple accounts, ways of putting things, forms of logic, applications of principle, and so on. We need not ask whether any utterance is worthy of our belief, for utterances are not the kinds of things about which we need ask the question, "Do I believe?" They are ways of being. Upon hearing a beautiful melody we do not ask whether we should believe it or not; nor do we ask whether we believe in the moves of a dancer or the athlete's deflection of a soccer ball. Rather, we are open to myriad melodies; we appreciate numerous forms of dance; and we are absorbed by many different games. We are immersed in the ongoing confluence of relating.

•

I look for the forms
things want to come as...
not so much looking for the shape
as being available
to any shape that may be
summoning itself
through me
from the self not mine but ours.
                    —A. R. Ammons

•

The critic returns: "OK, I am drawn to the image, and Ammons' words add a nice luster. However, can people truly live without a stable sense of the real, the reasonable, and the right? Will they not succumb to anxiety and spineless indirection if they lack a firm sense of self?" I have long heard such warnings, but I am not compelled by the idea of some basic human need for structure. What is the nature of a child's life prior to being told, "this is true," or "that is real?" Are children anxious and upset because they lack a "firm sense of identity?" Is the child immobile before hearing, "that's logical," or acquiring a "moral principle?" Prior to the intrusion of the real and the right, there was enormous flexibility, unlimited delight, and uncontained curiosity. Any object in the room might become a "dragon" at one moment, a "castle" the next, and soon a "hiding place." It is when we become certain that "this is a chair" that the world becomes one-dimensional. In the room of the real there are no exits.

•

And yet, I pause: Perhaps the critic is right in one respect. If we live within a tradition that places a premium on structure, coherent identity, and authoritative knowledge, we may often find ambiguity uncomfortable. I think here of Ralph. When I learned of his plan to become a psychiatrist I was aghast. Ralph was one of the most authoritarian people I knew. He was instantly ready to provide the last word on any topic. And he insisted that his word was the only truth. What kind of therapist would he become? Where were his capacities for sensitive listening, for fluid movement in the subtleties of co-action?

Years later I had an opportunity to speak with Ralph. He had indeed become a psychiatrist, and boasted of a burgeoning practice. I was very curious. Upon questioning him further I learned that most of Ralph's clients were from the lower-middle class, and often lacked a high school education. They came to therapy seeking authoritative answers to their problems, and Ralph had just such answers in waiting. If they complained of depression, sexual dysfunction, or uncontrollable anger, he set them straight with a diagnosis, and made clear behavioral prescriptions. Each week he would examine his clients to ensure they were following his orders. They often did so, and their problems seemed to slide away.

•

To what extent, in the present world, should our therapeutic practices nourish an appreciation of ambiguity, and the joy of improvisation? My ultimate hope is for therapy that can liberate participants from static and delimiting conventions of understanding and facilitate unthrottled engagement in the ongoing flow of relationship. As I see the therapeutic challenge, it is to facilitate participation in the continuous flow of co-creation.

Beyond Language: The Challenge of Effective Action

Among my favorite stories from the therapy world is one that is variously told about the revered therapist Milton Erickson;

> During a brief visit to Milwaukee, Erickson was asked by a worried nephew to pay a visit to his aunt, an older woman who was both depressed and suicidal. What advice could he give her? During the visit to her imposing, Victorian mansion, Erickson found the woman gloomy and despondent; she seldom left the house except to attend Sunday church services. Erickson asked if he might tour the house. He found it dark and grimy, with shades drawn and little sign of activity. However, Erickson did notice that the woman grew African violets, a lone signal of vitality. Could anything be done to help this woman before his departure?
>
> Erickson told the woman that her nephew had been worried about her depressed condition. But, he said, he didn't think this was the real problem. Rather, it was her failure to be a good Christian. She was resentful, and asked how he could say such a thing? She was an avid church-goer. He replied that here she was with time on her hands, a wonderful way with plants, and it was all going to waste. He then made the following suggestion: She should bring home the church bulletin each Sunday, and then visit each person in the congregation when there was a special event—such as a birth, a marriage, or death in the family. She should bring with her on these visits a gift of an African violet plant she had grown.

Some years later Erickson received from the nephew a Milwaukee newspaper, containing an article with the following headline:
African Violet Queen Dies, Mourned by thousands

•

I find this a touching story, but far more is implied: Here is a case in which there was not a single hour of therapeutic interchange. In a few short minutes one simple action was suggested. And this action led to a full and appreciative integration of the woman into the community. A new form of life was given birth. In my view this story makes clear the limitations of therapy built exclusively around verbal exchange. Our practices today still carry strong residues of Freud's "talking cure." Freud believed that with an especially crafted form of conversation, it was possible to bring about fundamental changes in psychological functioning. And, because all of one's actions are directed by mental activity, to transform the mind was to change behavior. In one form or another, such assumptions have informed most schools of therapy since Freud's time. Only the views of mental transformation differ. Thus, for Freud, words had the power to bring about transference; for Jung, self-discovery; for Rogerians, organismic valuing; and for cognitive therapists a better grip on reality. In all cases, the transformations achieved within the confines of the office are pivotal; with psychological change in place, it is held, the individual can participate more adequately in cultural life.

Yet, it is precisely this view of minds bound within bodies that the present volume places in question. From the relational standpoint, therapy is not so much about altering the mind as it is enhancing resources for viable relationships. Yet, we must ask, what are the potentials and the limits of purely linguistic exchange. If therapy limits itself to "doing language" is this not arbitrarily restricting its potentials? We acquire the ability to play a guitar, cook, or slice a golf ball out of a sand trap from repeated attempts to do these things. But if therapy is primarily concerned with relational recovery, where is the practice in participation?

•

I have a neighbor who senses a powerful force dominating the world about her. It is a force, she tells me, that destroys the economy and the environment, and most people are unable to escape its grip. She tells me the world is threatened. She also expresses distress that she has no friends. To alleviate her anxiety about the menace, she is sedated (in effect, treated as a schizophrenic). However, when she speaks to me about this "powerful force," I find myself resisting skepticism. After all, hers is one construction of the world among many. And, if I encourage her, she is pleased to fill out the picture. Now, my neighbor is fully capable of many things—buying groceries, cooking, riding a bicycle, playing tennis, reading books, and so on. And I wonder: what if she could acquire the simple skill of selective revelation? What if she could learn that others would be unsettled by her perceptions and avoid her as a result? The ability to control the public expression of one's private world is essential to viable relationships. It is a skill that should not be so difficult for her to acquire, and far more successful relations might result. How many of us have learned to be silent about our private dialogues?

•

There are significant steps toward an action-centered therapy. The potentials were long ago made apparent in the success of Alcoholics Anonymous and other 12-step programs of personal transformation. Although such practices leave one with a singular self-narrative, a narrative that sustains the tradition of bounded being, such programs do place their major emphasis on eliminating harmful drinking patterns. It is not simply the ways in which A.A. meetings teach the participant to avoid drink. In addition, monitors are supplied to provide supportive assistance whenever the temptation is strong. Programs specifically designed to reduce outbursts of anger are similarly focused on developing a new repertoire of action. Cognitive/behavior therapists have further added to the repertoire of possibilities. Many specialize in helping clients find ways to relax or distract themselves in the face of anxiety-provoking situations. Others ask their clients to keep diaries of their daily activities, and to try out new and more adaptive ways of responding to threatening situations. Again, the emphasis shifts from language to living.

•

Buddhist practices represent a major addition to practices available to contemporary therapists. They do not teach so much a way of talking as a way of being. For example, Jean Kristeller and her colleagues help the obese avoid binge eating by training them to focus more fully and carefully on their food.[40] Participants may be invited to meditate at length on the taste and texture of a single raisin. They may also learn to attend closely to the difference between two foods, and become conscious of how one might

---

[40]Kristeller, J. L., Baer, R. A., and Quillian-Wolever, R. (2006). Mindfulness-based approaches to eating disorders. In R. A. Baer (Ed). *Mindfulness and acceptance-based interventions: Conceptualization, application, and empirical support.* San Diego, CA: Elsevier.

choose between them. As discussed in Chapter 4, Kabat-Zinn and his colleagues have developed meditation practices for helping clients live more easily with pain. The important point is that such practices may be activated at any point during the course of daily life when one feels a surge of hunger or of pain.

A strong invitation to action-focused therapy is also found in the performance-oriented work of Fred Newman and his colleagues at the East Side Institute. As they see it, human action is primarily a social performance, that is, action within a world of co-constructed meaning.[41] Human development, on this account, is a process of expanding one's capacities for performance. To develop new capacities is "revolutionary" from their point of view, in the sense that it permits one to move beyond existing conventions. Therapy is dedicated, then, to expanding the client's capacities for effective performance. Working in groups is preferred to one-on-one therapy because it is performance *with* others that counts. Carrying the metaphor of performance further, the Institute sees stage performance as contributing to development. On the stage one is free to experiment with multiple identities and to risk the pratfall. In their support of performance, the Newman group has generated the All Stars Talent Show Network, a network that enables young, urban, African Americans to put on an annual talent show. The youth not only perform in the show, but organize the production, promotion and ticket sales. All activities constitute growth-oriented performance.[42]

•

In expanding the potentials of action oriented therapy much would be gained by collaborating with specialists in improvisation training, At this point, most improvisation training is theatrically oriented.[43] However, the potentials of improvisational education are enormous in implication. In a world of complex relationships and mercurial fluctuations in meaning, we must increasingly rely on improvisation for effective co-action. Repetition and reliability may be impediments to successful relationships in the ongoing flow of life.

[41]Newman, F. (1994). *Performance of a lifetime: A practical-philosophical guide to the joyous life.* New York: Castillo; Holzman, L., and Newman, F. (2003). Power, authority and pointless activity (The developmental discourse of social therapy) In T. Strong, and D. Paré (Eds.) *Furthering talk: Advances in discursive therapies.* New York: Kluwer Academic/Plenum.

[42] In an engaging variant, Gaetano Giordano, a Rome therapist, has his clients generate a video drama, with each playing the role of him or herself.

[43] See, for example, Gwinn, P., and Halpern, C. (2003). *Group improvisation: The manual of ensemble improv games.* New York: Meriwether; Hodgson, J. R. (1979). *Improvisation.* New York: Grove Press.

10

Organizing: The Precarious Balance

If your job were composed of mindless chores, meaningless orders, and alienated relationships, you would not freely choose it. For survival purposes many people do work under such conditions, and they long for escape. Yet, if we look at the ways in which most organizations are evaluated, that is, in terms of costs and benefits, such factors as mindlessness, meaninglessness, and alienation seldom figure in. These are not matters of the bottom line. At the same time, as most seasoned managers know, inattention to such factors risks the failure of the organization. The organization may limp along, it may be minimally effective, but its longevity is questionable. The difficult question is: What gives life to an organization? What brings about the kind of committed engagement that inspires its participants, and enables the organization to become the best that it can be?

In the past century there have been two major answers to these important questions. The first stresses the individual employee's intrinsic motives. As it is said, the individual possesses native instincts for growth, creativity, achievement, and so on. From this perspective the organization will thrive when it generates contexts enabling individual instincts to flourish.[1] The second answer stresses the impact of the environment on the person. Here it is proposed that the individual is motivated when offered rewards,

[1]The classic work is Herzberg's two-factor theory of worker satisfaction. Herzberg, F. (1959). *The motivation to work*. New York: Wiley. Maslow's hierarchy of needs is also a popular resource. Stephens, D. (Ed.) (2000). *The Maslow business reader*. New York: Wiley.

incentives, or comfortable working conditions.[2] Our traditions tell us, then, that individual engagement is driven either by intrinsic or extrinsic motivators.

•

But consider again: What if I had been reared in solitary—without any relationship to another human being? What work would I find intrinsically worth doing? Would I derive joy from typing away at a keyboard or spending hours examining markings on a page—just as I am doing now? And why should I achieve anything if the very concepts of achievement, success, or progress were unknown to me? If I had never known another human being, is there anything that would give me joy in my work, or that I would "just naturally" choose to do? Consider as well the impact of external motivators. If I were reared in solitary, what extrinsic rewards would fire my enthusiasm? Offer me a larger office, and I would shrug my shoulders; promise me a millions of dollars and I would wonder why that is interesting at all.

•

Julian greets the morning by nudging me awake with his paws. While I am in dreamland, he is preparing to empty his bladder and enjoy the breakfast that will follow. After the morning rituals, and a breakfast of my own, I repair to my desk and settle in for a morning's work. Julian crawls under the desk and readies himself for his morning nap. I once thought, with mild contempt, that I simply had a lazy dog; why wasn't he accomplishing something, like chasing squirrels, interrogating the bushes, or barking at possible dangers? But now I am not so sure. I sometimes wonder if Julian is quietly asking himself, "Why are humans such idiots? We have had such a nice breakfast, it is a marvelous time to relax, and he sits there all morning slaving away."

•

When we pose questions about why people act as they do, we so often answer by stressing *either* the intrinsic pull of heredity *or* the extrinsic push of environment. Why is it so difficult to formulate an intelligible answer to the question of "why" that relies on neither heredity nor environment? An answer can be found in the logic of bounded beings, whose relationships

---

[2]In the organizational sphere, this view is often traced to Taylorism, and the image of the factory as an in-put, out-put machine. On this account, the machine parts (the workers) will function according to in-puts, or environmental rewards.

are essentially those of cause and effect. Following a 16th-century scientific view of the cosmos as one great machine, there were only two reasons for the movement of an entity, the one external and the other internal. On the one side, a stone dropped from a mountaintop is propelled to earth by the external force of gravity; on the other, a bird dropped from the same point will glide to earth by virtue of its intrinsic capacities. But here we suspend this early view of science and its assumptions of bounded units. Rather, we ask: If organizational vitality issues from the confluence of relationships, what follows in terms of practices?[3]

The present chapter opens discussion on this question. First, I will draw together some of the major ideas from preceding chapters as applied to the organizing process. This introduction will also establish a leitmotif of the chapter, a concern with the precarious balance between fluid and frozen relations. It is within the flow of collaborative action that vitality and direction are spawned. However, in the attempt to solidify the fruits of co-action, relations are frozen. The future is jeopardized. The major challenge is to achieve a balance between the fluid and the fixed, the process of ordering and its ultimate realization.[4] With these concerns in place, I will then turn to four specific domains of practice: organizational decision-making, leadership, performance evaluation, and the relationship of the organization to its environment. How can a relational approach to practice sustain vitality? I will not be alone in these discussions. Just as in the preceding treatments of knowledge, education, and therapy, relational issues are robust among organizational scholars and practitioners. Their voices will be reflected here.

Organizing: Life Through Affirmation

It is through relational coordination that the organization comes to life. Organizations live or die in the swarm of daily interchange—in complimenting and criticizing, passing and retaining information, smiling and frowning, asking and answering, demanding and resisting, controlling

---

[3]For more on the co-creation of organization, see D. Grant, C. Hardy, C. Oswick, and L. Putnam (Eds.) (2004). *Handbook of organizational discourse.* London: Sage; Hosking, D.M., and McNamee (Eds.) (2006). *The social construction of organization.* Copenhagen: Copenhagen Business School.

[4]Resonant with the balance proposed here is a longstanding concern in organizational studies between balancing the opposing tendencies toward order and chaos. However, the collaborative flow emphasized here may simultaneously give rise to order (that upon which we can agree) and chaos (each co-creation represents a transformation of tradition).

and consenting.[5] What injects meaning into one's work is derived neither from the individual alone, nor environmental forces, but from participation in the swarm. Thus, what counts for some is selling soap, designing a new modem, or boosting corporate profits; for others, writing a novel, composing a song, or saving souls prove absorbing. As we participate, so do we create the value of various activities and outcomes—or not. Depending on the relationships, we would joyously work 12 hours a day or blow ourselves apart with a bomb.[6]

•

> Organizing is a conversational process, an inescapably self-organizing process of participation in the spontaneous emergence of continuity and change.
>
> —Patricia Shaw

•

Consider first the new recruit into an organization—a business, a team, a club, or a non-profit. It is not the rules, laws, or directives that will bring about vitality of action. Nor is it necessarily the process of formal training, mentoring, or modeling. The individual may learn to perform correctly, but without desire, care, or enthusiasm. The significant question is how to bring about fully engaged participation.

•

> Of all the organizations in which I have participated during my life, perhaps my least favorite was the military. When I graduated from college, the law demanded two years of service. Fulfilling my father's wishes, I became an officer in the U.S. Navy. Shipboard life was almost perfectly ordered; the unit functioned with a satisfactory degree of efficiency and efficacy. Nothing outstanding; nothing terrible. Ho-hum docility prevailed. As far as I could see, none of my mates was committed to the organization; none wished to remain in service for longer than required. We received our orders from officers

---

[5]For further discussion of the micro-practices of conversation out of which organizations develop, see Shaw, P. (2002). *Changing conversations in organizations: A complexity approach to change*. London: Routledge; Streatfield, P. (2001). *The paradox of control in organizations*. London: Routledge; and Grant, D., Hardy, C., Oswick, C., and Putnam, L. (Eds.) (2004). *The Sage handbook of organizational discourse*. London: Sage.

[6]In the field of organizational studies we must credit Mary Parker Follett as one of the first to understand that the well-being of the organization does not originate in the individual minds of the participants, but in the relational process. See Pauline Graham's, *Mary Parker Follett, Prophet of management*. (Frederick, MD: Beard, 1995).

on high, who received theirs from a central office. We did as we were told; to do less was to risk censure. Personal opinions and insights were not invited. The officers' meals together were largely confined to business, with all conversations monitored by the senior officer, lest they stray into matters of sex, politics, or religion.

Yet, there was vitality on board. It was there in the small informal and unmonitored groups—both in the case of the enlisted men and junior officers. It was created in dialogues of antipathy, derisive joking about life on board, damaging gossip about the senior officers, and sharing ways to "beat the system." Here there was mirth, irony, emotional expression, and self-sacrifice. It was, then, a *negative vitality*, a joyous process of organizing that was indeed *set against* organizational goals.

•

I do not believe that organizational engagement can be "produced." Those in charge cannot cause others to be vitally engaged. If work is to inspire, collaborative effort is required. When training is viewed as a top-down effort—with the trainer educating the fledgling—the possibilities for collaboration are diminished. When training is dominated by a single voice, carrying the organizational viewpoint, the fledgling listens, but with minimal involvement (see also Chapter 8). He or she may register information, but there is no invitation into the co-active process of creating meaning. In effect, monologue may lead to coordinated activity, but without commitment.[7]

•

In Chapter 6 I discussed a number of ways in which positive and productive relations may be achieved. For now, I wish only to elaborate on one of the most important means of inviting engaged participation: *affirmation*. When one is affirmed as a contributor to the process of meaning-making, the door is opened to engaged participation. Affirmation may take many forms, from a mere smile or nod of the head, to a fully voiced appreciation of another's actions. I am not referring here to affirmation as a means of boosting the individual's self-esteem. It is a welcoming into the process of meaning-making that is important. Nor does affirmation entail agreement; rather, it is the acknowledgement that there is value in the utterance that counts.

[7]A useful account of the significance of discourse use in building organization is found in Kegan, R., and Lahey, L. (2001). *How the way we talk can change the way we work*. San Francisco: Jossey-Bass.

As a multi-being, the newcomer is a carrier of multiple relations (Chapter 6), relations endowing the individual with multiple skills, insights, values, and so on. Thus, when the organization affirms the fledgling, it also affirms a relational background. In this moment the individual's relational life is given presence, and the individual feels "at home." It is not the narcissistic "I" who is drawn into the process of organizing, but the relational network in which the individual is embedded. When affirmed, the individual is more likely to share ideas, values, and logics. In this way the organization becomes both richer in potential and more fully connected to the web of meaning outside its walls. We will return to this issue again later in the chapter.

•

How did I come into a "love of ideas," and a profession as a scholar? The material costs and benefits scarcely made it attractive. The hours are long, the pay is mediocre, and after years of intense graduate study one may labor as a junior faculty member for another seven years without any guarantee of a secure future. Why choose such a profession? For me it began with a grammar school teacher. It is not what she taught me from the front of the classroom. It was her glowing reaction to my classroom report on how the outcome of the "war between the states" (as we called it) could have been reversed. Then there was a high school teacher who "deeply enjoyed" an article I had written for the school newspaper. Still later it was a college professor who was excited to debate a paper I had prepared for class. Such coveted affirmations fueled the present fire.

•

Affirmation also sets in motion the possibility of reciprocation. If you find my ideas interesting, for example, you also invite my caring attendance to your ideas. With mutual affirmation set in motion, the organization becomes a reservoir of enthusiastic engagement. Every relationship becomes a potential source for creating value. For example, the profession of car rentals has no intrinsic value. It could simply be "a job." A company slogan, such as "We try harder" attempts to inject value into the organization, but the slogan itself is monological. It does not invite the participants into conversation. It is when a close colleague says, "Hey, we got a good thing going here. Wouldn't it be great if we could beat those other guys this month," that the seeds of vitality are planted. Here the phrase, "beat those other guys" is drawn from a life-giving tradition outside the organization. Given another's affirmation, it injects a new value in the organization, something worth doing here and now.

With mutual affirmation the way is also open to bonding with one's colleagues. This was the case with the negative vitality I encountered with my Navy buddies. As we joked and gossiped, we came to share a sense of the real and the good, what is worth doing on board. We began to define ourselves as friends and to depend on each other in stressful times. Some of these friendships were for life. When mutual affirmation becomes a common fixture in an organization, and not just in its back rooms, the way is prepared for a communally shared narrative. It is not "my life," as opposed to the organization. I become one with others, whether it is the two of us, our team, our unit, and so on. We begin to ask how "we" are doing, and what is important for us. This world becomes significant to us, it matters, and we may honor this significance with expressions of emotion—cheering at success, becoming teary-eyed at retirements, and so on. When bonding is linked to organizational goals, the potentials are profound.

•

> You could capture all my research findings (on good relationships) with the metaphor of the salt shaker. Instead of filling it with salt, fill it with all the ways you can say yes, and that's what a good relationship is. "Yes," you say, "that is a good idea." "Yes, that's a great point. I never thought of that." "Yes, let's do that if you think it's important."
>
> —John M. Gottman

Beware the Organization

The affirming flow of relationship is a major source of vitality, and from this flow may spring commitment, direction, and bonding. It is so in classrooms, on teams, in neighborhoods, and in formal organizations. Yet, why is it that the workplace is so often tedious, empty, and suffused with conflict? Why did the exciting team of one year turn stale the next, the exhilarating neighborhood become boring, or the creative working group grow moribund? Moreover, is this trajectory inevitable? How can vitality be sustained across time? Such questions are complex and inexhaustible. However, let us again consider the issue from a relational perspective.

At the outset, we confront an irony. When relationship gives rise to shared realities and values, there is a strong tendency to assure continuation. No one wishes the exhilaration and productivity to end; we want to "nail it down." Thus we strive to sustain the trusted patterns and admonish those threatening to slip away. The organizational member who shirks, who fails to follow the rules, or whose allegiances are elsewhere becomes the subject of gossip, correction, and possible rejection. Simultaneously, it is by solidifying the patterns of relationship that organizational work is accomplished. It is when we are "all on the same page," that we know what to do. Clear and valued goals, knowledge of one's job, and mutual understanding of the functions that are filled, are essential to organizational efficacy. Yet, it is this same impulse to "hold on to what works" that carries the potential for destroying the vitality of the relationships. Recall here the preceding discussion of bonding and barricades (Chapter 6). Solidifying a relationship can impede the flow of creative co-action. Barriers are erected that can ultimately erode vitality and efficacy. Consider several of the important losses:

Suppression of Voices

As multi-beings, we enter organizations with myriad logics, pockets of knowledge, passions, and so on. Yet, as we are drawn into the organization's constructions of the real and the good, many of these potentials can be lost from view, simply shaved away as one is absorbed into the rituals, traditions, and standard operating procedures. We enter with enormous possibilities, and from them the organization extracts just those potentials needed to meet its needs. The remainder are irrelevant or irritating.

•

Lead, follow, or get out of the way.
—Thomas Paine

•

This flattening of potential is also hastened by the individualist orientation dominating most organizations. Individuals are generally hired to serve a particular function. Like bolts and levers in a machine, their job is defined so as to contribute to the "smooth and effective running" of the organization. A singular, coherent, and knowable individual is the ideal. It is just such individuals who can be trusted in their function. Other passions and potentials are irrelevant or possibly dysfunctional. Yet, as potentials for expression are eliminated, so does vitality wane.[8] Organizational participants are reduced to bland and predictable robots.

•

[8]For an account of the motivational significance of filling the dreams of employees as they are imported into the organization, see Kelly, M. (2007). *Dream manager*. New York: Hyperion.

I worked for a time as a consultant to a business executive with whom I couldn't seem to "connect." We were an effective team, but simply doing our job. While waiting in his office one day, I saw on his desk a puzzling snap-shot of a small hill of painted stones. When Arne arrived I asked him about the origins of the photo. He paused for a few moments, smiled wistfully, and slowly began to tell me about a private passion. He owned a little house on a secluded farm. On weekends and holidays he repaired to his sanctuary and took up his beloved pastime, painting the stones in the field. Over time the paint would weather, but he was not dismayed. It only gave him an opportunity to take up his brush again. As he unfolded the tale he began to laugh about his "totally useless pastime." His laughter was infectious, and soon we were howling in unison. Arne's disclosure was not only the beginning of lasting friendship, but of a sparkling work relationship.

The Organization Against Itself

When any cluster of people—great or small—becomes bonded, there is a simultaneous creation of an outsider. To sustain the specialness of "our group," those outside will necessarily be "less than great," or "second rate." As outsiders, they will be less valued and less affirmed. Communication recedes, and coordination is eroded (see Chapter 6). Under these conditions, groups can easily become alienated and antagonistic. These separations may occur between functional divisions of a corporation, between levels of an organization, and between sub-divisions separated geographically. They may also occur when colleagues become close friends. Even among Internet cronies in an organization, silent and privileged bonds may develop, thus insulating them from surrounding relationships. Separation is virtually assumed in relations between union and management. To be sure, the participants draw vitality from their compatriots, but the result is a negative vitality.

•

Mary and I once served as consultants for a large pharmaceutical firm. Their problem was a growing fragmentation between the home office and their 50 satellites spread around the world. As the home office executives described it, many of the satellite groups resisted their directives; they didn't seem to realize the importance of uniform practices, nor understand the economic logic necessary for success. Our visits to the satellites confirmed the picture of fragmentation. Often we found within the satellites a high degree of morale, and the sense that the home office didn't understand their situation or the culture of their organization. They took pride in their superior knowledge, and made fun of what seemed the "second rate intelligence" of managers in the home office. Here indeed was a negative vitality, and the result an alienation from the central offices. There was high morale within each satellite, but the result was an erosion of the whole.

Separation from Cultural Context

Organizations often take immense pride in themselves, their accomplishments, and their high degree of morale. Herein lie the seeds of another irony: the more effective the organization in achieving these ends, the greater the risk of losing connection with the outside world essential to continued survival. As the organization becomes a bounded entity, clear in its definition of what is *in* as opposed to *out*, that which is outside loses priority. Its realities, values, and logics cease to count for those inside.

In my own career I have seen this most strikingly in relationships between universities and the surrounding community. So often these relationships are cool, sometimes overtly hostile, each group holding its own internal reality as superior to the others. But such animosity is also present when a real estate developer unilaterally decides to construct condominiums, a corporation closes down a factory, or the government decides to build a wall separating nations. Even when city planning is carefully designed to benefit the citizenry, the very unilateral nature of the action may signal disregard for those who are supposed to benefit. The result is often resistance. When organizing gives way to "the organization," the walls become prisons.

•

Behold, how good and joyful it is, brethren,
to dwell together in unity.

—Early Anglican verse

•

As we find, when the flow becomes frozen, that process responsible for vital and effective outcomes can ultimately drain life and potential from the organization. Required, then, is a delicate balance between the continuous process of ordering and the injurious outcome of order itself, between creating and conserving, between traveling toward a destination and arriving.[9] But how is such a balance to be achieved; how can we build and sustain vitalizing relationships without simultaneously bringing about their demise? As I will propose in what follows, sustaining vitality requires continuous transformations of the ordinary, and these are primarily achieved by extending the perimeters of dialogue. Crossing the boundaries of convenient conversations is crucial, along with tapping the potentials of multi-being. In the coming discussion, I take up four significant features of organizational life: decision-making, leadership, evaluation, and public relations. My concern in each case is with relational practices that maintain the precarious balance.

Decision-Making as Relational Coordination

One of the earliest forms of large-scale organization was military in nature: Large numbers of men were mobilized under conditions of do or die. From the Peloponnesian wars to the present, the primary form of the military organization was, and continues to be, the pyramid. The plans of battle are developed at the pinnacle of the structure, orders are disseminated downward through the various functional units (e.g. infantry, supplies, medical), and large numbers of men follow the orders. Failure to follow orders could yield execution. Information relevant to the success of the plans is conveyed upward through the pyramid.

The metaphor of the pyramid continues to inform much organizational practice today. Often referred to as "command and control," the view dominated the organizational sphere for much of the 20th century. However, recent decades have been marked by growing discontent. Possibly influenced by the emerging sensitivity to democracy and diversity in the workplace, there are strong moves toward flattening or decentralizing the contemporary organization. Even within military circles there are doubts about the practical adequacy of command and control. As they move into

---

[9]Relevant here is the concept of the *chaordic* organization, one that exists in a space that is partially ordered and partially chaotic. The vision of the chaordic organization largely emerges from the biologically based view of living systems as self-organizing. See, for example, Jantsch, E. (1980). *The self-organizing universe: Scientific and human implications of the emerging paradigm of evolution.* New York: Pergamon. The major difference between the biological view and the present is that the former tends to view the chaordic state as a an inherent process of self-organization, while I strongly emphasize the chaordic condition as one that may or may not be achieved, depending on practices of collaboration.

the field, ground forces inevitably encounter surprises, and battlefields often border on chaos. In such cases, troops must improvise or die.

•

From a relational standpoint it is useful to view the organization as a potentially fluid field of meaning-making. Theoretically, the flow of meaning is continuous and uninterrupted. As individuals move from one relationship

Responding to my request to use playing cards to illustrate the modern organization, Professor John Rijsman from Tilburg University created this structure. While depicting the traditional pyramid, the Rijsman design also underscores the less obvious feature of relational interdendence.

Courtesy: Anne Marie Rijsman

to another, they will bring with them ideas, rationalities, and values from other conversations. Practically, however, people tend to congregate with certain colleagues more frequently than with others. This may be the result of their geographic proximity, their work group, a long history in the organization, personal friendship, and so on. In any case, as these clusters come into agreement about what is "really" the case, and what is "really" worth doing, the flow of meaning-making slows to a halt. There is a formation of "we" that insulates and separates them from "the others."[10]

Put in these terms, the inadequacy of the pyramidal structure is most glaring. Decisions made on high are typically monological. They do not issue from the relational clusters that create the realities and values through which daily work is accomplished. The decisions are imposed on this process. Such announcements as, "The budget must be cut by 10%," "We are closing down the unit," or "The benefits package is going to be reduced," are often thrust into the clusterings as if they had commanding presence. Yet, according to the logic of co-action, pronouncements such as these have no meaning apart from those who respond. They come into meaning as others interpret them, and those at the top do not control the interpretations. Within the various clusters, orders from elsewhere may not be accepted as reasonable and desirable; they may in fact be constructed as "mindless," "insensitive," "punitive," or "misguided." There may be forced compliance within the clusters, but the stage is then set for negative vitality.

•

The major challenge of decision-making, then, is to mobilize collaborative processes in the service of effective action.[11] This means facilitating coordination across clusters in such a way that new meanings, values, and motives may be mobilized. The rewards of collaborative decision-making are substantial. There is first the fact that decisions will not be alien arrivals into the conversations that make up the organization. They will carry the voices

[10]In other terms, these clusters represent small centers of power within the organization. For more, see Gergen, K. J. (1995). Relational theory and the discourses of power. In D. Hosking, H. P. Dachler, and K. J. Gergen (Eds.) *Management and organization: Relational alternatives to individualism.* Aldershot, UK: Avebury.

[11]Relevant is Boje, Oswick, and Ford's comment "Rather than consider organizations as some 'thing' that exists independent of language and that is only described and reported on in language, (we) start from the point of view that organizations can be understood as collaborative and contending discourses. Boje, D., Oswick, C., and Ford, J. (2004). Language and organization: The doing of discourse. *Academy of Management Review, 29,* 571. This view has roots in earlier writings on organizational culture. However, rather than viewing cultures as fixed entities, a relational view holds that "culturing" is a continuously unfolding process.

of the participants. When decisions are implemented, they will represent logics and values in which the participants are already invested. Second, as multi-beings, each participant in an organization carries a unique array of skills, opinions, values, and information. Every participant is also a representative of other communities. He or she possesses outsider knowledge that can vitally enrich decision-making. Finally, there is the matter of organizational vitality. By including organizational participants in the co-active process, and affirming their contributions, their investment in the organization may blossom. Decision-making will promote the kind of buy-in that is vitalizing.[12]

•

People support what they create.
—Stephen Littlejohn and Kathy Domenici

•

In what follows I want to share several practices that have impressed me in the way they contribute to collaborative decision-making. First, there are practices emphasizing the expression of multiple voices. Then I turn to practices highlighting the importance of appreciation.[13] (For a discussion of practices specifically concerned with conflict, the reader may wish to return to Chapter 6.)

Polyphonic Process: Lifting Every Voice

In organization studies the emphasis on participation is often captured by the metaphor of the *polyphonic* (many voiced) organization.[14] As Robert Rodriguez summarizes, polyphony exists in those "moments when people from different social realities come together and each person's voice is solicited, allowed to speak, heard, and valued equally to co-create the

---

[12]For more on the way in which participation can increase the creative capacity of groups, see Sawyer, K. (2007). *Group genius: The creative power of collaboration.* New York: Perseus.

[13]For more on relational decision-making see Straus, D. (2002). *How to make collaboration work.* San Francisco: Berrett-Koehler; Kaner, S. et al. (2007). *A facilitator's guide to participatory decision making* (2nd ed.). New York: Jossey-Bass; Ford, J. D., and Ford, L. W. (1995). The role of conversations in producing intentional change in organizations. *Academy of Management Review, 20,* 541–570. Although more psychological in its orientation, helpful insights may be found in Panzarasa, P., Jennings, N. R., and Norman, T. J. (2002). Formalizing collaborative decision making and practical reasoning in multi-agent systems. *Journal of Logic and Computation, 12,* 55–117.

[14]For more on the polyphonic organization, see Gergen, K. J., and Gergen, M. (in press). Polyvocal organizing: An exploration. In C. Steyaert (Ed.) *Dialogic organizing.* New York: Springer.

future."[15] Mary Ann Hazen proposes that an organization becomes poly-phonic when people celebrate their differences. She uses the carnival tradition of Mardi Gras to illustrate the point. In the festival, people from many different walks of life come together to dance, play, sing, and laugh.[16] On the level of day-to-day decision-making, the practical implications are clear: Establish dialogues that include as many participants as practicable. Any manager who finds him or herself alone at the desk, formulating an autonomous decision, poses a threat to organizational life.

Unfortunately our individualist tradition often stands in the way of collaborative decision-making. First, if we see the world in terms of bounded beings, each out for his or her own welfare, we become suspicious of one another. What are they really trying to accomplish when they speak, what's their pay-off, how will I be affected? We are also thrown into competition; if my opinions don't prevail, others will win out. When it is me against you, I will scarcely be open to your opinions. And at times, I may be reticent to voice an opinion on various topics. If my opinions prove faulty (a goal of my competitors), it will suggest that I possess an inferior mind. The challenge, then, is to generate practices that avoid the strangulating tendencies of the individualist tradition.

•

Leo, the CEO of a large subsidiary of an international corporation, recently shared with me an impressive illustration of relational decision-making. Leo was ordered by his parent organization to reduce the costs of the subsidiary by 15%. He was staggered by the demand, and deeply frustrated when he found it was non-negotiable. He considered hiring a large consulting firm to advise him on how to make such reductions. Laying off employees was the most obvious solution, but which ones, and when? And, it was also clear that if he announced a down-sizing decision to the organization, he himself would duplicate the kind of treatment he had received from the parent organization. Such an announcement would foster an atmosphere of fear, anger, and dejection.

With his staff, another route to decision-making was devised. Essentially the organizational members would be enlisted into the decision making process. They would provide inputs into how the organization could be made more cost effective. Fourteen discussion

[15]Rodriguez, R. (2001). The social construction of polyphony within organizations (p. 5). Unpublished doctoral dissertation, Benedictine University.

[16]Hazen, M. A. (1993). Towards polyphonic organization. *Journal of Organizational Change Management*, 6, 15–22.

groups were thus created, each composed of members from all sectors and levels of the company. The groups gathered information, conducted interviews, and periodically met with each other. External consultants were hired only to orchestrate the complex process of communication and scheduling. Ultimately the discussion groups generated a seven-volume summary containing their research and recommendations. The executive board ultimately accepted more than 75% of the teams' recommendations. Down-sizing was minimal; ingenious re-organization was everywhere in evidence; the economic goal was achieved, and enthusiasm was maximal. Virtually all sectors of the company were represented, and when the final policies were announced, broad acceptance and affirmation prevailed.[17]

•

It is useful here to distinguish between two kinds of polyphonics. The first is that of the *bounded expression*, with each organizational participant responsible for voicing his or her opinion. Often this orientation is reflected in accounts of democracy in the workplace, and in debates between management and workers. The presumption here largely follows from the tradition of bounded being, in which we anticipate that people possess (or should possess) a singular, coherent voice, "my opinion," "my attitude," or "my view." On this account, the individual who expresses multiple viewpoints is scattered and unfocused; to express doubts in one's offering is to lack the strength of conviction; inconsistency is the sign of a lesser mind. Yet, this tradition also stifles the enormous potentials for multi-being. We must recognize, then, the potential for *unbounded expression*. As multi-beings we possess antithetical values and visions, self-doubts, and conflicting reasons. Although there are gains to be made through singular expressions, they are limited. In giving voice to multi-being we invite the expression of multiple logics and values—reflecting the multiple traditions of which people are a part. The practical challenge is to generate conditions in which participants are free to express a full range of views and values, even when contradictory.[18]

---

[17]In his innovative work, Theodore Taptklis solicits stories from participants at all levels of an organization, which are then made available as an archive. The stories often treat discoveries that participants have made which they feel would help others in the future. See Taptklis, T. (2005). After managerialism. *E-CO, 7,* 2–14.

[18]As many see it, this orientation to decision-making is also a major contributor to knowledge-making in the organization. See, for example, Kawamura, T. (2007). Managing networks of communities of practice for organizational knowledge creation: A knowledge management imperative in the era of globalization. *Annales des Telecommunication, 62,* 734–752.

The possibilities for unbounded expression are suggested by this collage, created as a gift from a son to his mother. The mother, Roberta Iversen, does not possess a singular voice, but a multitude, including the voices of all her family members.

Courtesy: John Iversen

The possibilities for unbounded expression have scarcely been explored. However, a useful move in this direction is represented in the popular decision making heuristic developed by Edward deBono.[19] Using a metaphor of six hats, a decision making group may be invited into periods of exchange in which the participants are invited to speak in a particular manner. Thus, one person wears the White Hat and is invited to simply share relevant information, such as a recent opinion poll result; the person with the

[19]DeBono, E. (1985). *Six thinking hats*. Boston: Little Brown.

Yellow Hat is asked to share optimism, what is good about the decision they are entertaining; then, the Black Hat character may speak out on what the downside or dangers might be; the Red Hat person may wax subjective, speaking about relevant feelings, hunches, and intuitions; the Green Hat is invited to share creatively, to brainstorm on what could be done, and to imagine alternatives; finally, the Blue Hat wearer can speak about how the conversation is going, what has been accomplished, and where the group should go now. In many cases, the entire group wears one of the hats for a period of time and then switches to another. The beauty of this heuristic is not only that it opens up the arena of multi-being, but that it vastly enriches the range of ideas and sentiments considered in any decision.

•

Theresa Bertram, the past director of a very large and successful gerontology foundation, shared her story of polyphonic participation. The foundation was responsible for the well-being of a large community of elders, including the delivery of 800 meals on wheels. Theresa describes the way in which the organization had reached a stagnation point, maintaining an effective program, but without the zest of full engagement. She then found herself struck by the views of a consultant who spoke of tapping the latent energies of the staff and board members. As a result she held a retreat in which the staff and board could have a new form of conversation: Rather than taking care of business as usual, they told stories and shared dreams of new and better futures. The result was not only an electrifying of their relationships, but the realization that the very people to whom they provided care might also harbor such stories. In fact, as she described, the foundation's care-taking might actually stifle the creative participation of the population they were trying to serve.

A further program was then initiated in which the elderly could share their hopes and dreams for their life in the community. These stories were brimming with innovative ideas. A new policy resulted, one that granted to the community of elders a major voice in how they were to be served. The result was a profound change in the vitality of the retirement community members. The participants became deeply involved in planning. They developed special events, invited their own speakers, managed their budget, selected menus for social occasions, and more. The bus schedule, formerly arranged by the program director, was now unscheduled, and the bus was made available to take the residents wherever they wished to go. Among the selected destinations were the town meetings. Here the elderly became a political voice, expressing their views on basic issues confronting the community at large. Polyphonic voicing and vitality walked hand in hand.[20]

Decision-Making Through Appreciative Inquiry

A number of central themes in this book come together in the widely shared decision making practice of Appreciative Inquiry (AI). A premium is placed on broad participation, with mutually affirming dialogue as the centerpiece. The rationale for the practice is best understood in contrast to the strong traditional emphasis on problem solving. Too often one hears, "We have a problem with marketing," "Our CEO has no imagination," "Our costs are too high," and so on. One imagines that if all the problems were solved, the organization would run perfectly. Yet, from a relational standpoint, problems are the result of co-action. There are no problems in themselves, but only those that people come to define as problems. The question, then, is whether "problem talk" is an ideal way of going on in the organization. For one, a focus on "the problem" often mushrooms. By talking about a problem people soon one find other problems to which it is related. Solving the problem of product development, for example, depends on solving the problem of marketing, which depends on finding able personnel, which depends on.... Soon one confronts an insurmountable array of difficulties. Further, in the focus on problems we also begin to find fault with each other; there is denial and defense, and an accumulation of fear, depression, and distrust. Finally, in a problem focus we lose our sense of positive direction; as problems absorb our attention, our goals move to the margins of concern. The organizational dream is perpetually postponed as pessimism wins the day.

If "deficit discourse" bleeds life from the organization, what forms of talk can move the organization effectively and enthusiastically into the future? The practice of Appreciative Inquiry is based on the assumption that by inquiring into the strengths, successes, values, hopes, and dreams of the participants, the organization can be transformed. As David Cooperrider and Diana Whitney describe, "The single most prolific thing a group can do, if it aims to consciously construct a better future, is to make the 'positive change core' of any system the common and explicit property of all."[21]

[20]For illuminating contributions to ways in which dialogue with clients or patients may improve health-care systems, see the work of the Picker Institute: www.pickereurope.org.

[21]See Cooperrider, D. L., Sorensen, P. F., Whitney, D., and Yaeger, T. F. (2000). *Appreciative inquiry: Rethinking human organization toward a positive theory of change* (p. 5). Champaign, IL: Stipes.

The focus is on an organization's most central strengths and resources, those that breathe life into it.

Appreciative inquiry can be used for many different purposes: to determine the future of an organization, set the organization on a new course, resolve conflict, create an enthusiastic sense of cooperation, and more.[22] The typical AI session is divided into four phases. In what is called the *Discovery phase*, members of the organization are typically paired off and asked to share stories with each other. For example, they might be asked to describe a time when they were most excited by their work, when the organization was most fully alive for them, or when collaboration with others was most exhilarating and effective. In an organization facing internal conflict, participants might be drawn from each of the conflicting groups and asked to share stories of times when they worked well with someone from the other group, enjoyed the other's company, or were enriched by each other. In the *Dream phase*, the stories are first shared in small groups, and the primary themes are subsequently communicated in larger groups. In this phase the organizational members locate within these stories a collective vision of a commanding future. "If these are the kinds of relations that have given us vitality," it is asked, "what kind of organization can we create that would embody these ideals."

In the *Design phase*, the members begin to ask what kind of specific changes, policies, mechanisms, or the like might be placed in motion to achieve these ideals. Here they begin to work together in hammering out specific details. Otherwise alienated or hostile members of the organization are now collaborating in building a positive future in which they all have an investment. The form of dialogue has entirely changed. Finally, in the *Destiny phase*, groups take on the responsibility of moving visions into action. Often the proposed changes are extensive, aimed at management practices, evaluation systems, customer service, work processes, and so on. However, specific initiatives must be set in place to bring about such changes. The entire process typically ignites enthusiasm and good will. Importantly, AI locates the roots of the future within grounds of the past;

[22]For more detailed accounts, see Cooperrider, D. L., Whitney, D., and Stavros, J. M. (2003). *Appreciative inquiry handbook.* Bedford Heights, OH: Lakeshore Communications; Whitney, D., and Trosten-Bloom, A. (2003). *The power of appreciative inquiry.* San Francisco: Berrett-Koehler; Fry, R., Barrett, F., Seiling, J., and Whitney, D. (2002). *Appreciative inquiry and organizational transformation.* Westport, CN: Quorum; Watkins, J., and Mohr, B. (2001). Appreciative inquiry: Change at the speed of imagination. San Francisco, CA: Jossey-Bass Pfeiffer; For a succinct guide to practice, see Barrett, F., and Frye, R. (2005). *Appreciative Inquiry: A positive approach to building cooperative capacity.* Chagrin Falls, OH: Taos Institute Publications.

the participants are not indulging in mere pipe dreams, but drawing from their multiple potentials to generate realistic possibilities for the future.

•

Practitioners have also developed means of expanding the practice to include entire organizations. The mounting of an *AI summit*,[23] as it is called, has been used with groups of more than a thousand participants. While many AI projects are conducted within the corporate setting, there are numerous applications within schools, churches, non-profit organizations, medical settings, the military, communities, and more. AI advocates also find the appreciative orientation can vitally enrich relationships in daily life. The emphasis on the positive core of marriages, families, and friendships not only sustains vitality, but is invaluable in helping family members through stressful times.[24]

•

Enthusiasm for AI practices is globe-spanning. Some even credit entire shifts in cultural politics to the pervasive use of such practices.[25] For example, the extensive use of AI in Nepal is credited with the avoidance of civil war. However, like all practices, its success or failure must be understood in the contexts of meaning upon which its intelligibility depends. For example, many resist the practice because they feel it gives insufficient room for the expression of their anguish. If their story of maltreatment and injustice is not heard, they say, then they cannot be understood. Their relational history is not sufficiently affirmed. Others feel that there is insufficient space for minority voices. In the move from Discovery to Design, the vision of the future is necessarily simplified. In the simplification, differences of opinion may have been eliminated. Further, like all practices, when they become standardized and repeated, their meaning is altered. The initial participation in the practice is often exciting and productive. By the third participation it may become a cumbersome routine, and possibly seem manipulative. Standardized practices always reduce the potentials of co-action. Such issues continue to drive innovation in AI practices.

•

[23]Ludema, J. D., Whitney, D., Mohr, B. J., and Griffin, T. J. (2003). *The Appreciative inquiry summit: A practitioner's guide for leading large-group change.* San Francisco: Berrett-Koehler.

[24]See Stavros, J. M., and Torres, C. B. (2005). *Dynamic relationships: Unleashing the power of appreciative inquiry in daily living.* Chagrin Falls, OH: Taos Institute Publications. For family life, see Dole, D. C., Silbert, J. H., Mann, A. J., and Whitney, D. (2008). *Positive family dynamics: Appreciative inquiry questions to bring out the best in families.* Chagrin Falls, OH: Taos Institute Publications.

[25]See, for example, http://appreciativeinquiry.case.edu/community/link.cfm, http://www.imaginenepal.org/organizer.htm.

In conclusion, a relational orientation to decision-making emphasizes collaboration as the key element, not only in reaching more fully informed conclusions, but in sustaining the balance between creating and conserving. Collaborative decision-making thrives on polyphonic participation. Ideally this means opening decision-making to as many participants as practicable, and encouraging participants to share the richness of their multi-being. When carried out appreciatively the process is vitalizing and there is maximal buy-in. This emphasis on "decision-making without end" also softens the boundaries of various clusterings or groups within the organization. And it is here that the relational approach joins hands with the learning organization movement. As Peter Senge and his colleagues propose, "A learning organization is a dynamic organization of cooperating human beings in a state of continuous transformation."[26] In learning organizations, the continuous collection and exchange of information, opinion, and value means that all assumptions are subject to continuous challenge. The conversation is forever open. It is against this backdrop that we turn now to issues of leadership.

From Leadership to Relational Leading

The subject of leadership has a long history. Indeed, over 200,000 books have treated this subject. Do we not know quite enough; is there anything to add? From a relational standpoint, we are barely at the beginning. This is so because the vast bulk of writing on leadership primarily represents variations on the single melody of bounded being. From the classical "great man" theories, to recent accounts of the traits of great leaders and successful managers, most theories presume that leadership potential resides within the individual person.[27] It is not simply that the view carries with it a range of unfortunate consequences (Chapter 1). From a relational standpoint, the individualist view is fundamentally misleading. None of the qualities attributed to good leaders stands alone. Alone, one cannot be inspiring, visionary, humble, or flexible. These qualities are achievements of a co-active process in which others' affirmation is essential.

---

[26]See especially, Senge, P. (1994). *The fifth discipline: The art and practice of the learning organization*. Sydney, Australia: Currency (p. 9).

[27]The one significant alternative to the view of leadership as inherent in the individual, is to view leadership as a result of "the situation." It is not the characteristic of the leader that is important on this account, but the situation that happens to place a person in a significant role at a particular time. Yet, this view also sustains the tradition of bounded being. It voices the environmentalist pole of the heredity/environment binary account of human behavior. See, for example, Simonton, D. K. (1987). *Why presidents succeed: A political psychology of leadership*. New Haven: Yale University Press.

A charismatic leader is only charismatic by virtue of others who treat him or her in this way; remove the glitter in their eyes and the "charisma" turns to dust. An "intelligent decision" is only intelligent if there are agreeable collaborators.[28] To say anything about the leader as a single human being misses the relational confluence from which the very possibility of "the leader" emerges. As James O'Toole and his colleagues remind us:

> When we speak of leadership, the likes of Mohandas Gandhi and Martin Luther King, Jr., spring to mind. We don't immediately remember that, during the struggle for Indian independence, Gandhi was surrounded and supported by dozens of other great Indian leaders, including Nehru, Patel, and Jinnah, without whose joint efforts, Gandhi clearly would have failed. We also forget that, far from doing it all himself, King's disciples included such impressive leaders in their own right as Jesse Jackson, Andrew Young, Julian Bond, Coretta Scott King, and Ralph Abernathy.[29]

It must be added, however, that each of these surrounding figures required the collaborative support of countless others. Leadership resides in the confluence.

•

The vision of "great leaders" is largely the result of the command and control structures inherited from the past. However, as many believe, this structure is no longer effective in the contemporary world. When information is limited, the aim is clear, and conditions are stable, command and control may be adequate (though seldom energizing). However, consider the contemporary conditions:

- Because of technological developments, information accumulates more rapidly, becomes increasingly complex, is less reliable, and is more rapidly outdated.
- The speed of change, in economic conditions, government policies, and public opinion, outpaces assimilation. Long-term strategic planning becomes increasingly ineffectual.
- New organizations, new products, new laws, new systems of accountability, and new communication systems constantly shift the terrain of competition and cooperation.

[28]The demise of the former Soviet Union is a fascinating case in point.
[29]O'Toole, J., Galbraith, J., and Lawler, E. E. (2002). The promise and pitfalls of shared leadership. In C. L. Pearce and J. A. Conger (Eds.) *Shared leadership* (p. 251). Thousand Oaks, CA: Sage.

– The increasing diversity of differences—ethnic, cultural, religious—provides expanding opportunities for both growth and for conflict.
– The opinion climate can rapidly change, and the range of opinions to which the organization must be sensitive constantly expands.

•

We cling to the myth of the Lone Ranger, the romantic idea that great things are usually accomplished by a larger-than-life individual working alone.... Whether the task is building a global business or discovering the mysteries of the human brain, one person can't hope to accomplish it, however gifted or energetic he or she may be. There are simply too many problems to be identified and solved, too many connections to be made.

—Warren Bennis and Patricia Ward Biederman

•

These conditions of rapid and often chaotic change now give rise to new visions of leadership. Abandoned are the endless and often contradictory lists of what it takes to be a good leader. In their place we find increasing emphasis on collaboration, empowerment, dialogue, horizontal decision-making, sharing, distribution, networking, continuous learning, and connectivity.[30] In effect, there now exists a cadre of organizational scholars and practitioners who variously reflect a deep concern with relational process. In my view, we may usefully replace the concept of leadership with that of *relational leading*. While leadership denotes the characteristics of an individual, relational leading refers to the ability of persons in relationship to move with engagement and efficacy into the future. It is not the single individual who is prized, but animated relations. If significant movement is to take place within an organization, it will emerge from the generative interchange among the participants. To be sure, individuals may be designated leaders, but the process of leading is ultimately relational.

•

[30]See, for example, Drath, W. (2001). *The deep blue sea: Rethinking the source of leadership*. San Francisco: Jossey-Bass; Spillane, J. P., and Diamond, J. B. (2007). *Distributed leadership in practice*. New York: Columbia Teachers College Press; Raelin, J. A. (2003). *Creating leaderful organizations*. San Francisco: Berrett-Koehler Publishers; Spillane, J. P. (2006). *Distributed leadership*. San Francisco: Jossey-Bass; Schiller, M., Holland, B., and Riley, D. (2001). *Appreciative leaders*. Chagrin Falls, OH: Taos Institute Publications.

> Power is never the property of an individual; it belongs to a group
> and remains in existence only so long as the group keeps together.
> When we say of somebody that he is "in power" we actually refer to
> his being empowered by a number of people to act in their name.
> The moment the group, from which the power originated to begin
> with...disappears, "his power" also vanishes.

—Hannah Arendt

•

What does relational leading mean in terms of daily practice? At the outset,
it is clear that relational leading is not the task of a specific individual.
Rather, it emerges from within the micro-processes of everyday interchange. Ideally it should become a way of life within the organizational
culture—just there in the ordinary ways in which we go on together.
Clearly the practice of affirmation would be a primary asset. At this juncture, however, I wish to focus on three additional, but less obvious practices:
positive sharing, adding value, and reality building.

Positive Sharing. At the outset, initiatives for change emerge most
effectively from the broad sharing of visions, values, and insights.
Establishing congenial contexts for expression sets conversational wheels
in motion. The greater the number of voices entering the conversation,
the greater the sophistication of the outcome. More will be known about
possibilities and potentials. Further, there will be greater ownership of the
outcome by the participants. A senior official can move an organization to
action, but members may move woodenly and inflexibly toward the
specified end. If major ideas for change are hatched in high places, ideally
these should be widely shared and discussed before implementation. When
treated like a pawn, one behaves like a pawn. As conditions change and
plans are no longer adequate, pawns simply await orders.

In their illuminating research, Alexandra Michel and Stanton Wortham
compared the organizational practices of two investment banking organizations.[31] The first trained their executives in the traditional way, with
an emphasis on rules of effective performance, and the responsibility of
each individual for his or her own accounts. Executives could thus be compared in terms of their performance; an ethos of super-stars prevailed. The
second organization used an organizational-centered model of training.
In this case the participants were trained to treat each other not as potential

[31]Michel, A., and Wortham, S. (2008). *Bullish on uncertainty: How organizational cultures transform participants*. New York: Cambridge University Press.

competitors, but as resources for learning. The stress on rules was replaced by a more situated or contingent view of what might be effective. Not only was there a stress on sharing information and opinion, but in principle, any executive could substitute for any other on a given account. The ethos of competition and conflict was replaced by an emphasis on collaboration. Policies aimed at reducing uncertainty were replaced by an emphasis on learning from contexts of ambiguity, and moving sensitively and reflexively with the flow of events. As their research suggests, executives in the organization centered bank functioned under less stress of evaluation, were more positively motivated, and were far more flexible and imaginative in their work.

•

Adding Value. Engaged activity does not begin with the proposal of a single individual—"I think it would be a good idea to... ."—but with a proposal and its affirmation by at least one other person. "That's interesting," "I never thought of that before," "That just might be what we need," "Let's explore that idea." All of these replies inject value into the other's utterance. Animation begins here. Affirmation is not the only means of adding value. *Positive elaboration* is also a powerful motivator. "Let's think about what this would mean to... ." "I can see where this might help to...." As an idea is elaborated—detailing its potential, adding useful information, overcoming possible hurdles—an inviting future takes shape. Further value is added by making *relevant associations*: "That reminds me of...." "They tried something similar in X organization, and... ."[32] Frontal critique should be avoided. It is not simply the individual making the proposal who will suffer at the hands of critique, but indeed the entire climate of conversation. Critique will often lead to the impasse of an idea; collective excitement will begin to wane. By adding value, elaborating, and associating, ideas will take wing; Enthusiasm will pervade. This does not mean avoiding critical ideas. However, such expressions are most effective in the form of an alternative vision, and most promisingly one that builds on what has already been offered. "I think we are moving in a good direction, but you know, if we thought about the possibility of Y, it might do everything that X accomplished, but avoid some of its problems."

•

[32]For an engaging discussion of adding value, using jazz improvisation for inspiration, see Barrett, F. J. (1998). Creativity and improvisation in jazz and organizations. *Organization Science*, 9, 605–622.

Without my personal and professional relationships inside and
outside the company, virtually none of the things in my life would
have been accomplished... . Hewlett-Packard itself is a good example
of the power of relationships. It was founded on a relationship of love
and respect between two people. This is not the Hewlett company or
the Packard company, but the Hewlett-Packard company. The order
was decided not by higher or lower, greater or lesser, but by the flip
of a coin. And the company grew through hundreds of significant
relationship. Not just relationships with peers, but relationships up
and down the hierarchy... . We cannot make or keep good
relationships unless we listen. And listen wholly without preparing
the next remark, without thinking about getting gas on the way
home or whether our child did well on her math quiz. We must shut
off the incessant judgment machine urging us to decide who's
smarter, right, most likely to succeed. We must fall into each other's
eyes. When we do this, magical things happen. Things far greater
than we could have imagined.

—Barbara Waugh, Recruiting Manager, H & P

•

Reality Building: Positive sharing and adding value are excellent ways
to animate and direct organizational energies. However, it is also essential
that participants share in their constructions of the realities in which they
exist. Two specialized forms of talk can make a telling contribution to
reality building. First there is narration. Recall from the preceding account
of bonding (Chapter 6), the significance of moving from "I" to "we" in the
stories we tell about ourselves. This is no less the case in organizations. The
more conversational reference to "we" and "ours" (as opposed to "I" and
"mine"), the more likely the buy-in to the organizational goals. However,
there is more to narration in the way of carving significant futures. Members
of an organization are often content with the status quo. At least they know
what to do and they are reasonably effective in doing it. Why change; or at
the least, why dance with a new devil rather than the devil at hand?
Leadership implies direction, and to have a direction is to be moving from
one condition to a new, more valued one. Needed, then, is a narrative that
will explain the significance of this new state, and show the way. "This new
plan will help us to serve our customers better, and we can make it work
by ... ." "We are barely getting by in our present situation, and if we move
in X direction we can really prosper." A good narrative may inject zest into
future goals.

Understanding the organization as moving from the present into a
positive future is only one form of narrative. Narratives may also be used to

inject value into the present condition, and thus to prepare the way for the future. For example, there is the common *from the ashes* narrative, in which "We came from nothing, but look at us now," or the *rebound story*, in which "We were brought low, but we are resilient." Each situates the present in terms of the past, and in doing so adds value to present pursuits. Such stories of the past may also be linked to the future, thus mobilizing efforts for new initiatives. "We have struggled from nothing, to find ourselves tenth in the world.... . I think we can do even better." "We were hit hard, and have almost recovered...but I think this is an opportunity to do better than just recover." To bring such narratives into common conversations is to energize the organization.[33]

•

Another useful vehicle for reality building is the metaphor. A metaphor is a figure of speech that defines one thing in terms of another, as, for example, defining various aggressive activities as "a war on drugs," or "a war against terrorism." Metaphors can be powerful tools not only for focusing on an issue, but for setting new courses of action.[34] The metaphor of the *pyramid* is commonly understood, and invites with it a posture of deference to those above, and distance from those below. The metaphor of the organization as a *smoothly functioning machine* is also popular, and it does draw attention to the interdependency of differing units. However, it also has the unfortunate consequence of giving the participants the sense of being simple and replaceable parts. The metaphor of the organization as a *family* has different implications from seeing it as a *team,* or "*lean and mean*". At the same time, it is important that there be broad agreement on the major metaphor. If the members of an organization believe they are participating in a family, and top management, (the "parents"), unilaterally decides to down-size the organization, a major fall-out may ensue. It is wrong to abandon your children![35]

•

[33]For more on narratives in organizational life, see, Czarniawska, B. (1997). *Narrating the organization: Dramas of institutional identity.* Chicago: University of Chicago Press; Denning, S. (2005). *The leader's guide to storytelling.* San Francisco: Jossey-Bass; Gabriel, Y. (Ed.) (2004). *Myths, stories and organizations: Premodern narratives in our times.* New York: Oxford University Press.

[34]For more on the importance of metaphors in organizational life, see Morgan, G. (2006). *Images of the organization* (updated edition). Thousand Oaks, CA: Sage; Grant, D., and Oswick, C. (1996). *Metaphor and organizations.* London: Sage.

[35]For a case example of the dissension generated by violating the dominant metaphor, see Smith, R. C., and Eisenberg, E. M. (1987). Conflict at Disneyland: A root metaphor analysis. *Communication Monographs, 54,* 367–380.

This sketch invites us to view the organization in terms of relational flow. Shared agreements and bonding may occur at any location in the organization, but with the potential to impede the flow.

These three contributions to leadership—positive sharing, adding value, and reality building—are not reserved for any single person or position. Ideally they should be encouraged throughout the organization. This is not to say that all are equal in their potential for contributing. Persons occupying senior positions in traditional organization are often advantaged. Their connections are more numerous, and their words may carry more weight. Special skills may be required, then, to serve as a coordinator of coordinations. Skills in narration and metaphor, for example, may be very useful.[36] Especially vital, however, is the challenge of establishing conditions for sharing, valuing, narrating, and coalition making.

•

> Leadership communications begin as monologue. If they are
> successful they turn into dialogue, and then conversation.
>
> —Stephen Denning

From Evaluation to Valuation

> I have two daughters who work for large corporations. If there is one
> facet of their job that unsettles them, it is the performance
> evaluation. Perhaps all of us have occasional fears of inadequacy.
> Life in an individualistic culture prepares us for such fear, but a
> performance evaluation can stir these fears into frenzy. My daughters
> work very hard; they are dedicated and responsible; I tell them there

[36]For more on discursive skills in management, see Shotter, J., and Cunliffe, A. L. (2003). The manager as practical author II: Conversations for action. In D. Holman, and R. Thorpe, (Eds.) *Management and language: The manager as practical author*. London: Sage.

is nothing to fear. But they scarcely hear me; they cannot. Who knows what their assessors may be thinking?

•

The evaluation of individual performance is an unquestioned part of organizational life. Rituals of evaluation are not only regular and expected, they are typically required. How else, we ask, can we give feedback and correct for deficiencies? Indeed, we believe that without evaluation, many individuals could cease to be motivated, and their work quality would deteriorate. But how accurate is this assumption? Is it true that performance would really suffer without individual assessment? Is it possible that assessment may even be injurious to effective performance? Consider some of the outcomes of performance evaluation for relationships in the organization:

— *Keeping my opinions to myself.* "If I share a good idea, someone else may claim it as their own. They would get a better evaluation than me. If I share a controversial idea, I may be scorned, and my evaluations will suffer."
— *Looking out for #1.* "My major task is to look out for myself. My evaluations are on the line, thus my job, and my family's well-being. My colleagues are expendable."
— *Undermining others.* "If I help others, they may receive better evaluations than me. It will be to my benefit to criticize them behind their backs. "
— *Trusting no one.* "You can't trust what anyone tells you. They are all out for themselves, just like me. If they praise me, it is just flattery; if they help me, it means they think I am weak; whatever they do, it's for themselves."

•

Nor is it clear that performance evaluations are effective in generating improvements. If an individual is slow to submit a major report, a timely reminder may be very helpful. It would contribute even more to organizational life to inquire into the reasons for the tardiness and to find ways of helping out.[37] However, if the problem is noted two months later in a performance evaluation, it will have no corrective value, and will leave only a residue of anxiety about the future. Further, evaluating someone after a period of several months is treacherous. As a teacher, for example, I find

[37]As Jane Seiling proposes, most purposes of evaluation could be met through constructive conversations within the organization. See her dissertation, *Moving from individual to constructive accountability*. Unpublished doctoral dissertation. Tilburg University, 2005.

myself virtually unable to evaluate a student's contributions to classroom discussions at the end of the semester. I cannot recall all the class sessions, all the contributions, and all the silences. Recollections are scanty and haphazard; evaluation is a travesty. And so it is in organizations.

•

As I have argued, mutually affirming relationships are the source of organizational vitality. If so, traditional evaluative practices are detrimental to organizational health. Should they be abandoned altogether? After all, performance evaluation essentially derives from the presumption of bounded being. On this account, it is the individual we evaluate because individuals are responsible for their actions. Yet, we now understand that actions always emerge from a matrix of relationships. In principle, the individual never acts alone. However, the ultimate aim of evaluation is to ensure effective functioning of the organization, to correct for deviations, and to stimulate maximum performance. The question we now confront is whether there are means of achieving such ends without the damaging practice of traditional evaluation? Traditional forms of evaluation drive wedges between people. Are there alternative practices that could energize collaboration?

•

To explore, let us first replace the concept of *evaluation* with *valuation*. To evaluate is to position oneself as an independent judge of another's significance or worth. "*I* am an objective judge of *your* ability." In contrast, to value another is to lend significance to their voice; it is to affirm their contribution to the relationships from which the vitality of the organization is derived. Valuing contributes to coordinated action. If valuing the person encourages cooperative and creative participation, how is it to be achieved in actual practices? The search for alternatives to performance evaluation is only at its beginning. However, those attempting to use an appreciative approach offer useful insights.[38] The following kinds of activities are particularly promising:

– Invite organizational members to share what it is about their job that they do well and enjoy doing. Periodic questions of this sort will keep in the forefront the well-springs of value for the individual, as well as their contributions to the organization.

[38]Preskill, H., and Tzavaras Catsambas, T. (2006). *Reframing evaluation through appreciative inquiry.* London: Sage; Anderson, H. et al. (2008). *The appreciative organization.* Chagrin Falls. OH: Taos Institute Publishing.

- Ask peers and supervisors to share what the individual does best and what he or she contributes to the organization. Communicate these opinions to the individual. Learning how your colleagues value your presence can be enormously powerful. Consider 360 degree valuation.
- Ask individuals to articulate those talents and strengths they bring to the organization, and how it is they may best make use of these in their work. In this way members communicate to each other what can be appreciated in their work.
- Work in groups to discuss how best to support one another in reaching performance goals and objectives. Here individuals become sensitized to ways they may appreciate others with whom they work.
- Ask individuals to describe what help or support they receive from each of those with whom they closely work. When these statements are shared with others, they contribute to productive bonding.

•

Jill Machol of D&R International, Ltd. describes a successful attempt to build in an appreciative component to evaluation:

> We asked each employee to document their accomplishments for the year— specifically, not listing just the task, but also the value the individual had added—and also asked each manager to document the employee's accomplishments to the extent possible. Then, the manager and employee met and exchanged lists. The focus was on the conversation regarding any accomplishments that were on one list but not the other and also on ways in which performance on particular accomplishments could have been even better, thus leading into development needs (including coaching and mentoring) for the future…. Finally, the managers were asked to write up two to three paragraphs documenting the conversation, attach both lists, have both the manager and employee sign, and turn the whole thing into human resources. The process was not time consuming and engaged everyone in looking in a positive way at what had been accomplished during the year.

•

The critic wants a word: "Very sweet, indeed. But with all this emphasis on valuing, how will people learn about their shortcomings, what they need to improve?" This is a good question. But realize that most rituals of evaluation are born of distance and distrust. They inform a person that he or she is not fully acceptable, and that continued scrutiny is necessary. In contrast, the valuing process invites the individual into a relationship of trust and security. Relations of this sort typically bring out the best in people. When individuals are valued, they are more likely to be sensitive to the needs and desires of those with whom they work. They care about them. They are likely to detect those ways in which their work falls short in the eyes of their colleagues. Rather than being resistant or resentful, they will endeavor to correct their deficiencies. Finally, questions about how participants can best support each other, as outlined above, may pinpoint specific areas of improvement but without personal faulting. There may be corrective and caring coaching.

·

> I had heard about Tracy before she entered my class. She was said to
> be talented, but rebellious and uncaring about her studies. Romance
> and clubbing seemed her major pursuits. Tracy's first paper for my
> class carried traces of both artistry and apathy. I chose to blind myself
> to the latter, and directed my comments almost exclusively to her
> moments of excellence. In the next paper, it appeared that Tracy was
> writing "for me." She wanted me to recognize her ideas and to
> appreciate them. I was pleased to do so. Then, after a period in which
> she was absent more often than present (a romance gone sour),
> I spoke with her privately. I told her how much I appreciated her
> ideas, and how interesting I found them. Her final paper for the
> course was outstanding, one of the best I had ever seen. Later I had
> an opportunity to view Tracy's transcript for that semester. Unlike
> the poor showing of the previous three semesters (during which she
> was faced with academic probation), her grades were blossoming.

·

From a relational perspective, appreciative approaches to evaluation are a valuable beginning. But exciting potentials remain untapped. So far, such practices remain tied to the tradition of bounded being. That is, they draw attention to the positive capabilities of individual performers. The next important step is to shift this attention away from the individual to relationships. For example, consider the possibility that pairs of participants meet together and ask, "What is it about our relationship that is valuable, that gives it life, that brings forth our best work? What do we see as an ideal for our relationship, and how might we more fully achieve this ideal?" Such questions remove the individual from the center of judgment; they create the reality of the relationship; and they invite a growth-oriented conversation. The challenge for the future is to move *relational valuing* into practice.

The Organization-in-the-World

Every storefront on a city street represents a declaration of independence. *We* are a pharmacy, *we* are a pizza parlor, *we* are a grocer, and so on. To insure independence, walls separate one organization from the next. And so it is for larger organizations, schools, government offices, and man- ufacturing plants. Each typically resides within a structure, its surfaces designed to shelter and protect the precious within from the unknown without. For each organization there is a privileged domain of the "in here" separated from "out there."

In these everyday commonplaces we are again immersed in the logic of bounded being. It is not individual persons in this instance, but indepen- dent organizations. And when we construct the organizational world in this way we invite many of the same illnesses that beset the individualiza- tion of society. *We* exist within the walls, and *they* without. Once the sepa- ration has been struck, those within the organization confront the outside with three major options: they are *with us*, *against us*, or *irrelevant*. If they are with us, the relationship is solely instrumental: "How much can they contribute to us and at what cost?" If they are against us, the primary ques- tion is how to subdue (or possibly eliminate) them. The irrelevant simply remain so. This orientation of adversarial instrumentality is coupled with a form of organizational narcissism: "We exist in order to strengthen and expand ourselves." Nothing beyond the organizational well-being counts. A self-concerned organization invites relations of calculation, suspicion, antagonism, and dispassion.

•

> At its worst, this is the world of Enron, a business that lied, swindled, and exploited the public for its own profit; it is the world of every political enclave that "digs dirt," stonewalls, or sabotages an opposing party to strengthen itself; it is the world of an advantaged economic class that increases its wealth at the expense of the have-nots; and it is the world of every religious group that condemns all other religions to expand its own following. "Survival of the fittest" is not a description, but a battle cry.

•

In this relationship between organization and the world, the challenge of balancing tendencies toward organizing and organization is critical. In the very attempt to create a powerful organization—a perfectly func- tioning machine—the grounds are prepared for its failure. The major problem here is that of detachment from context. As the realities and values within the organization become all consuming, so do the worlds of those outside become irrelevant, alien, or antagonistic. On a small scale this is the failure of organizations to understand the market, of professional entertainers to comprehend the values of their audiences, or political parties to appreciate the climate of opinion. All may suffer as a result. On a grander scale, it was the failure of the Marxist government in the Soviet Union to appreciate the commonly circulating opinions of the people, and the failure of Apartheid government of South Africa to comprehend the intensity of global antagonism. In each case powerful, self-seeking structures crumbled. Perhaps nowhere in recent history have the results of disconnected realities been more disastrous than in the rise and fall of Nazi Germany.

•

The major challenge, then, is to bring the organization and its environment into mutually productive synchrony. How are the outside voices to enter so that boundaries are softened and organizational vitality is sustained? There is a traditional answer to such answers, and it issues from the logic of bounded being. More specifically, it lies within the instrumental orientation described above: "How can we influence or control outside opinion so that *we* are favored?" This is primarily the logic of marketing managers, directors of public relations, and political spin-doctors. The task is to gather information about "them," and to determine how *we* can shape *their* responses. From a relational standpoint, however, the challenge is to replace this casual view with the logic of co-action. It is to ask, "How can we *together* generate a well-being?"

•

Relevant here is sociological research on *structural holes*.[39] As reasoned, certain people within an organization have access to the flow of information in other groups. Persons in such positions represent "holes" in the organizational structure, that is, openings through which information can flow in and out. As much research attests, structural holes are essential to the vitality of the organization. For example, research demonstrates that higher company performance is achieved when top managers have significant relationships beyond their firm and industry; there is a higher patent

[39]Granovetter, M. S. (1985). Economic action, social structure, and embeddedness. *American Journal of Sociology, 91*, 481–510. See also, Burt, R. S. (2001). Structural holes versus network closure as social capital. In N. Lin, K. S. Cook, and R. S. Burt (Eds.) *Social capital: Theory and research.* Hawthorne, NY: Aldine and Gruyter.

output in organizations with joint ventures or alliances; accounting firms have higher survival rate if they have strong partner ties to client sectors; semi-conductor firms have a higher probability of innovation if they establish alliances with firms outside their own technological area; small job manufacturers are more competitive if they have sources of advice beyond the firm; companies with fewer structural holes grow less rapidly; new product teams function more productively when their members have contacts beyond the team; biotechnology companies have higher earnings and survival chances if they have a greater number of alliances and more partner firms.[40] In short, boundary-spanning relationships may be essential to the life of the organization.

•

Yet, the scholarship on structural holes doesn't take us far enough. The presumption remains that the point of having such openings is to strengthen one's own organization. A relational perspective invites us to expand our vision. It is not the well-being of single organizations that is at stake, but the broader relational flows that sustain and vitalize not only cultures, but the conditions of global existence more generally. The challenge, then, is to facilitate the co-active process in which the very borders between inside and outside are blurred. Two illustrations from my recent experience demonstrate the potentials on the local level:

– A large manufacturing company in Vienna was constantly and critically scrutinized by the press. They were attacked for profiteering, making questionable claims for their products, and for exploiting their workers. Whenever the company attempted to defend its policies, the press located reasons for mistrust. Antagonism prevailed. Reaching an impasse, the company adopted a different policy. Rather than fearing and loathing the press, they decided to invite members of the press into meetings where company decisions were made. In this way the press might come to understand the logics and values of the organization from the inside. And too, as decisions were made in the presence of the press, managers might be more acutely aware of public implications. The result was a transformation in both the organizational logics and the attitude of the press toward the organization. The antagonistic relationship dissolved; organizational practices were transformed.

[40]For a full review, see Burt, R. S. (2000). The network structure of social capital. In R. I. Sutton, and B. M. Staw (Eds.) *Research in organizational behavior*. Greenwich, CT: JAI Press.

— An anti-vivisectionist group picketed a biological research company, decrying the research practices that destroyed animals. From the perspective of the demonstrators, harmless animals were being sacrificed for the purpose of boosting profits. From the company's vantage point, however, their research was leading to the development of drugs that could save the lives of thousands of people. There was no means of reaching accord on the ethical issues at stake. However, rather than continuing the head-on confrontation, the company invited the demonstrating group to join them in mounting a public exhibit in which both sides of the issue would be presented. The demonstrators agreed, and for several months the groups worked side by side to generate a worthy exhibit for the public. During this period an important change began to occur. The representatives of the opposing groups began listening to each other, treating each other with respect, and valuing each other's inputs on how to improve the exhibit. The organizational boundaries began to dissolve. Interestingly the research organization later developed an internal group to represent the demonstrators' views at their meetings. The "outside" voice was now "inside."

•

I like these stories; they represent innovative ways of coordinating the organization with the world, and doing so for the benefit of both. Yet, such concerns with coordination may also go beyond the level of single organizations. Those who see ways of bringing multiple organizations into synchrony with each other and the public world are visionary. I am impressed, for example, with the Making Connections initiative of the Annie E. Casey Foundation.[41] Functioning in almost a dozen cities, the foundation sets in motion dialogues designed to bring low-income families out of poverty, and simultaneously build more promising futures for the young. The hope is that these accomplishments may also have positive ripple effects, such as lowering the crime rate and the incidence of illness. The initiative first locates business concerns that can offer employment. Brought into relationship are also health services, day care centers, and financial advisors for local families. Further, a special attempt is made to build relations within the communities, such that its inhabitants can rely on each other for support. The attempt, then, is to alter an entire area of the inner city through coordinated efforts of multiple institutions and neighborhoods.[42]

[41]See www.aecf.org/MajorInitiatives/MakingConnections.aspx
[42]Although there are significant positive outcomes resulting from this initiative, close study reveals that good jobs are not in themselves sufficient. See Iversen, R. R., and Armstrong, A. L. (2007). *Jobs aren't enough*. Philadelphia: Temple University Press.

Efforts at coordination may also move from the community to regional sectors. For example, the Swedish government has made a major commitment to bring about sustainable development for large regions of the country.[43] These efforts are not simply devoted to economic improvement, but as well to environmental well-being, gender equality, and integrated society. In this context, attempts are made to bring businesses (both large and small), together with universities, cultural institutions, local government officials, and artists to create regional change.

The vision of full-flowing coordination may also be extended to the global level. The efforts of such organizations as the Business as an Agent of World Benefit program,[44] and the United Nations Global Compact are future-oriented.[45] Here the attempt is to enlist major businesses in programs dedicated to creating better world conditions. Given that the top 300 multinational businesses own 25% of the world's assets, the implications are enormous. At the same time, many corporations believe that it is good business to improve world conditions. General Electric, for example, has made major investments in wind power; Toyota's success is stimulating auto makers everywhere to produce more fuel efficient cars; Wal-Mart reduced the amount of packaging for their items, with an energy effect equal to removing 200,000 trucks from the road. It is too early to know whether such efforts can be sustained without large profit margins. However, world betterment could well become a mark of organizational pride. It is inspiring to imagine that one day we might replace traditions of self-gain with practices of fully relational welfare.

[43]See www.internat.naturvardsverket.se/documents/issues/report/pdf/8176.pdf
[44]See www.bawbglobalforum.org/
[45]See www.unglobalcompact.org/

Four

From the Moral to the Sacred

II

Morality: From Relativism to Relational Responsibility

My aim in these last two chapters is to open dialogue on the moral and spiritual implications of relational being. I do not take this step with ease. My colleagues are primarily scholars in the social sciences. Within this milieu, moral and spiritual commitments are generally viewed with suspicion. Sound scholarship in this tradition attempts to describe, reveal, and explain the world, not to make judgments about how people should live their lives. Or, as frequently put, scholarship should be concerned with *what is the case*, and not *what ought to be*. On this view, our tools of analysis and our rigorous methods may ultimately yield clarity on the world as it is, but matters of "what is the good" will always dwell in the shadows of subjectivity.

Issues of spirituality are particularly problematic. The scholarly tradition is largely a child of the Enlightenment, thus playing a major role in the critique of what are seen as the strangulating effects of Dark Age religious dogmas. Scientific research is often seen as the apex of Enlightenment thought, and now serves as one of the most powerful voices of secularism in the contemporary world. Scientific commitments to materialism, objectivity, and determinism, for example, typically serve as deterrents—if not antagonists—to religious or spiritual traditions.[1] The scorn heaped by

---

[1] There are exceptions to this general avoidance of spiritual issues in both the natural and social science. Under the initiative of the Templeton Foundation (www.templeton.org), significant efforts have been made to enlist both scientists and theologians in discussions that would

scientists upon "intelligent design" theory is but one recent example. Even in religious studies, scholars largely write and teach *about* various spiritual traditions. To *advocate* would threaten one's very status as scholar. To celebrate one's spiritual beliefs borders on proselytizing, and as it is said, would place blinders on the student's capacity for rational and objective judgment.

•

In this context, would it not be wiser to rest the case for relational being as it is? Won't the proposals of the preceding chapters lose force by adventuring into murky issues of morality and spirituality? For some readers this may indeed be the result. But as I see it, such adventuring is essential. As outlined in Chapter 7, in its Enlightenment thrust, the scholarly world approaches a dangerous insularity. In daily life we continuously confront issues of moral and spiritual concern. Issues of war, the environment, immigration, abortion, the death penalty, the minimum wage, bloated salaries, pornography, and the like immerse us in complex moral issues. There is no escaping the question of how we *should* live. To avoid issues of *ought*, as science invites us to do, is to abandon responsibility to the relational world that makes science possible at all.

Similarly, we confront a world in which religious beliefs play an enormously important role, not only in terms of people's deepest commitments, but in terms of the life and death of millions. It is not enough for the scholarly community to smugly view religious traditions as havens of mythology. If scholarly work is to make a significant contribution to the culture that sustains it, open dialogue is imperative. Failing to take up such dialogue is to establish yet another island of practice, separated from others by an ocean of alienation.

Nor is it intellectually defensible to make a strong distinction between moral subjectivity and scientific objectivity. In spite of longstanding claims to the contrary, there is no separating "is" from "ought." Scientific communities are no different from spiritualist communities in creating an intelligible reality—for example, atoms, social structures, and the unconscious in the former case, and spiritual awareness, the sacred, and divine guidance in the latter. Most importantly, both enterprises are

unite their efforts. For the most part, however, these efforts have viewed science as a secure knowledge base to which theological thought must be adequate. There are also a number of ambitious efforts of transpersonal social scientists to provide a grounding for spiritual experience and belief. See, for example, Wilbur, K. (2006). *Integral spirituality: A startling new role for religion in the modern and postmodern world.* Boston: Shambhala. However, such efforts are generally disregarded by the scientific profession.

value-saturated, with scientists placing value on reliable prediction and many religions valuing worship and compassion. Unfortunately, because they have largely functioned as separate territories, both traditions have sought only to expand their borders and to educate the world into their own circumscribed forms of life. From a relational perspective, however, we need not ask which is the more valid with respect to its account of the world or which strives toward the highest values; one can only purchase validity and value with the currency accepted within the relevant community. Rather, we may ask, what are the global consequences of these discourses? What happens to our relational lives when we inhabit one as opposed to (or along side of) the other?

•

One of the greatest, most fundamental problems all religions
face in our times is their relationship to science.

—Keiji Nishitani

•

The consequences of scientific discourse and its accompanying practices are everywhere with us. For the most part, science proceeds without question within the society more generally. There is gratitude for the contribution science has made to curing disease, harnessing energy, fostering technologies of transportation, and so much more. Yet, there are critics who argue that the scientific perspective has suppressed deliberation on values and spirituality, led to the exploitation of the earth, invited a materialist orientation to life and to human relations, and more.[2] Likewise, from diverse points of view, the discourse of the sacred has had both positive and negative consequences.[3] Millions have derived a sense of purpose and value from a spiritual or religious orientation to life, and find their contribution to sustaining a moral society invaluable. At the same time, teaming numbers have been, and continue to be, slaughtered in the name of religion. These are not only issues demanding continuous dialogue, but as we

[2]See, for example, Nelson, L. H., and Nelson, J. (Eds.) (1996). *Feminism, science, and the philosophy of science.* Dordrecht: Kluwer; Aronowitz, S. (1988). *Science as power: Discourse and ideology in modern society.* Minneapolis, MN: University of Minnesota Press; Keller, E. F. (1986). *Reflections on gender and science.* New Haven, CT: Yale University Press; Haraway, D. (1991). *Simians, cyborgs, and women: The reinvention of nature.* New York: Routledge.

[3]See for example, Dawkins, R. (2006). *The god delusion.* New York: Bantam; and Hitchens, C. (2007). *God is not great: How religion poisons everything.* New York: Twelve Books, Hachette Book Group.

abandon questions of which is superior as an account of the world, both communities may usefully open themselves to alternative intelligibilities. Thus far in this book I have followed the scholarly path. In the present context I find it necessary to engage the traditions of the sacred.

•

> My reasons for including spirituality in this book are also born of relationships; many of my cherished friends and colleagues are deeply committed to spiritual traditions. To disregard their investments is not only a constricting of our relationship, but an interruption in the broader relational flow of which we are a part. It is to place an unnecessary wedge between the communities of relationship that we bring to each other. Here my hope is to soften the boundaries of separation.

•

In the present chapter I confront the challenge of the moral good. I begin with a critical challenge to those striving to establish moral foundations or fundamental ethical principles to guide human conduct. In place of this problematic effort, I will explore the moral implications of relational being. Here we first recognize the potential of all relations to generate moral goods. We may term this process, *first-order morality*. I then grapple with the challenge of moral relativism. For, as we find, in generating first order commitments to the good, we also create an exterior domain that is less than good. Alienation sets in, and if sufficiently threatening, we attempt to control or eliminate the "evil other." There is a rupture in the flow of co-action. I then open discussion on *second-order morality*, a non-foundational ethic for sustaining the very possibility of co-creating the good. In effect, we move toward a position of responsibility for relationships themselves. I complete the chapter with a brief discussion of relational responsibility in practice.

The Challenge of Moral Conduct

The problem of evil is a common fixture of daily life. The morning news is rife with reports of assaults, murders, political suppression, wars, and even genocide. We seem deluged with wrongdoing, and little capable of doing much about it. Nor is the challenge of the moral good simply "out there" in the news. It is squarely in front of us—in the way people drive their cars, fail in their promises, cheat on their taxes, waste energy resources, tell racist jokes, disregard the needy, and so on. It is also there in our families, as parents struggle with children who lie or bully, children struggle with absent or uncaring parents, and spouses struggle with each other's shabby behavior.

The close companion to our moral anguish is an abiding sense of "if only." If only people were committed to moral or ethical principles, if only they were conscious of right and wrong, if only they could abandon their evil ways, if only they could love each other. And so it is that we try to impart our ideals to our children, support our religious institutions, develop rules and sanctions in organizations, propound laws, and build an increasing number of prisons. In the scholarly world our contribution takes the form of reasoned arguments for various principles or virtues. From Aristotle to MacIntyre, Nussbaum, and McCloskey, philosophic deliberation has been a continuing presence.[4] Yet, lamentably, this enormous range of effortful activity seems to make little obvious difference. We are never without a plenitude of evil.

•

Of course, all these attempts to mold, shape, invite, and control, are in the service of generating a moral or virtuous society. But let us consider the opposite possibility: Virtually all these efforts to bring about the good society simultaneously contribute to presumption of bounded or separated beings. At least in Western culture, virtually all principles, punishment, and praise are directed toward individual actors. In courts of law we traditionally hold the individual responsible for his or her actions. In organizations, it is to the individual that we point in saying, "The buck stops here." And in daily relations, we hold individuals responsible for being late, rude, drunk, rapacious, or insensitive. The moral atom in Western culture is fundamentally the individual. And in this way, the tradition of moral worth creates a reality of separation—me standing here, and you there.

As proposed in Chapter 1, in a world of fundamental separation, personal well-being is a matter of utmost concern. I must first care for myself, and at base, your well-being is primarily your affair. Indeed, in a world of limited goods, your welfare may compete with mine. In this context we can understand why indeed Western moral codes place such a high value on "doing good for others." From the early Old Testament exhortation to "Love thy neighbor as thyself" to Levinas' vision of fundamental obligation to the other,[5] the presumption is that moral good is achieved

[4] See, for example, MacIntyre, A. (1988). *Whose justice, which rationality?* Notre Dame: University of Notre Dame Press; McCloskey, D. N. (2007). *The bourgeois virtues: Ethics for an age of commerce.* Chicago: University of Chicago Press; Nussbaum, M. (1990). *Love's knowledge, essays on philosophy and literature.* New York: Oxford University Press.

[5] See, for example, Levinas, E. (2005). *Humanism of the other.* Evanston: University of Illinois Press.

through love, caring, charity, and dedication to others' well-being. Such imperatives make sense to us primarily because we presume that human beings "just naturally" seek their own welfare. Thus, while I am sufficiently immersed in Western culture to resonate with such proposals, we must also recognize the way in which they contribute to the tradition of bounded being. With each invitation to be thoughtful, caring, or compassionate, and with each reminder to "do unto others...." we are simultaneously informed that we are separate, and that our natural instinct is self-gratification.

•

Consider the common appeal to be charitable, to love others, or to care for them. We are all drawn by such appeals; at one time or another many of us have wished to dedicate our lives to helping others. The invitation, then, is to play out a grand narrative of moral worth. We achieve a sense of transcendent value through dedication to the well-being of others. However, we must also realize that this is a narrative in which the giver is the privileged one. It is "I" who gives, and who is therefore blessed. In this narrative the receiver is only advantaged in a material way. There is no gain "in heaven" to have one's hunger satisfied or illness cured. And woe unto the receiver who is ungrateful. To scorn the donor who has sacrificed for you is to invite the scorn of all. The story of loving your neighbor, then, is a not a story about relationship, but a hero story of the self.

•

Are there viable alternatives to establishing and reinforcing moral codes for directing and controlling individual conduct? Let us consider the possibility from the standpoint of relational being.

Immorality Is Not the Problem

We commonly suppose the world suffers because there are people who possess a flawed sense of conscience, who pursue their goals without regard for the consequences to others, or are simply "bad eggs." It is their actions that must be controlled or eliminated. However, let me propose the opposite hypothesis: We do not suffer from an absence of morality in the world. Rather, in important respects we suffer from its plenitude. What can save such a proposal from absurdity? Consider the issue from a relational standpoint: If we trace all that we hold meaningful in life to relationship, then we must also view relationships as the source of our visions of good and evil. All viable relationships will generate at least rudimentary understandings of right versus wrong. Such understandings are essential to sustaining patterns of coordination. Deviations from accepted patterns constitute a threat. When we have developed harmonious ways of relating—of speaking and acting—we will come to value "our way of life." That which encroaches upon, undermines, or destroys this way of life becomes an evil.

•

It is not surprising that the term *ethics* is derived from the Greek, *ethos*, or essentially, the customs of the people; or that the term *morality* draws from the Latin root, *mos*, or mores, thus equating morality with custom. The accepted conventions constitute the basis for the good.[6] Rational justification comes later.

•

Let us view this process of generating goods within a relationship as an establishing of *first-order morality*. To function within any viable relationship will virtually require embracing values inherent in its patterns. When I teach a class of students, for example, first-order morality is at work. We establish and perpetuate what has become the "good for us." There are no articulated rules in this case, no moral injunctions, no bill of rights for students and teachers. The rules are all implicit, but they touch virtually everything we do, from the tone and pitch of my voice, my posture, and the direction of my gaze to the intervals during which students may talk, the loudness of their voice, the movement of lips, legs, feet, and hands. One false move—the voice is too loud, a gaze becomes a leer, feet shuffle too loudly, lips make the sound of a kiss—and any of us becomes the target of suspicion.[7]

•

In the case of first-order morality alone, one cannot choose evil. That is, in the hypothetical case of being fully immersed within a single relationship, and that relationship alone, one could not step outside the existing patterns of coordination to do otherwise. To do so would simply be unintelligible. The nonsense of "doing evil" is pervasive. For example, in the case of the classroom, I would neither kick nor punch a student; my students would neither tumble on the floor nor throw chairs from the window. We do not engage in these activities because they are forbidden; we fail to do them because they are unintelligible to us. It would never occur to the members of the class to throw a chair out the window. We continue to carry on

---

[6]For a more extended treatment of this equation, see Eliade, M. (1987). *The sacred and the profane: The nature of religion.* New York: Harcourt Brace Jovanovich.

[7]See also, Peperzak, A. (1997). *Before ethics.* New York: Prometheus Books.

normal classroom life because it is our way of life. In effect, morality of the first order is essentially *being sensible* within a way of life. In the same vein, most people do not think about murdering their best friend, not because of some principle to which they were exposed in their early years and not because it is illegal. Rather, it is virtually unthinkable. Similarly it would be unthinkable to break out in a tap dance at a religious service or to dip one's head into the soup of a dining companion. We live our lives largely within the comfortable houses of first-order morality.

Moralities Are the Problem

So, we might ask, what is the source of evil action? Why is wrong-doing everywhere apparent? Ironically, the answer is to be found in the outcomes of first-order morality. Wherever people come into productive coordination, first-order morality is in the making. As we strive to find mutually satisfactory ways of going on together, we begin to establish a local good, "the way we do things." As a result there are myriad traditions of the good, and everywhere people congregate successfully they may set in motion new possibilities. The result is the production of disparate goods in the major religious traditions of the world, along with the traditions of government, science, education, art, entertainment, and so on. There are also the countless localized traditions of the good, inhering in families, friendships, and communities. All sustain visions of moral conduct, some sacred and others secular, some articulated and others implicit. And, layered upon these are newly emerging and rapidly expanding visions of the good: pro-life, women's rights, anti-globalization, anti-war, anti-vivisectionist, anti-psychiatry, vegan, environmentalist, gay rights, and so on. There is no end to valuing.

•

It is in the multiplication of the good that we find the genesis of evil. First the stage is set for what might be called *virtuous evil*. By this I refer to one's embracing the virtues of a tradition that is simultaneously declared evil by another. For example, the pro-choice advocate is virtuous within this tradition, but evil within the camp of pro-life, the anti-psychiatrist is scorned by the psychiatric profession, the fundamentalist Christian discredited by the fundamentalist Muslim, and so on across the spectrum of goods. In a universe of plural goods, *any* virtuous action is subject to the antipathy of a multiplicity of alternative traditions.

Typically we act virtuously within the relations at hand, and avoid the gaze of those who would find such virtue an evil. Even the rooms of a home may be used to conceal what are reasonable and desirable actions in one relationship (e.g. with one's spouse) but odious in other relationships (e.g. with one's children). For many of us, virtuous evil haunts our daily consciousness. This is so because we bear the traces of countless relations, all incubating devices for their own vision of the good (see Chapter 5). In every commitment to an action we relegate the traces of countless competitors to a lesser status. And thus: It is a good thing that I complete my work at the office, but it is also a good thing that I am at home with my family. It is good to arrive on time for a dinner invitation, but it is also good to obey the speed limit. It is good to feel the pleasure of someone's love, but it is also good to feel the pleasure of someone else's love. It is good to defend one's country, but it is also good to avoid killing others. In every choice I am both moral and immoral. For every relationship of which I am a part, I am also part of another relationship for whom my present actions may be misbegotten. Because we are immersed in multiple goods we are potentially alienated from any activity in which we engage. We carry into any relationship—even those of great importance to us—the capacity to find its conventions empty or even repulsive. At every moment, the voice of a disapproving judge hovers over the shoulders.

•

Struggles of conscience are not struggles between
good and evil but between competing goods.

•

Let us shift the focus to more heinous actions—robbery, extortion, rape, drug dealing, or murder. It is here we find a dangerous transformation in the quest for the good. The petty transgressions of daily life are often disregarded, renegotiated, or forgiven. However, in the case of these more destructive actions, the impulse is toward elimination. This is typically accomplished through various forms of defense (surveillance, policing), curtailment (imprisonment, torture), or more radically, through extermination (death penalty, invasion, bombs). It is with the impulse toward elimination that we shift from the register of virtuous evil to what may be viewed as *evil virtue*, that is, in the name of virtue eliminating evil that is deemed virtuous by others.

•

Anger is the price that we pay for being attached
to a narrow view of being right.
                                        —John Kabat-Zinn

•

By far the most obvious and most deadly outcome of the urge to eliminate evil is the hardened shell separating relational clusters—families, communities, religions, nations, ethnic traditions, and so on. Echoing the discussion of bonding and barricades (Chapter 6), those committed to stamping out the "evil other" gain value in the eyes of their mates for punishing and destroying others. Extinguishing evil is an intoxicating elixir. At the same time, those who are targets of elimination often move to collective reprisal. As the condemned come to realize their common plight, their own moral position gains weight and becomes more fully articulated. Now they counter-attack in the name of virtue. The result, of course, is the familiar scenario of mutual destruction. "You are mutilated, and it is good," "I have destroyed your children, and I am blessed."

•

> Once the dance of death is underway,
> the other is not the major enemy.
> It is the tradition of choreography.

Toward Second-Order Morality

As discussed, the production of the good establishes the conditions for the "not good," or evil. In effect, so long as there are coordinated actions generating harmony and fulfillment, alienation and conflict are waiting at the door. Given the rapid development and proliferation of communication technologies—email, cell phones, the world-wide web, and the like—the potential for conflict rapidly increases. With each new relationship, new formations of valuing (and devaluing) are placed in orbit; groups can easily sustain such connections across time and geographic borders. As the world becomes smaller, it also becomes more fragmented. However, while agonistic tension is virtually inevitable, hostility, bloodshed, and genocide are not. Conflicting goods will always be with us. The challenge is not that of creating a conflict-free existence, but of locating ways of approaching conflict that do not invite mutual extermination. Given the circumstances of human coordination, how do we go on?

•

One inviting possibility is to join the search for a universal ethic, embraced by all, and enabling us to transcend our animosities. I have some sympathy with this view. For example, given my cultural history, a universal ethic of love, compassion, care, or sacrifice for others, springs rapidly to the fore. Within a somewhat more secular vein, I also have great admiration for the human rights movement. At the same time, I have significant reservations about the outcome of these various pursuits. Even when there is broad agreement in the universal good, the result is a hierarchy in which good and evil serve as the antipodes. It is also a hierarchy designed for control of the less than good. In effect, universal goods are premised on the intent to eliminate some form of action that seems reasonable and right from at least one other point of view.[8] Once a nation or a people become targeted for rights violations, there is once again a distancing.

•

Even in the commitment to universal love
we condemn actions of hatred.

•

The divisive potential of abstract goods is intensified by the fact that they do not tell us when and how they can be applied. One cannot unambiguously derive concrete action from an abstract virtue or human right.[9] There is nothing about the value of justice, equality, compassion, or freedom that demands any particular form of action. And thus any action condemned in the name of an abstract value may also be used to defend the same value. In the name of freedom, the U.S. government has suppressed its minorities (e.g. African and Native American), incarcerated law-abiding citizens (e.g. Japanese Americans in WWII), and invaded other nations without provocation (e.g. Iraq). And what horrors have been set loose on earth by those invoking the name of Jesus or Mohammad. Exhortations to love one another, to seek justice, to promote equality may all be calls to action against the evils of the world, but these actions may be bloody indeed.[10]

On the other hand, there are many who are quite willing to accept multiple moralities as a continuing fact of social existence. As intoned, "There are many ways of seeing the world; let us live with mutual respect." Yet, this view is fiercely criticized for its "moral relativism." Moral agnostics who seem to hold that one moral stance is "just as good" as any other are scorned. They stand for nothing; they resist nothing. They have no

[8]Related is Hauke Brunkhorst's argument that to achieve human rights would require a "juridification of global society." See his, *Solidarity: From civic friendship to a global legal community* (Jeffrey Flynn, Trans.). Cambridge, MA: MIT Press, 2005.

[9]For a discussion of the inadequacy of abstract moral principles, see Nussbaum, M. (2001). *The fragility of goodness: Luck and ethics in Greek tragedy and philosophy.* Cambridge: Cambridge University Press; and Logstrup, K. E. (1997). *The ethical demand.* Notre Dame, IN: University of Notre Dame Press.

[10]As Jeffrey Perl points out, the call to justice may often serve as an impediment to peace. (*Common Knowledge*, 8:1 (2002)). As Cardinal Lustiger adds, "Regrettably, the most noble declarations of principle can serve merely to justify the most abject abuses." (*Common Knowledge*, 11:1 (2005), p. 22.)

Let him howl
He has it coming…
He's the robber, the killer, the pedophile
The monster among us.
Not one of us, never was
Never listened, never heard me
Not even as a baby.

Courtesy: Regine Walter, Artist

investment in the future, nor do they join in opposition to injustice. In my view, such criticisms of "relativism" are very much overdrawn. If moral relativists are defined as those who believe all moralities are equally valid or equally justified, I must admit that I have never met one.[11] Let us replace the epithet of moral relativism with the more credible concept of *moral pluralism*. Moral pluralists are quite willing to embrace a given moral tradition, even if it cannot be justified in all worlds. They are quite open in preferring a particular form of life, and working toward a future that realizes these values. However, for pluralists this preference does not provide justification for eliminating alternative traditions. The pluralist typically opts, then, for *tolerance*. One is invited to understand other traditions and to appreciate why they believe as they do. The Buddhist philosopher, Thich Nhat Hanh, resonates with this approach in his advocacy of an enlightened stage of *omni-partiality*. Here the ideal is to respond to those who practice any moral tradition with compassion.[12]

I am drawn by this ideal, but in my view the tolerance and compassion favored by pluralism does not take us far enough. It is easy to tolerate when others' "moral failings" are minor or unintrusive. However, very often they are not, and the wellsprings of tolerance are quickly drained. When we (in the West) confront what we see as sexual slavery, racial prejudice, suppression of women, and rampant slaying in other cultures, we are disturbed. As Westerners we can scarcely tolerate the conditions of life imposed by the Taliban in Afghanistan; in the same way Muslim fundamentalists are understandably appalled by what they see as the sexual depravity of the West. In spite of the Western emphasis on liberty, we have not tolerated the expansionism of Nazi Germany, apartheid in South Africa, or genocide in Bosnia. And we are boisterously proud of our actions. Moral pluralism is but a sleeping tiger.

•

At this point it is useful to return to the vision of relational being. As proposed, it is through collaborative action that moral value is given birth. Through co-action we emerge with visions of a satisfying life; we achieve harmony, trust, and direction. Herein lie the grounds for first-order morality. At the same time, as we generate enclaves of the good, we also tend to create an exterior, the less than good. In more extreme form, in establishing the good, evil is under production. And as we are moved to control, punish, incarcerate, and ultimately to eliminate evil, so are those who are under

[11]For a recent compendium of scholarly writing on this issue, see Volume 13 of *Common Knowledge*, 2007, on *A "dictatorship of relativism?"*
[12]See Ellsberg, R. (Ed.) (2001). *Thich Nhat Hanh: Essential writings*. New York: Orbis.

threat drawn into defense. In effect, a major outcome of conflict among first-order moralities is the severing of communicative connection. In this severing, the potentials for generative co-action are destroyed. As the eliminative impulse is set in motion, we move toward mutual annihilation. We slouch toward the end of meaning.

•

To eliminate all those whose values are not identical to one's own, would leave but a single voice...and an empty silence.

•

It is precisely here that we may invite into being a process of *second-order morality*, that is, *collaborative activity that restores the possibility of generating first-order morality*. Second-order morality rests not on a logic of discrete units, but of relationship. From this standpoint there are no acts of evil in themselves, for the meaning of all action is derived from relationship. Holding single individuals responsible for untoward actions not only represents a failure to confront the relational conditions from which the act has emerged, but results in alienation and retaliation. In the case of second-order morality, individual responsibility is replaced by *relational responsibility*, a collective responsibility for sustaining the potentials of coordinated action.[13] To be responsible to relationships is, above all, to sustain the process of co-creating meaning. In relational responsibility we avoid the narcissism implicit in ethical calls for "care of the self." We also avoid the self/other split resulting from the imperative to "care for the other." In being responsible for relationships we step outside the individualist tradition; care for the relationship becomes primary.

•

Second-order morality restores
the possibility of morality of any kind.

•

The critic is at the door, "It seems to me that that this proposal for a second-order morality simply reestablishes the problems of both individualism and universal ethics. Isn't it equivalent to declaring that *individuals*

---

[13]See McNamee, S., and Gergen, K. J. (1999). *Relational responsibility: Resources for sustainable dialogue.* Thousand Oaks, CA: Sage Publications. This position resonates in significant degree with what Bergum and Dossetor call "relational ethics." However, in championing an ethic of care and respect for the other, echoes remain of the individualist tradition. See Bergum, V., and Dossetor, J. (2005). *Relational ethics: The full meaning of respect.* Hagerstown, MD: University Publishing Group.

ought to be responsible for the process of sustaining coordinated relation-ships? And if so, haven't you just established another hierarchy of the good in which the errant individual is deemed inferior and in need of correc-tion?" These are reasonable criticisms and need to be addressed. First is the question of whether relational responsibility once again thrusts the indi-vidual into judgment. In reply, from a relational standpoint there are no individual persons to be held accountable. Relational responsibility must itself issue from coordinated action. Practices of relational responsibility are made intelligible within relationships. The individual person may acti-vate scenarios of caring for the relationship, but unless coordinated with others, the actions do not count. And, is second order morality not another universal ethic? Not if it is consistent with its own premises. The ideal of second order morality is in a non-foundational foundation. We move toward a foundational ethic for going on together, but without declaring this ethic as absolute, true, or ultimately grounded. Second-order morality is not a wedge for reinstating universal hierarchy; it is an invitation for mutual exploration.

Relational Responsibility in Action

As we find, tendencies toward division and conflict are normal outgrowths of relational life. Prejudice is not, then, a mark of a flawed character—inner rigidity, decomposed cognition, emotional bias, and the like. Rather, so long as we continue the normal process of creating consensus around what is real and good, classes of the undesirable are under construction. Wherever there are tendencies toward unity, cohesion, brotherhood, commitment, solidarity, or community, so alienation is in the making. We should forgive ourselves the inability to achieve conflict-free societies and a harmonious world order. These shall always remain beyond our reach. Rather, given strong tendencies toward conflict, the question is: How can we proceed in such a way that ever emerging conflict does not yield aggres-sion, oppression, or genocide—in effect, the end of meaning altogether?

•

The challenge of second-order morality is care for relationship. But what does this mean in terms of action? As proposed, abstract concepts such as second-order morality carry no necessary entailments in terms of action. Here we confront the limits of moral theorizing. Theory unwedded to practice is an impecunious suitor. Let us, then, abandon the search for those stone-inscribed words from the wise or mighty that will set all aright. Rather, let us reverse the process. Let us begin by exploring practices that, on the face of it, seem effective in achieving second-order morality.

We may then set practice into conversation with theory. What do these practices tell us about the possibilities of relational responsibility? And as we deliberate once again on the ethic, what new practices may be implied? Can the conversation between theory and action move us toward a more relationally viable world?

•

What actions might thus be congenial with responsibility toward relationship? In significant degree, we have been treating this issue for the past four chapters. In each case we have taken up practices—in knowledge-making, education, therapy, and organizations—that bring people into positive coordination. All such practices contribute to a world in which distance is replaced by relational immersion. Most prominently, however, Chapter 6 featured a number of dialogic practices specifically attempting to transit conflicting boundaries of meaning to restore peace. The work of the Public Conversations Project, Narrative Mediation, and Restorative Justice projects were all featured. One might view these as exceptional in their realization of relational responsibility. At this juncture, however, I wish to add one further dimension to the domain of practice, specifically touching on initiatives that bring otherwise fragmented communities together. It is within this new wave of public practices that we find important realizations of second-order morality.

From Co-Existence to Community

Many critics have called attention to what they see as a loss in community participation over the past century. Richard Sennett's *The Fall of Public Man* and Robert Putnam's *Bowling Alone* are two of the most prominent contributions.[14] As they see it, with the loss of community vitality, the democratic process is undermined. Much in keeping with arguments developed in preceding chapters, without opportunities for free and open deliberation, the individual voter is unable to weigh the pros and cons of important issues.[15] To think independently of any relationship is not to think at all.[16] Most important for present purposes, the lack of community

[14]Sennett, R. (1992). *The fall of public man.* New York: Knopf; Putnam, R. D. (2000). *Bowling alone: The collapse and revival of American community.* New York: Simon and Schuster.

[15]For further elaboration of the essential need for a civil society, see O'Connell, B. (1999). *Civil society: The underpinnings of American democracy.* Lebanon, NH: University Press of New England.

[16]See also Sandel, M. J. (1982). *Op cit.*

represents disruptions in the flow of collaborative action. People become secure in their isolated niches, and outside of their small enclaves there are simply faceless numbers who are either irrelevant or threatening. In this context, efforts to re-build community connection represent second-order morality in motion. In bringing otherwise indifferent or alienated people together to explore their common concerns, the wheels of co-action are again set in motion. As people come to share experiences and values, and to reflect on their differences, the boundaries of separation are blurred. The crystallized grip of first-order morality is loosened.

•

> In human societies there will always be differences of views and interests. But the reality of today is that we are all interdependent and have to co-exist on this small planet. Therefore, the only sensible and intelligent way of resolving differences and clashes of interests, whether between individuals or nations, is through dialogue.
>
> —The Dalai Lama

•

I will not attempt to review the many fascinating initiatives to re-build community emerging in recent years.[17] Illustrative, however, are the efforts of Reuniting America (www.reunitingAmerica.org), an organization working across the country to increase opportunities for collective deliberation. They specialize in bringing leaders from otherwise opposing traditions—religious, political, ethnic—into *transpartisan* search for new and more harmonious policies. The Minnesota Active Citizenship Initiative (www.activecitizen.org), organizes citizen-leaders who can take collaborative practices into their community and work environments. The emphasis here is on practices that enable various institutions—business, religious, non-profits, and the like—to collaborate in making a contribution to the greater civic good. The Imagine Chicago project (http://imaginechicago. org) brings together the peoples of poor inner-city communities to explore positive potentials, and to work with institutions throughout the greater city to create a positive future. The Chicago model is now transported throughout the world. The Arlington Forum (www.arlingtonforum.org), attempts to create a civic society in Arlington, VA, and simultaneously

---

[17] For a useful overview, see Sirianni, C., and Friedland, L. A. (2005). *The civic renewal movement: Community-building and democracy in the United States.* Dayton, OH: Kettering Foundation Press. Also see, Davis, A., and Lynn, E. (2005). *The civically engaged reader.* Chicago, IL: Great Books Foundation. (www.greatbooks.org); see also Putnam, R., and Feldstein, L. (2003). *Better together: Restoring the American community.* New York: Simon and Schuster.

offers tools and resources for initiatives in other communities. In Arlington, for example, they have generated community-wide discussions on issues such as real estate development, minority student achievement, and school culture. The World Café (www.theworldcafecommunity.net), is a global network of people voluntarily engaged in establishing inclusive conversations about people's concerns—both local and global. Special practices for building fruitful conversations are offered world-wide. The International Institute for Sustained Dialogue (www.sustaineddialogue.org), is organized to bring alienated groups together from around the world; their work includes a concerted program to bring Arab, American, and European groups together. All these attempts invite participants to move beyond their comfortable conventions of the good and to affirm the intelligibility of alternatives.[18] In these moments of affirmation, the seeds are planted for the regeneration of first-order morality.

•

It is a cold winter evening and I am returning to my hotel in
Amsterdam. There is a large crowed gathered in the Leidseplein and
I am curious. Here I find a small ice-skating rink, and a hockey
match ensuing between two men's teams. The boisterous shouting
from the crowd is mixed with spasms of laughter. "Why are they
laughing," I ask the man standing beside me. "Because this is a game
between the cops and robbers," he smilingly responds. He sees that
I am puzzled and explains that these are teams in a city hockey
league, and among the teams there is one from the city police force,
and another composed of ex-convicts. I am intrigued, and he goes on
to explain that petty criminals in Amsterdam help the police to
impede serious crime such as drug-dealing, mob violence, and the
like. In return, the police lend an understanding ear to the life of the
petty criminal. They co-exist in the service of the greater good.

•

One of the most important challenges for community building lies in the area of religion. The term, *religion* has its roots in the Latin *religare*,

18For further resources in building community dialogue, see Schoen, D. and Hurtado, S. (Eds.) (2001). *Intergroup dialogue, Deliberative democracy in school, college, community, and workplace.* Ann Arbor: University of Michigan Press, along with the work of the Co-Intelligence Institute (www.co-intelligence.org); Democratic Dialogue (www.democraticdialoguenetwork. org); Civic Evolution (www.civicevolution.org); and the Pioneers of Change (http://pioneersofchange.net). A unique attempt to include youth in the process of community change—thus breaking generation barriers—can be found in Flores, K. S. (2008). *Youth participatory evaluation: Strategies for engaging young people.* San Francisco: Wiley.

meaning to tie or bind again. Yet, ironically, because of strong tendencies to wrap religious beliefs in the mantle of fundamental truth, religious movements frequently function as societal winnowing machines. Cherished is the wheat of righteousness, and discarded or destroyed is the remaining chaff. Strong pressures are exerted to reduce doubts and sustain belief. Schisms and the resulting multiplication of sects and denominations are common. If true to its origins, might religions not seek to remove separations between peoples and nourish a sense of community without end?

•

> I am told that there was a street in Nashville on which there were three churches, the Church of God, the Church of the One God, and the Church of the One True God.

•

The ecumenical movement once invited common deliberation among the multiple faiths of the world. Yet, as I see it, this movement has largely given way to an effort solely by Christian denominations to unite under a single banner. Such unification does move toward reducing alienation, but at the cost of creating another schism of far more dangerous potential. Thus, from a relational perspective, we must treasure the work of such organizations as the Inter-Faith Action for Peace in Africa, attempting to bring traditional African religions together with Buddhism, Hinduism, Islam, Judaism, and Christianity for purposes of promoting peace; the Interfaith Community for Action in Wellesley (ICAW), bringing volunteers from Christian, Muslim, Jewish, and Hindu communities together with local government to provide safe and drug-free environments for youth; the Interfaith Action initiative in Rochester, N.Y. (www.buildingfaith.com), bringing various church groups together with representatives of various ethnic groups to initiate collaborative program of action to reduce the spread of violence in the city; and the Interfaith Action group in Evanston, IL (www.interfaithactionofevanston.org), bringing together all the faiths in feeding the hungry and caring for the homeless.[19]

•

> Religious pluralism involves more than the mere co-existence of multiple traditions... it requires engagement across traditions.
> —Robert Wuthnow

[19]For further information on inter-faith action, see the website of the Harvard University Pluralism Project, www.pluralism.org.

Beyond the Beginning

I have only sampled here from an ever-increasing array of efforts to cross boundaries of distance and animosity. Everywhere there is talk of dialogue and its potentials for healing in a world of pervasive conflict. From a relational perspective, these are significant contributions to achieving second-order morality, a condition in which we restore the possibilities of collaboration and the genesis of the good. However, in many respects I feel that we are only crossing the threshold of possibility. In part, this is so because humankind has barely become conscious of the relational basis of its realities and values. History supplies us with numerous means of declaring and defending what is the case. Languages of science, faith, personal experience, divine illumination, reason and so on, all function to protect, sustain, and expand particular traditions. Discourses of "is true," "is real," "is moral," and the like, all have the capacity to drive wedges between people. At this juncture in history we struggle toward the possibility of accepting a position as "both true *and* false," "real *and* mythical," "moral *and* immoral." It is said that civilization took a major step forward when war was replaced by rational argument. Yet, rational argument still remains a vehicle for opposing sides to seek their own advantage. Argument is often war by other means. The present challenge, then, is to generate practices of dialogue that may replace both war and argument as vehicles for confronting contentious differences. We have many brave beginnings, but can they flourish?

•

At moments I am pessimistic. The tendency of large and powerful institutions to draw distinct boundaries around themselves is strong indeed. Governments, religions, and businesses are steeped in the logic of bounded being. Almost irrevocably they are "out for themselves, their own good, their future well-being." And thus the achievements of thousands of grass-roots attempts to speak across realms of the good can be wiped away with the closing of a plant, the firing of a single rocket, strong words from the Vatican, or government saber rattling. A major challenge, then, is to develop means of bringing large institutions into dialogic relations with the broader communities of humankind.

•

I also have optimistic moments. As multi-beings, we carry with us myriad potentials for relating—a teeming array of moral goods, reasons, emotional expressions, motives, experiences, memories, and the like. As a result, each of us carries some part of those whom we otherwise oppose. Traditions of argument may thrust us headlong into battle over some particular difference, and in doing so, reject the enormous potentials for affinity that otherwise exist. Even as we listen to alien arguments, we acquire the capability to repeat them. They are now features of our own vocabulary. Thus, the routes to crossing boundaries are more numerous than the highways we have allowed to divide us. We have well-worn traditions for resisting each other and terminating the flow of meaning. However, we also have an enormous reservoir of collaborative potentials awaiting congenial circumstances of expression. The challenge is to discover and develop means for unleashing the flow.

12

Approaching the Sacred

I began this book by proposing that the distinction between self and other is an artificial one, simply one way of making the world intelligible. Although Western culture has been richly rewarded in its presumption of the individual self, we also have found this tradition limiting in its potentials, and often injurious in its consequences. Although forms of communalism have long stood as engaging alternatives to individualism, here too there are significant reasons to resist. The entity of the community is no less bounded than the individual self. In relational being, we transcend both traditions.

With a vision of relational being in place we also entered a radical clearing. As I have argued, it is not only the concepts of self and community that have their origins in relationship; rather, all intelligible action owes its existence to relationship. Or, to put it otherwise, no/thing truly or fundamentally exists for us outside our immersion in relational processes. Relationship stands before all. Yet, upon enter this clearing, where all things are emergents of relationship, one discovers that new and significant challenges arise. Given the profound significance of relationship, how can we understand its workings, grasp its essential nature, or control its potentials? Is this not the major challenge? Doesn't the future of our very planet depend on our ability to nurture and sustain relationship?

•

The preceding chapters have indeed grappled with this challenge. We have explored relational process in both theory and practice. However, the discerning reader will have surely realized an implicit irony in these accounts: to describe, theorize, and illustrate relationship, I have relied on a discourse of independent entities. Every page of description and explanation has been replete with "he," "she," and "it" as if these were separable entities. To be sure, I have tried to remove the traditional assumption that relationships are formed by individual entities. Insistently I have proposed that relationship precedes entities. But the language continuously mocks my attempts. To describe and explain relationship my language demands a segmenting of the world into independent entities. Try as I might to transcend separation, the language of nouns and pronouns sends me sprawling.

•

> The limits of my language form the limits of my world.
> —Ludwig Wittgenstein

•

We now approach a pivotal moment of recognition: In our attempt to comprehend relationship, we have at hand only those intelligibilities provided by relationship itself. There is no "getting it right" about the nature of relationship, for in our exploration we cannot escape our particular traditions of understanding. We cannot break through the veil of words to stare directly into the light. We have the sense that there is something "behind" or "responsible for" the process of generating meaning, but this source cannot be grasped directly. It is at this juncture that we begin to glimpse the possibility of a sacred dimension to relational being. If the origin of all that we take to be real and good, all that is nourishing, lies within a process beyond articulation, we approach what many view as a spiritual consciousness. It is to exploring this potential that the remainder of this chapter is devoted. I approach the subject tangentially. That is, rather than directly grappling with issues of the sacred, I consider a family of metaphors that place relationship in the vanguard of understanding. Here a significant dimension is added to relational understanding, along with an appreciation of practical, moral, and spiritual potentials. With these metaphors in hand, we are more fully prepared to explore a converging consciousness of the sacred. I will conclude the chapter by considering the implications for action—here and now.

•

> When we look for something we can describe as its final identity,
> we find that the pot's very existence—and by implication that of all

other phenomena—is to some extent provisional and determined by convention.

—The Dalai Lama

Metaphors of the Relational

Let us suspend the quest for conclusive answers to such questions as "What is relationship," "What are its basic components," or "How does it function?" Let us avoid the temptation of clarity. "To know that..." is the end of the conversation, and when conversation is terminated so is the genesis of meaning. And, if there is no "final understanding" about relationship, then we may welcome all attempts to articulate its character. Rather than winnowing away the incorrect or misleading accounts, as the search for knowledge is wont to do, we may celebrate multiplicity. Each new account will open up possibilities, sharpen our attention, and expand our potentials for action. We benefit enormously from new entries into our continuing dialogues on such issues as the nature of good and evil, justice, and the future. Such contributions sustain the conversation, keeping us ever humble, flexible, and creatively poised.

•

In the preceding pages I have made much of the concept of co-action, and the collaborative constitution of the real and the good. Indeed, it is by unpacking the implications of this concept that we ultimately confronted the limits of explanation. However, this account of relational being is only one possible way of breaking the boundaries of separation, and illuminating the potentials of relational existence. I wish, then, to share glimpses into six significant metaphors that have sparked my enthusiasm over the years.[1] Each vision opens a space of appreciation, and together they richly laminate the potentials of understanding and action. This brief accounting will provide the legs for further steps toward the sacred.

•

I value the fact that a work of art can allude to things or states of being without in any way representing them.

——Martin Puryear

[1]Useful in thinking through the issue of relational metaphors are the works of Rosenblatt, P. C. (1994). *Metaphors of family systems theory*. New York: Guilford; and Olds, L. E. (1992). *Metaphors of interrelatedness. Toward a systems theory of psychology*. Albany: State University of New York Press.

The Procreative Act

For many people the most compelling realization of relational being is revealed in the act of procreation. Here the message is clear: Human life is brought into being through the relationship of two beings, biologically the bearers of egg and sperm. Herein lies the primordial moment of co-action. Many writers—both ancient and modern—speak to the experience of sexual intimacy as an ultimate form of unity; some find the experience thrusts them into a state of cosmic oneness.[2] A biological understanding of procreation also informs us that there are no self-contained individuals; all bodies carry the imprint of preceding relationships. By extension, the procreative relationship carries the immediate imprint of four other beings, and they the ingredients of all those before them. To view our bodies as bounded singularities is illusory; they contain multitudes.

•

> To heal is to make whole, as in wholesome; to make one again; to unify or reunify: This is Eros in action. Eros is the instinct that makes for union, or unification.
>
> —Norman O. Brown

•

The metaphor of procreation is particularly important in its capacity to generate a powerful sense of "oneness" in the here and now of daily life. It is also a richly evocative metaphor within the West, as it invests this oneness with a spiritual dimension. Sexual union suggests not only a joining of bodies and spirits, but of all humanity, and wraps it in an awe-inspiring sense of mystery. The metaphor also offers resources for resisting the prevailing movements that mechanize and commercialize the sexual act.[3] Yet, I also resist reducing the enormous potentials of relational being to a single form of activity, one that precludes many sectors of the population. The scope is also narrow, and the implications for action ambiguous. As the preceding chapters make clear, a compelling vision of relational being should ideally inform all our activities.

---

[2]Nik Douglas and Penny Slinger's volume, *Sexual secrets: The twentieth anniversary edition: The alchemy of ecstasy* (Destiny Books, 1999), explores the Tantric tradition, in which sexual union brings forth a consciousness of union with all things. As they point out, the very term, "tantra," means "interwoven." Remaining within the sexual act, as opposed to completing it, thus constitutes a form of meditation. See also, Anand, M. (2003). *The new art of sexual ecstasy: Following the path of sacred sexuality.* London: HarperCollins.

[3]See for example, Marcuse, H. (1962). *Eros and civilization.* New York: Vintage.

Systems Theory

The sciences have largely been devoted to studying the causal relationship between various independent entities, for example, the effects of rainfall on vegetation, oil prices on the price of stocks, parental care on the child's self-esteem, and so on. This model is also expanded in most sciences to account for the impact of multiple causes. However, a major advance in this orientation is represented by what is commonly called systems theory. Systems thinking begins when one realizes that all effects are also causes of other effects. Thus, rainfall may affect vegetation, and plant growth may affect wild-life, which in turn may affect the consumption of vegetation. Attention shifts away from single cause/effect relations to larger patterns of inter-related sequences. Systems analyst, Anatol Rapaport, describes a system as "a whole which functions as a whole by virtue of the interdependence of its parts."[4]

The systems orientation has moved in many directions. In his work, Rainbow Arch, the sculptor, Kenneth Snelson, demonstrates that when placed in a particular relationship, otherwise independent pieces of aluminum and stainless steel defy the force of gravity.

Courtesy: Kenneth Snelson

    [4]See Buckley, W. (Ed.) (1968). *Modern systems research for the behavioral scientist: A sourcebook.* Chicago: Aldine. xvii; Ludwig von Bertalanffy's 1968 volume, *General systems theory: Foundations, development, applications.* New York: George Braziller.

In the 1950s a multi-disciplinary movement developed to explore the possibility that certain properties or laws were common to all systems. Because of its abstract character, and the open space it provided for theorists in many different disciplines, no single theory emerged. Rather, systems thinking gave rise to a family of concepts, variously developed in different disciplines. For example, the concept of *feedback loop* became focal for many; this notion denoted cases in which an effect loops back to become an input to the causal source. In the case of human relationships, for example, a husband's anger may cause his wife's withdrawal, which in turn serves to prolong the husband's angry outbursts, which leads to further withdrawl by his wife. In this way the system maintains itself. Others stress the difference between *open* and *closed systems*, the former vulnerable to inputs from the outside and the latter resistant to outside information. Families are generally open, in this sense, while many machines are not. Cybernetics is a term largely used in engineering and biology to account for the way in which feedback functions within systems to enable them to achieve specific ends.

For many therapists, the concept of *second order cybernetics* later became pivotal.[5] Here the concern shifted to how an observer constructs models of cybernetic systems, and more specifically, how the therapist understands the family system. The result of this approach was sobering to consider: Therapists cannot be objective in their approach to clients; through their communications and observations they become part of the family system. In more recent times the concept of *the self-organizing system* has moved across the sciences to become a popular metaphor for understanding the tendency of units to become organized into larger wholes.[6] Coupled with a general view of systems as self-organizing is the widely shared idea that as a system becomes increasingly *complex* in its organization so does its adaptive capacity increase.[7]

The systems theory metaphor represents a major contribution to the vision of relational worlds. It has also been practically useful, not only in engineering, but in suggesting linkages between seemingly independent entities. For example, in the field of mental health, rather than viewing the

[5]Von Foerster, H. (2003). *Understanding understanding: Essays on cybernetics and cognition*. New York: Springer-Verlag.

[6]See, for example Luhmann, N. (1999). *Social systems*. Stanford, CA: Stanford University Press; Holland, J. (1998). *Emergence: From chaos to order*. New York: Perseus Books; Sole, R.V., and Bascompte, J. (2006). *Self-organization in complex ecosystems*. Princeton: Princeton University Press.

[7]For discussion of complexity theory and its relational implications see Stacey, R. (2003). *Complexity and group processes: A radically social understanding of individuals*. London: Brunner-Routledge.

single individual as mentally ill, the systemically oriented therapist will explore ways in which the problems of the "designated patient" are intimately related to his or her relationship to other family members. It is this orientation that has led to the broadly shared concept of *dysfunctional family*, in contrast to the dysfunctional individual. Yet, while rich in practical implications, it should be noted that in most systemic thinking the units in the system are fundamentally bounded, and their relationship one of cause and effect. In the dysfunctional family, for example the parents act upon the child, who in turn acts upon the parents. For the practitioner this orientation often invites a strategic as opposed to a collaborative approach to producing change. The practitioner asks, how can I effect change in the system?

While most systems theory is secular in its focus, there are exceptions. In their book *Angels fear: Toward an epistemology of the sacred*, Gregory Bateson and his daughter, Mary Catherine, began to suggest a sacred potential of systems ideas.[8] They envisioned a system of the whole, an all encompassing, and awe-inspiring inter-relation of all. Appreciation of the whole could be a valuable corrective to the kind of dichotomizing orientation (e.g. self/other, mind/matter, animate/inanimate) that pervades daily life.

•

Is there a line or sort of bag of which we can say that "inside" that line or interface is "me" and "outside" is the environment or some other person? By what right do we make these distinctions?

—Gregory Bateson

Actor Networks

Bearing traces of systems theory are two more recent and important innovations. The first derives from a longstanding sociological interest in social networks. Here it is not the individual who counts but the pattern of relations among persons. Concepts of sociometry, graph theory, and path analysis have all played a significant role in the development of network analysis.[9] For present purposes, the most interesting variation on network theory is *actor network theory* (ANT), which emerged from the social studies of science.[10] Here, for example, scholars attempt to understand the ways

[8]New York: Macmillan, 1987.

[9]For a summary of early work, see Wasserman, S., and Faust, K. (1994). *Social network analysis: Methods and applications*. Cambridge: Cambridge University Press.

[10]See, for example, Law, J., and Hassard, J. (Eds.) (1999). *Actor network theory and after*. Oxford: Oxford University Press; and Latour, B. (2005). *Reassembling the social: An introduction to actor-network-theory*. Oxford: Oxford University Press.

in which various technologies are embedded in broader networks of events. The effort has resulted in two significant departures from traditional systems theory. First, many systems analysts are only concerned with the causal relations within a single class of entities—such as the parts of a machine, participants in an organization, or members in a family. ANT differs in that it seeks to relate elements across classes, for example, human actions, discourse, technical objects, the weather, and so on. In this way ANT treats humans and non-humans as in relation with one another; they are all interacting participants in the system. Although many systems analysts views causality as linear (A causes B causes C), ANT contrastingly holds that any element in the system has the capacity to enroll the actions of any other element in its functioning. We may use a machine to accomplish a given task, but the machine can also "use us" to accomplish its mission. The elements making up a network are termed *actants*, and as theorists propose, inanimate objects are equivalent to people in their possession of causal power.

The generative power of the ANT metaphor is considerable. For example, we typically attribute the concept of gravity to Isaac Newton. This account of history extends the individualist heritage and its valorization of great men. From the perspective of ANT, however, we are drawn to the fact that Newton scarcely functioned alone. He required astronomical data gathered by others, the geometry of Euclid, the astronomy of Kepler, and the mechanics of Galileo, along with a laboratory, living quarters, food, and even an apple tree.[11] In effect, very much like the idea of confluence developed in Chapter 2, we must attribute Newton's concept of gravity to an entire network of inter-related elements, of which the concept of gravity is simply one part. The vision of such networks vastly expands our conception of the relational matrix.

Distributed Cognition

Similar to ANT in its emphasis on person/object relations is a lively development in cognitive theory. The cognitive movement in psychology is a gem in the crown of Western individualism. The movement draws reflected light from the Cartesian tradition, holding reason as the wellspring of human behavior. However, in modern times, most cognitive psychologists are drawn to the metaphor of the mind as a form of computer or information processing system. Thousands of books and articles attest to the power of this metaphor, and its supportive cultural context.

[11]See White, M. (1998). *Isaac Newton: The last sorcerer*. London: Fourth Estate.

The relational turn began as a few innovative scientists shifted their attention from the computer in the head, to the relationship between the person and the computer on the desk. In this light a new question emerged: Does the computer make you smarter? You can quickly see the implications. For example, recall the times when your machine has made you feel stupid: "I can't understand this format," "I don't know how to do Y." More important are the computer's positive contributions to your abilities. If you are like me you are grateful for the computer's memory for spelling. Many programs will also improve your grammar. Computers will do my mathematical work in a split second. And this is to say nothing of the vast email exchanges that can be revisited, long after they have left but a minor trace in consciousness. In terms of intelligence, my computer and I are one.

The result of shifting the idea of intelligence from person to person/object relationship gives rise to the concept of *distributed cognition*.[12] From this perspective, rational activity does not reside alone in the individual head but may be distributed across an array of persons and objects. The practical utility here is considerable. For example, you begin to see that a child's learning in school is not simply an internal process, but is the outcome of his or her relationship to teachers, classmates, available books, video games, lighting, temperature, and so on. It is not "I who learn," but rather, learning takes place out of the entire agglomeration. In this light, we now have multiple ways to think about improving education.[13] Our emphasis shifts from individual students to the larger context in which learning takes place. A more dramatic example comes from the domain of air traffic control. Consider the fact that almost 70% of the cases in which an airplane has crashed can be traced to pilot error (as opposed, for example, to mechanical failure). Yet, from the standpoint of distributed cognition, the pilot is not a lone operator. Rather, one begins to see "intelligent flying" as distributed over the pilot, the co-pilot, the instrument panel, the crew, the messages from air traffic controllers, the flow of information from one sector to another, and so on. Invited, then, is the development of new

---

[12]See, for example, Salomon, S. (Ed.) (1993). *Distributed cognitions: Psychological and educational considerations*. New York: Cambridge University Press; and Middleton, D., and Engestrom, Y. (Eds.) (1996). *Cognition and communication at work: Distributed cognition in the workplace*. Cambridge: Cambridge University Press.

[13]The classic contribution to this orientation is Lave, J. (1988). *Cognition in practice; Mind, mathematics and culture in everyday life*. New York: Cambridge University Press. See also Chapter 8 of the present volume.

practices of aircraft control, based on the analysis of all the contributing elements of the system and their inter-relationships.[14]

•

Theories of distributed action are powerful additions to the family of relational metaphors, primarily because they extend the vision of relationship beyond the realm of the human interchange. The myopic focus on individual action favored by the tradition of bounded being is replaced by a vision of thoroughgoing interdependence of persons and objects. Further, the practical implications are substantial. However, like systems theory in general, these developments ultimately sustain the view of a world composed of discrete entities. The entities (persons, technologies, information, etc.) tend to be of paramount importance; the network or system represents their specific arrangement. It follows in many cases that certain persons may make a more important contribution to system functioning than others. Indeed, some may fail, in which case these dysfunctional units must be re-tooled or eliminated. The individual unit remains under scrutiny.

Biological Interdependence

Systemic and distributed metaphors expand our vision to include relations between people and objects. However, developments in biology and eco-philosophy focus attention on the relationship of humans to other living matter. On the biological side, the major breakthrough took place in research on evolution. Darwin's widely accepted theory characterized living species as each struggling for survival, with the fittest species surviving while others perished. Within this tradition, we are invited to use other living creatures to sustain the human species. From social Darwinism to Nazism and to the present, this form of thinking also pervades our vision of relationships among humans. We divide the world into races, and ask ourselves about their relative superiority or inferiority in intelligence. We worry about the way immigration will dilute or obliterate the species of which we are a part. We ask whether other peoples represent threats to our survival. Again, we are reminded that we live in a world of fundamental separation, and highest priority must be given to our own well-being.

In the 1980s evolutionary biologists began to question the Darwinian assumptions about the relationship among species. With careful attention

[14]See, for example, Hutchins, E., and Klausen, T. (1996). Distributed cognition in an airline cockpit. In Y. Engstrom and D. Middleton (Eds.) *Cognition and communication at work.* New York: Cambridge University Press.

to detail, an alternative view emerged. The relationship was not one of competition, but *co-evolution*. That is, the survival of various species could be linked to the survival of other species, with whom they existed in a mutually symbiotic relationship. For example, the hummingbird is vitally dependent on flowers for life-giving nectar, but the flowers are dependent on hummingbirds for spreading the pollen that facilitates their reproduction. Further, as biologists ask, can we not view interdependence as spread over a range of species? For example, aren't both the hummingbird and flower dependent upon other species of flora and fauna? Such questions gave rise to the concept of *diffuse co-evolution*, emphasizing broad patterns of interdependence among living things.[15] To be sure, the human species is included in this growing map of interdependence. The important implication is that we are not independent competitors; rather, our survival is a matter of broad interdependence.

•

All living beings are akin to one another.
—Pythagoras

•

It is only a short step from this emphasis on living creatures to a concern with ecology, and most especially the patterns of interdependence between living organisms and their environment. Thus, we add to the biological vision of interdependence environmental factors such as rainfall, temperature, soil quality, water supplies, and so on. Ecological study has enormous consequences in terms of programs for sustaining various forms of life—animal species, forests, lakes, fish, glacier ice, and the like. As the ecology movement makes clear, we exist in a delicate balance with nature. This view was amplified in the *Gaia hypothesis*, to wit, it is not simply various regions on earth to which we must attend, but to the earth as a whole. In effect, the entire earth is a life-form in which there are precious balances of temperature, oxygen, and the like that are sustained (or not) by the activities of human and plant activity.[16] Global warming is but a case in point.

For *deep ecologists* such relational awareness demands an entire rethinking of our cultural values and institutions. Required is an abandonment of the value of self-gain, and in its place, a fundamental commitment is required to sustain the habitat as a whole. For deep ecologists, all living

[15]See Durham, W. H. (1992). *Coevolution: Genes, culture and human diversity*. Palo Alto: Stanford University Press.

[16]Lovelock, J. E. (1979). *Gaia: A new look at life on earth*. Oxford: Oxford University Press.

beings have the right to live and to flourish.[17] Such ideas and ideals have sparked global movements for sustainability, Green party politics, Green peace activism, nature conservancy, eco-feminism, and more.

•

We find that we are interwoven threads in
the intricate tapestry of life, its deep ecology.
—Joanna Macy

•

The biological construction of relationship is a vital entry into the compendium of relational metaphors. It links the human and the natural habitat in a compelling way. It is also a construction on which the future of the planet depends. Unlike systems approaches, the ecology movement has strong moral implications. Stress is variously placed on putting the earth first, animal rights, and the intrinsic value of nature.[18] And, for many, there are significant spiritual implications within the ecological metaphor.[19] In nature, it is proposed, there is a spiritual presence, an indwelling of God.

•

I believe that earth and sky, human beings and other beings,
everything that lives and grows in its own time and according to its
own nature, is pulsing with a green life force that is sacred, that is
eternal, that is God.
—Mark Wallace

•

Clearly, the biological metaphor is enormously rich in both practical implications and moral and spiritual evocations. One might wish, however, less in the way of the righteous antagonism often tendered by these movements. There is a strong tendency to blame the other, as in, "*You* are spoiling the environment; *your* greed is causing global warming." Processes of second-order morality are needed in which greater care is given

[17]See Drengson, A., and Inoue, Y. (1995). *The deep ecology movement: An introductory anthology (Io; No. 50)*. Berkeley: North Atlantic Books.

[18]See, for example, Singer, P. (Ed.) (2005). *In defense of animals: The second wave.* (1975) Oxford: Blackwell; Bari, J. (1994). *Timber wars.* Monroe, ME: Common Courage Press.

[19]See, for example, Wilbur, K. (2001). *Sex, ecology, spirituality: The spirit of evolution* (2nd ed.). Boston: Shambala; Wallace, M. (2005). *Finding god in the singing river: Christianity, spirit, nature.* Minneapolis: Augsburg Fortress Publishers.

to creating relationships with those who are held in blame. Critical assault is a poor invitation to productive coordination.

Process Philosophy

As earlier proposed, the character of spoken and written language makes it difficult to escape the view that the world is composed of separate entities. The language is itself a threshing device, separating what might otherwise be viewed holistically. Process philosophy represents a significant attempt to reassert an appreciation of wholes, but with particular attention to cross-time transformation. Consider: The biological metaphor, much like that of systems theory, tends to view the world as composed of discrete entities, objects, or compositions enduring across time. It is this separation of enduring entities that also permits one to speak of cause and effect. In contrast, consider the view of the early Greek philosopher, Heraclitus:

> By cosmic rule, as day yields night, so winter becomes summer, war becomes peace, and plenty gives way to famine. Fire penetrates the lump of myrrh, until the fire and myrrh die away, but to rise again in the smoke called incense.

Here we find a vision of continuous, and uninterrupted flow. Many philosophers have since added dimension to Heraclitus' vision. Hegel's view of human history moving forward through a dynamic of thesis/antithesis/synthesis is but one. Influenced by developments in quantum mechanics, Alfred North Whitehead's volume, *Process and reality: An essay in cosmology*, continues to command attention.[20] In terms of the present work, process philosophy makes two noteworthy contributions. As Whitehead reasons, the fundamental reality is one of continuous change. What we take at any moment to be an enduring reality is the momentary coming together of "occasions of experience." With each new moment, the unity may change, so that reality is in a constant state of becoming. Much like the concept of confluence, as proposed in Chapter 2, Whitehead views each moment as a *concrescence*. However, Whitehead's emphasis on continuous becoming adds an important dimension to understanding.

•

The many become one and are increased by one.
—Alfred North Whitehead

•

[20] Whitehead, A. N. (1929). New York: Macmillan.

The process orientation also asks us to reconsider the traditional concept of knowledge. As outlined in Chapter 9, the view of bounded and enduring units invites a view of knowledge in which truth is the ultimate goal. Yet, to determine what is true, objective, or real is simultaneously to curtail discussion. The process of co-action is terminated. In contrast, through the lens of process philosophy we can see the limits of truth seeking. If the cosmos is essentially a grand transformative process, then no/thing can be known in the sense of fully secure knowledge. All that exists is in continuous motion. Thus, conversation on what exists must never be terminated

•

> Perpetual movement
> Endless change!
> You are all there is left to be enlightened about
> Ah, ten years of study—all for nothing.
> —Ko Un

•

Process philosophy adds a significant dimension to relational accounts, and particularly in its challenge to understanding the world in terms of separate entities. It lends intelligibility to a relational understanding in which objects or entities are not the fundamental building blocks of some larger whole. Similar to the concept of co-action, process precedes the bounded unit. Boundaries, in this sense, can be understood as artificial ruptures in the relational flow. Although controversial, many have extended Whitehead's interest in the theological implications of process philosophy. They propose that God is immanent in the emerging world of our experience, but is simultaneously more than this universe.[21] Thus far, however, the action implications of process philosophy remain underdeveloped.

The Buddha Dharma: Inter-Being

A final contribution to this family of relational metaphors has ancient origins but commands increasing interest in an increasingly complex world. In the teachings of Gautama Buddha (5th century BC), the four noble truths occupy a space of pivotal importance. The first truth recognizes the prevalence of human suffering. The second truth attributes the cause of suffering to human desires. If we desired nothing for ourselves we would

---

[21]See, for example, Cobb, J. B., and Griffin, D. R. (1976). *Process theology: An introductory exposition.* Philadelphia: Westminster Press; Pittenger, N. (1968). *Process-thought and Christian faith.* New York: Macmillan.

suffer little. It follows in the third truth that if one escapes the thrall of desire (including the very concept of self), suffering can be alleviated. The fourth noble truth directs one to a range of practices (the Eight Noble Paths) designed to accomplish not only the end of suffering, but a harmonious life. The one practice now virtually synonymous with the Buddhist tradition is meditation. With the practice of intense or "mindful" concentration (e.g. the movement of breath, the emptying out of all mental content) there is not only liberation from the demands of our desires. There is also an alleviation of suffering.[22]

•

Resonating with the thesis of co-action, Buddhists propose that as we remove ourselves from daily cares we come to realize the artificiality of the distinctions or categories on which they are based. In effect, our linguistic distinctions are responsible for both our desires and disappointments. We see that in conceptualizing wealth, love, status, or progeny as desirable, we establish the grounds for disappointment and distress. Further, we come to see that the division between self and non-self is not only misleading, but contributes to the character of our suffering. (Consider the common anguish resulting from the sense of personal failure.)

Over time one becomes conscious (Bhodi) that there are no independent objects or events in the world. These are all human constructions. When we suspend the constructions, as in meditation, we enter a consciousness of the whole or a unity. More formally, one enters consciousness of what Buddhists call *codependent origination*, or the sense of pure relatedness of all. Nothing we recognize as separate exists independent of all else. As the Vietamese master Thich Nhat Hanh puts it, we come to an appreciation of *inter-being*, that "everything is in everything else." Consider the waves of the ocean. In our vision we can separate the waves as they come rolling into shore. They each seem to have an individual identity. However in their evanescent existence they cannot be separated from neighboring waves, and these from still others. Or to extend this vision, each wave is ultimately within all others. And, it is proposed, to discover the arbitrary nature of our distinctions, and the possibility for their suspension, gives rise to an all-encompassing compassion. If I am in you, and you within me, then mutual caring should replace antagonism.

I am deeply drawn to Buddhist views. Within them, a strong spiritual sense pervades, but without attempting to establish the reality of a bounded

---

[22]For further resources, see Kwee, M. G. T., Gergen, K. J., and Koshikawa, F. (Eds.) (2006). *Horizons in Buddhist psychology*. Chagrin Falls, OH: Taos Institute Publishing; Bodian, S. (2008). *Wake up now: A guide to the journey of spiritual awakening*. New York: McGraw Hill.

A visual metaphor for the state of inter-being is found in the ancient Hindu image of Indra's net. The net is suspended above the heavenly palace of Indra, the god of the natural forces that nurture all life. It extends in all directions, and at each knot in the net is placed a jewel that reflects the image of all the other jewels in the net. The beauty of each jewel contains and expresses the beauty of all. The present rendition is Indra's net for a networked world.

or remote God. Given the earlier exposition of co-action, I am also drawn to the emphasis on humanly created meaning, and its potentials to imprison us.[23] However, I feel the various meditative practices currently in use are limited; they tend to focus on individual change, with the anticipation that personal change will contribute to a more viable world of relationships. The individual's meditational practices, it is said, will lead to compassion for others. To be sure, such practices can be very useful in suspending

[23]For more on the relationship between Buddhism and constructed realities, see Gergen, K. J., and Hosking, D. M. (2006). If you meet social construction along the road, a dialogue with Buddhism. In M.G.T. Kwee, and F. Koshikawa, *Op cit.*

degenerative relations (taking a "time out"). However, the demands of relational life are enormous and complex. If the productive flow of meaning is to be sustained, a rich array of resources is required. Building promising futures together would seem to require skills in pro-active participation. The challenge as I see it is to generate meditative, mindful practices that include multiple parties.

The Sacred Potential of Relational Being

The inability to capture in words the nature of relationship provided an invitation to appreciate multiple metaphors of relational existence. Each of these approaches to understanding—procreation, systems theory, distributed being, biological theory, process philosophy, and Buddhism—offers a significant means of moving beyond a world of independent entities to considerations of relational wholes. We find in each orientation different potentials for understanding and action. The procreative focus renders the relational concrete; the systems and distributed approaches have great scientific and practical value; the biological orientation stimulates both research and programs of environmental sustainability; process philosophy facilitates dialogue between scientists and theologians: and Buddhism offers theory and practice for a good life. There are still further metaphors we could have added to the above. For example, African culture offers us the concept of *ubuntu*, which emphasizes care and compassion for all. Echoing earlier chapters of this work, the ubuntu spirit is carried in the phrase, "I am who I am because of who we all are." Also relevant is the concept of *Ba* as developed by the Japanese philosopher, Kitaro Nishida. Ba refers roughly to a condition of pure relationship, in which all participants are united in the sharing and synthesizing of subjectivity.[24] Moments of high group solidarity would be illustrative of Ba. There is also the metaphor of *the carnival*, in which festive sensuality becomes the route to a primordial conjoining.[25] There is no "best," or "only" way of comprehending the relational source of all vitality. We have only avenues of implication.

•

[24]Nishida, K. (1990). *An inquiry into the good*. (Trans. By M. Abe and C. Ives). Orig. published, 1921. New Haven: Yale University Press.

[25]See, Bakhtin, M. (1993). *Rabelais and his world*. (Trans. H. Iswolsky). Bloomington: Indiana University Press.

The harmony past knowing
sounds more deeply than the known.
                    —Heraclitus

•

The recognition of an unfathomable, originary source is scarcely new; it has been alluded to for centuries and around the world. This recognition is often accompanied by a profound sense of awe, humility, and mystery. For 19th-century romanticists such as Wordsworth, Coleridge, and Schiller, nature provided inspiration to the creative artist. There was the soaring grandeur of the Alps, the rushing of a waterfall, or the rich colors of a sunset. Such experiences could not be described, but approached only indirectly—through art or poetry. Romanticists spoke in terms of the "sublime," that is, beyond limining or the making of distinctions. More recently, scholars have found sources of the sublime in the wondrous accounts of physics,[26] and in the vast expansion of connectivity brought about by communications technology.[27]

This consciousness of a profound presence, beyond articulation, is suffused with a sense of the sacred. For many, this sense of mystery and awe before an unfathomable origin is nothing less than a consciousness of the divine. The view is an essential part of the Judeo-Christian and Muslim traditions. "How unsearchable are His judgments and how inscrutable His ways!" we find in the book of Romans (11:33). This sensibility is also writ large in the 5th-century development of *negative theology*. Here theologians reasoned that no words were capable of describing or representing the Divine. In effect, any account or image would necessarily be a misleading distortion. One might describe that which was not the divine (*via negativa*), but not the divine itself.[28] Similarly, in the Kabbalistic tradition, the Creator is viewed as unknowable. And within the Sufi tradition one may strive for a state of "annihilation" in which distinctions are abandoned and one joins an unutterable unity of One.[29]

[26]Cannato, J. (2006). *Radical amazement: Contemplative lessons from black holes, supernovas, and other wonders of the universe*. Notre Dame: Sorrin Books.

[27]Gergen, K. J. (1996). *Technology and the self: From the essential to the sublime*. Thousand Oaks, CA: Sage. In D. Grodin and T. R. Lindlof (Eds.) (1995). *Constructing the self in a mediated world*. Thousand Oaks, CA: Sage.

[28]This view is also articulated in the work of the 12th-century Jewish scholar, Moses Maimonides. In his work, *The Guide for the perplexed*, he proposes that to identify the attributes of God is to engage in anthropomorphism (London: Routledge & Kegan Paul Ltd., 1904).

[29]Yazdi, M. H. (1992). *The principles of epistemology in Islamic philosophy, knowledge by presence*. Albany: State University of New York Press.

The consciousness of a divine presence—beyond description—is also echoed today in postmodern theology. Here the capacity of words to map or mirror an independent world is called into question. Rather, it is proposed, words gain their meaning from their relationship with other words. If words do not serve as maps or mirrors, it is reasoned, then theological writings cannot reveal the nature of the divine.[30] The divine is not to be found in sacred texts; searching Biblical writings to locate "God's meaning" is a specious practice. Rather, as some postmodern theologians propose, we should turn our attention to the absences and illogicalities of such texts; the very fact that we cannot fix *the* meaning brings us closer to the sacred. As Mark Wallace proposes, the significance of the sacred may be carried in Biblical accounts or narratives, but not if we view them as records of historical fact. Rather, they convey a wisdom that is open to continuous dialogue and reinterpretation.[31]

In the Hebraic tradition a similar view holds that since God is the creator of all that exists, the divine is separate and beyond spatio/temporal substance. Because the divine is no palpable thing, no direct description is possible. The Hindu tradition also touches on the divinity of the un-voiceable. In the spiritual teachings of the Upanishads, dating from the 8th century BC, the Supreme Cosmic Spirit is said to be beyond comprehension. Thus emerged the sacred chant, *neti-neti*, meaning that the Supreme Being is "not this, not that;" no description of the divine constitutes its measure.

•

Ultimate meaning resides in silence as unuttered truth.

—Chris Hermans

•

We find, then, a longstanding sense of a divine presence, beyond definition. Most important for the present, this sense of the sacred is equated with relational unity. Such a conclusion was suggested in the earlier discussion of ecology, process philosophy, and Buddhism. In each case, proponents linked visions of a relational whole with a spiritual presence. The sacred does not dwell within singular or bounded entities as such—with

---

[30] See, for example, Taylor, M. (1982). *Deconstructing theology.* New York: Crossroad Pub Co; Winquist, C. (1999). *Epiphanies of darkness: Deconstruction and theology.* Aurora: Davies Group Publisher; Coward, H., and Foshay, T. (Eds.) (1992). *Derrida and negative theology.* Albany: State University of New York Press. See also Marion, J. (1991). *God without being.* Chicago: University of Chicago Press.

[31] See, Wallace, M. (2002). *Fragments of the spirit: Nature, violence and the renewal of creation.* Harrisburg, PA: Trinity Press; Owen, H. P. (1971). *Concepts of deity.* London: Macmillan.

some "more blessed" than others—but within a condition of ultimate relatedness. Such views are ancient in origin. Consider the 3rd century BC writings of the Tao:

> Looked at but cannot be seen—it is beyond form;
> Listened to but cannot be heard—it is beyond sound;
> Held but cannot be touched—it is beyond sensation.
> The depthless evades definition
> And leads into a single unity.

In the Christian tradition this sense of fundamental relationship is closely associated with the concept of *perichoresis*, or the holy trinity of the Father, the Son, and the Holy Spirit. Rather than viewing these as entities split from each other, each partakes of the other. God is essentially three in one, one in three. Also prominent are writings associated with the pantheist tradition, stretching from the early work of Heraclitus and Plotinus, through Spinoza, and Ralph Waldo Emerson. Briefly put, for pantheists there is no separate entity or bounded being called God (the theist tradition). Rather, all is God and God is all.[32]

A similar sensibility can be found in Sufism in which God is said to be devoid of any specific form or quality, yet inseparable from every phenomenon. For the more recent movement in eco-theology this wholeness is to be found in nature. It is in the wholeness of nature that the sacred is to be found.[33] In Margaret Wheatley's words, "Life's true nature is wholeness…. In a sacred moment I experience the wholeness."[34]

•

> All things are linked with one another,
> and this oneness is sacred.
> —Marcus Aurelius

Toward Sacred Practice

The impossibility of grasping the nature of relational process invites both awe and humility. That which is essential to all that we hold dear cannot be owned, penetrated, or articulated. In the consciousness of the relational

[32]See Levine, M. P. (1994). *Pantheism: A non-theistic concept of deity.* London: Routledge.

[33]See Hallman, D. G. (Ed.) (1994). *Ecotheology: Voices from South and North.* Maryknoll, NY: Orbis Books; Edwards, D. (2006). *Ecology at the heart of faith.* Maryknoll, NY: Orbis.

[34]Wheatley, M. (2002). *Turning to one another: Simple conversations to restore hope to the future* (p. 130). San Francisco: Berrett-Kohler.

we come to find a sacred potential. The implications for our practices of daily life are substantial. Merciade Eliade (1959) argued compellingly for the significance of sacred experience in human history.[35] For Eliade the process of sacralization lends value to our actions. When actions are suffused with the sense of the sacred, they acquire a vital sense of ought. The kinds of factual declarations more common to the profane world lack this potential. As Morris Berman has added, the modernist vision of the world—most fully represented in the scientific emphasis on prediction and control—has robbed humanity of a major source of valuing.[36] As Berman sees it, the scientific perspective distances the person from nature. We observe nature as if it is independent from us, and as a result, we study and use nature for our own purposes. The result has been disastrous for the planet and for human relationships. As I am suggesting, it is relational process that carries with it a sacred dimension. That which contributes to the growth and extension of relational process acquires aspects of the divine.

•

It is easy enough to drive the spirit out of the door,
but when we have done so, the salt of life grows flat
—it loses its savor.

—Carl Jung

•

At the same time, there is a longstanding tendency within many religions to place the divine at a distance, temporal and/or spatial. For some it is the distance of the past, with God defined as an originating source responsible long ago for our present existence. Such displacement of the divine may also be into the future, with the anticipation of a heavenly existence to come. And, for many, the Divinity is somewhere "on high," a sky-god far removed from the banalities of the merely mortal. Yet, these various displacements of the divine also generate separation between the challenges of the here and now and the worship of a holy elsewhere. Such a conclusion risks rendering the moment at hand irrelevant.

From a relational standpoint we may leap this chasm of separation between the sacred and social life. We realize the artificial character of bonded and separated beings, and stand in awe of the relational process from which these very concepts draw significance. We recognize that it is out of ongoing relationship that we have created the conception of a remote

[35]Eliade, M. (1968). *The sacred and the profane: The nature of religion.* San Diego, CA: Harvest Books.
[36]Berman, M. (1984). *The reenchantment of the world.* New York: Bantam.

God—an identifiable and sometimes gendered being, possessed with agency, love, anger, forgiveness, omnipotence, wisdom, and other diverse attributes assigned by the various cultures of the world. We are invited, then, to view the divine as *a process* within which we exist and from which we cannot be separated. The sacred is not distinct and distant, but immanent in all human affairs.[37]

•

From a friend: "if someone asked me where I worship, I would answer: through my relationships, inside my body through yoga/meditation/movement and outside in nature, where unique beauty fills the senses each day for those with eyes to see it."

•

This view of sacred presence has substantial relevance to daily life. Specifically we are invited to see our actions as potential expressions or realizations of the sacred. The thesis of relational being, as developed in these pages, places special significance on the process of co-action, the mutual creation of meaning. In particular, when our actions contribute to the continuous generation of meaning—to coordination rather than alienation—we are engaged in sacred practice. Through positive coordination we engage in the very processes from which issue meaning, value, and the continued sustenance of the sacred. Holiness is neither a state of heaven nor mind, but may be realized in our next moment together.

Nor is this emphasis restricted to human relations alone. As indicated throughout this work, and most clearly in the present chapter, the boundaries between human and non-human are also artificial. Human relations cannot be separated from relations with nature. When we speak of the co-active generation of meaning we must include the entirety of nature. In Martin Buber's words, "The relation with God...includes and encompasses the possibility of relation with all otherness."[38]

•

[37]Here the present thesis draws sustenance from theological and philosophical conceptions of immanence, holding that the divine does not occupy a transcendent position beyond what there is, but is to be found within it. Visions of immanence are shared across a spectrum of religions, including Christianity, Judaism, Hinduism, and Buddhism. For many, the divine force from which life springs is immanent within such life. In more secular form, but also relevant to the present thesis, is the more recent writing of Gilles Deleuze. In his 1980 work with Felix Guattari and Brian Massumi, *A Thousand plateaus* (Minneapolis: University of Minnesota Press), an ontology is developed in which there are neither structures nor causal agents, but continuous movement, forming and unforming.

[38]Buber, M. (1947). *Between man and man* (p. 65). London: Kegan Paul.

What are the more specific implications for our daily actions? On the simplest level it may mean expanding our appreciation for all that contributes to any moment of pleasure or satisfaction. In savoring the tastes of good food, for example, we may contemplate the way in which the enjoyment of these tastes has been prepared by a relational history extending for generations. We may appreciate those who have labored to produce the foodstuffs, transported it, examined it, stored it, and organized its sales. Consider as well the conditions of the earth that have made such foodstuffs possible, and have established as well the of conditions for us to be living this moment of enjoyment. To such moments of appreciation we should also add concern with the ways in which relational synchrony has not yet been achieved. In what ways does our moment of pleasure impede the relational flow? For example, what are the conditions of the migrant worker responsible for harvesting, and what is the carbon footprint left by the transporting of foodstuffs? This expanded, appreciative, and critical consciousness is effectively a state of worship.

Let us move from such worshipful moments to our actions together. As the pages of this volume suggest, when our actions invite and sustain the process of generating meaning, we contribute to a sacred state of being. For example, in the simple acts of listening with care, affirming the other, and giving expression to the multiple relations of which we are a part, there is a divine spark. Likewise, the therapist who helps to restore generative coordination within the client's relationships, the researcher who gives voice to the marginalized, the school teacher who facilitates classroom dialogue, the manager who expands the range of those included in making decisions, all share in the sacred.

•

If humankind lived as though all of creation
were honored relations, the world would be healed overnight.
—Susan McElroy

•

As the preceding chapters have emphasized, the creation and sustenance of meaning within relationships runs the perpetual risk of establishing new boundaries: the right within versus the wrong without. Thus, we may especially honor those actions traversing the barricades of conflicting traditions of the good. Relations between groups—religious, political, tribal, ethnic—have brought untold misery in the history of civilization, and the future hangs in the balance. The route from separation to alienation, and then mutual destruction, is a route to the demise of meaning altogether.

Dialogic practices that restore the flow of productive meaning are vitally needed. Similarly honored are practices that bring humans and their environment together into a mutually sustainable world. All such actions are realizations of second-order morality—a revitalizing of the relationship among relationships. All harbor sacred potential.

The Coming of Relational Consciousness

> We have to face the fact that either all of us are going to die together, or we are going to learn to live together—and if we are to live together, we have to talk.
>
> —Eleanor Roosevelt

To approach human beings exclusively as separate or bounded units—whether individual selves, communities, political parties, nations, or religions—is to threaten our future well-being. To understand the world in which we live as constituted by independent species, forms, types, or entities is to threaten the well-being of the planet. Such are the implications of the preceding pages. As I have also proposed, the most commanding alternative to these realities of separation is that of relational being. It is through relational process that whatever we come to view as independent beings are given birth. Understanding persons and nature in terms of bounded units is but one outcome of this more fundamental process of coordination. Whatever value we place upon ourselves or others, and whatever hope we may have for the future, depends on the welfare of relationship. As Martin Buber once wrote, "In the beginning is the relationship."[1] Without care of relationship we also risk an ending.

To bring these proposals into focus, my chief target of criticism was the Enlightenment vision of independent selves. My concern was with the

[1]Buber, M. (1937). *I and thou*. New York: Free Press.

many ways in which the presumption of individual agents—with gifts of inherent reason, motivation, and passion—generates untold suffering. Alienation, loneliness, conflict, self-doubt, selfishness, and manipulative relations were among the impairments. This account prepared the way for the relational alternative. The concept of coordinated action, or co-action, was pivotal. As proposed, it is through coordinated action—not individual minds—that meaning originates. It is within coordinated action that we find the source of all that we take to be real, rational, or good. Yet, as I proposed, this does not mean abandoning the rich vocabulary of the mind inherited from past generations. Rather, the challenge is to reconfigure our understanding of this vocabulary. On closer inspection, we find that virtually all faculties traditionally attributed to the internal world of the agent—reason, emotion, motivation, memory, experience, and the like—are essentially performances within relationship. Indeed, it was concluded, in all that we say and do, we manifest our relational existence. From this standpoint, we may abandon the view that those around us cause our actions. Others are not the causes nor we their effects. Rather, in whatever we think, remember, create, and feel, we *participate* in relationship.

Owing perhaps to the undulations of daily life, I have never been content with the Enlightenment ideal of the "coherent mind." And, it has seemed to me, if we are embedded within multiple relationships, coherence is an enemy of fluidity. We carry with us traces of myriad relationships, past and present, existing or imagined. These traces essentially equip us with multiple and often conflicting potentials for action. The value placed on coherence, then, is derived from our participation within particular relationships. The local relationship generates its own realm of the real, rational, and good. And it is within such relationships that bonds develop—friendships, marriages, communities, clubs, teams, religions, military units, political parties, and so on. We value those who are trust-worthy and reliable within these relationships. If this seems reasonable, we then confront a fundamental irony. While these bonded relations are vital to our well-being, the process of bonding often generates barricades separating us from them. And because of these barricades, the flow of col-laborative action is obstructed. Most unfortunately, these artificial sep-arations often bring with them animosity and a slide into mutual elimination.

At that juncture, my concern shifted to forms of practice. In my view, if the vision of relational being is to have significance, it must be wedded to the ways we live our lives together. Of focal concern are practices that invite productive co-creation of meaning, and most especially, that break the barriers of antipathy. Attention was directed here, for example, to prac-tices for navigating the rocky waters of relationship, building community, and replacing conflict with coordination. Extended attention was given to relation-building in scholarly research, education, therapy, and organizations. And yet, throughout this exploration I was haunted by an uneasiness at the narrowness of scope. Yes, we had touched on multiple sites of coordinated action. But, at the edge of consciousness lay an enormous expanse of the unspoken. There were so many additional arenas in which significant developments were taking place. How could they be ignored?

The wheels began to turn. My research had revealed hundreds of practitioners exploring practices for and enriching relational process. However, when I considered these efforts in light of this domain of the unspoken, it became evident that I had underestimated the coming of relational consciousness. Was I not identifying a movement of far greater scope than first imagined? To be sure, there were already well-known and well-developed movements championing community development[2] and democratic participation.[3] I have also been impressed with the open source movement in the computer world, an active movement to decentralize technologies so they might be available to all people.[4] In spite of their being lodged in an individualist tradition, all of these demonstrated an investment in inclusive participation. However, from the local to the global, there was also evidence of a far greater and more clearly relationship-centered expansion of consciousness. I am struck, for example, by such developments as the following:

> **The National Coalition for Dialogue and Deliberation**. This recently emerging group is dedicated to supporting organizations and individuals engaged in the use of dialogue to benefit society. They "envision a society in which systems and structures support and advance inclusive, constructive dialogue and deliberation."[5] The NCCD membership represents organizations that have created forms of dialogue now used in numerous communities, schools, businesses, religions, and the like, to assist in the collaborative creation of the future. For example, participating groups such as the Co-Intelligence Institute, the Institute for Democratic Dialogue and

[2]See, for example, Etzioni, A. (1993). *The spirit of community: Rights, responsibilities and the communitarian agenda*. New York: Crown; Bell, D. (1993). *Communitarianism and its critics*. New York: Oxford University Press.

[3]See, for example, the World Movement for Democracy, www.wmd.org, the Democratic Dialogue Network, www.democrativedialoguenetwork.org., and *the International Journal of Public Participation*.

[4]See, for example, Weber, S. (2005). *The success of open source*. Cambridge: Harvard University Press.

[5]See www.thataway.org

Deliberation, the Neighborhood Assemblies Network, 21st Century
Dialogue, and the Compassionate Listening Project, all facilitate
interchange and the civil sharing of concerns.

The International Academy of Collaborative Professionals. This
organization emerged from the work of myriad grassroots groups to
locate means of replacing litigation and other contentious means of
problem-solving with collaborative practice. The academy is
primarily composed of professionals from legal, mental health, and
financial sectors. They work internationally to provide resources for
education and networking. For them, "Human relationships are
foremost in our work at all times." An excellent example of the work
supported by the Academy is collaborative law. Especially useful in
cases of divorce and custody issues, lawyers attempt to replace the
disruptive practice of litigation with civil discussions in which all the
significant stakeholders participate. In the case of medical
malpractice, collaborative law attempts to reduce the growing gap of
distrust between patients and physicians by facilitating conversations
that generate common understanding.[6]

Grassroots Conflict Reduction. In Chapter 6, I briefly treated the
work of several collaborative practices for reducing or managing
conflict. These were representative of a globe-spanning movement to
locate alternatives to brute force approaches to conflict. Because
large-scale organizations—including governments, religions, political
parties, tribes, and the like—are often inept in moving beyond an
ideology of self-gain, these groups have taken it into their own hands
to develop and propagate collaborative means of approaching
conflict. Among hundreds of such organizations, the following
are particularly noteworthy: the Alliance for Peacebuilding
(www.allianceforpeacebuilding.org), which brings together peace
building organizations from around the world to share information
and innovation; the Search for Common Ground (www.sfcg.org),
with active projects in 17 countries; the Global PeaceWorks
organization (www.center2000.org), which gathers volunteers from
multiple religions together to serve local communities; and
PeaceXPeace (www.peacexpeace.org), which connects women from
around the world to work locally for peace.[7]

[6]See Clark, K. (2007). The use of collaborative law in medical error situations, *The Health Lawyer*, June issue, 19–23.

[7]For more on the political implications of communal collaboration, see Saunders, H. H. (2005). *Politics is about relationship*. New York: Palgrave Macmillan.

Regional collaboration. It has long been recognized that traditional units of geographic division—principalities, counties, states, and nations—are all limited in what they can achieve. With increased sensitivity to issues of interdependence—economic and environmental most central—there has been accelerating movement toward regional collaboration. For example, the Great Lakes Regional Collaboration resulted from growing alarm at the dissipation of the Great Lakes. Meetings bring together representatives of the national government, state governors, local mayors, and tribal chiefs, among others, to implement programs for restoring and sustaining the lakes. Regional organizations such as this are most common in the Scandinavian countries. In Sweden, Bjorn Gustavsen specifically draws attention to the shift from top-down regional planning to the importance of working in inclusive networks.[8]

Social Networks. The concept of the social network has long been a fixture in the social sciences, with analysis generally illuminating the pattern of linkages among individuals or groups. However, with the development of the Internet, the concept of social network has sprung from library shelves to become a dynamic entry into everyday life. In this case social networks are typically composed of persons who share a particular interest or social category, who make their identity public, and participate in communication with others in the network. The most visible of these networks in the U.S. are MySpace, with over 100 million participants, Facebook with 150 million users, and Twitter with 15 million devotees. In the social network, the Cartesian dictum is replaced by "I am linked, therefore I am." Not all such networks are outlets for interpersonal pleasure. For example, SixDegrees.org., started by actor Kevin Bacon, joins with the Network for Good to offer outlets for over a million charities to connect with supporters.

The Globalization of Relational Enlightenment

These movements and initiatives are not only based on an appreciation of what may be wrought by human connection, but actively increase the flow of co-action in the world. As I see it, these few exemplars are but small

[8]Gustavsen, B. (1996). Action research, democratic dialogue, and the idea of "critical mass" in change. *Qualitative Inquiry, 2*, 90–103.

indicators of a global movement of substantial significance, a movement that promises only to increase in momentum. There are three driving engines for this movement, each of which places relationship in the forefront of consciousness. Each points as well to the necessity of relational well-being for the world's future. Consider:

Communication Technology

The chief stimulus in expanding relational consciousness is undoubtedly the availability of low cost, instantaneous means of learning about or communicating with people from around the globe. Central in significance is the Internet, a globe-spanning network carrying electronic mail, websites, blogs, games, music, art, live conversations, and other resources to publicly accessible computer outlets throughout the world. There are now well over a billion users of the Internet worldwide, most of them relying on e-mail communication. In the U.S. over 70% of the population now relies on Internet services. The Internet also provides entry into the World Wide Web, an immense domain of readily accessible "documents" carrying text, images, videos, voice, and more. It is estimated that today there are more than 100 million websites, with the amount of information accumulating each year equaling 30 feet of books per person for the entirety of the world's population. The average Internet user in the U.S. now spends approximately 100 hours a month on-line.

The implications for relational being are breathtaking. For one, each new contact or website expands the potentials of multi-being. From the Aljazeera website I absorb certain logics and values from the Arab world; from the Conservative Outpost a dash of right wing Republicanism; from the ACLU the latest on the protection of free speech; from You Tube, zaniness from around the world, and so on. In the same way, an e-mail message from Russia thrusts me into a certain form of relationship, different in character from relating with a colleague in Japan, Argentina, China, or India. Daily there are accretions in my potentials for saying and doing, and thus my capacity for sensitive coordination in other relationships. As I become a bridge, so do millions of others. The potential for effective co-action expands exponentially. The result is not only a profound increase in ongoing connectivity, but the world's people become increasingly capable of effective collaboration.

Globalized Organizing

When high-speed communication technologies are linked to skills in coordination, the stage is set for an unlimited acceleration in the process of organizing. From the individual who seeks others who share an exotic interest, to large industries or governments, the technologies facilitate the coordination of realities, visions, and agendas. The small business can expand, a medium-sized business can develop markets abroad, and a large business grows larger through globalization. It should come as little surprise that there are over 300 thousand websites now treating the importance of collaboration in the workplace. Increased organization takes place at all levels—the community, the state, the regional, the national, and the international. There is a globally expanding network of police that parallels the expansion of globally organized crime and terrorism. There are now over 1,300 websites for religions seeking connection around the world. To appreciate the rate of growth in international organizing, consider that in 1950 there were estimated to be approximately a thousand U.S. organizations—governmental and non-governmental—with active, intercontinental programs. There are currently over 60,000 such organizations. (Ironically, with the expansion in globalized organizing, there is a global expansion in anti-globalization groups.) The message writ large is that sustaining or enhancing well-being requires collaborative efficacy. "Networking" becomes a way of life, while the values of autonomy and independence slip into history.

Environmental Threat

The third major stimulus for relational consciousness is not the opportunity for increased efficacy, but the threat to the environment wrought by such increases. It was perhaps the 1962 publication of Rachel Carson's *Silent Spring*[9] that ignited concern over the environmental ravages resulting from the systematic exploitation of the habitat. As the human population has continued to expand—its technologies of control ever more effective, and the demands for industrial production ever increasing—so have we also witnessed the pollution of our air and water supplies, the erosion of land, massive deforestation, the extinction of animal and plant species, the exhaustion of fish population, and more. For many, the concepts of progress, expansion, and profit have turned sour. In their place, sustainability has become the necessary alternative. Yet, with the more recent and alarming increment in global warming, sustainability no longer seems an adequate goal. We now confront a choice between productive collaboration or catastrophe. The efforts of isolated individuals, communities, states, or nations are insufficient. There are no land masses that are exempt from

[9]New York: Houghton Mifflin.

environmental threat. In effect, a viable future will depend on the collaborative capacity of the world's peoples.

I began this volume with the hope of offering resources for moving beyond the Enlightenment view of the human being. To view the self as a center around whom others orbit is no more misguided than holding the earth to be the center of the universe. We move then, toward a *New Enlightenment* in which the valuing of the self is replaced by the prizing of relationship. Nor is this an Enlightenment particular to Western culture. There is reason to hope and to anticipate that we are embarked on a global transformation in consciousness. Let us replace the Hobbesian dystopia of "all against all," with a vision of "all with all." When relational well-being is the center of our concern we approach a life-giving future.

INDEX

potential of, 370
sustaining process of, 301
transformative, 191–98
Diamond, J. B., 333*n*30
discipline(s)
  barricaded, 221
  debilitation and, 208–10
  hybrids of, 216–19
  of knowledge, 206–21
  transcending, 213–21
  weaving, 214–16
discourse
  of agency, 80
  of intentions, 80
  of mind, 60–61, 70–74
  relationships and mental, 70–74
  of truth, 189
Discourse on Method (Descartes), 64
dissonance, cognitive, 135
distrust, 13, 15
  fundamental, 14
  self-gratification and, 14
Dole, D. C., 330*n*24
Domenici, Kathy, 323
Donald, Merlin, 77
Donaldson, G. A., 263*n*33
Dossetor, J., 364*n*13
Dostoyevsky, Fyodor, 141
Douglas, Nik, 375*n*2
Drath, W., 333*n*30
Drengson, A., 383*n*17
dualism, xxi
  mind-world, xxiii–xxiv, 56*n*20, 205
Durham, W. H., 382*n*15

Eakin, J., 176*n*11
Earley, P. C., 244*n*4
economic theory, 21
Ede, L., 260*n*29
education, 201, 214. *See also* learning; teachers
  aims of, 241–45
  circles of participation in, 245–47
  cognitive apprenticeship in, 251
  collaborative, 259–62
  community differences and, 244–45
  cooperative, 264–65
  curriculum-centered, 247–48
  dialogic classroom in, 249–51
  facilitation/coaching model of, 252
  graduate, 215–16
  liberation/empowerment vision of,
    251–52, 252*n*15
  relationally effective, 243
  relational-oriented, 247–48
  relationship placed prior to individual in,
    243, 245–46
  student/family relationship and, 246–47
  student/teacher relationship in,
    248–50, 254–55
Edwards, D., 73*n*10, 391*n*33

Eisenberg, E. M., 182*n*17, 337*n*35
Ekman, P., 105*n*17
Eliade, M., 357*n*6, 392
Eliot, T.S., 93
Elkind, David, 175
Ellis, C., 231*n*36, 237*n*47
Ellsberg, R., 363*n*12
Ellsworth, P., 105*n*17
emotional scenarios, 107–11
emotions, 96, 137. *See also* love
  as biological, 115–21, *119*
  co-action and, 99
  disrupting dangerous dances of, 111–15
  in history/culture, 98–102
  as human constructions, 100
  identifying, 99, 115–16
  as performance, 102–6
  reason v., 181
  registers of, 114
  states of, 98
  universal, 101–2
empowerment, 252–53
enchantment, of relationships, 179–81
Engestrom, Y., 380*n*12, 381*n*14
enlightenment, relational, 400–1
Enlightenment, relational, xvff, 400–1
Epston, David, 299
Erickson, Milton, 291
ethics, 25, 27, 357, 364
Etzioni, A., xxiv, 398*n*2
evaluation. *See also* self-evaluation
  appreciative approaches to, 341–43
  individual, xiv
  of organization, 310
  of performance, 339–40
  site of, 12
  threat of, 10
  traditional forms of, 340
  unrelenting, 8–10
  valuation from, 339–43
evil
  actions, 140, 358–59
  eliminating, 360, 363–64
  virtue, 359
experience, memory and, 83–90, *85, 89*
explanation
  of agency, 53
  causal, 50–53
exploration, appreciative, 168–70
expression
  bounded, 325
  of inner world, 14
  of memories, 87–88
  unbounded, 326–27

The Fall of Public Man (Sennett), 366
Farber, S., 288*n*19
fascism, 19
Faust, K., 378*n*9
feedback loop, 377